HISTORICAL ANTHROPOLOGY

Oxford in India Readings in
Sociology and Social Anthropology

GENERAL EDITOR
T.N. MADAN

HISTORICAL
ANTHROPOLOGY

edited by
SAURABH DUBE

OXFORD
UNIVERSITY PRESS

OXFORD

UNIVERSITY PRESS

YMCA Library Building, Jai Singh Road, New Delhi 110 001

Oxford University Press is a department of the University of Oxford.
It furthers the University's objective of excellence in research,
scholarship, and education by publishing worldwide in

Oxford   New York

Auckland   Cape Town   Dar es Salaam   Hong Kong   Karachi
Kuala Lumpur   Madrid   Melbourne   Mexico City   Nairobi
New Delhi   Shanghai   Taipei   Toronto

With offices in
Argentina   Austria   Brazil   Chile   Czech Republic   France   Greece
Guatemala   Hungary   Italy   Japan   Poland   Portugal   Singapore
South Korea   Switzerland   Thailand   Turkey   Ukraine   Vietnam

Oxford is a registered trademark of Oxford University Press
in the UK and in certain other countries

Published in India by Oxford University Press, New Delhi

ISBN-13: 978-019-569071-2
ISBN-10: 019-569071-0

Typeset in Giovanni 9.5/11.5 by Jojy Philip
Printed in India at Ram Printograph, Delhi 110 051
Published by Oxford University Press
YMCA Library Building, Jai Singh Road, New Delhi 110 001

For Ishita
one reason or many

Contents

Preface

History is my vocation, anthropology was my fate. Fortuitously, the coming together of the two in my life has accompanied their formidable mating at large over the past two decades.

Recent times have witnessed profound changes in the practice of anthropology, sociology, and history. Among the major motivations for these transformations have been increasingly heightened emphases on the place of 'process', 'practice', and 'power'—or the three 'Ps', as these are sometimes known—in understandings of social worlds. In the actual elaborations of such emphases and understandings, a key role has been played by acute intersections between anthropology and history, leading to a rather broad field of historical anthropology.

Scholars of South Asia have often stood at the forefront of the development of the crucial questions and particular persuasions of historical anthropology. At the same time, in terms of the institutional organization on the subcontinent of the twinned enquiries of anthropology and sociology, historical anthropology remains only an ambiguously, uncertainly demarcated terrain. Dense histories of the formation and sedimentation of the disciplines are at stake here.

Historical Anthropology seeks to rethink the long-established, constitutive split between anthropology and history. Yet, the volume takes up the task neither to merely mark out one more disciplinary specialization—or, indeed, still another sub-discipline—nor to simply discuss historical anthropology in terms of the methodological convergences between anthropology and history, cast as two already known, readily prefigured enquiries. The aims of the work are wider. On the one hand, here are to be found efforts to approach historical anthropology in a manner that reconsiders its constituent disciplines and their wider interplay. On the other hand, on offer is a wide-ranging domain of anthropological and historical endeavour, turning on the shared sensibilities that underlie its substantive contributions. Together, the book attempts to critically unravel—rather than comfortably foreclose—the imaginative arena of historical anthropology, pointing toward its productive possibilities, not only in the past and the present but in times to follow.

Historical Anthropology has been uncomfortably long in the making, from its inception and gestation through to its realization and publication. The fault is mine, but there are reasons. I was trained in history while becoming oriented to anthropology from the middle of the 1980s, and have straddled the two since the 1990s. Thus, when Professor T. N. Madan initiated the idea of the present volume for his series a few years ago, I fairly jumped with excitement. It was not difficult to choose the pieces for the volume—although there were some hiccups, at the beginning and the end. Yet, it was the writing of the Introduction to the volume that confounded and consumed me. Reading a great deal was not the challenge. Nor was digesting what I had read all that uncomfortable. It was the structuring of the introductory piece in terms of thinking through the routine approaches to the disciplines and their interplay that proved the problem. After the anxieties and epiphanies, I have learned much and unlearned more, especially undoing my previous certainties about anthropology, history, and historical anthropology. For better or worse, some of this is reflected in the pages that follow.

To Professor Madan I owe immense gratitude for trusting me with the volume and sincere apologies for the delay in completing it. He has been a remarkable series editor: patient, supportive, incisive. Many thanks also to Amma, Dadu, Winnie, and Pooh—for another home, great meals, splendid times, and frenetic *achar* eating. Leela Dube first saw to it that I do not ride roughshod over the history of anthropology and has subsequently aided my journeys into the pathways of these pasts. Were he still here, S. C. Dube would have been happy and proud—and questioning and critical—about the volume: registering loss is bitter-sweet remembrance.

Professor Bernard Cohn and Dr K. S. Singh went away before seeing the volume. I am convinced that they too would have been generously supportive yet constructively querying about it. In Barney's absence, Abbey Cohn has been solidly behind the venture. I would be remiss not to express my warm thanks also to the OUP team. Heroically, in the midst of our mutual travels, Vandana Madan produced a comprehensive index within a couple of weeks, also magnanimously forgetting our childhood squabbles. Professors Sudhir Chandra and Mark Thurner as well as the participants in my seminars at El Colegio de México and Cornell University were responsive interlocutors. The gratitude extends to all the contributors to the volume, for answering importune emails, pursuing publishers for permissions, agreeing to my editing of their pieces, and providing many insights through their wider work. Among these contributors is Ishita. Of course, I owe her another book. For the present, this one must suffice.

Acknowledgements

The publisher acknowledges the following for permission to include articles/extracts in this volume.

Princeton University Press for Bernard Cohn, 'Cloth, Clothes, and Colonialism: India in the Nineteenth Century', in Bernard Cohn, *Colonialism and its Forms of Knowledge: The British in India*, Princeton, 1996, pp. 106–43.

Oxford University Press for Ranajit Guha, 'Negation', in Ranajit Guha, *Elementary Aspects of Peasant Insurgency in Colonial India*, New Delhi, 1983, pp. 51–66.

Oxford University Press for K.S. Singh, 'The Making of a Prophet: June 1894–July 1895', in K.S. Singh, *Birsa Munda and His Movement, 1874–1901: A Study of the Millenarian Movement in Chotanagpur*, Calcutta, 1983, pp. 45–56.

Oxford University Press for Paul Greenough, 'Conclusion', in Paul Greenough, *Prosperity and Misery in Modern Bengal*, New York, 1982, pp. 261–75.

Orient Longman for Ravindra K. Jain, 'Bundela Genealogy and Legends: The Past of an Indigenous Ruling Group', in Ravindra K. Jain, *Between History and Legend: Status and Power in Bundelkhand*, Hyderabad, 2002, pp. 1–33.

Sage Publications for Ishita Banerjee-Dube, 'Reading Time: Texts and Pasts in Colonial Eastern India', *Studies in History*, 19 (1), 2003, pp. 1–17.

Sage Publications for Susan Visvanathan, 'Reconstructions of the Past among the Syrian Christians of Kerala', *Contributions to Indian Sociology*, 20 (2), 1986, pp. 241–60.

State University of New York Press for Saurabh Dube, 'A Contested Past', in Saurabh Dube, *Untouchable Pasts: Religion, Identity, and Power among a Central Indian Community, 1780–1850*, Albany, 1998, pp. 115–39.

Oxford University Press for Gyanendra Pandey, 'The Bigoted Julaha', in Gyanendra Pandey, *The Construction of Communalism in Colonial North India*, New Delhi, 1990, pp. 69–107.

Oxford University Press for Malavika Kasturi, '*Bhumeawat* and Rajput Rebellion', in Malavika Kasturi, *Embattled Identities: Rajput Lineages and the Colonial State in the Nineteenth-Century North India*, New Delhi, 2002, pp. 172–83.

Oxford University Press for Ajay Skaria, 'Anxious Pleasures of Livelihood' and 'Shared Kingship and Loss', in Ajay Skaria, *Hybrid Histories: Forests, Frontiers and Wildness in Western India*, New Delhi, 1999, pp. 63–94.

Oxford University Press for Veena Das, 'Time, Self, and Community: Features of the Sikh Militant Discourse', in Veena Das, *Critical Events: An Anthropological Perspective on Contemporary India*, New Delhi, 1995, pp. 118–36.

Duke University Press for Ann G. Gold and Bhoju Ram Gujar, 'Shoes', in Ann G. Gold and Bhoju Ram Gujar, *In the Time of Trees and Sorrows: Nature, Power, and Memory in Rajasthan*, Durham, 2002, pp. 105–25.

Oxford University Press for Nandini Sundar, 'The Dialectics of Dussehra: *Raja* and *Praja* in the Bastar Polity', in Nandini Sundar, *Subalterns and Sovereigns: An Anthropological History of Bastar 1854–1996*, New Delhi, 1997, pp. 47–76.

Oxford University Press and Stanford University Press for K. Sivaramakrishnan, 'Geographies of Empire: The Transition from "Wild" to Managed Landscapes', in K. Sivaramakrishnan, *Modern Forests: Statemaking and Environmental Change in Colonial Eastern India*, New Delhi and Stanford, 1999, pp. 80–90.

University of Chicago Press for John D. Kelly, 'Gaze and Grasp: Plantations, Desires, Indentured Indians, and Colonial Law in Fiji', in L. Manderson and M. Jolly (eds), *Sites of Desire/Economies of Pleasure: Sexualities in Asia and the Pacific*, Chicago, 1997, pp. 72–98.

Princeton University Press for Peter van der Veer, 'The Moral State: Religion, Nation, and Empire in Victorian Britain and British India', in

P. van der Veer and H. Lehmann (eds), *Nation and Religion: Perspectives on Europe and Asia*, Princeton, 1999, pp. 17–40.

Princeton University Press for Nicholas B. Dirks, 'The Policing of Tradition: Colonial Anthropology and the Invention of Custom', in Nicholas B. Dirks, *Castes of Mind: Colonialism and the Making of Modern India*, Princeton, 2001, pp. 149–72.

Oxford University Press for Shail Mayaram, 'Partition and Violence in Mewat: Rites of Territorial and Political Passage', in Shail Mayaram, *Resisting Regimes: Myth, Memory and the Shaping of Muslim Identity*, New Delhi, 1997, pp. 179–98.

Hurst for Emma Tarlo, 'Is *Khadi* the Solution?', in Emma Tarlo, *Clothing Matters: Dress and Identity in India*, London, 1996, pp. 94–126.

Introduction
Anthropology, History,
Historical Anthropology

SAURABH DUBE

The relationship between anthropology and history has been chequered and contradictory. The alliance between them has also been passionate and productive.[1] Displaying limited comprehension and lingering mistrust of the other discipline, the two have often talked past one another.[2] Conversely, at different times and in distinct locations, important practitioners of these bodies of knowledge have underscored their key convergences, highlighting the necessity of crossing borders and straddling boundaries that separate them.

Over the last three decades, the interchanges between these enquiries have acquired fresh purposes in theoretical and empirical studies. The conjunctions have been accompanied by key considerations of the history of anthropology and the anthropology of history. At stake has been a serious rethinking of the status of the two disciplines. This has included the cautious questioning of contemporary celebrations of interdisciplinary departures—of the 'anthropological turn' in history and of the 'historical turn' in anthropology—as being insufficiently conceptualized.

The anthropology and history of South Asia have reflected these patterns, but they have also reworked such tendencies, imbuing them with specific salience. Here, significant studies of the 1960s and 1970s brought together processes of history and of culture and society as part of mutual analytical fields. More recently such emphases and orientations have been critically worked upon. As anthropologists and historians have rethought theory, method, and perspective, archival materials have been read through anthropological filters and fieldwork has been harnessed to the historical imagination, significantly opening up questions of the nature of the 'archive' and the 'field'. Anthropological agendas have been yoked to historical accounts of the interleaving of meaning and practice in distinct terrain, across time. Historical sensibilities have informed ethnographic explorations of the interplay between culture and power in diverse places, through time. Such blending has produced hybrid narratives—rendering the strange as familiar and accessing the familiar as strange, the better to unsettle our notions of strangeness and familiarity regarding historical and contemporary worlds.

This collection brings together a range of writings that intimate the terms, terrains, and trajectories of the enmeshments of anthropology and history. The work offers to students and scholars a wide-ranging domain of anthropological and historical endeavour, gathered under the rubric of historical anthropology—unravelling its departures, charting its contexts, exploring its characteristics, and tracking its predicaments and possibilities. At the same time, the book does more, too, since it also attempts to open up the terms of historical anthropology.

In terms of the organization of disciplines concerning South Asia, what I am calling historical anthropology remains only an uncertainly demarcated form of scholarly enquiry, especially on the subcontinent. Registering this fact but abjuring the temptation to establish still another cross-disciplinary sub-field, I will proceed by raising critical questions, rather than providing settled solutions, regarding historical anthropology. It only follows that I seek as much to probe the business-as-usual of the anthropology and history of India as to present the consequences of the meeting and mating of these enquiries, including their profound, mutual transformations.

How are we to understand historical anthropology? Is it a form of knowledge principally entailing archival research *and* fieldwork, themselves framed as pre-figured and already known procedures that subsequently find productive combination in this interdisciplinary terrain? Is historical anthropology, then, only an enquiry that conjoins the methodologies and techniques of two taken-for-granted disciplines? As Brian Axel has argued,

in all the bustle to try and figure out how history and anthropology can use each other's techniques (and thus, supposedly, constitute a historical anthropology), what most often goes without comment is the presumption that history and anthropology are whole and complete in themselves. Here, we regard such a presumption as a problem—one leading to the very common way of speaking about historical anthropology as exemplifying the dialogue between history and anthropology.[3]

My own efforts involve approaching historical anthropology in a manner that rethinks its constituent disciplines and their wider interplay. This Introduction is divided into three main parts, each with their own several sections. The first part, 'Lasting Legacies', explores formative orientations of anthropology to time and temporality, and of history to culture and tradition. It does this by approaching anthropology and history not narrowly as hermetic disciplines, but as configurations of knowledge and modalities of knowing that have often entailed mutual presuppositions about social worlds that shore up and shelter them. Of critical import here are temporal hierarchies and oppositions as well as epistemological ambivalences and excesses of anthropology and history under formations of modernity. The second part, 'Critical Departures', considers the more recent transformations of anthropology and history. This is done not simply by tracing the dialogue between the two but by attending to their critical makeovers and mutual renovations, which signal convergent dispositions yet also divergent articulations. Indeed, the account is not framed as a heroic narrative of the progressive departures in anthropology and history, but one that registers the ambiguities and contradictions in this terrain. The third part, 'Formative Conjunctions', discusses important developments in the study of pasts and communities, empire and nation, and culture and power in South Asia, as part of a wider interplay between anthropology and history.[4] Here, too, rather than an exclusive concern with methodological convergences between these forms of enquiry, the account turns on their shared sensibilities that underlie the substantive contributions of such scholarship. This serves to broaden rather than restrict the emergent field of historical anthropology, pointing toward its productive possibilities.[5]

LASTING LEGACIES

I have noted that conversations between anthropology and history are usually approached by regarding the two as *disciplines*. But their shared entailments are no less the attributes of common assumptions and mutual denials, which have deep provenance and broad implications. On the one hand, neither time nor temporality is the exclusive prerogative of the historian, each finding diverse configurations in anthropological practice. Indeed, ethnography has opened up the taken-for-granted nature of time and temporality. Yet, it has also spatially segregated these categories into distinct domains of myth and modernity, imbuing them with static significance when they refer to the former. On the other hand, the concepts of culture and tradition might have shored up anthropology, but they have been variously present in history-writing, especially as received notions and ready devices of comprehension and explanation. Acting as discursive shorthands in historical narratives, culture and tradition have carried contending connotations through particular projections of historical action. These issues require further unpacking, including examinations of the reciprocal principles propping up history and anthropology.

Anthropology and Time

For a very long time now, anthropological understandings have displayed varied dispositions toward issues of temporality and history, from willing disregard and uneasy excision to formative ambivalences and constitutive contradictions. Yet time itself has never been absent from such comprehensions. Today there is wide acknowledgment of the epistemic violence that attended the birth and growth of modern anthropology. Here were to be found temporal sequences, based on evolutionary principles and racist presuppositions, which projected hierarchical stages of civilizations, societies, and peoples. At the same time, it is worth considering if such hierarchically ordered, evolutionary mappings of cultures and societies—turning on the 'savage' and the 'primitive'—were excised from disciplinary formations with the emergence of fieldwork based 'scientific' anthropology in the first half of the twentieth century.

First, the apparent ruptures of functionalist and structural-functionalist anthropology with evolutionist (and diffusionist) principles, on the grounds of their speculative procedures, had wider consequences. They no less entailed a wider suspicion towards—the placing of a question mark on—history as such within the discipline.[6] Now the practice of anthropology could proceed in contradistinction to the writing of history. Second, these tendencies were conjoined with the influence of Durkheimian sociology in the shaping of structural-functionalist tenets. Such conjunctions led to pervasive presuppositions that societal arrangements were better understood in abstraction from their historical transformations. They called forth and rested on analytical oppositions between 'synchrony' and 'diachrony', or 'statics' and 'dynamics', where in each copula the former term was privileged over the latter notion concerning the object of anthropology. Third, these emphases were further bound to wider anthropological predilections towards seeking out continuity and consensus, rather than change and conflict, in the societies being studied. Fourth and finally, the ambivalence toward the temporal dimensions of structure and culture within the discipline was implicitly founded on broad disjunctions between, on the one hand, Western societies grounded in history and reason, and, on the other, non-Western cultures held in place by myth and ritual.

Such premises came to underlie particular protocols of salvage anthropology, also shoring up formative dispositions of the ethnographic enterprise. Of enormous significance were pervasive procedures of anthropological practice that have forged a tendentious timeless 'tradition' through narrative techniques and analytical projections of a lasting 'ethnographic present'. It only followed that intrusive disciplinary presumptions came to sharply separate the dynamic time of the ethnographer's society from the static temporality of anthropological objects, procedures also affecting the historical enterprise.[7] Together, in widespread ethnographic orientations, change and transformation usually entered 'native' structure in exogenous ways.

Johannes Fabian has pointed to the repeated ways in which anthropological inquiry has construed its object as the irremediable other, through measures turning on temporality: the ethnographic object is denied the 'coevalness of time' with the instant of the anthropologist subject.[8] In other words, the (observing) subject and the (observed) object are precisely separated through time to inhabit distinct temporalities, the historical time of the former always ahead of the mythic time of the latter. Here, the temporal divide has meant that not only anthropological objects but also ethnographic practice have emerged as being out of time, albeit in ambivalent and disjunctive ways. On the one hand, the temporal dimensions of anthropological writing have appeared effaced through their elision with both the taken-for-granted time of the modern subject and the objective time of scientific knowledge. On the other hand, the temporality of anthropological others—their time/timelessness—could only emerge as being external to and lagging behind the time of the writing of ethnography.[9] All this has defined the 'savage slot' and the 'native niche' of anthropology that have been constitutive of the discipline.[10]

None of this is to deny that such schemes have been attended by contentions and exceptions within the discipline. These are exactly related to the formations and tensions of anthropology, incisively articulated by George Stocking, Jr.:

... the greatest retrospective unity of the discourses subsumed within the rubric 'anthropology' is to be found in the substantive concern with the peoples who were long stigmatized as 'savages', and who, in the nineteenth century, tended to be excluded from other human scientific disciplines by the very process of their substantive-cum-methodological definition (the economist's concern with the money economy; the historian's concern with written documents, etc.)...to study the history of anthropology is to...describe and to interpret or explain the 'otherness' of populations encountered in European overseas expansion. Although thus fundamentally (and oppositionally) diversitarian in impulse, such study has usually implied a reflexivity which reencompassed the European self and alien 'other' within a unitary humankind. This history of anthropology may thus be viewed as a continuing (and complex) dialectic between the universalism of 'anthropos' and the diversitarianism of 'ethnos' or, from the perspective of particular historical moments, between the Enlightenment and the Romantic impulse.[11]

At stake, then, are attempts to reconcile tensions between 'generic human rationality' and 'the biological unity of mankind' on the one hand, with the enormous variation of cultural formations on the other, issues to which I shall return. The immediate point is that the constitutive presuppositions and procedures concerning time within the ethnographic enterprise require staying with longer. They intimate the persistent influence of evolutionist understandings on contemporary anthropology.[12] At the same time, beyond purely disciplinary considerations, they insinuate pervasive 'meta-geographical' projections. Turning on time, such projections draw on developmental visions of history of academic bents, quotidian persuasions, and their persistent interchange. Authoritatively if ambiguously, they carve up social worlds into enchanted terrains of tradition and disenchanted domains of modernity.

Hierarchies of Time

At stake, in fact, is nothing less than the hierarchical ordering of timespace as part of the wide-ranging interplay between modern knowledge, anthropological understandings, historical blueprints, and their quotidian configurations. Consider the manner in which patterns of history and designs of culture have been understood in the past and the present through formidable oppositions between static, enchanted communities and dynamic, modern societies. At first, the duality might seem to be little more than an ideological plank of modernization theory, counter-posing (primarily non-Western) tradition with (chiefly Western) modernity. But the antinomy has wider implications and deeper underpinnings.[13] It is not only that the duality has animated and articulated other enduring oppositions, such as those between ritual and rationality, myth and history, community and state, magic and the modern, and emotion and reason.[14] It is also that as lasting legacies of the developmental idea of universal, natural history and an aggrandizing representation of an exclusive, Western modernity, such antinomies have found varied expressions among the distinct subjects that they have named, described, and objectified since at least the eighteenth century.[15] Representations emanating from the European Enlightenment have played a key role here.

It would be hasty and erroneous to see the European Enlightenment of the seventeenth and eighteenth centuries as all of a piece. For example, contending strains of rationalism in France and of empiricism in Britain lay at the core of this movement of ideas. Similarly, the Enlightenment hinged on different conceptions of universal and natural history. Indeed, following prescient, wide-ranging historical analyses it might be more useful to speak in the plural: of *Enlightenments*.[16] Here were to be found, too, challenges to the predominantly rationalist procedures of a primarily French provenance through varieties of *Counter-Enlightenments*.[17] For a long time now it has been generally accepted that the period of the Enlightenment was accompanied by ideas and processes of the secularization of Judeo-Christian time.[18] Actually, such secularization of Judeo-Christian time during the Enlightenment was an emergent and consequential idea, but a circumscribed and limited process.[19]

In this context, discrete yet overlaying developmental schemes underwrote grand designs of human history, from the rationalist claims of Francois-Marie Arouet Voltaire and Immanuel Kant through to the historicist frames of Giambattista Vico and Johann Gottfried von Herder.[20] There was profound contention among such schemas, yet in different ways they each projected developmental blueprints of universal history.[21] Such contrary strains and convergent emphases were bound to the fact, many times overlooked, that the Enlightenment was as much historical as philosophical, as much about the rewriting of history as about the rethinking of philosophy. The consequences were limited yet significant. On the one hand, throughout the nineteenth century but also afterwards, Judeo-Christian and Messianic time and temporality did not lose their influence in Western worlds.[22] On the other hand, by the second half of the nineteenth century, at the very least in the Protestant West, secularized time could acquire a naturalized aura and developmental thought was distilled (uncertainly yet potently) as historical progress.[23]

It followed that time came to be increasingly mapped in hierarchical ways to plot peoples and cultures in the movement of history that was primarily projected as the passage of progress. Frequently articulated

by the *Ur*-opposition between the primitive and the civilized, in place
here nonetheless was neither a singular Western 'self' nor an exclusive
non-Western 'other'. Rather, at play in this terrain were the cultural
severalty of Western selves and the historical hierarchies of non-Western
otherness. In this scenario, many groups were still stuck in the stage of
barbarism and savagery with few prospects of advancement. Other
societies had reached the ascending steps of civilization yet lacked the
critical foundations of reason. Still other peoples had evolved to the
higher reaches of humanity through advantages of race and rationality
and propensities of history and nationality. Indeed, it was the past and
the present of this last set of peoples, comprising the enlightened
European elect, that was seized upon and rendered as a looking glass at
large. In this mirror was envisioned the universal history of human
destiny—a destiny ultimately represented as groups and societies either
failing before or rising to the stage of modernity.

Ruptures of Modernity

Put simply, the idea of modernity entails the unfolding of a break with
the past. This story turns on fault lines, intimating ruptures with ritual
and magic, and breaches with enchantment and tradition.[24] Following
influential understandings, modernity, as an epochal concept, has been
seen as embodying a distinct and new status from preceding periods,
insinuating essentially novel orientations to the past, present, and
future.[25] Such a picture carries its own truths, but it also presents modernity in principally idealized terms. To begin with, authoritative and
commonplace understandings of modernity project it as a phenomenon
generated purely internally within the West, albeit one that was later
variously exported to other parts of humanity. It follows that precisely
this measure serves to override the dynamic of the colonizer and the
colonized, race and reason, and Enlightenment and empire that
underlies modernity as history. These twin procedures announce salient
registers of hierarchical mappings of time and space. In both conscious
and inadvertent ways, the registers involve two simultaneous measures.
Rehearsing the West as modernity, they equally stage modernity '*as*
the West'.[26]

The idea of modernity as a coming apart from the past rests on the
imagination of ruptures within Western history. But it cannot help also
turning on, explicitly or implicitly, the importance of disjunctions of
the West with non-Western worlds. On the one hand, the caesura
defined by modernity as the new beginning is shifted into the past,
'precisely to the start of modern times' in Europe.[27] This break is a

formative horizon and a receding past. Indeed, it is ahead of this threshold that the present is seen as being renewed in its vitality and novelty under modernity. On the other hand, exactly when the present is privileged as the most recent period, the novelty and vitality of modernity are threatened by spectres of the 'medieval', the 'superstitious', the 'eschatological', and the 'prophetic' meandering in its midst. These spirits are a prior presence or covenant *and* an ongoing horror or delight. Each attempt to contain them in the present entails marking them as an attribute of the past. Concerning the contemporary world, my reference is to the ways in which, in dominant representations, the Taliban and Al-Qaeda are simultaneously 'coeval' and 'medieval'; and the manner in which the pervasive 'enchantments' today of the 'indigenous' and the 'tribal' are at once every bit contemporary yet entirely anachronistic.

The meanings, understandings, and actions that fall outside the disenchantment-driven horizons of modernity have to be plotted as lagging behind this novel stage. Here, spatial mappings and temporal measurements of the West and the non-West come to rest on the trajectory of time, an axis that claims to be normatively neutral but is, in fact, profoundly hierarchical. This is to say that the precise notion of modernity as a rupture with the past carves up social and historical worlds into the enchanted and the modern, further naming and animating other oppositions such as those between ritual and rationality, myth and history, and magic and modernity. There are many entanglements and critical implications of the duality of the primitive (or native) and the civilized (or modern), an antinomy constitutive of the anthropological enterprise but also crucial for the historical discipline. The pervasive place in social worlds of oppositions of modernity underwrites their forceful presence within the disciplines.

Modern Antinomies

Why should the antinomies of modernity have played an important role in the mapping and making of social worlds? To begin with, it should be clear that these oppositions emerged embedded within formidable projects of power and knowledge, turning on modernity, Enlightenment, empire, and nation. These have been motivated projects 'not simply of looking and recording but of recording and remaking' the world, as Talal Asad tells us.[28] Indeed, at stake have been differently motivated projects of diversely recording and remaking the world in their distinct images of history and modernity. Unsurprisingly, in this terrain modern oppositions have themselves assumed persuasive analytical authority *and* acquired pervasive worldly attributes, being variously articulated with mappings of modernity as a self-realizing project of progress and a self-evident embodiment of history.[29]

I have been suggesting the salience of registering the place of the oppositions of modernity in the moulding of social worlds. At the same time, it is equally important to attend to the contending elaborations of the analytical, ideological, and everyday separation between enchanted or traditional cultures and disenchanted or modern societies. The contentions are present at the core of post-Enlightenment thought and non-Western scholarship, each including critiques of the West in the past and the present. Indeed, the actual elaborations of the hierarchical oppositions of modernity have imbued them with contradictory value and contrary salience. Here are to be found ambivalences, ambiguities, and excesses of meaning and authority. All of this is registered by the *particular* unravelling of divergent traditions of understanding and explanation at the heart of modernity as ideology and history. My reference is to the opposed tendencies that have been described as those of rationalism and historicism, of the analytical and the hermeneutical, and of the progressivist and the romantic.[30] It is critical to track the frequent combination in intellectual practice of these tendencies in order to trace the contradictions and contentions and ambivalences and excesses of modern knowledge(s). Together, such interleaving expressions reveal that the terms of modernity are assiduously articulated, but that they are also out of joint with themselves.

Ethnography and Temporality: Three Masters

In tune with these considerations, let me turn to some of the contradictions and contentions that have characterized ethnographic orientations to time and temporality. I shall focus on aspects of the work of Franz Boas, E.E. Evans-Pritchard, and Pierre Bourdieu, three masters of the anthropological craft who represent different historical moments, explanatory efforts, and epistemological styles in the pasts of the discipline. My choice of these scholars has much to do with their particular engagements with temporality and time.

We have noted the racial assumptions that underlay evolutionary anthropology in the later nineteenth and early twentieth centuries. The single greatest early disciplinary challenge to such schemes and presuppositions was issued by Franz Boas (1858–1942).[31] At the beginning of the twentieth century, Boas defined anthropological knowledge as consisting of 'the biological history of mankind in all its varieties; linguistics applied to people without written languages; the ethnology of people without historic records; and prehistoric archaeology.'[32] Across his career, he added to all these forms of enquiry. At the same time, Boas' distinctive contribution to anthropology derived from his insistence on the diachronic dimensions of the discipline.[33] As George Stocking has argued, 'For Boas, the "otherness" which is the subject matter of anthropology was to be explained as the product of change of time', an insistence that covered his unifying definition of the discipline.[34] Here were to be found his critique of evolutionary assumption, 'a neo-ethnological critique of "the comparative method" of classical evolutionism'.[35]

Today, there is appreciation not only of how Boas construed a domain of enquiry mostly free of biological determinism to lay the basis for the modern disciplinary conception of culture as pluralistic and relativistic, but also of how his particular turn to the diachronic, the historical, and the temporal signified a road mainly not taken by anthropology during most of the twentieth century.[36] Indeed, Boas' orientation to anthropological knowledge can emerge in current commentaries as primarily building on nineteenth-century romantic and hermeneutic traditions in European science, philosophy, and history.[37] Yet it would not do to simply celebrate Boas' critique of evolutionary and racialist presuppositions from the vantage point of our present. Nor would it be enough to emphasize only the romantic underpinnings of his anthropology. In fact, the work of Boas is best understood as straddling the dualism between progressivist and romantic traditions, at once braiding together while retaining a tension between these opposed tendencies. Here are to be found the salient entwinings of contending schemes of modern knowledge, which have variously shored up anthropology.

On the one hand, in the work of Boas, the progressivist stance was profoundly manifest in key nineteenth-century liberal beliefs, which stressed scientific knowledge and individual freedom. They expressed Boas' broader historical vision and developmental viewpoint. He believed in cumulative rational knowledge that underlay innate human progress. Here, human progress was understood not in a generalized manner but as intimating specifically the growth of what Boas called 'our own' Western modern civilization.[38] Indeed, this perspective was marked by a fatalistic attitude toward technologically based historical development as not only pushing forward Western civilization but as confronting and vanquishing 'technologically primitive cultures'. At the same time, Boas' universalistic rationalism also led him to assert the existence of 'general values' that were 'cumulatively realized' in the history of human civilization and 'variously realized' in different human cultures. Thus, Boas' well-known questioning of his own Western civilization and his belief in the alternative values of other cultures went hand-in-hand with the anthropologist's lack of submission to cultural relativism and his faith in a non-contingent realm of scientific truth.[39]

On the other hand, throughout Boas' career, cross-cutting this optimistic, rationalist, and universalistic progressivist stance was a more pessimistic, emotional, and particularistic romanticist disposition. Arguably, the latter sensibility could not but inform both Boas' dissatisfaction with Western civilization and the manner in which such 'alienation' found expression in his anticipation of a pluralistic conception of culture that was itself based on recognition of 'the legitimacy of alternative value systems'. At stake in this sensibility was an aesthetic undercurrent—reinforced by Boas' life experiences yet carrying wider resonances—that made him acutely 'aware of the role of irrational factors in human life'. These tendencies were articulated positively in the variety of human forms of culture, but they were expressed negatively in the way particular customs of determinate groups could be retrospectively rationalized as universal norms, including in the case of race. Unsurprisingly, Boas' lifelong devotion to the study of culture and race, especially the exclusivity they each defined, stressed the profoundly contingent conditioning by history of these phenomena.[40]

Taken together, Boas' thought derived motive force from its everrestless juxtaposition of wider progressivist and romantic tendencies, its almost inevitable interleaving of universalistic and rationalist orientations with particularistic and emotional dispositions. Note the contrasts. Boas 'retained all his life a rather idealized and absolutistic conception of science' that was unambiguously non-contingent: but he also granted a necessary, contingent value to specific cultural groupings. Boas singularly conjoined human progress and technologically based historical process with Western civilization: but he equally defended the 'mental capacity' of 'primitive man' to participate fully in 'modern civilization'.[41] Boas exclusively envisioned rational advance in the image of Western civilization: but he crucially affirmed the values of non-European cultures and established thereby 'a kind of Archimedian leverage point' for a critique of his own civilization.[42] According to established anthropological lore, Boas' career had a dramatic end. At a luncheon in New York, Boas had just begun to say, 'I have a new theory of culture…', when he fell dead in mid sentence. In death as in life, Franz Boas encapsulated not only the ambiguities but also the ironies of anthropology—in an acute way, his own manner.

The contrary dispositions constitutive of the anthropological enterprise were no less characteristic of the work of the British anthropologist
E.E. Evans-Pritchard (1902–1973), widely known as 'EP'. In conventional
anthropological wisdom, the work of Evans-Pritchard has been
approached as consolidating the structural–functional enquiry initiated
by A.R. Radcliffe-Brown. Here, there is acknowledgement of EP's earlier
interactions with Malinowski and there is recognition that from the
1950s onwards his work followed different pathways of theory and
explication. The latter included Evans-Pritchard's famous endorsement
of anthropology as a humanistic (and not natural-scientific) discipline,
as well as his assertions of the close linkages of anthropology with
history.[43] They extended to the questions EP raised concerning the
inability of anthropologists to enter the minds of the people they studied;
the limits of their scholarly motivations that often mirrored the ethno-
centric assumptions of their own cultures; and the narrowness of
biological, sociological, and psychological theories of religion.[44] At the
same time, despite such avowals of the shifts in Evans-Pritchard's anthropology, the centrepiece of his contribution to the discipline is yet often
assumed to consist of his development of structural–functionalism,
reflecting the hagiography of this paradigm.[45]

In front of such currents, I would like to indicate a distinct approach
to Evans-Pritchard's work, an approach that turns on critically registering how his writings were shaped by their salient interleaving of
hermeneutic strands and analytical strains. Such an orientation to EP's
anthropology does not deny, for example, the place of his monograph
on the Nuer as a flagship endeavour of structural–functionalist analysis.[46] Nor does it overlook the fact that Evans-Pritchard's work bore
close connections with the formative presuppositions of both
structural–functionalism and functionalism considering society as an
integrated system. Rather, the disposition being outlined seeks to open
up the terms of understanding of EP's arguments and analyses.

In his discussion of time, Evans-Pritchard drew upon the work of
both Durkheim and Malinowski.[47] In *The Nuer* as well as in an essay
on time reckoning among these peoples, EP famously developed the
notion of 'oecological' time.[48] This notion emerged closely bound to
time-reckoning concepts, conveying 'social activities' or a 'relation
between activities to one another'.[49] Here time's passage is perceived
through a lens of cultural concepts referring to activities—that is,
through time-reckoning systems—rather than through an actual
immersion in activities.[50] Yet, time also consists, for EP, of the 'rhythm'
of basic activity cycles linked to natural cycles: daily cattle movements
and seasonal passages between villages and camps as well as the

distinctive tempo of each season. In this sense, time appears as motion or process and not simply static units or concepts of reckoning time.[51] Together, two sets of emphases work in tandem in Evans-Pritchard's elaboration of oecological (or everyday) time.

Conversely, when EP turns to long-term, structural time, his gaze entirely shifts away from activities which, recall, provide a sense of concrete movement. Rather, EP now comes to focus exclusively on conceptual frames. This is to say that structural time is not about an incremental movement but rather that it is fundamentally non-cumulative, so that the genealogical grid of the Nuer creates only an immobile 'illusion' of time.[52] Drawing on the insights of Nancy Munn, I am suggesting that Evans-Pritchard's structural time is not qualitative and concrete but quantitative and geometrical. It is a static version and vision of time that occludes the concrete and lived space of activities.[53]

At stake here is a constitutive split, a formative discrepancy. On the one hand, in *describing* oecological time, EP brings to bear on his discussion key spatiotemporal activities, including, for example, phased movements between village and camp. This is, broadly speaking, the hermeneutic moment in Evans-Pritchard's understanding(s) of time. On the other hand, precisely this 'co-constitution' of time and space in activity is ignored and suppressed within EP's formalist frames, so that structural time appears as an abstract geometry of social distance.[54] This might be broadly spoken of as the analytical moment in Evans-Pritchard's conception(s) of time. Needless to say, the hermeneutic and the analytical tendencies are profoundly entwined in EP's anthropology. Indeed, it is such entwining that provide EP's considerations of time with their motive force and their critical limitations. The Nuer peoples in EP's hermeneutic hands have their own concrete, everyday time. The move serves to found time in the image of social diversity and cultural heterogeneity, implicitly opening up thereby pervasive, common-sense, and taken-for-granted terms of time as a simply homogeneous measurement with no qualitative distinctions. But the Nuer peoples, according to EP's analytic, also do not have long-term time. The measure raises key questions regarding his analytical framework as bearing the profound impress of lasting projections, discussed earlier, of primitive places (the Nuer and their oecological time) and modern spaces (the West and its long-term time).[55]

The interplay between hermeneutic dispositions and analytical tendencies—as well as the opposition of the enchanted and the modern—no less marks the influential corpus of the French sociologist-philosopher Pierre Bourdieu (1930–2002). Bourdieu combines phenomenological, Weberian, and Marxian dispositions to underscore the temporal dimensions of social practices and practical actors, including through his notion of 'structuration', arguing that totalizing frameworks of fixed 'rules' of action take time out of practice. Yet, precisely such hermeneutic moves crucially crisscross in Bourdieu's work with analytical orientations that bring into play implicit oppositions between the 'traditional' and the 'modern', collective rhythms and individual action, and 'space' and 'time'. Here, in framing time through agent-oriented filters, Bourdieu contrasts pre-capitalist, traditional Algeria as marked by 'foresight' only of the immediate future (already 'implicit in the directly perceived present') *with* capitalist, modern societies where 'forecasting' entails an indefinite future, 'a field of possibilities to be explored...by calculation.' Moreover, in his later work, the emphasis on exploring practices through a focus on both the irreversible, enduring time of activities and the agent's strategic manipulation of this time disappear when Bourdieu turns his gaze toward collective (calendric) rhythms and periodization, which are explained through symbolic homologies that now readily dissolve into a generalized 'logic of practice'. Finally, Bourdieu's writings not only do not escape the analytical oppositions of time and space but they principally privilege the former over the latter.[56] None of this is to suggest that a focus on the entwining of hermeneutic and analytical dispositions holds the single key to understanding traditions within anthropology and history, but to regard it as a possible means of reconsidering the past and the present of the disciplines and their portrayals.[57]

Temporality and Anthropology:
Indian Instances

Turning to the anthropology and sociology of India, it would be easy to show that these disciplinary practices have been chiefly conducted at a remove from historical considerations, broadly privileging the ethnographic present. Much of this would be doubtless true, but it is possibly more important to consider the contradictory and contingent ways in which history and temporality have entered anthropological writing on the subcontinent. Indeed, keeping in view the ambivalences of ethnography, discussed above, makes it possible to approach the pasts of anthropology in India with a distinctive set of questions.

     Let me begin with an instance that brings home such considerations: anthropologist S.C. Dube's first monograph, *The Kamar*.[58] This developed from the self-trained Indian ethnographer's Ph.D. dissertation, the thesis and the manuscript being written and revised in the second half of the 1940s. Now, the study can be upbraided as a variety of salvage anthropology in the colonial frame, denying temporality to its object— the Kamar, hunter-gatherers and shifting-cultivators living in the southern part of Raipur district in Chhattisgarh —through the means of evolutionary assumption. At the same time, I would like to critically open up *The Kamar* toward other readings, which stay with the tensions that have been formative of anthropology on the subcontinent. Here is to be found the ambiguous yet pervasive play in such scholarship of temporality and history—and of empire and nation—that requires further examination.

   The Kamar lies at the cusp of the end of colonial rule and the arrival of Indian Independence. The study was shaped by assumptions of the prior primitive, the savage slot, and the native niche within colonial/modern ethnography, presuppositions and projections that we encountered earlier. Yet the book equally referred to Kamar life-ways as embedded within wider societal processes. The work cast its subjects as caught within the larger terms of nationalist transformation. Nonetheless, it constantly returned to an essential Kamar tradition. The point is that such tension is not merely a shift of accent in the study between portions written before and after Indian Independence, nor is the tension simply disabling. Rather, the tension is formative of the book, running through its chapters. *The Kamar* captures and contains the ambiguities and ambivalences of S.C. Dube's thought and writing—themselves indicative of anxieties of his discipline—at a critical juncture, uneasily braiding anthropological demand and nationalist desire.

   It should not be surprising that the formative tensions and productive ambiguities of *The Kamar* are bound to the style, structure, and sentiment of the work. Dube considered that primitive cultures were not static but dynamic, especially since culture itself was an adaptive mechanism. Here the notion of the primitive entailed twin registers. On the one hand, it signified backwardness upon an evolutionist axis, a self-explanatory schema, assumed in place, a priori, the dominant vision of anthropology and nation at the time; on the other, it registered cultural difference, coeval with the ethnographer, in the space of the nation, which invited empathetic understanding. Thus, in the study, the imperative to describe the Kamar way of life before it changed crisscrossed with the impulse to record the changing way of life of the Kamar, the dual dispositions pulling apart but also coming together.[59] I am not suggesting that Dube's first ethnographic monograph prematurely reconciled these contrary tendencies. Rather, the point is that the text is the site where such contradictory pressures are visible, the terrain where these tensions were set in motion, which serves to further reveal and unravel the conjunctions and disjunctions between anthro-pological frames and nationalist formulations.[60] All this raises key questions for critical considerations of anthropological (and socio-logical) practice on the Indian subcontinent, particularly of scholarship in the shadow of empire and nation.

Consider the fact that the work of important Indian anthropologists and sociologists, whose reputation was already well established in the pre-Independence era, was frequently shaped by implicit presup-positions and explicit projections regarding the civilization and history of the subcontinent. Here, scholars as diverse as Nirmal Kumar Bose, G.S. Ghurye, and Iravati Karve combined readings of Hindu, classical texts with insights from ethnographic, field materials. Their scholarship initiated thereby different enquiries into common concerns such as the integration of 'tribes' into Hindu society, also addressing issues involving arrangements of kinship along pan-regional lines in the sub-continent.[61] Similarly, in the writings of Radhakamal Mukerjee, D.P. Mukerji, and D.N. Majumdar, all of whom were based in Lucknow, distinct considerations of cultural tradition and its transformations were enmeshed with inherently varied articulations of the terms of history and civilization of India.[62]

My point is that it is easy but hasty to prejudge such scholarship as antiquated knowledge, which was firmly superseded after the 1950s by an increasingly specialized practice of the anthropology/sociology of India. Instead, the more difficult yet productive task entails tracking the specific, shifting ways in which notions and understandings of tradition, history, and civilization were played out in this terrain. Indeed, to undertake these efforts would be to unravel the archival lineaments of Indian anthropology, especially its engagements with and articu-lations of empire and nation, Western categories and nationalist considerations. None of this suggests simple celebrations of such scholarship. Rather, it implies the need for critically yet cautiously entering the protocols of this knowledge and its forms of knowing, in order to trace their constitutive considerations and contradictions, their formative ambivalences and excesses.[63]

From the 1950s onwards, writings in the anthropology/sociology of the subcontinent came to be cast in ever more synchronic moulds, particularly under the influence of functionalist, structural–functionalist, and structural analyses. In both implicit and explicit ways, such emphases put a question mark on what now appeared as the speculative procedures and commonsense projections—particularly concerning history, civilization, and tradition—within earlier scholarship. At the same time, it would be much too sanguine to assume that considerations of the terms of Indian civilization and tradition, including often-implicit articulations of patterns of history, simply disappeared from the newer writings.[64] Rather, these were variously folded into the creases of more tightly organized, synchronically structured, and self-confidently social-scientific analyses. Once again, it is critical to unravel the presence of notions of Indian civilization and tradition—and the implied projections of history—as shaping influential accounts of the village and social structure on the subcontinent in anthropology after Independence.[65]

Aspects of the influential writings of Louis Dumont assume significance here. The French intellectual's crucial contributions to scholarship include his articulation of Indian society as underpinned by the framework of the hierarchical man, *homo hierarchicus*.[66] Important for Dumont are the principle of *dharma*, the command of caste, and the order of hierarchy. Underpinned by the mandate of dharma, the structure of caste is manifested consciously in the ideology of hierarchy. This ideology finds its key form in the opposition between the pure and the impure, and assumes its critical characteristic in the separation of status and power, further defining a continuous hierarchy as the core value of the Hindu/Indian ethos. These primary principles also provide the basis for the range of Dumont's readings, which extend from particular understandings of the relationship between caste and sect through to discussions of religion and politics in South Asia.[67] Dumont's synthetic writings on South Asia draw on historical materials of an 'Indological', textual variety, further conjoining them with ethnographic insights.

Among his critics and supporters, Dumont's work served to orient important emphases of Indian anthropology in specific ways, emphases that only occasionally tended toward but mainly stayed away from historical readings.[68] At the same time, interlocutors of Dumont have rarely touched on the protocols of his own uses of history. Broadly speaking, the supporters applauded the richness of Dumont's writings, including as carrying forward his prior proposal—made together with David Pocock—that the sociology of India was best founded at the intersection of Indological and ethnographic research.[69] But they were hardly concerned with the historical dimensions of Dumont's textual readings.[70] In contrast, the various critics of Dumont took him to task, for example, for providing a Brahminical view of Indian society and for privileging the ritual hierarchy of purity and pollution in ways that excluded the 'material' bases of caste and authority or overlooked the 'cultural' constitution of kingship and power.[71] Yet these criticisms, too, suggested at best that Dumont's readings were a-historical—without staying further with the burden of such a-historicity, to imply that his work amounted to an outright rejection of history.

Ahead of these tendencies, I would like to suggest that it is crucial to attend to the terms of history in Dumont's seminal scholarship. While a detailed discussion of such issues is outside the scope of this Introduction, let me once again raise a few overlapping sets of questions here.[72] First, in what ways do Dumont's rendering of Indian/Hindu society imply an exclusive reading of Indological texts and a singular construction of history, which work in tandem? Does Dumont deploy textual–historical materials—along with other bodies of writings—to aggrandize and buttress his conception of Hinduism, which betokens a civilizational core and an encompassing ethos? Second, more specifically, do Dumont's projections of the past crucially underlie his proposals regarding caste and sect, and householder and renouncer, categories that are rendered in his earlier work as interacting ideal-types and that are cast in his later writing as complementary dualities? If this is the case, how do such ruses of history and articulations of oppositions shore up the place of caste and the position of sect as at once conforming to overweening constructions of Hinduism and expressing its exclusive history? Put differently, in what ways do Dumont's claims on history underpin his intonations of the essential continuity of the Hindu civilization, to underplay the differences embodied by caste and sect (in the image of a unified Hindu order) and/or to dissolve the distinctions of these formations (into a continuous Hindu ethos)?[73] Third and finally, the critical tenor of my queries notwithstanding, are there perhaps moments in Dumont's writing where his articulations of historical materials exceed his analytical schematics? At such moments, do his uses of history extend beyond supplying narrow illustrative material for aggrandizing projections of the unity and continuity of Hindu civilization, and provide instead glimmers of contested and contradictory elaborations of Hinduism, including of caste and sect?

History and Culture

I have noted that just as terms of time and temporality have been differently present at the core of anthropology, so also the writing of history has variously entailed projections of culture and tradition. It is to the latter issue that I now turn. Here it is important to reiterate that the writing of history, no less than anthropology, has borne the profound impress of the hierarchical oppositions of modernity and acutely expressed the contradictions and contentions of modern knowledge, also underscoring the reciprocity of these enquiries.

First, processes of the institutionalization of the discipline in the
Euro-American world in the nineteenth century—as also their significant antecedents—meant that history-writing emerged as bearing
the flag of the nation. Not only was the discipline often endlessly, ethno-
centrically inward-looking, but it was shaped by sharp distinctions
between the civilized and the backward in framings of peoples and
nations. Second, it followed that in Western arenas the relatively few
historical accounts that were undertaken of distant, generally colonial,
territories frequently presented such pasts as footnotes and appendices
to the history of Europe. Third, the histories construed in colonized
countries and newly independent nations were themselves often
envisioned in the image of a progressive West, albeit using unto their
own purposes the hierarchies and oppositions of an exclusive
modernity.[74] Fourth and finally, important strands of history-writing
could express hermeneutic, historicist, and counter-Enlightenment
impulses, but their relationship with an exclusive, hierarchical Western
modernity was double-edged. Such histories acutely articulated notions
of culture, tradition, and the *volk* (folk)—generally of the nation—to
critically question the conceit of an aggrandizing reason that they saw
as the leitmotif of the Enlightenment. Conversely, such articulations
of hermeneutic, historicist, and counter-Enlightenment tendencies
themselves could not escape, as we have seen, the developmental
schemes of a somewhat singular history centred on Europe.[75]

What about more contemporary history-writing on India? Here,
too, the notions of culture and tradition find rather particular manifestations, including their being turned into empty placeholders or
their being articulated in attenuated ways. First consider historical
accounts that are principally un-reflexive about their presuppositions
or/and frame themselves in primarily analytical modes. In two
important essays, Gyanendra Pandey has focused on the failure of
modern history-writing to adequately address the pasts of sectarian
religious violence in colonial and postcolonial India, particularly the
violence that constituted the Partition of the subcontinent.[76] He sees
this lack as a larger problem of historiography that subordinates the
everyday experience of violence and pain to histories of transition of
modernity, state, reason, and progress. We could agree or disagree with
Pandey's sweeping condemnation of history—or, following Foucault,
'historian's history'—that is rendered as 'History', the dark and ominous
reflection, in a mirror held up by the author, of 'Modernity'.[77] Yet, it is
important to register that Pandey points towards how pervasive blueprints of modernity and progress, state and nation, and reason and
civilization are built into the structure and *telos* of diverse historical

narratives. The blueprints not only underlay the existence and the experience of everyday and extraordinary moments of violence, but they do so by at once naturalizing and excising the transformations of culture(s) and tradition(s) in which the violence is embedded. Here, violence, culture, and tradition are ghosts, spectres that are assiduously attempted to be exorcised by history-writing but whose haunting presence is constitutive of the historian's narrative.[78]

In these historical accounts the exact articulations of violence, culture, and tradition are ignored yet assimilated—as inconsequential episodes and inconvenient aberrations—to endless narratives of inevitable transitions. Thus, colonial representations of 'native' unrest and nationalist writings on sectarian strife share common ground, since each offers explanations cast in terms of the criminality, backwardness, primitive passions, and ready unreason of the people. Equally, there are close connections between modern historians of different ideological persuasions in their depiction of the violence that accompanied the Partition of the subcontinent into India and Pakistan. There is little room in these accounts—constituted, variously, by a quest for underlying structures, a privileging of forces of change, and a preoccupation with the actions of great men—for discussing the trauma or meaning of sectarian violence, including critical considerations of the terms and transformations of cultures and traditions of which they form a part. Unsurprisingly, violence and pain—and their mutual entailments with culture and tradition—are relegated here to the realm of 'otherness', an otherness that formatively haunts history-writing of the Indian subcontinent.[79]

The terms of culture and tradition also pose problems for history-writing that actively espouses these category-entities. As we shall see, a salient place in the development of historical anthropology of South Asia is occupied by the collective Subaltern Studies project. An important departure of the project involved its reconstruction of the forms of culture and consciousness present in the initiatives and movements of subordinate groups. At the same time, as I have discussed elsewhere, the difficulties in the earlier work within subaltern studies contain links with the place of culture and tradition within the project.[80] Here, culture often appeared as an a-priori element rather than as a critical category in the writing of history. On the one hand, in this corpus, cultures of subalterns remained somewhat static frameworks of belief and behaviour, ironically corresponding to an earlier anthropological notion of culture as an 'entire way of life'—largely unchanging and broadly homogeneous blueprints of thought and action, which underlay the passivity and resistance of subordinate groups. On the other hand, through the preoccupation with the autonomy and agency of the subaltern, articulated by dualities between resistance and domination and the subaltern and the elite, meaningful practices of subordinate groups before authority appeared as simply opposing domination, so that the cultures and traditions of the subalterns were placed outside the productivity of power. It is precisely such issues that have emerged as critical questions in the recent transformations of anthropology and history, and it is to these departures that I now turn.

CRITICAL DEPARTURES

In recent times writings of anthropologists and historians have shaped incisive readings of meaning and power in the past and the present. Indeed, over the last two decades or so it has become a matter of critical orthodoxy that from the 1970s onwards a vigorous emphasis on practice, processes, and conflict has replaced the prior privileging of structure, rules, and consensus within ethnography. Similar claims can be found today concerning historical narratives immaculately embracing anthropological sensibilities. Such understandings point toward important disciplinary transformations over the past three decades. At the same time, by overplaying the uniqueness of ethnography and history in our own times they also underplay the difference and diversity in the pasts of these disciplines.

Ambiguities of Anthropology

Earlier in this Introduction, I have sought to clarify some of the distinctions in the history of anthropology. The point now is that from the 1940s to the 1970s, transformations within ethnography were influenced by processes of counter-colonialism, de-colonization, and other struggles against imperialism and racism. This context shaped emergent critiques of reigning paradigms within the discipline.[81] Here was, on the one hand, an interchange between the autonomy and logic governing continuities and changes within disciplinary traditions, and, on the other, processes of history and politics affecting inherited understandings of the world.

I have elsewhere explored these questions by examining the vexed relationship between action and structure, especially within functionalism, structuralism, and the questioning of these theoretical traditions.[82] Let me recapitulate the discussion. Functionalism and structuralism have been prominent paradigms within the social sciences, the former till the 1960s and the latter till the 1970s.[83] The two traditions have understood 'structure' differently. Yet both have accorded primacy to the object(s) of structure over the subject(s) of history, emphases that worked in tandem with their privileging of synchrony over diachrony. All this defined the a-temporal predication of human action upon underlying structure in these theoretical traditions, which overlooked the interleaving of structure and agency through time.[84] Over the past three decades, the interrogations of these traditions have resulted in vigorous emphases on practice, process, and power in anthropology, including through articulations of historical materials.[85]

My point here is that the questioning of such paradigms—where social action was predicated on sociological structure—should not be approached as an inexorable disciplinary process set in motion only after the late 1960s. Consider, for example, the discrepancy between classical functionalist apprehensions of social action and the emphatic agency of non-Western subjects as witnessed in counter-colonial movements, nationalist struggles, and other practices of colonized subalterns. Arguably, this gap called forth diverse shifts within British anthropology since at least the 1930s.[86] These included the efforts of the Rhodes Livingstone Institute in Africa to move the locus of ethnographic enquiry from tribes to proletarians.[87] They extended to the emergent interrogation of functionalism within British anthropology, especially its many Manchester variants, which formed part of attempts to understand anew conflict, process, and action in social orders. In this terrain, questions of structure and practice appeared in newer ways in theories of (individual) action and analyses of (collective) processes, particularly from the 1950s.[88] Together, at stake were varied endeavours to grapple with the shifting contexts of anthropology; to respond to wider political and historical transformations affecting the discipline; and to think through the autonomy of analytical traditions.[89] Such efforts could not simply shake off the long shadow cast by functionalist schemes. At the same time, they announced critical engagements with inherited visions and models of social action and anthropological practice.[90]

Ambiguities and contradictions were no less characteristic of efforts to reconfigure the anthropological discipline after the experience of the 1960s. Recall that this decade saw the intense articulation of anti-racist and civil rights movements and of anti-imperialist and radical student actions, which found varied expressions in Western and non-Western worlds. At the very least implicitly, such events and processes pointed once more to tensions between the somewhat abstract focus on underlying structures within influential scholarship and the clearly palpable nature of human action in social worlds. At the same time, the late

1960s and the 1970s also saw the immense success in sociology and anthropology of explanatory frameworks according precedence to the unfolding of structures and systems in understandings of history and society. This was the case with 'world-system' and 'dependency' theories that projected the irrevocable logic of world capitalism as orchestrating the conduct of historical actors in the metropolis and the colony.[91] In such schemas the exact analytical avowal of history and power could go hand in hand with a ready privileging of structure/system and an unsteady undermining of action/practice. To reiterate, such ambiguities and contradictions must be kept in view while considering the turn within anthropology to practice, process, and power.

Reconfigurations of Anthropology

These qualifications in place, it is now possible to approach the more recent reconfigurations of anthropology. The 1970s saw critical explorations of the linkages between structure and practice, formulations that thought through the acute enmeshments of social reproduction and cultural transformation. Such efforts could take the form of critical sociological reflection; they could also imaginatively conjoin ethnography and theory to rethink issues of structure and practice, rules and processes.[92] It followed that by the beginning of the 1980s, ethnographic and sociological scholarship increasingly turned to practice as a key category, a concept that helped to mediate the oppositions of society and individual and social structure and historical action.

The emergent emphasis on practice appeared linked with a heightened sensitivity to temporal processes and historical considerations in anthropological inquiry. Such tendencies derived impetus from world-systems theory and Marxist models, including their structuralist variants. Yet they extended to distinct dispositions of ethnographic practice, especially considerations of the temporal textures of cultural formations and societal transformations.[93] Salient anthropological writings that engaged the historical record focused on non-Western subjects of colonialism and capitalism. Here, the meanings and practices of these subjects did not emerge as simple responses to colonial projects and capitalist processes. Rather, such actions and apprehensions were explored as critical attributes of the contradictory elaboration of colonialism and capitalism, themselves understood as historically and culturally layered fields, in apparently marginal terrain. Far from cut-and-dried distinctions between Western and non-Western worlds, here were to be found discussions of sustained interchanges between these terrains.[94] Above all, such scholarship could involve implicit and explicit recognition that not merely social processes but anthropological analyses were enacted in time

Much of this diverse scholarship highlighted the presence of power and recalcitrance in configurations of meaning and practice. In emergent yet critical ways, under challenge were procedures of ethnographic practice that framed their objects of enquiry as contained within, and themselves insinuating, bounded and coherent entities, especially by drawing pervasive distinctions between traditional orders and modern societies. Nothing better illustrates the shifts within anthropology on account of the freshly laid emphasis on relationships of power—and on terms of practice and process—than the recent rethinking, revaluation, and reworking of the concept of culture, a category of categories in ethnography, especially in its American avatar.

Shifting definitions of culture have characterized the pasts of anthropology. These have emerged from within broad, long-lasting anthropological orientations toward culture as a shared system of values, beliefs, symbols, and rituals of a people. They have extended to the refinement of such a notion in the influential work of Clifford Geertz, which saw culture as the '"webs of meaning" within which people live, meaning encoded in symbolic forms (language, artefacts, etiquette, rituals, calendars, and so on) that must be understood through acts of interpretation analogous to the work of literary critics.'[95] Now, while it is important to register the centrality of changing definitions of culture for the discipline, this is not the place to rehearse its shifting genealogies in the pasts of anthropology. My point concerns the basic re-drawings of the category of culture since the 1970s, which have been in tune with urgent emphases in critical ethnography on history and temporality and power and process.

We might begin with three general, interconnected criticisms of earlier anthropological orientations that totalized culture. First, such dispositions frequently presented culture not only as essentially coherent but as virtually autonomous from diverse modalities of power, including in characterizations of 'stateless' societies. Such procedures underplayed thereby formations of dominance, contentions of authority, and terms of dissonance *within* arrangements of culture, critical distinctions that entailed, for example, power relations of community and gender and race and office. Second, it followed that culture often appeared here as inescapably discrete and inexorably bounded. This is to say that non-Western culture was marked off from broad patterns of societal change—involving, for instance, articulations of colonialism, capitalism, nation, and modernity—and it was envisioned as sets of imaginings that chiefly looked inwards and turned on themselves. Third and finally, these problems were connected to the fact that authoritative ethnographic understandings did not approach the values, beliefs, symbols, and rituals that they examined as embedded within temporal processes, themselves formed and transformed by historical subjects. Rather, the elements of culture were rendered as principally untouched by the shifts and mutations, ruptures and continuities that shaped the past and the present.[96]

Such questionings of anthropological articulations of culture emerged linked to the rethinking of its Marxist conception as an ideational superstructure that derives from a material base. Now, in pointing to societal and political processes, Marxist understandings— along with anthropological ones—had broken with 'aesthetic' appre- hensions of culture as referring to works of art and architecture, painting and design, and music and literature. At the same time, by predicating the superstructure on the base, the orthodox Marxist schema rendered culture as epiphenomenal, while imbuing abstractions such as modes of production with a life of their own.[97] Overlooked thereby was the indissoluble nature of social and historical processes. The critical ethno- graphic rethinking of orthodox Marxist—and of earlier disciplinary —understandings of culture emphasized that such processes have consisted of specific practices of historical subjects within relationships of power. These practices and relationships entail tacit stocks of know- ledge and changing contours of meaning, so that the entire ensemble defines culture.

From a different direction, the 'reflexive' turn in the 'experimental' ethnography of the 1980s brought forth questions of 'authority' in the 'representation' of culture.[98] There were strategies here of the multiple evocation of ethnographic voices in the writing of anthropology, registering especially the complicities of power between the ethno- grapher and the informant.[99] There was also interrogation of the terms and techniques of anthropological work that configured culture as sticking to a particular group and as circumscribed in a discrete locale.[100] These emphases have been followed by critiques of anthropology as itself an alterity-engendering mechanism that has exoticized and reified —and institutionalized and produced—cultural difference unto its own ends.[101] Unsurprisingly, all this has led discussions of the writing *of* culture toward demands for writing *against* culture, where culture is seen as implicated in dominant projects—from anthropological schemes to imperial regimes to nation-state routines—that make a fetish out of cultural difference.[102]

Such critical engagements have only been carried forward in recent years. There has been increasing recognition not only of the intensely differentiated nature of 'local' culture(s) and knowledge(s) but of their insistent interplay with wider formations of region, state, nation, and globalization. If such intimations were present earlier, critical articulations of culture in anthropology today have emerged interwoven with a growing interest in transnational processes of empire, diaspora, and modernity, each acutely entailing entangled identities and hybrid histories.[103] At stake are ironies and challenges for rethinking culture.

It has become apparent that culture should not be approached only as an analytical device but as a concept-entity that has been central to the imaginings and practices of the very people the notion has sought to define and describe. From the fourth world to the first world—from impoverished indigenous peoples to privileged ethnic constituencies; and from violent religious militants to their equally zealous opponents —here are to be found subjects who have variously, vigorously laid claims on 'culture' to express its terms in intriguing, powerful ways. Such urgent assertions of culture—and of 'custom', 'identity', 'civilization', and 'tradition'—have featured at once in projects of unity and division, involving strategies of survival and designs of destruction.[104] All this has raised key questions concerning culture in configurations of modernity in the present and the past.

Of course, such critical engagements with the concept of culture are hardly all of a piece. Elaborated at different moments in recent decades, they have been characterized by salient contentions among themselves. I am also not implying that the critiques have been necessarily fair, patient, and modest in their rebuttal of prior traditions. It would be silly not to learn from the possibilities and pluralities of older discussions of culture within anthropology. At the same time, the interrogative endeavours that I have presented are indicative of the recent reconfigurations of the discipline, from their querying of the formative assumptions of anthropology through to their own blind spots in the practice of ethnography.

The conjoint emphases on process, practice, and power have reinvigorated the study of such staples of the discipline as religion and ritual, magic and witchcraft, symbolism and law, and kinship and kingship.[105] Many of these writings have combined historical readings with an ethnographic imagination.[106] Several others have gone about their tasks by thinking through temporal elaborations that inhere in the present.[107] Together, explorations of state, nation, and globalization, as well as reconsiderations of colonial cultures, imperial archives, and vernacular modernities, have made a striking appearance on the ethnographic stage. This has resulted in remarkable accomplishments, empirical and analytical, theoretical and methodological, in the work of anthropology. For the purposes of this volume, such renovation of the discipline over recent decades has been especially evident in the construal of wide varieties of historical ethnographies and anthropological histories, which have themselves undergone transformations through time. I will return to these tendencies later.

To register the recent reconfigurations of anthropology and to acknowledge its critical contributions is not to overlook the deep dissensions and formidable fault lines that continue to characterize the discipline. This is to say that the emphases on practice, process, and power intimate the recasting of anthropology, but their actual elaborations also announce that the discipline remains heterogeneous, even split, to the core. The contemporary transformations of ethnography bear contending influences from the past. Across anthropology, earlier traditions of analysis have been rethought but this has not meant that prior proclivities toward favoured frameworks have been abandoned. At the same time, the current makeovers of anthropology as a fraught terrain are the result of contentious crossovers in the present. The distinct dispositions to practice, process, and power in anthropology today extend beyond exclusively disciplinary logics. The impact on ethnography of the wider 'linguistic' and 'interpretive' turns in the social sciences, which were partly anticipated by certain versions of anthropology, has served to divide the discipline. The same is true of ethnographic engagements with anti- and post-foundational thought and literary criticism and their endless disciplinary rebuttals. Here are to be found opposed orientations to the operations of power, their nexus with knowledge, the nature of their productivity, their connections with historical practice, and their shaping of social subjects.

Such disciplinary reconfigurations have been closely bound to wider changes in the world at large. I indicate three key developments here. First, it was noted above that anti-colonial nationalism and de-colonization in newly independent nation-states were powerful examples of the making of history. Implicitly, at the very least, they challenged ethnographic projections of the timeless natives and their enchanted terrain.[108] There was refusal of and ambivalence towards integrating such reminders of the agency of anthropological subjects as a part of ethnographic practice. But the reminders were nonetheless consequential for emerging critiques of anthropology. Especially in the wake of student movements and protests in the academy against the Vietnam War, there was increasing interrogation of (what Johannes Fabian called) the 'scandal' of Western domination.[109] Such questioning extended to the place of anthropology in the outrage, including considerations of the complicity of the discipline with colonialism.[110] Disciplinary criticisms of the anthropological enterprise could go hand in hand with political sympathy for third-world peoples, even though the transformation of the latter within ethnographic endeavour into subjects (of practice, process, and power) was more protracted and contradictory than is often imagined.

Second, precisely as the critical tendencies that I have described were gathering force in academic terrain, the newly independent (and other, non-Western) nations had been unravelling in ways that suggested that sympathy and solidarity were simply not enough to understand their societies and polities. In particular, questions of the authoritarianism and corruption of the nation highlighted the requirements of more critical perspectives on state, governance, culture, and society in these arenas. Indeed, very soon the spirit of third-world solidarity—manifest in proclamations and sensibilities of the Bandung era for two decades after the middle of the 1950s—was itself in retreat. In this context, the probing of anthropology from within (and outside) the discipline since the 1960s has had distinct consequences. As we have seen, such developments and debates led to the emergence of the 'experimental' ethnography of the 1980s, influenced by literary–critical readings, while equally informing the recasting of anthropology of subjects of empire, nation-state, and modernity, approached as processes and histories.

Third and finally, recent disciplinary departures have had much to do with the changing face of the contemporary world, from the fall of the Berlin wall to the expressions of ethno-nationalisms in Eastern Europe, and from assertions of majoritarian nationalisms in South Asia to the events of 11 September 2001 and their aftermath. At stake throughout have been diverse calls for a changing anthropology for a changing world. On the one hand, these calls have been assimilated to simplistic dismissals of earlier anthropological traditions as being entirely flawed and complicit with institutional power, procedures that have also overlooked the fact that it is not only in recent years that the world has begun to change but that this has been the case for a very, very long time now. As a result, over the past fifteen years a certain kind of ethnographic wisdom has shared in the contemporary conceit that 'overplays the uniqueness of our own times', also singularly judging the relevance of anthropological enquiry as based on the alleged novelty of the theme of research.[111] On the other hand, taking up the challenge of rethinking and reworking ethnographic practice, a variety of anthropologies have not only drawn on social and political theory but also often considered afresh the pasts of the discipline. They have imaginatively articulated thereby a wide range of key questions that are critical to the contemporary world.[112] Such contrary tendencies and transformations, characterizing academic arenas and social worlds, have been no less crucial in the makeovers of the discipline of history.

History: Ambiguities and Reconfigurations

I have noted that narratives describing anthropological endeavours from the 1970s onwards as breaking with the past—by being increasingly oriented to practice, process, and power—can be too exclusive in focus and scope. Similar problems can underlie singular storylines of the heroic rise of social/cultural history, which function most pervasively as pedagogical frameworks, manifest in the classroom and the seminar. Here are to be found projections of such history-writing as becoming more and more democratic, progressively inclusive of hitherto marginalized subjects (both research themes and human constituencies) of the past, and consequently as ever more embracing other disciplines, especially anthropological methods. Such narratives frequently start off with the privileged place of politics in the institutionalization of history as a discipline from the second half of the nineteenth century onwards, and emphasize that in such scholarship social and cultural history-writing had a residual role, including as the practice of history with the politics left out. Next, they focus on major breakthroughs in historical scholarship that progressively expanded the subject matter of history from the 1930s onwards to draw in wide-ranging dynamics of society and culture, also including in their fold subaltern subjects, while initiating a dialogue with the social sciences, especially anthropology, sociology, and psychology. Discussions of the 'masters' and 'schools' marking such breakthroughs involve mention particularly of the work of: the *Annales* School in France;[113] the erstwhile British Communist Group of Historians;[114] historians of Europe and scholars of African-American slavery in the US;[115] and prominent historical tendencies in Europe, especially Italian 'micro-history' and '*Altagsges-chichte*' ('history of everyday life').[116] Finally, it is against this backdrop that such storylines sketch the problems and potentialities of social/cultural history, including the dialogue with anthropology or sociology, in diverse institutional contexts in the here and now.

Once more, the difficulties with such storylines are not that they are simply wrong but that they are highly tendentious. Construed from the vantage point of the present and implicitly cast in teleological moulds, they overlook the constitutive ambivalences and contradictions, silences and tensions, and problems and possibilities at the core of developments in the discipline of history—from the privileged place of political and diplomatic history in the past to the greater prominence of cultural and social history in the present. At stake are persistent contentions and excesses of history-writing as a form of modern knowledge.

To begin with, prior and present political histories have carried their own, varied articulations of culture and society and tradition and modernity. These can entail key conjunctions of hermeneutic and analytical tendencies and of romanticist and progressivist sensibilities. Such conjunctions have formed part of the institutionalization of the historical discipline, including the privileging of an exclusively demarcated domain of the 'political', but they have also resisted the turning of historical knowledge into a merely subordinate ally of overwrought social scientific schemes. A single example should suffice. The writings of the early nineteenth-century French philosopher–historian Jules Michelet have been criticized as the work of a mere 'romantic' who poetically idealized a popular 'people' in his account of the French Revolution. Or, they have been celebrated for uncovering a new object–subject of history, turning on collective mentalities and anonymous forces in the unfolding of the past. Yet, such readings ignore Michelet's actual procedures of research and writing, which arguably recast both 'hermeneutic' and 'scientific' methods in order to create a genuinely 'modernist' historical scholarship. Michelet's history-writing, Jacques Rancière has argued, brought to the fore the salient but repressed 'subject of history', also intimating the requirements of historical research to live up to its threefold contract—'scientific, political, and literary'—with modern political democratic constituencies.[117] Indeed, by ignoring Michelet's 'method' and assimilating his writing to pre-figured schemes, modern historians were 'able to continue the age-long tradition of keeping the "the poor" in their place—outside of history—and of pretending to be relating nothing but facts—and ignoring their meanings.'[118] To read a historian such as Michelet (or Herder or Ranke, and many, many others) without succumbing to inherited historiographical schemas is to begin to track the pathways that have been opened up, yet are mainly forgotten within historical practice. It is also to think through the un-thought predilections and un-enunciated assumptions of the historical discipline.

Unsurprisingly, ready projections of the triumphant rise of social and cultural history are often insufficiently critical, especially regarding their invocations of 'schools' and 'masters' of the historical craft. They do not sufficiently probe the constitutive conceits of such traditions. Consider the *Annales* School of history-writing in France, which has existed since 1929 into the present, and was important in breaking with earlier event-based narratives of political history. Drawing on wide

sociological considerations and especially impressed with the formulations of Emile Durkheim, the *Annales* not only suggestively, vastly
opened out the scope and subject of history-writing but also created
influential versions of long-term, 'structural' history. At the same time,
it is important to ask if the histories crafted by Lucien Febvre and Fernand
Braudel, two of the formative figures of the *Annales* School, were not
shaped by critical burdens.[119] Did their precise achievements also
perhaps deprive 'history of its human subject, its links to a generally
political and specifically democratic agenda, and its characteristic mode
of representing its subject's manner of being in the world, namely,
narrative'?[120] It is also worth reflecting on how Braudel's seminal
writings have not only rendered entire regions of the Mediterranean
world as islands floating outside the currents of civilization and history,
but further cast as a-historical the sphere of everyday 'material culture',
especially when compared to the historical dynamism of early modern
mercantilism.[121] At work here are weighty distinctions between the
'backward' and the 'civilized', entailing hierarchical mappings of time
and space that we encountered earlier.

Similarly, it is crucial to recognize that the work of the British socialist
historian E.P. Thompson has imaginatively unravelled the contours of
culture and consciousness of the 'plebian public' in eighteenth-century
England, including the transformations of time among these subjects
with the advent of the measurement of time-in-labour as part of new
regimes of capitalist and industrial manufacturing processes.[122] Yet, it
is critical to register that Thompson's writings tend to locate eighteenth-
century plebian culture along an irrevocable axis of historical
modernization that sets up too solid an opposition between the
'tradition'-bound moral economy of the plebian public and the market-
driven economy of 'modern' capitalism.[123] This axis further governs
Thompson's construal of non-Western orientations to time in the
second half of the twentieth century, which are seen simultaneously as
lagging behind the time of the West and as insinuating a hapless tradition
waiting to be inevitably overcome by modern history.[124] Clearly, we are
in the face of apparently normatively neutral but actually profoundly
ideological hierarchies, oppositions, and hierarchical oppositions
of modernity.

None of this is to deny the profound transformations of history-
writing in the past few decades. Rather, it is to approach such changes
by cautiously considering the unstated, uncritical assumptions and the
formidable, underlying conceits of the discipline. Here, the enduring
extension and palpable prominence of social/cultural history in more
recent times need to be understood as part of the wider expansion after

the Second World War of the historical discipline, which has been true of anthropology and sociology too. The expansion has included a steady increase of professional specialization and a significant growth of job opportunities, which have shored up the delineation and development of identifiable social and cultural fields of history-writing. At the same time, such spreading out of social/cultural history has been no less the result of abiding yet manifold intellectual interests, archival engagements, cross-disciplinary concerns, and political commitments, including impulses toward the democratization of history-writing.[125]

The sheer variety of these procedures and processes makes it very difficult to provide here a consistent, detailed account of their trajectories. Yet, it is possible to selectively present some of the key tendencies in this terrain. To begin with, the elaboration of important trends in social/cultural history in the 1960s and 1970s, including their critical reconsideration of the discipline, might be usefully understood as part of common attempts with different emphases to construe accounts that focused on subjects hitherto marginalized from the historical record.[126] All this was further accompanied by at least two related developments. The first concerned attempts to seek out distinct archival materials and to read historical sources in innovative ways—also opening up questions of the varieties and validities of 'sources' of history—especially considering the paucity and perversity of the record of the pasts of marginal subjects. The other involved a dialogue with other disciplines, from anthropology and sociology to demography and psychology, which also led history-writing in new directions.[127]

Now, these processes were neither inexorable nor exclusive. Even as there were wide varieties of critical conversations both within history-writing and with other disciplines, the newer forms of historiography could also approach and understand cultures, subalterns, related disciplines, and history itself in tendentious and limited ways.[128] Actually, the new modes of history-writing emerged principally, albeit in different ways, as alternative articulations of the history of the nation. The work of Christopher Hill and E.P. Thompson attempted to recast authoritative understandings of English history by bringing to the fore, respectively, patterns of popular, radical religious dissent in the seventeenth century, and frameworks of meaning and practice of the plebian public in the eighteenth century, each scholar tracing the approbation and interrogation of authority among such subordinate subjects.[129] The writings of Eugene Genovese and Lawrence Levine sought to restore to Afro-American slaves their own modalities of culture and action, consciousness and agency in order to critically rethink the history of the US nation, which in its conservative and liberal renderings

had overlooked the experiential textures of slavery and cast the slave
population as objects rather than subjects of (national) history.[130] The
central task that the subaltern studies collective set itself was to explore
'*the failure of the* [Indian] *nation to come into its own*', especially focusing
on the place of the subaltern in the history of the Indian nation that
had failed its dispossessed peoples.[131] These historiographical tendencies
imaginatively extended the terms of the dominant coupling of history
and nation under modernity, but they were also unable to break with
bonds simply, easily.

Rather than being disabling, the ambiguities have been productive.
Indeed, the developments in history-writing discussed above have been
followed by an even wider opening up of critical histories over the past
two decades. As in the case of anthropology, these more recent makeovers
of history-writing have been severally influenced by shifting political
contexts, the 'linguistic' turn in the social sciences, and key crossovers
with anti-foundational perspectives.[132] The consequences have been
truly wide-ranging: from the expansion of imperatives of 'minority'
histories through to new historical accounts of the colony and nation,
the body and sexuality, and the prison and discipline; and from critical
reconsiderations of concept–entities of modernity and the state through
to the radical rethinking of the terms of theory and the disciplines,
including history-writing.[133] All of this is elaborated in the account
that follows.

FORMATIVE CONJUNCTIONS

The discussion so far has already indicated several of the grounds for
the crossovers between anthropology and history. I now trace the
conjunctions between these disciplines by focusing first on the initial
terms of their interplay in scholarship on India. Next, I will consider
issues of genealogies and communities, empire and nation, and culture
and power. Broadly reflecting the distinct sections of the volume, these
themes overlay one another.

Formations

Critical accounts of the institutionalization and elaboration of anthropological and historical scholarship concerning India are yet to be
written, although we have notes towards such endeavour.[134] As implied
earlier, such accounts would need to clarify the reciprocal principles
shoring up the anthropology and history of the subcontinent, especially
the configurations of time and history in the former and of culture and
tradition in the latter, each entailing preoccupations with questions of

civilization and nation. The accounts would further need to probe the particular ways in which historians and anthropologists marked off their respective disciplines, the one from the other. That said, I now turn to scholarly tendencies in work on the subcontinent that variously initiated conversations between anthropology and history, tendencies that are precursors to the more recent crossovers between these disciplines.[135]

The increasing specialization of Indian anthropology from the 1950s onwards led to its clear demarcations from history.[136] At the same time, precisely in this scenario, there were distinct efforts by some anthropologists to engage historical issues. The efforts were less concerned with blurring disciplinary boundaries and more with expressing anthropological considerations by drawing on historical materials and understandings, many of which remained suspect to the professional historians of the time. Until well into the 1960s, these efforts were often influenced by wider formulations of interactions between 'great' and 'little' traditions.[137] Such work included the study of patterns of 'local' history in north India;[138] bardic castes and their genealogical accounts;[139] the social structure of a village in early nineteenth-century western India;[140] and historical linkages between state formation, royal myths, and tribal integration.[141] It came to be extended in the 1970s to explorations of the formations of myth, legend, and kinship in royal genealogy, as well as of social structure, kingship, territory, and property in pre-colonial central India.[142]

Unsurprisingly, across most of the twentieth century, the institutionalization and unravelling of professional history-writing of the subcontinent also proceeded at a distance from anthropological enquiry.[143] After Independence, the developments in the study of ancient and medieval Indian history have been rich and revealing, including the more recent emphasis on 'social formations' in this terrain, but only a few scholars in these fields have engaged the terms of anthropology.[144] As for history-writing on modern India, earlier studies of British administrators and administration were honed further, yet also supplanted by fiercely contending scholarship on nationalism (and communalism), accounts that drew on the steadily increased availability from the early 1960s of previously classified materials. This decade and the following one were further marked by impressive achievements in the writing of economic history, which had its corollaries for understandings of societal patterns. From the middle of the 1960s, influenced by divergent strains of Marxism, including Maosim, and in the context of radical upheavals across the world, the social sciences witnessed a wider concern with the place of the peasantry in economic development, historical change, and revolutionary transformation.[145] These concerns had their effect on historical writing on peasant society, usually entailing questions of economic history, yet also concerned with issues of culture and power. The impact extended to social–political history-writing on counter-colonial movements and popular nationalisms of peasant groupings, working classes, and adivasi communities.[146] As we shall see, all this set the stage for critical debates within history from the late 1970s onwards that recast the discipline, including by initiating conversations with critical theory and anthropological understandings. It is also the case, however, that prior to these trans-formations, productive engagements with anthropology were very rare in historical scholarship on modern India conducted on the sub-continent. They appeared forcefully in the work of a single scholar. The administrator-academic K.S. Singh—only marginally a member of the historian's guild—implicitly and explicitly drew on anthropological considerations to focus on colonial transformations of adivasi society and the terms and textures of adivasi anti-colonial responses and movements.[147]

At the same time, from at least the beginnings of the 1960s, the entanglements between these disciplines have found varied articulations in American scholarship on modern and contemporary South Asia. Here a crucial role has been played by the wide-ranging work and critical inspiration of Bernard S. Cohn, who over time straddled and subverted the boundaries between anthropology and history.[148] Belonging to the first generation in post-Second World War US anthro-pology that was trained to conduct sustained fieldwork in Indian villages, Cohn nonetheless resisted the lure of a purely synchronic study. For example, his doctoral work on the Chamars of the village of Senapur in north India, conducted in the 1950s, attended to processes of social change among these subalterns.[149] Within a matter of a few years Cohn extended his enquiries into diverse questions of history and anthro-pology, based on varied crossovers between these disciplines.[150] Across the 1960s, these studies entailed explorations set in northern India, concerning, for instance, the relationship between revenue policies and structural change, the levels of political integration in pre-colonial regimes, and the shaping of local life and legal practice by systems of colonial law. Most of this work rested on archival materials, yet it was also influenced by Cohn's earlier fieldwork in the region.[151]

Such emphases were followed by other departures as Cohn shifted his attention more and more to 'the historical anthropology of colonial society itself'.[152] Here, Cohn's prior concern with investigating the historical bases of social relations in South Asia was never simply forgotten. Rather, it found newer configurations. For example, during the 1970s, Cohn's work on the development and deployment of colonial knowledge of India engaged with the 'ethnosociology' of his colleagues McKim Marriott and Ronald Inden.[153] Such dialogue is evident in Cohn's seminal essay on the Imperial Assemblage of 1877, held to proclaim Queen Victoria the Empress of India, wherein he explores the logics and forms of Indian society precisely as he elaborates the cultural constitution and historical transformation of rituals and symbols of colonial authority and imperial power.[154] Yet it is also the case that Cohn came to increasingly recognize colonial cultures of rule as fundamentally restructuring Indian society. Together, in essays written after the 1980s on themes as diverse as colonial usages of language, the law, and clothing, Cohn focused on wide-ranging dynamics between knowledge and power and the colonizer and the colonized.[155] Cohn wrote two playful and provocative programmatic pieces charting the relationship between history and anthropology, which saw him at home in both these disciplines.[156] These garnered wide circulation, much as Evans-Pritchard's reflections on the theme had found a generation earlier. At the same time, it is in the entire body of Cohn's work that we find the several signposts and emergent formations of historical anthropology.

This is all the more true since Cohn's researches were frequently followed and sometimes accompanied by work on related questions by other scholars, especially his students. Of course, such enquiries were often also influenced by other scholarly tendencies. Nonetheless, they can all be seen as articulating a wider set of issues that had been brought to the fore by Cohn's writing, teaching, and supervision.[157] Here is to be found scholarship explicitly yet variously based on conjunctions between anthropology and history: from the study of patterns of social and economic transformation across the nineteenth and twentieth centuries in a single village in the Punjab through to explorations of the historical structure of local-level political groupings and their interactions with state governmental machinery in parts of northern India;[158] and from discussions of worlds of temples across time through to an 'ethnohistory' of a 'little kingdom'. Each of these works helped to rethink caste and kingship by focusing on royal and godly honours, favours, and services, including processes of their redistribution, which were constitutive of differential groups, ranks, and identities.[159] These departures were accompanied by other studies that also combined anthropology and history as part of distinct scholarly traditions. Conducted both within and outside the US academe, such scholarship elaborated questions of sect, caste, and their transformations;[160]

configurations of kinship and kingship in South India;[161] and the
ideological nature of official and ethnographic (colonial) representations of India.[162]

From the latter half of the 1970s, critical departures were afoot in
the history of the subcontinent. Reassessments of the pasts of Indian
nationalism were often central to such endeavours.[163] At the same time,
on offer were convergences of significance. Especially important were
imaginative readings of historical materials: from conventional archival
records, including reports of colonial administrators, through to earlier
ethnographies as sources of history; and from previously maligned
vernacular registers of history through to diverse subaltern expressions
of the past. Such readings could problematize the very nature of the
historical archive as well as initiate conversations with other orientations, including those of structural linguistics and critical theory.[164]
No less salient were key acknowledgements of the innately political
character of history-writing. Together, new questions were raised and
possible conversations underscored, including with ethnographic
inquiry, augmenting thereby the study of South Asia.[165] All this has
influenced the recent crossovers of history and anthropology, the
articulations of historical anthropology.

Genealogies

The critical rethinking of history as concept and entity has been at the
heart of historical anthropology. Here, I outline four overlapping sets of
developments that have elaborated such questions. While deriving from
the wide-ranging intersections of historical writing with anthropological endeavour, these departures have further drawn in perspectives
of critical thought and social theory.

In the first place, it has been increasingly noted that forms of historical
consciousness vary in their degree of symbolic elaboration, their ability
to pervade multiple contexts, and their capacity to capture people's
imaginations. Such recognition does not fall back on oppositions
involving cyclical notions of the past as characteristic of the East and
linear conceptions of history as constitutive of the West. Nor does it
merely measure distinct notations of time across cultures, with the
latter projected as separate, bounded entities. Rather, it precisely probes
such overwrought schemes, which carve up social worlds into
enchanted terrains of myth and disenchanted domains of modernity.
It does this especially by tracking the articulations and understandings
of history as made up of interleaving, conflict-ridden processes of
meaning and authority.[166] On offer are explorations of the variability
and mutability that can inhere in the perceptions and practices of the

past of historical communities as well as enquiries into the persistence of oppositions between myth and history in authoritative projections, explorations and enquiries that are attentive to the incessant interchange between power and difference.[167]

Second, it has been variously admitted for some time now that history does not just refer to events and processes out there, but that it exists as a negotiated resource at the core of shifting configurations of social worlds.[168] Closer to our times, elaborating the oppositions of modernity, the clamour over the past in assertions of authority and alterity has provided a further twist to these patterns. To foreground such appropriations and enunciations of the past as important issues for anthropology and history is not to submit to a view that each of these visions is equally true. Instead, it is to track the uses of the past and their contending validities in the making of worlds and to trace the presence of power in the production of history.[169]

Third, imaginative explorations of the pasts of subaltern peoples and elite groups combined with energetic interrogations of univocal conceptions of universal history have made for compelling consequences. There has been an opening up of critical questions considering the coupling of history-writing with the idea of the nation under modern regimes. Must all histories be national histories? Why does historical endeavour, including its critical manifestations, continue to be shaped by the impress of the nation? What should be the forms taken by an alternative practice of history-writing?[170] Such queries have been accompanied by sustained examinations of the haunting presence of a reified West in widespread beliefs in historical progress. Is the record of history mainly a register of the work of progress in some societies and of its lack in others? How are we to comprehend underlying expectations of progress in the past and of development in the present—the passage forward in time framed as the hallmark of history—in scholarly schemes and quotidian understandings? What has been the place of Europe as entailing the point of departure and arrival on the road to progress and modernity in Western and non-Western arenas? In short, all this has put a question mark on pervasive projections of the West and the nation as history, modernity, and destiny.[171] Such terms of discussion have engaged and extended the critiques of an adjudicatory reason and the enduring oppositions of modern knowledge. They have also formed part of critical, imaginative renderings of state, nation, modernity, and globalization. These are points to which I will return.

Fourth and finally, it has become evident that to draw on and participate in such many-sided endeavours of rethinking the disciplines is not necessarily to shy away from the task of writing history, especially in ethnographic and critical modes. In approaching the past and the present, such efforts of history-writing can bind the impulse to cautiously probe and affirm with the desire to carefully narrate and describe, while being responsible to the challenge of thinking through intractable issues such as those of memory and trauma. The endeavours take requirements of evidence and fidelity to facts truly seriously. Yet they can also sieve historical evidence through critical filters and construe unexpected facts that speak in the uneasy echoes of limiting doubt rather than deal in aggressive certainties.[172] Such wide-ranging articulations of history are expressed on different registers in *Historical Anthropology*.

Communities

It should hardly be surprising that reconfigurations of history have been accompanied by reconsiderations of community in the mutual transformations of historical knowledge and anthropological under-standing. Here, the astute probing of pervasive projections of community as an ineluctably anachronistic, tightly bounded entity—one featuring face-to-face interaction among its members; entailing allegiance to hoary custom and primordial tradition; tending toward consensus in its expression; and broadly opposed to modernity—has had compelling consequences. Communities have come to be understood as active participants in wider processes of colonialism and empire, state-formation and modernity, and nation and nationalism. They have been unravelled as historical players that imbue such processes with their own terms and textures, articulating the 'oral' and the 'written'—and 'tradition' and 'custom'—in intriguing ways. In a related manner, com-munities have been rescued from aggrandizing analytics that have construed them as endlessly enacting integration and consensus in their constitution and elaboration. Rather, communities have been understood as embedded in diverse relationships of meaning and power, as accessing and exceeding authority in order to negotiate, question, and subvert—in heterogeneous, changing ways—schemes of dom-inance that shore up social worlds.

Three sets of distinct yet overlaying orientations have influenced such reconsiderations, meaning also of course that in historical anthro-pology communities have been elaborated in different ways. To begin with, ethnographic and historical studies have focused not only on 'the symbolic constituents of community consciousness' but also on the 'symbolic nature of the idea of community itself', especially as expressed in formulations of its boundaries.[173] At the same time, the emphasis on the symbolic construction of community has been accompanied by attempts to write greater heterogeneity into the concept. This has involved explorations of the many meanings of community construed by its members, including their symbolization and elaboration of boundaries as providing substance to their differences and identities. It has also entailed tracing the constitutive location of community within wide-ranging processes of power as well as tracking its internal divisions as articulated along axes of property, gender, and office.[174]

Such accents have crisscrossed with varied portrayals of communities as questioning and contesting dominant projects of meaning and power, including those turning on empire and nation. This has been particularly true of scholarship on the Indian subcontinent, where an important influence has been exercised by the collective subaltern studies endeavour. Now, I have noted that earlier incarnations of this project could be limited in their conceptions of the action, culture, and tradition of subaltern communities, also attending only inadequately to the internal fissures of these groupings while presenting them in homogeneous ways. At the same time, these preoccupations with the agency, autonomy, and resistance of subaltern communities have led to wider results. Both within and outside the subaltern studies enterprise, they have entailed critical recognitions and imaginative renderings of such communities as salient historical actors, unravelling their challenge to authority in a historically and ethnographically layered manner.[175] More recently, there has been a larger shift within subaltern studies from reconstructing the pasts of subordinate groups towards probing colony and nation as monumental expressions of modern power. The figure of the community has made distinct appearances here. The discussions have extended from the place of community as a key constituent of modernity that yet inherently escapes its disciplinary power through to its contemporary transformations as bound to emergent techniques of governmental administration;[176] and from the presence of community as an always/already 'fragmented' phenomenon through to its inextricable weaving with narratives of nation.[177] Once more, a variety of scholarship now explores the articulations of community with gender and race, modernity and state, and political thought and social theory.

Indeed, recent reconfigurations of the category have derived further support from the thinking through of enduring oppositions of modern worlds, discussed earlier, including the antimony between community and state. Such scholarship has been influenced by critiques of a subject-centred reason, a meaning-legislating rationality, and their hierarchical

dualities. It has also expressed acute challenges to analytical binaries of
modern disciplines, querying enticing renderings of otherness and
enduring projections of progress, which are closely tied to totalizing
templates of universal history and exclusive blueprints of Western
modernity.[178] The effects of such procedures have been felt in the critical
and contending rethinking not only of community and history but
also of empire and nation and culture and power.

Empire and Nation

Neither colony and empire nor nation and nationalism are new to
anthropology and history.[179] At the same time, the critical crossovers
between history and anthropology in recent times have led to newer
renderings of these categories and entities. Concerning colony and
empire, we might begin with two broad tendencies that have overlapped
but also diverged. Both these tendencies have built on and broken with
prior anthropological and historical analyses that debated the complicities between anthropological practice and colonial projects,
constructed detailed accounts of economic systems and social structures
spawned under empire, and tracked the responses of the colonized to
processes of colonization.[180]

On the one hand, an impressive body of recent research has thought
through persistent presuppositions regarding colony and empire as
highly articulated schemas of economic exploitation, social control,
and political domination. The newer analyses have instead elaborated
colony and empire as chequered and contested processes of culture
and history. They have also critically attended to the practices, meanings,
symbols, and boundaries in colonial locations of Euro-American
peoples such as missionaries, administrators, and settler communities,
in order to track the constitutive contradictions and contrary elaborations of colonial cultures. On the other hand, an influential corpus has
drawn on literary criticism and critical theory in order to focus on
imperial representations, especially of colonized peoples, as formative
of wider projects of discursive domination under colonialism. Such
work has further highlighted the complicity between earlier imperial
imaginings and contemporary academic renderings of non-Western
terrain. Often articulating anti-humanist perspectives, important
interventions here have variously questioned the ethics of according
unchallenged efficacy to colonial projects. Several critical studies have
also drawn upon historical materials to trace the interplay between the
construction, elaboration, and institutionalization of racial boundaries,
gender identities, and class divisions in explorations of imperial
imaginings, colonial cultures, and postcolonial arenas.[181]

Both these tendencies have variously influenced discussions of colony and empire in South Asia. At the same time, in the context of scholarship on the subcontinent, a distinct divide—frequently framed as a formidable fault-line—between competing conceptions of colonialism has often equally influenced work on empire.[182] Here, salient writings on the eighteenth and early nineteenth centuries in India, which have revised our understanding of this period, primarily predicate questions of colonial cultures on issues of state formation and processes of political economy. Unsurprisingly, this work can accord something of an innate heuristic privilege to continuities in state and society between Indian regimes and colonial rule. Conversely, in a great deal of innovative work on Indian pasts at the heart of subaltern studies and postcolonial scholarship, the terms of colonial power often appear as unassailable propositions of history. It follows that in such work wider considerations of colonial cultures do not accord well with the presumed principles of imperial power, which can afford an a-priori analytical prerogative to the introduction by colonial rule of putative ruptures in subcontinental history. Now, it is crucial to register that the former emphases intimate the importance of attending to the particular attributes and limits of colonial processes, and that the latter arguments announce the salience of probing the wider stipulations and effects of imperial power. For it is in this way that we can stay with the productive possibilities of these contrary orientations, including in order to better approach the contributions in this volume that deal with questions of colonialism and empire.

In the study of colony and empire in South Asia, what are the shifts that have been made possible by current intersections of history and anthropology? To begin with, these transformations are keenly manifest in critical refusals to treat the pasts of colonies as mere footnotes and appendices to the history of the metropolis, a pervasive tendency that has projected the latter as providing the former with Western civilization and European governance. Rather, recent writings have explored the intimate linkages between the metropole and the colony. Such explorations have carried forward earlier examinations and contemporary discussions of imperial histories and colonial cultures as deriving from far-reaching interactions between the colonizer and the colonized. They have crucially considered the mutual shaping of European processes and colonial practices, imaginatively analysing also how developments in distant empire could influence changes at the core of the metropole.[183]

Moreover, current work in historical anthropology has acutely interrogated projections of colonialism as a homogeneous project, a monolithic endeavour. It has variously explored the critical divisions between different agents of colonialism, diverse agendas of empire. As has been noted, here are to be found discussions of the representations and practices—and the boundaries and contradictions—of imperial agents, settler communities, and evangelical missionaries in colonial locations, which is to say a focus not only on colonized populations but also on colonizing peoples.[184] At the same time, intimations of the plural articulations of empire have informed understandings of the transformations of caste and kingship—and community and kinship —under colonial rule.[185] They have undergirded considerations of environmental transformations under imperial regimes.[186] Together, such emphases have further suggested the importance of tracking how the conflicting interests and the contending visions of empire of differentially located actors could often times drive a single colonial project.

Finally, diverse dimensions of colonial cultures have found critical expression in historical anthropology. At stake are varied, overlapping forms entailed by colony and empire, which have themselves been heterogeneously explored within the field: the numerous modalities of knowledge and power as expressed in colonial discourses and practices;[187] imperial articulations of space, crime, and the body;[188] and the politics under empire of art, popular representation, travel, museums, and consumption.[189] The critical spirit of such work has been extended by two other developments. On the one hand we have writings in history and anthropology that have focused on the forceful work of gender as variously inflecting and influencing, shaping and structuring the processes of colonialism's cultures, including the terms of sexuality and race under empire.[190] On the other hand is the manner in which not a few of the analyses discussed above have rethought the past and the present of the disciplines, especially keeping in view their linkages with cultures of colony and nation.[191]

Critical conjunctions between anthropology and history have played an important role in reformulations of approaches to nation and nationalism. Salient writings have thought through prior presuppositions and present predilections regarding nations and nationalisms as expressing innate ideas, primordial patterns, and timeless designs. They have also interrogated the ways in which wide varieties of renderings of the past can be differently yet intimately bound to authoritative— indeed, biographical—portraits of nation-states and nationalist endeavours, each understood as image and practice. In such questioning a key role has been played by acute recognitions that nations, nationalisms, and national cultures are historically and socially constructed artefacts and processes. This is to say that although nations and nationalisms are among the most consequential features of modern times, they nonetheless display attributes of what Benedict Anderson has called 'imagined communities', often entailing processes that centre on 'print capitalism' and reorientations to time and space under modernity.[192] Following such recognitions and articulating anti-essentialist sensibilities, there have been astute studies of the historical construction of nations, nationalisms, and national cultures as projects and processes of power. Here ethnographies and histories have come together with sociological discussions and literary explorations not only to query familiar understandings of these categories and entities but to do this by tracking their varied creations and formidable fabrications.[193] At the same time, other related endeavours have highlighted the importance of tracing the ways in which the ideological practices and pedagogical performances that assiduously construe nation and nationalism acquire a forceful presence in the world, assuming pervasive worldly attributes.[194]

These emphases have been accompanied by analyses stressing the distinctions and differences at the core of elaborations of nations and nationalisms, particularly considering their subaltern expressions, anti-colonial manifestations, and gendered dimensions. The subaltern studies project and associated scholarly developments have led to rich explorations of the idioms and trajectories of wide varieties of subaltern endeavours. Against the grain of nationalist propositions and instrumentalist projections concerning the politics of the lower orders, these analyses have shown that in the broader terrain of anti-colonial politics, subaltern ventures followed a creative process of straddling and subverting the ideas, symbols, and practices defining dominant nationalism. Such initiatives articulated thereby a supplementary politics with distinct visions of the nation and particular expressions of nationalism that accessed and exceeded the aims and strategies of a generally middle-class leadership. Unsurprisingly, extending the terms of these discussions, it has been emphasized that middle-class anti-colonial nationalisms embodied their own attributes of difference and distinction, ahead of likenesses of the nation in the looking glass of Europe. By drawing on yet reworking European democratic and republican traditions and Enlightenment and post-Enlightenment principles, such endeavours translated and transformed the ideals of the sovereign nation and the images of the free citizen through forceful filters of the subjugated homeland and the colonized subject.[195] With distinct accents, other critical approaches have unravelled issues of the presence of gender and the place of women in formations of nation and articulations of nationalism. The focus has extended, for instance, from the mapping of the nation in terms of domesticity and the gendered construal of the homeland as a feminine figure through to the terms of participation of women in nationalism and the ambiguities attending their definition as citizen–subjects.[196] In this way, the analytic of gender has incisively interrogated the attributes of authority and alterity at the heart of nations and nationalisms in their dominant and subaltern incarnations—in the past and the present.

All this has further meant that salient work within historical anthropology has probed the stipulations and contentions of nation and state, examining especially their familiar, revealing, and intimate associations but also their unfamiliar, contingent, and contending connections with modern power and global transactions. Rather than accepting the space and the time of the nation as settled analytical coordinates, recent writings have explored the interplay of imperatives of nation and nationalism with transnational processes, critically examining how the one can be inextricably embedded in the other.[197] Still other studies have focused on the nation-state as entailing sets of frequently conflicting disciplines to normalize and order society, bringing to the fore what Hansen and Stepputat have summarized as three 'practical' languages of governance and three 'symbolic' languages of authority, which are together crucial for understanding state and nation.[198] The pedagogies, performances, and practices of power of state and nation have been critically unravelled through scholarship that has focused on the quotidian configurations and everyday articulations of these concepts and entities.[199]

Such different yet interconnected emphases have clarified that, across shifting contexts and terrains, propelled by distinct agendas and aspirations, nations and nationalisms have articulated wide varieties of historical practice and disciplinary power. At the same time, incisive discussions of nation and nationalism—as well as those of history and community and colony and empire—have pointed toward the need for critical considerations of modernity, its processes and persuasions. Unsurprisingly, salient writings within history, anthropology, and historical anthropology have presciently probed the analytical abstractions and the formalist frames that incessantly attend understandings of modernity. They have intimated that, ahead of exclusive images of modernity, its divergent articulations and representations have emerged linked to particular historical processes, where such generative practices and meanings need to be thought down to their expressions on the ground. Equally, this work has highlighted that the diverse manifestations of modernity have been frequently influenced by singular likenesses of Western modernity. Thus, formations and elaborations of modernity are increasingly discussed and debated today as contradictory and contingent processes of culture and power, as chequered and contested histories of meaning and mastery.[200]

Culture and Power

After the discussion so far, the notions of culture and power hardly require further exegesis. Yet it is important to note the tangible tensions concerning these terms that abound in the terrain of historical anthropology. Here, approaches according analytical primacy to processes of political economy and state formation contend with orientations attributing theoretical privilege to discursive orders and representational regimes. Each puts a different spin on culture and power, reading and rendering them in distinct ways.

In basic terms, we might distinguish between two tendencies. On the one hand, strongly influenced by critical theory—especially the work of Michel Foucault and Jacques Derrida, but also the writings of philosophers and critics from Martin Heidegger to Edward Said—a key corpus has focused on formations and regimens of modern power. Such scholarship has especially tracked the discursive entailment and constitutive embedding of power in projects and provisos of, for example, empire and modernity and state and nation. Here extraordinary efficacy has often been accorded to dominance and its dissonance, so that practices and processes construed by historical subjects have primarily appeared as encompassed by power and its productivity. On the other hand, distinct dispositions have focused on the contingent and contradictory elaborations of societal processes and cultural practices as enacted by historical subjects. Such practices, processes, and subjects have been explored as at once part of and themselves articulating relationships of power, but without turning power into a fetishized force and omnipresent totality. Here are to be found examinations of the vexed relationships between culture, structure, action, and event, including the ways in which each of these terms mediates history. Here are to be discovered, too, discussions that cast the metropole and the margins and the dominant and the subaltern as part of mutual analytical fields, including by tracking the transformations of time within anthropology.

Now, the contending tendencies that I have outlined actually come together in the precise crafting of historical anthropologies. But the two often also talk past one another. Here, I would submit, there are no ready resolutions. Rather, it is critical to think through such conjunctions and disjunctions in order to better understand historical anthropology and its ongoing transformations.

NOTES

1. I use the term anthropology to refer to social and cultural anthropology in their widest sense, also including those writings in the sociology of India that are shored up by ethnographic sensibilities. Ethnography is used here as shorthand for practices constitutive of social and cultural anthropology.

2. This is especially reflected in the manner in which stark statements of specific authors are turned into leitmotifs for discussing one's own and the other discipline. Such statements include Maitland's comment that 'by and by anthropology will have the choice of becoming history or nothing'; Radcliffe-Brown's assertion that for the most part history 'does not explain anything at all'; and Trevor-Roper's dismissal of the history of Africa (except for the European presence there) and of pre-Columbian America as 'largely darkness' that never could be 'a subject of history'. For the difficulties of conducting discussions by invoking such statements, usually quoted out of context, see Shepard Krech III, 'The State of Ethnohistory', *Annual Review of Anthropology*, 20 (1991), pp. 345–6.

3. Brian K. Axel, 'Introduction: Historical Anthropology and its Vicissitudes', in Axel (ed.), *From the Margins: Historical Anthropology and its Futures* (Durham, Duke University Press, 2002), p. 13.

4. Together, the three parts of the Introduction might be thought of as three concentric circles, where each part is encompassed by the preceding one. Of course, I would prefer the Introduction to be read from the beginning through to the end. Yet, readers interested chiefly in the developments in the historical anthropology of the Indian subcontinent could move first to the last division ('Formative Conjunctions') and then retrace their steps to the earlier two parts (although keeping in view that these two parts also explore issues of anthropology and history of South Asia).

5. Clearly, this Introduction is not merely a record of the dialogue between anthropology and history in scholarship on South Asia. At the same time, I seek to expand the notion of disciplinary dialogue and dissension, precisely through critical reconsiderations of anthropology and history. This also means that my efforts engage yet extend the emphases of several influential discussions of the interplay between anthropology and history, writings that should be of interest to readers of this collection. Brian K. Axel, 'Introduction: Historical Anthropology and its Vicissitudes'; Saloni Mathur, 'History and Anthropology in South Asia: Rethinking the Archive', *Annual Review of Anthropology*, 29 (2000), pp. 29–46; John Kelly and Martha Kaplan, 'History, Structure, and Ritual', *Annual Review of Anthropology*, 19 (1990), pp. 119–50; Peter Pels, 'The Anthropology of Colonialism: Culture, History, and the Emergence of Western Governmentality', *Annual Review of Anthropology*, 26 (1997), pp. 163–83; Ann Laura Stoler and Frederick Cooper, 'Between Metropole and Colony:

Rethinking a Research Agenda', in Frederick Cooper and Ann Stoler (eds), *Tensions of Empire: Colonial Cultures in a Bourgeois World* (Berkeley, University of California Press, 1997), pp. 1–56; James D. Faubion, 'History in Anthropology', *Annual Review of Anthropology*, 22 (1993), pp. 35–54; Krech III, 'The State of Ethnohistory', pp. 345–75; and John Comaroff and Jean Comaroff, *Ethnography and the Historical Imagination* (Boulder, Westview, 1992).

6. The Introduction distinguishes between 'functionalism' (of Malinowski) and 'structural–functionalism' (of Radcliffe-Brown) as analytical procedures, but it also considers together the shared orientations of these traditions to temporality in the practice of anthropology. See S.N. Eisenstadt, 'Functionalist Analysis in Anthropology and Sociology: An Interpretive Essay', *Annual Review of Anthropology*, 19 (1990), pp. 243–4; Adam Kuper, *Anthropologists and Anthropology: The British School 1922–1972* (London, Allen Lane, 1973), pp. 92–109; Joan Vincent, *Anthropology and Politics: Visions, Traditions, and Trends* (Tuscon, University of Arizona Press, 1990), pp. 155–71; and George Stocking, Jr, *After Tylor: British Social Anthropology 1888–1951* (Madison, University of Wisconsin Press, 1995), pp. 233–441.

7 Indeed, not only anthropological but also historical writing can set up a sharp separation between the principally dynamic time of modern subjects and the relatively static temporality of all others. Hans Medick, '"Missionaries in the Rowboat?" Ethnological Ways of Knowing as a Challenge to Social History', in Alf Lüdtke (ed.), *The History of Everyday Life: Reconstructing Historical Experiences and Ways of Life*, trans. William Templer (Princeton, Princeton University Press, 1995), pp. 41–71.

8. Johannes Fabian, *Time and the Other: How Anthropology makes its Object* (New York, Columbia University Press, 1983). See also Comaroff and Comaroff, *Ethnography and the Historical Imagination*, pp. 1–9; and Nicholas Thomas, *Out of Time: History and Evolution in Anthropological Discourse*, Second Edition (Ann Arbor, University of Michigan Press, 1996).

9 Here I am engaging and extending the critical arguments of Fabian, *Time and the Other*.

10. On the notion of the 'savage slot' of anthropology, see, Michel-Rolph Trouillot, 'Anthropology and the Savage Slot: The Poetics and Politics of the Otherness', in Richard Fox (ed.), *Recapturing Anthropology: Working in the Present* (Santa Fe, School of American Research Press), pp. 17–44. On the 'native niche' of the discipline, see Saurabh Dube, *Stitches on Time: Colonial Textures and Postcolonial Tangles* (Durham, Duke University Press, 2004).

11. George Stocking, Jr, 'Paradigmatic Traditions in the History of Anthropology', in Stocking, Jr, *The Ethnographer's Magic and Other Essays in the History of Anthropology* (Madison, University of Wisconsin Press, 1992), p. 347.

12. Thomas, *Out of Time*.

13. At the very outset, I should clarify that such mappings of the 'enchanted' and the 'modern' are connected to dominant apprehensions of the 'disenchantment of the world'. The latter constitutes the watershed between custom-bound 'tradition' and rationality-driven 'modernity', something of a formative horizon of the modern subject, whether in scholarly schemes or in commonplace

conceptions. This means that the *enchantments* of enchanted spaces certainly refer to an innocent paradise within several nativist and primitivist projections and specific Romantic and anti-modernist understandings. Yet they no less connote superstition and backwardness, or the precise other of a celebrated reason, on the other side of the epistemic breach. In the same way, for a long time now the *modern* of modern places has been construed as a privileged terrain acutely reflecting the bright light of reason and Western civilization, but also instituted as the fall of humanity under modernity. On these questions as well as on my specific use of 'space' and 'place', see Dube, *Stitches on Time*.

14. Catherine Lutz, *Unnatural Emotions: Everyday Sentiments on a Micronesian Atoll and their Challenge to Western Theory* (Chicago, University of Chicago Press, 1988); Comaroff and Comaroff, *Ethnography and the Historical Imagination*; and Saurabh Dube, *Untouchable Pasts: Religion, Identity, and Power among a Central Indian Community, 1780–1950* (Albany, State University of New York Press, 1998).

15. This is not to ignore prior formations of the modernity of the Renaissance and the New World, issues discussed in Saurabh Dube and Ishita Banerjee-Dube (eds), *Unbecoming Modern: Colonialism, Modernity, Colonial Modernities* (New Delhi, Social Science Press, 2006).

16. Roy Porter, *The Creation of the Modern World: The Untold Story of the British Enlightenment* (New York, Norton, 2001); J.G.A. Pocock, *Barbarism and Religion: Volume Two, Narratives of Civil Government* (Cambridge, Cambridge University Press, 1999); and Donald R. Kelley, *Faces of History: Historical Inquiry from Herodotus to Herder* (New Haven, Yale University Press, 1998). See also, Sankar Muthu, *Enlightenment against Empire* (Princeton, Princeton University Press, 2003).

17. Here I am not only referring to Isaiah Berlin's seminal discussion of the philosophical 'Counter-Enlightenment' but also bringing into view the more pervasive, quotidian, often clerical, 'counter-Enlightenment'. Darrin M. McMahon's work underscores the importance of such counter-Enlightenment representations in delineations of the Enlightenment itself. Similarly, even at the level of historical and philosophical thought, while it is important to distinguish between Enlightenment and counter-Enlightenment tendencies, it is imperative to take leave of those procedures that treat these traditions as hermetically sealed off from one another. Indeed, it is by taking such simultaneous steps that we encounter the Enlightenment and the counter-Enlightenment tendencies in their precise concreteness, murkiness, and mutual admixtures. Isaiah Berlin, *Against the Current: Essays in the History of Ideas* (Princeton, Princeton University Press, 2001), pp. 1–24; Darrin M. McMahon, *Enemies of the Enlightenment: The French Counter-Enlightenment and the Making of Modernity* (New York, Oxford University Press, 2002). See also John H. Zammito, *Kant, Herder, and the Birth of Anthropology* (Chicago, University of Chicago Press, 2002).

18. See, for example, Fabian, *Time and the Other*, especially pp. 26–7, 146–7.

19. Even in terms of eighteenth-century Enlightenment thought, consider the emphases of Carl Becker regarding the reconfigured place in this terrain of the

much earlier Augustinian City of God: the more popular French writings about the past appeared as a new history yet constructed within the edifice of a 'medieval' crypto-Christian vision of universal world order. Carl L. Becker, *The Heavenly City of the Eighteenth-century Philosophers* (New Haven, Yale University Press, 1932). It is also important to register that the Enlightenment philosophers could not by themselves bring about the secularization of Judeo-Christian time in broader social and political contexts. For example, after the French Revolution, efforts to establish the historical–temporal rupture between the past and the present entailed wide-ranging measures of governance. This was the case with the French Republican calendric reform, which 'defined a "new" world that opposed the Judeo-Christian tradition, grounding calendric time in another vision of the socio-economic foundation of political power.' Nancy D. Munn, 'The Cultural Anthropology of Time: A Critical Essay', *Annual Review of Anthropology*, 21 (1992), p. 110. All this still leaves open questions of the means by which the temporal ideas of the philosophers and the calendar reforms of the state came to be understood and articulated by citizens and subjects. These processes have borne their own textures and temporalities, pointing to the limited and contentious nature of the secularization of Judeo-Christian time.

20. The term 'historicism' is often used today—as it has been in the past—to readily, summarily indicate totalized and totalizing orientations to the world. Instead, in writing of 'historicism' my reference is to a practice of philosophy and history that developed through critical orientations to aggrandizing claims of an abstract reason and natural law, also entailing other mutual procedures to be discussed shortly. Such practices and procedures were profoundly manifested in the work, for example, of Vico and Herder. They found diverse yet acute manifestations across the nineteenth century, the time when the term was first invented, and they can be seen as continuing up to the present in heterogeneous ways.

21. The point is that not only rationalist, analytical schemes but contending historicist, hermeneutic traditions articulated in distinct ways the terms of developmental, universal history. See, for example, Kelley, *Faces of History*, pp. 211–62.

22. Concerning only the United States—where the Puritan and Protestant model of the secularization of the world has been particularly influential—see, for instance, R. Laurence Moore, *Touchdown Jesus: The Mixing of Sacred and Secular in American History* (Louisville, Kentucky, Westminster John Know Press, 2003); and Vincent Crapanzano, *Serving the Word: Literalism in America from the Pulpit to the Bench* (New York, New Press, 2000).

23. I am neither attributing an inexorable quality to these developments nor denying that such processes have possessed contradictory and critical pasts. See, for example, Stocking, Jr, 'Paradigmatic Traditions', pp. 346–52; and Fabian, *Time and the Other*, pp. 12–16.

24. Saurabh Dube, 'Introduction: Enchantments of Modernity', in Dube (ed.) *Enduring Enchantments, South Atlantic Quarterly*, 101, 4 (special issue) (2002), pp. 729–55.

25. Jürgen Habermas, *The Philosophical Discourse of Modernity: Twelve Lectures,*

trans. Frederick Lawrence (Cambridge, Mass., MIT Press, 1987); Reinhart
Koselleck, *Futures Past: On the Semantics of Historical Time*, trans. Keith Tribe
(Cambridge, Mass., MIT Press, 1985), pp. 3–20.

26. Timothy Mitchell, 'The Stage of Modernity', in Mitchell (ed.), *Questions of
Modernity* (Minneapolis, University of Minnesota Press, 2000), p. 15, emphasis
in the original.

27. Habermas, *Philosophical Discourse of Modernity*, p. 5. It is important to
remember that Habermas is summarizing significant historical and philosophical writings here.

28. Talal Asad, *Genealogies of Religion: Discipline and Reasons of Power in Christianity
and Islam* (Baltimore, The Johns Hopkins University Press, 1993), p. 269.

29. For an elaboration of the issues raised in this paragraph, see Dube, *Stitches on
Time*, chapter 7.

30. Each of these copulas is broadly homologous to the other. Rationalist and
progressivist dispositions—privileging the capacity of reason and seeking to
remake the world in its image—have emerged as often bound to the analytical
model: 'the analytical (*analysis* being basically a mathematical and logical
term), requiring the selection and isolation of factors, political or economic
…[that are] given privileged explanatory status.' In contrast, the hermeneutical
model has entailed 'interpretation on the analogy of reading a text in its
literary and philological fullness (as distinguished from logical analysis)', treating
history itself as 'a matter not of seeing, as tradition and etymology would
have it, but rather of reading, deciphering, and interpreting.' Hermeneutical
protocols have been frequently linked to expressions of historicism. Here,
historicist procedures have variously played out critiques of an abstract
and aggrandizing reason; reassertions of the centrality of language and
historical experience; the principle of individuality (while often pursuing a
universal history); and acute inclinations toward hermeneutical understandings. This is to say that there are also distinct formations and discrete
intimations of what Isaiah Berlin has notably described as the 'Counter-
Enlightenment', 'the great river of romanticism' running from the eighteenth
into the nineteenth centuries, its waters no less overflowing into the times and
terrains that have come after. Kelley, *Faces of History*, pp. 247, 262; Berlin,
Against the Current.

31. See George Stocking, Jr, 'Anthropology as *Kulturkampf*: Science and Politics in
the Career of Franz Boas', in Stocking, Jr, *The Ethnographer's Magic*, pp. 94–8.
I have learnt much from Stocking's work in the discussion of Boas that follows.

32. Franz Boas, 'The History of Anthropology', in George Stocking, Jr, *The Shaping
of American Anthropology, 1883–1911: A Franz Boas Reader* (New York, Basic
Books, 1974), p. 35.

33. There are three interconnected reasons behind my exploration of the work of
Franz Boas rather than that of later Boasians such as A.L. Kroeber (or E. Sapir
or P. Radin), which can be understood as more frontally expressing historical
and historicist considerations. First, my concern with the diachronic and the
temporal—in this case as expressed in Boas' writings—extends beyond only

anthropological 'uses' of history. Rather, I wish to underscore how the temporal and the diachronic were bound to the wider interplay between hermeneutic and analytical, romanticist and progressivist, tendencies. The epistemological dualism of Boas assumes enormous significance here. Second, precisely this constitutive tension between 'history' (and a careful hermeneutic) and 'science' (and induction from elements) was crucial for the unravelling of the broader Boasian tradition: for example, Leslie Spier, Melville Herkovits, Ruth Benedict, Clyde Kluckohn, Radin, Kroeber, and Sapir were all differently influenced by, what Stocking calls, their 'Boasian upbringing', articulating the family traits in distinct ways. The work of Kroeber or Sapir, including its attitudes toward history and historicism, must be approached as part of such contending unfolding of a common genetic make-up. Third and finally, it follows that it would be simply insufficient to focus on, say, Kroeber's articulations of history, since taken as a whole his work 'went through phases in which now one, now another [Boasian] genetic tendency was most clearly manifest.' These extended from his pronouncement on the 'superorganic' in 1917 through to his rather later work on civilizations and overarching trends in global history, with his quantitative reconstructionism of the late 1920s and his assertion of a holistic historicism just a few years after falling in between. Of course, to understand such shifts and phases in Kroeber's corpus in terms of the interchanges between hermeneutic and analytical dispositions in scholarship would be very interesting, but such an exercise is outside the scope of this Introduction. This is also true of the work of a scholar such as Ralph Linton, who combined the influences of Boas and Radcliffe-Brown. See A.L. Kroeber, 'The Superorganic', *American Anthropologist*, 19 (1917), pp. 163–213; A.L. Kroeber, *An Anthropologist Looks at History* (Berkeley, University of California Press, 1963); and Stocking, Jr, 'Ideas and Institutions in American Anthropology', in Stocking, Jr, *The Ethnographer's Magic*, pp. 118–50.

34. Stocking, Jr, 'Paradigmatic Traditions', p. 347.

35. Ibid., pp. 352–3.

36. Stocking succinctly considers such disciplinary departure(s) from Boas' emphasis on the diachronic and the historical. Here are to be found transformations of key tendencies in Boasian anthropology as increasingly inclined from the 1920s onwards towards a synchronic study of integration of cultures and of the relation of 'culture' and 'personality' as well as a widening breach between British and US anthropology, albeit one where both traditions overplayed synchrony, although with different emphases (ibid., 353–7). See also, Stocking, Jr, 'Ideas and Institutions in American Anthropology', pp. 134–49; and Stocking, Jr, *After Tylor*, pp. 233–441.

37. For a hint of such a reading, see Marshall Sahlins, *Culture in Practice: Selected Essays* (New York, Zone Books, 2000), pp. 20–2.

38. Franz Boas, *Anthropology and Modern Life* (New York, W.W. Norton, 1928), p. 206.

39. Stocking, Jr, 'Anthropology as *Kulturkampf*', pp. 110–11.

40. Ibid., 111.

41. Ibid., 110–12.

42. 'The need for such an external reference point was one of the leitmotifs of Boas' career, and it tended to carry with it a double standard of cultural evaluation: a universalistic one in terms of which he criticized the society in which he lived and a relativistic one in terms of which he defended the cultural alternative' (ibid., 112–13).

43. See E.E. Evans-Pritchard, 'Social Anthropology' and 'Social Anthropology: Past and Present', in Evans-Pritchard, *Social Anthropology and Other Essays* (New York, The Free Press of Glencoe, 1962), pp. 1–134, 139–57; E.E. Evans-Pritchard, *Anthropology and History* (Manchester, Manchester University Press, 1961). The essay titled 'Social Anthropology: Past and Present' is the Marett Lecture delivered by EP and published in *Man* in 1950. Not unlike *Anthropology and History* a decade later, this essay led to a series of exchanges in the pages of *Man* in the early 1950s, with Kroeber, Edmund Leach, Raymond Firth, and Meyer Fortes, among others, joining the debate. The keen reader should find these exchanges of interest. See also note 89 below, and T.N. Madan, 'Review of *Anthropology and History* by E.E. Evans-Pritchard, *The Eastern Anthropologist*, 14 (1961), pp. 262–7.

44. E.E. Evans-Pritchard, *Theories of Primitive Religion* (Oxford, Clarendon Press, 1965).

45. This is far from denying that EP's work has been read in other ways. For example, at the beginning of the 1960s David Pocock made a case for the affinities of EP's writings with modern structuralism, including by focusing on the notion of classificatory 'oppositions'. David F. Pocock, *Social Anthropology* (London, Sheed and Ward, 1961), pp. 72–82.

46. E.E. Evans-Pritchard, *The Nuer: A Description of the Modes of Livelihood and Political Institutions of a Nilotic People* (Oxford, Clarendon Press, 1940).

47. For a discussion of the ways in which EP's articulations of time crystallized the 'un-resolvable ambiguities' concerning time in the work of Durkheim (and his associates) and of Malinwoski, see Munn, 'The Cultural Anthropology of Time', pp. 94–8. My arguments draw on Munn's brilliant essay, extending its insights through overlapping but distinct emphases.

48. Evans-Pritchard, *The Nuer*; E.E. Evans-Pritchard, 'Nuer Time Reckoning', *Africa*, 12 (1939), pp. 189–216.

49. Evans-Pritchard, *The Nuer*, pp. 96, 102.

50. Munn, 'The Cultural Anthropology of Time', p. 96.

51. Ibid.; Evans-Pritchard, *The Nuer*, pp. 98–103.

52. Evans-Pritchard, *The Nuer*, pp. 105–8.

53. Here is something of an implicit, un-thought opposition between time and space in Evans-Pritchard's formulations. Munn, 'The Cultural Anthropology of Time', pp. 97–8.

54. Ibid.

55. The nature of readings that I am proposing can also open up other tensions and possibilities of his anthropology. On the one hand, EP's remarkable historical study of the Sanusi yet shows significant continuities with his a-historical work on Nuer politics. On the other hand, EP proffered forms of

'processual' analysis beginning in the late 1930s in his work on witchcraft, magic, and sorcery in the Azande state. Arguably, such emphasis on process was only confirmed in his contribution(s) to *African Political Systems*, a work widely considered a flagship endeavour of the structural-functionalist paradigm. Here, EP's writings actually intimated a significant shift from the programme laid down by Radcliffe-Brown. See E.E. Evans-Pritchard, *The Sanusi of Cyrenaica* (Oxford, Clarendon Press, 1949); Kuper, *Anthropologists and Anthropology*, p. 163; E.E. Evans-Pritchard, *Witchcraft, Oracles and Magic Among the Azande* (Oxford, Clarendon Press, 1937); Meyer Fortes and E.E. Evans-Pritchard (eds), *African Political Systems* (London, Oxford University Press, 1940); and Vincent, *Anthropology and Politics*, pp. 258–65.

56. Pierre Bourdieu, *Algeria 1960* (Cambridge, Cambridge University Press, 1979), p. 8 (first published in French in 1963); Pierre Bourdieu, *Outline of a Theory of Practice*, trans. Richard Nice (Cambridge, Cambridge University Press, 1977); and Munn, 'The Cultural Anthropology of Time', pp. 106–9.

57. Thus, it is in these ways that we might revisit Claude Lévi-Strauss' influential corpus in terms of its combination of symmetrically modernist lines and distinctive aesthetic sensibilities. Indeed, Lévi-Strauss' influential separation between 'hot' and 'cold' societies— each insinuating distinct temporalities— notwithstanding, his discussion of the relationship between anthropology and history is more ambivalent and even suggestive in its own manner. See, for example, Claude Lévi-Strauss, *Structural Anthropology* (New York, Basic Books, 1963); and Claude Lévi-Strauss, *The Savage Mind* (Chicago, University of Chicago Press, 1966). At the same time, rather than providing further examples, let me only state that attention to such interlacing of contrary dispositions toward social worlds and their academic understandings can help us approach anew the different bodies of work discussed in this Introduction.

58. S.C. Dube, *The Kamar* (Lucknow, Universal, 1951). Here, my discussion draws on Saurabh Dube, 'Ties that Bind: Tribe, Village, Nation, and S.C. Dube', in Patricia Uberoi, Satish Deshpande, and Nandini Sundar (eds), *Disciplinary Biographies: Essays in the History of Indian Sociology and Anthropology* (Delhi, Permanent Black, forthcoming).

59. Consider that Dube wrote of the Kamars as 'seriously talk[ing] about Gandhi Mahatma, *the king of all kings*...endowed with greater magical powers to fight the white sahibs.' Yet, he described the Kamars as 'almost untouched' by the 'great political awakening which has given a new national consciousness to India during the last sixty years'. The narrative holds together, but it also strains at the seams. Dube, *The Kamar*, p. 166.

60. Interestingly, D.N. Majumdar was among the first anthropologists of India who sought to reconcile the tension between synchronic and diachronic approaches (T.N. Madan, personal communication). However, his work on a tribe in transition possibly did not explicitly influence the approach of *The Kamar*, although Dube's discussion with Majumdar left a mark on the work (Leela Dube, personal communication).

61. See, for example, Nirmal Kumar Bose, *The Structure of Hindu Society* (New Delhi, Orient Longman, 1975); G.S. Ghurye, *The Aborgines—So called—and*

their Future (Poona, Gokhale Institute of Politics and Economics, 1942); G.S. Ghurye, *Caste and Race in India* (Bombay, Popular Prakashan, 1969); Irawati Karve, *Kinship Organization in India* (Bombay, Asia Publishing House, 1953); and Irawati Karve, *Hindu Society: An Introduction* (Poona, Deccan College, 1961).

62. For a persuasive reading see, T.N. Madan, *Pathways: Approaches to the Study of Society in India* (New Delhi, Oxford University Press, 1994), pp. 3–36. Indeed, D.P. Mukerji explicitly articulated the Marxist approach in a book on history. Dhurjati Prasad Mukerji, *On Indian History: A Study in Method* (Bombay, Hind Kitabs, 1945). Consider also Radhkamal Mukerjee, *The Indian Scheme of Things* (Bombay, Hind Kitabs, 1951); D.N. Majumdar, *A Tribe in Transition: A Study in Cultural Pattern* (Calcutta, Longman, Green & Co., 1937); and D.N. Majumdar, *Caste and Communication in an Indian Village* (Bombay, Asia Publishing House, 1958).

63. For key efforts toward such readings see, for example, Madan, *Pathways*, pp. 3–36; and Ravindra K. Jain, 'Social Anthropology of India: Theory and Method', in Indian Council of Social Science Research, *Survey of Research in Sociology and Social Anthropology, 1969–1979* (New Delhi, Satvahan, 1985), pp. 1–50. See also Veena Das, *Critical Events: An Anthropological Perspective on Contemporary India* (New Delhi, Oxford University Press, 1995), pp. 50–4.

64. Redfield's formulations concerning 'great' and 'little' traditions of civilizations exercised an important influence here. It was while articulating this influence that Marriott asked: 'Can a village be comprehended and conceived as a whole in itself, and can understanding one such village contribute to an understanding of the greater culture…in which the village is embedded?' Robert Redfield, *Peasant, Society, and Culture* (Chicago, University of Chicago Press, 1956); McKim Marriott (ed.), *Village India: Studies in the Little Community* (Chicago, University of Chicago Press, 1955), p. 171.

65. I have addressed such questions in relation to S.C. Dube's writings on villages in India. Saurabh Dube, 'Ties that Bind'. The issues can be usefully extended to the seminal work of M.N. Srinivas. M.N. Srinivas, *Religion and Society among the Coorgs of South India* (Oxford, Clarendon Press, 1952); and M.N. Srinivas, *Social Change in Modern India* (Berkeley, University of California Press, 1966). See also Jain, 'Social Anthropology of India', pp. 8–11; and Satish Saberwal, 'Sociologists and Inequality in India: The Historical Context', *Economic and Political Weekly*, 14 (1979), pp. 243–54.

66. Dumont contrasts the *homo hierarchicus* of Indian (mainly Hindu) culture and the *homo equalus* (man-the-equal) of Western society. Louis Dumont, *Homo Hierarchicus: The Caste System and its Implications* (Chicago, University of Chicago Press, 1980). See also T.N. Madan, 'The Comparison of Civilizations: Louis Dumont on India and the West', *International Sociology*, 16 (2001), pp. 474–87. On the nuances in Dumont's arguments concerning 'holism', 'individualism', and their mutual entanglements, see Dube, *Stitches on Time*, pp. 121–2, 217 n. 62.

67. Dumont, *Homo Hierarchicus*; Louis Dumont, *Religion/Politics and History in India: Collected Papers in Indian Sociology* (Paris and The Hague, Mouton, 1970).

68. Among prominent anthropologist critics of Dumont, two in particular—Nicholas Dirks and Richard Burghart—explicitly turned to historical materials and arguments. See Nicholas B. Dirks, *The Hollow Crown: Ethnohistory of an Indian Kingdom* (Cambridge, Cambridge University Press, 1987); Nicholas B. Dirks, *Castes of Mind: Colonialism and the Making of Modern India* (Princeton, Princeton University Press, 2001); and Richard Burghart, *The Conditions of Listening: Essays on Religion, History, and Politics in India*, edited by C.J. Fuller and Jonathan Spencer (New Delhi, Oxford University Press, 1996). See also Dube, *Untouchable Pasts*; and Peter Van der Veer, *Gods on Earth: The Management of Religious Experience and Identity in a North Indian Pilgrimage Centre* (New Delhi, Oxford University Press, 1988).

69. Louis Dumont and David F. Pocock, 'For a Sociology of India', *Contributions to Indian Sociology*, 1 (1957), pp. 7–22.

70. Needless to say, such appreciations of Dumont have not been uncritical. See, for instance, Veena Das, *Structure and Cognition: Aspects of Hindu Caste and Ritual* (New Delhi, Oxford University Press, 1982), pp. 3–7, 46–9. See also T.N. Madan (ed.), *Way of Life: King, Householder, Renouncer* (New Delhi, Vikas, 1982); and Das, *Critical Events*, pp. 34–40.

71. For discussions of such critiques and questions, which include relevant references, see Dube, *Untouchable Pasts*, pp. 8–12; and Jens Lerche, 'Dominant Castes, Rajas, Brahmins, and Inter-Caste Exchange Relations in Coastal Orissa: Behind the Facade of the "Jajmani System"', *Contributions to Indian Sociology* (n.s.), 27 (1993), pp. 237–66. See also Dipankar Gupta, 'Continuous Hierarchies and Discrete Castes', in Dipankar Gupta (ed.), *Social Stratification* (New Delhi, Oxford University Press, 1992), pp. 110–41.

72. The wider, substantive grounds for these queries derive from Saurabh Dube and Ishita Banerjee-Dube, 'Spectres of Conversion: Transformations of Caste and Sect in India', in Rowena Robinson and Sathianathan Clarke (eds), *Religious Conversion in India: Modes, Motivations, and Meanings in India* (New Delhi, Oxford University Press, 2003), esp. pp. 224–30.

73. This prompts a related question: Do such procedures of Dumont envision Indian forms of Christianity and Islam in the mirror of Hinduism?

74. On this issue, see Dipesh Chakrabarty, 'Postcoloniality and the Artifice of History: Who Speaks for "Indian" Pasts?', *Representations*, 37 (1992), pp. 1–26; Frederick Cooper, 'Conflict and Connection: Rethinking Colonial African History', *American Historical Review*, 99 (1994), pp. 1519–26; and Sumit Sarkar, *Writing Social History* (New Delhi, Oxford University Press, 1997), pp. 30–42. See also, Gyan Prakash, 'Subaltern Studies as Postcolonial Criticism', *American Historical Review*, 99 (1994), pp. 1475–94. While registering certain exceptions, the surveys by both Cooper and Sarkar substantiate my claims.

75. The critical edge of my arguments notwithstanding, there is much to be learnt anew from all these different tendencies of history-writing. Specifically, the distinct entwining of hermeneutical and analytical impulses in different modes of historical endeavour requires especial attention.

76. Gyanendra Pandey, 'In Defense of the Fragment: Writing about Hindu-Muslim Riots in India Today', *Representations*, 37 (1992), pp. 27–55; and Gyanendra

Pandey, 'The Prose of Otherness', in David Arnold and David Hardiman (eds), *Subaltern Studies VIII: Essays in Honour of Ranajit Guha* (New Delhi, Oxford University Press, 1994), pp. 188–221.

77. Pandey, 'The Prose of Otherness'. The difficulty with this essay lies in its style of pronouncement. Thus, even as Pandey takes note of differences among historians of different persuasions, 'History' is rendered as entirely too singular. Such larger-than-life statements actually stem from the very singularity of the overarching framework that binds Pandey's essay, riding roughshod over marks of difference and heterodoxy in the nitty-gritty of historical practice.

78. Clearly, I am sieving Pandey's arguments and emphases through related yet distinct filters.

79. Ibid.; Pandey, 'In Defense of the Fragment'. The latter essay establishes that such elision of the meanings of violence and the contours of pain in everyday arenas continues into the present. On recent writings on the Partition seeking to redress such excision of terms of violence and pain in historical endeavour, see, for example, Urvashi Butalia, *The Other Side of Silence: Voices from the Partition of India* (New Delhi, Viking Penguin, 1998); Ritu Menon and Kamla Bhasin, *Borders and Boundaries: Women in India's Partition* (New Delhi, Kali for Women, 1998); and Gyanendra Pandey, *Remembering Partition: Violence, Nationalism and History in India* (Cambridge, Cambridge University Press, 2001).

80. Dube, *Stitches on Time*, esp. chapter 5.

81. See, for example, Vincent, *Anthropology and Politics*, pp. 225–9, 308–14.

82. Saurabh Dube, 'Terms that Bind: Colony, Nation, Modernity', in Dube (ed.), *Postcolonial Passages: Contemporary History-writing on India* (New Delhi, Oxford University Press, 2004), pp. 2–3.

83. Nonetheless, functionalist tenets and structural analyses did not simply disappear from the academic scene from the 1970s onwards. Rather, they have continued to variously exercise their influence on anthropology, also being differently reconfigured in the discipline. Eisenstadt, 'Functional Analysis in Anthropology and Sociology', pp. 243–51; Sherry Ortner, 'Theory in Anthropology since the Sixties', *Comparative Studies in Society and History*, 26 (1984), pp. 127–32, 135–41; and Vincent, *Anthropology and Politics*, pp. 335–41. For influential works recasting functionalism and structuralism within anthropology, see, respectively, Maurice Bloch, *From Blessing to Violence: History and Ideology in the Circumcision Ritual of the Merina of Madagascar* (Cambridge, Cambridge University Press, 1986); and Marshall Sahlins, *Islands of History* (Chicago, University of Chicago Press, 1985).

84. Bourdieu, *Outline of a Theory of Practice*, esp. pp. 4–9.

85. Not only functionalism and structuralism but also other important anthropological traditions of the time could variously privilege structure over action. On the one hand, different versions of the 'cultural ecology' approach, associated especially with Marvin Harris, externalized the dynamics of history— considered as practice and process—and meanings of actors from within their fold. On the other hand, the work of Clifford Geertz opened up distinct possibilities for anthropology and history, particularly through its stress on the

orientation of the actor, including meaningful action. Yet it also tended to remove temporality from the terms of practice within culture, including in his reconstructions of the (Balinese) past. Marvin Harris, 'The Cultural Ecology of India's Sacred Cattle', *Current Anthropology*, 7 (1966), pp. 51–64; Clifford Geertz, *The Interpretation of Cultures* (New York, Basic Books, 1973); Clifford Geertz, *Negara: The Theatre State in Nineteenth Century Bali* (Princeton, Princeton University Press, 1980); and Munn, 'The Cultural Anthropology of Time', pp. 98–100.

86. Such shifts followed upon the fact that from the end of the 1920s key British anthropologists were 'confronted not with tiny, bounded isolated [sic] populations, but with comparatively huge, extended, dispersed tribes and nations [in Africa]'. These societies possessed governmental mechanisms that posed a problem to colonial authorities seeking to effectively administer them, including by accommodating their 'traditional' forms of governance under the principle of indirect rule. This was the wider colonial context to important British anthropological work of the 1930s and 1940s, which chiefly centred on Africa. Kuper, *Anthropologists and Anthropology*, pp. 107–8.

87. The political nature of the setting up of the Rhodes Livingstone Institute could combine imperial administrators' deep scepticism of anthropological work (ibid., pp. 133–5). On the shifts in anthropological research initiated by the Institute, see Vincent, *Anthropology and Politics*, pp. 276–83; and for a more recent, critical assessment of this research, see James Ferguson, *Expectations of Modernity: Myths and Meanings of Urban Life on the Zambian Copperbelt* (Berkeley, University of California Press, 1999).

88. See, for example, Edmund Leach, *Political System of Highland Burma: A Study of Kachin Social Structure* (London, G. Bell and Sons, 1954); Max Gluckman, *Order and Rebellion in Tribal Africa* (London, Cohen and West, 1963); F.G. Bailey, *Caste and the Economic Frontier: A Village in Highland Orissa* (Manchester, Manchester University Press, 1957); F.G. Bailey, *Stratagems and Spoils: A Social Anthropology of Politics* (Oxford, Basil Blackwell, 1969); Fredrik Barth, *Political Leadership among Swat Pathans* (London, Athlone Press, 1959); J.P.S. Uberoi, *The Politics of the Kula Ring: An Analysis of the Findings of Bronislaw Malinowski* (Manchester, Manchester University Press, 1962); and Victor Turner, *Schism and Continuity in an African Society* (Manchester, Manchester University Press, 1957). See also Peter Worsley, *The Trumpet Shall Sound: A Study of 'Cargo' Cults in Melanesia* (London, MacGibbon and Keo, 1957). Consider too the orientation to the anthropological discipline as a humanistic one—along with an emphasis on issues of belief and meaning—as represented in Evans-Pritchard, *Social Anthropology and Other Essays*; and Evans-Pritchard, *Theories of Primitive Religion*. See also, Edmund Leach, 'Virgin Birth: The Henry Myers Lecture 1966', *Proceedings of the Royal Anthropological Institute* (1967), pp. 39–50.

89. It is as part of such wider rethinking of the discipline that we might consider Evans-Pritchard's famous endorsement of the intersections between the 'sister' disciplines of anthropology and history, the differences between which he found to be 'illusory'. Significantly, his claims were based on the grounds that

anthropologists were increasingly 'more interested than they used to be in communities which are far from simple and undeveloped....' Thus, anthropologists could 'no longer ignore history', as had been the case earlier, especially on account of the anti-historical bent of functionalist anthropology. EP's ruminations invited a rejoinder from Isaac Schapera, who argued that several functionalist anthropologists had actually been doing history for a long time. While conceding that there could be situations in which the historian's tools might be usefully deployed by anthropologists, Schapera added that ultimately the disciplines were different. Anthropology was concerned with the 'social present' and history with the 'social past'. The debate reveals that while British anthropology had left behind what Brian Axel calls its 'pre-war fetish of pre-colonial purity', history and change were nonetheless understood as entering native society principally on account of European influence. Evans-Pritchard, *Anthropology and History*, quotation from p. 19; Isaac Schapera, 'Should Anthropologists be Historians?', *Man*, 93 (1962), pp. 198–222; and Axel, 'Introduction: Historical Anthropology', p. 7. See also, I.M. Lewis (ed.), *History and Social Anthropology* (London, Tavistock Publications, 1968).

90.   Such transformations were no less evident in anthropology in the US after World War II, especially entailing disciplinary moves toward the study of 'complex civilizations'. The implications of these for the study of India, particularly those concerning formulations of 'great' and 'little' traditions, have been mentioned earlier and shall also be discussed later. My point concerns the critical significance in this context of studies of subalterns that articulated textures of temporality and history, a tradition of anthropology as represented in Sydney Mintz, *Worker in the Cane: A Puerto Rican Life History* (New Haven, Yale University Press, 1960); and Eric Wolf, *Sons of the Shaking Earth* (Chicago, University of Chicago Press, 1959). It is this tradition that has been taken forward later in writings in historical anthropology such as Sydney Mintz, *Sweetness and Power: The Place of Sugar in Modern History* (New York, Viking, 1985); Eric Wolf, *Europe and the People without History* (Berkeley, University of California Press, 1982); and William Roseberry, *Anthropologies and Histories: Essays in Culture, History and Political Economy* (New Brunswick, Rutgers University Press, 1989). Another academic field, crucially delineated in the 1950s in the US, which has combined history and anthropology with limitations and possibilities is that of 'ethnohistory', astutely surveyed in Krech III, 'The State of Ethnohistory'.

91.   Such models and theories interrogated the capitalist and imperialist continuities of Western domination in non-Western theatres through polarities of core and periphery, development and under-development. An able, recent survey is contained in Patrick Wolfe, 'History and Imperialism: A Century of Theory, from Marx to Postcolonialism', *American Historical Review*, 102 (1997), pp. 380–420. See also, Ann Stoler, '(P)refacing Capitalism and Confrontation in 1995', in Ann Stoler, *Capitalism and Confrontation in Sumatra's Plantation Belt*, Second edition (Ann Arbor, University of Michigan Press, 1995), pp. vii–xxxiv; and Dube, 'Terms that Bind'.

92.   For example, Bourdieu, *Outline of a Theory of Practice*; Philip Abrams, *Historical Sociology* (Ithaca, Cornell University Press, 1982); Anthony Giddens, *Central*

Problems in Social Theory (London, Macmillan, 1979); John Comaroff and Simon Roberts, *Rules and Processes: The Cultural Logic of Dispute in an African Context* (Chicago, University of Chicago Press, 1981); Ortner, 'Theory in Anthropology'; and Sahlins, *Islands of History*. See also, E.P. Thompson, *The Poverty of Theory and other Essays* (New York, Monthly Review Press, 1978).

93. Fabian, *Time and the Other*; Renato Rosaldo, *Ilongot Headhunting 1873–1974: A Study in Society and History* (Stanford, Stanford University Press, 1980); Sahlins, *Islands of History*; Bernard Cohn, *An Anthropologist among the Historians and Other Essays* (New Delhi, Oxford University Press, 1987); Gerald Sider, *Culture and Class: A Newfoundland Illustration* (Cambridge, Cambridge University Press, 1986). See also, Arjun Appadurai, *Worship and Conflict under Colonial Rule: A South Indian Case* (Cambridge, Cambridge University Press, 1981); and Dirks, *The Hollow Crown*.

94. For instance, Jean Comaroff, *Body of Power, Spirit of Resistance: The Culture and History of a South African People* (Chicago, University of Chicago Press, 1985); Stoler, *Capitalism and Confrontation*; and Michael Taussig, *The Devil and Commodity Fetishism in South America* (Chapel Hill, University of North Carolina Press, 1980). See also, Richard Price, *First-Time: The Historical Vision of an Afro-American People* (Baltimore, Johns Hopkins University Press, 1983); June Nash, *We Eat the Mines and the Mines Eat Us: Dependency and Exploitation in Bolivian Tin Mines* (New York, Columbia University Press, 1979). In history-writing, such issues found expression on complementary yet distinct registers. See, for example, Ranajit Guha, *Elementary Aspects of Peasant Insurgency in Colonial India* (New Delhi, Oxford University Press, 1983).

95. Sherry B. Ortner, 'Introduction', in Sherry B. Ortner (ed.), *The Fate of 'Culture': Geertz and Beyond* (Berkeley, University of California Press, 1999), p. 3. Geertz's emphases further implied that the concept of culture needed to be trimmed of its bloated attributes in order to ensure its continued relevance. Geertz, *The Interpretation of Cultures*, p. 4.

96. Writings that initiated such critical considerations include Talal Asad, 'Anthropological Conceptions of Religion: Reflections on Geertz', *Man* (n.s.) 18 (1983), pp. 237–59; Gerald M. Sider, 'The Ties that Bind: Culture and Agriculture, Property and Propriety in the New Foundland Village Fishery', *Social History*, 5 (1980), pp. 1–39; and Herman Rebel, 'Cultural Hegemony and Class Experience: A Critical Reading of Recent Ethnological–Historical Approaches (Parts one and two)', *American Ethnologist*, 16 (1989), pp. 117–36, 350–65.

97. This is not to deny the emergence of sophisticated versions of the base-superstructure model, especially the one offered by the French philosopher Louis Althusser. However, the basic problem with the base–superstructure metaphor is that it displaces or, at any rate, cannot adequately account for meaningful practice. This also holds true for Althusser's model. Louis Althusser and Etienne Balibar, *Reading Capital* (London, New Left Books, 1970); Raymond Williams, *Marxism and Literature* (Oxford, Oxford University Press, 1977), pp. 81–2; Raymond Williams, 'Base and superstructure in Marxist cultural analysis', *New Left Review*, 82 (1973), pp. 3–16; Thompson, *The Poverty of Theory*.

98.   It warrants emphasis that the reflexive moment and the experimental impulse
      in ethnography are tied to the wider turn from the 1980s onwards to critical
      theory within the humanities. This has taken the form of close engagements
      with Continental philosophy—once the preserve of departments of European
      literatures in the Anglo-Saxon academy—in the fields of literary criticism and
      cultural studies and the disciplines of history and anthropology. Such
      developments have variously influenced several of the recent departures
      discussed in this Introduction. Here, an important role has been played by the
      blurring of scholarly genres and the dismantling of disciplinary boundaries—
      as distinct from the methodological reaching out to other disciplines—including
      entailing a questioning of their foundations, for example, by Jacques Derrida.
      See, for instance, Jacques Derrida, *Writing and Difference*, trans. Alan Bass
      (London, Routledge and Kegan Paul, 1978), which also contains a key engage-
      ment with the work of Lévi-Strauss.
99.   None of this is to suggest that by registering the complicities between the
      ethnographer and the informant, reflexive anthropology had resolved the
      problem. Indeed, the key texts of the reflexive turn within the discipline stand
      haunted by formative tensions and constitutive ambivalences, especially ones
      turning on the play of power in the crafting of ethnographies. Here, the
      reflexive ethnographers arguably remain implicated in the precise relationships
      they indict. See, for example, James Clifford and George Marcus (eds), *Writing
      Culture: The Poetics and Politics of Ethnography* (Berkeley, University of California
      Press, 1986); George Marcus and Dick Cushman, 'Ethnographies as texts',
      Annual Review of Anthropology, 11 (1982), pp. 25–69; George Marcus and
      Michael Fischer, *Anthropology as Cultural Critique: An Experimental Moment in
      the Human Sciences* (Chicago, University of Chicago Press, 1986).
100. See George Marcus, 'The Uses of Complicity in the Changing Mise-en-scène of
      Anthropological Fieldwork' and Lila Abu-Lughod, 'The Interpretation of
      Culture(s) after Television', in Ortner (ed.), *The Fate of 'Culture'*, pp. 86–109,
      110–35.
101. Micaela di Leonardo, *Exotics at Home: Anthropologies, Others, and American
      Modernity* (Chicago, University of Chicago Press, 2000); Catherine Lutz and
      Jane Collins, *Reading National Geographic* (Chicago, University of Chicago
      Press, 1993).
102. John Pemberton, *On the Subject of 'Java'* (Ithaca, Cornell University Press,
      1994); and Ortner (ed.), *The Fate of 'Culture'*.
103. A broader elaboration of these twin issues is contained in Dube, *Stitches on
      Time*. See also Peter van der Veer, this volume; John Kelly, this volume; and the
      literature surveys in Robert Foster, 'Making National Cultures in the Global
      Ecumene', *Annual Review of Anthropology*, 20 (1991), pp. 235–60; Sally Engle
      Merry, 'Anthropology, Law, and Transnational Processes', *Annual Review of
      Anthropology*, 21 (1992), pp. 357–79; Robert W. Hefner, 'Multiple Modernities:
      Christianity, Islam, and Hinduism in a Globalizing Age', *Annual Review of
      Anthropology*, 27 (1998), pp. 83–104; and Ana Maria Alonso, 'The Politics of
      Space, Time, and Substance: State Formation, Nationalism, and Ethnicity',
      Annual Review of Anthropology, 23 (1994), pp. 379–400.

104. See, for instance, Faubion, 'History in Anthropology', p. 36; J.D.Y. Peel, 'Making History: The Past in the Ijesha Present', *Man* (n.s), 19 (1984), pp. 111–32. See also Ishita Banerjee-Dube, this volume.

105. This is clarified by the following essays, which also orient the reader to salient writings in the fields they discuss. William Reddy, 'Emotional Liberty: Politics and History in the Anthropology of Emotions', *Cultural Anthropology*, 14 (1999), pp. 256–88; Michael G. Peletz, 'Kinship Studies in Late Twentieth-century Anthropology', *Annual Review of Anthropology*, 24 (1995), pp. 343–72; Merry, 'Anthropology, Law, and Transnational Processes'; Krech III, 'The State of Ethnohistory'; Kelly and Kaplan, 'History, Structure, and Ritual'.

106. Here, concerning only studies focusing on colony and empire, for two surveys of the field, see Dube, 'Terms that Bind', pp. 6–12; Stoler and Cooper, 'Between Metropole and Colony'.

107. Considering only anthropological studies that implicitly and explicitly engage issues of modernity in South Asia, see, for instance, Akhil Gupta, *Postcolonial Developments: Agriculture in the Making of Modern India* (Durham, Duke University Press, 1998); Emma Tarlo, *Unsettling Memories: Narratives of India's 'Emergency'* (Delhi, Permanent Black, 2003); Thomas Blom Hansen, *Wages of Violence: Naming and Identity in Postcolonial Bombay* (Princeton, Princeton University Press, 2001); Arjun Appadurai, *Modernity at Large: Cultural Dimensions of Globalization* (Minneapolis, University of Minnesota Press, 1996); William Mazzaarella, *Shovelling Smoke: Advertising and Globalization in Contemporary India* (Durham, Duke University Press, 2003); and Purnima Mankekar, *Screening Culture, Viewing Politics: Television, Womanhood and Nation in Modern India* (New Delhi, Oxford University Press, 2000).

108. For instance, David Lan, *Guns and Rain: Guerillas and Spirit Mediums in Zimbabwe* (Berkeley, University of California Press, 1985); Comaroff, *Body of Power, Spirit of Resistance*.

109. Fabian, *Time and the Other*, p. x.

110. For example, Kathleen Gough, 'Anthropology: Child of Imperialism', *Monthly Review*, 19 (1968), pp. 12–68; Jairus Banaji, 'The Crisis of British Anthropology', *New Left Review*, 64 (1970), pp. 71–85; Talal Asad (ed.), *Anthropology and the Colonial Encounter* (London, Ithaca Press, 1973); and Dell Hymes (ed.), *Reinventing Anthropology* (New York, Pantheon Books, 1972).

111. Michel-Rolph Trouillot, 'North Atlantic Universals: Analytical Fictions, 1492–1945', in Dube (ed.), *Enduring Enchantments*, p. 840.

112. For example, E. Valentine Daniel, *Charred Lullabies: Chapters in an Anthropology of Violence* (Princeton, Princeton University Press, 1996); Catherine Lutz, *Homefront: A Military City and the American Twentieth Century* (Boston, Beacon Press, 2002); Michael Taussig, *Law in a Lawless Land: Diary of a Limpieza* (New York, New Press, 2003); and John Kelly and Martha Kaplan, *Represented Communities: Fiji and World Decolonization* (Chicago, University of Chicago Press, 2001).

113. Lucien Febvre, *New Kind of History: From the Writings of Febvre*, edited by Peter Burke (London, Routledge, 1973); Marc Bloch, *The Historian's Craft* (Manchester, Manchester University Press, 1954); Fernand Braudel, *The Mediterranean*

and the Mediterranean World in the Age of Philip II: Vols. I and II (London, Fontana/Collins, 1973); Emmanuel Le Roy Ladurie, *Montaillou: The Promised Land of Error*, trans. Barbara Bray (New York, Vintage Books, 1979); and Roger Chartier, *Cultural History: Between Practices and Representations* (Ithaca, Cornell University Press, 1993).

114. Edward P. Thompson, *Customs in Common: Studies in Traditional Popular Culture* (New York, The New Press, 1993); Christopher Hill, *The World Turned Upside Down: Radical Ideas during the English Revolution* (New York, Penguin Books, 1973); and Eric Hobsbawm, *Nations and Nationalism since 1780: Programme, Myth, Reality* (Cambridge, Cambridge University Press, 1993).

115. Natalie Z. Davis, *Society and Culture in Early Modern France: Eight Essays by Natalie Zemon Davis* (Stanford, Stanford University Press, 1977); Robert Darnton, *The Great Cat Massacre and Other Episodes in French Cultural History* (New York, Vintage, 1985); William H. Sewell, Jr, *Work and Revolution in France: The Language of Labor from the Old Regime to 1848* (New York, Cambridge University Press, 1980); Eugene D. Genovese, *Roll Jordan Roll: The World the Slaves Made* (New York, Pantheon, 1974); and Lawrence Levine, *Black Culture and Consciousness* (New York, Oxford University Press, 1977).

116. Carlo Ginzburg, *The Cheese and the Worms: The Cosmos of a Sixteenth Century Miller*, translated by John and Anne Tedeschi (Baltimore, Johns Hopkins University Press, 1980); Edward Muir and Guido Ruggiero (eds), *Microhistory and the Lost Peoples of Europe*, translated by Eren Branch (Baltimore, Johns Hopkins University Press, 1991); and Lüdtke (ed.), *History of Everyday Life*.

117. Jacques Rancière, *The Names of History: On the Poetics of Knowledge*, translated by Hassan Melehy (Minneapolis, University of Minnesota Press, 1994). See also, Jacques Rancière, *The Philosopher and His Poor*, translated by Andrew Parker (Durham, Duke University Press, 2004).

118. Hayden White, 'Foreword: Rancière's Revisionism', in Rancière, *The Names of History*, p. xvii. White is commenting on Rancière's reading of Michelet here.

119. It should be clear that in raising the questions that follow I am neither offering an overall assessment of the *Annales* tradition nor suggesting that its key practitioners have entirely effaced human practices, subordinating these to structural principles. Indeed, I am acutely aware of the diversity, difference, and discontinuity that have characterized the *Annales* scholarship as also its productive grappling with critical questions of the relationships between, for instance, structure and event and human agency and anonymous forces in the shaping of history. All this is clarified by the writings of the *Annales* cited earlier. Rather, my purpose is to guard against a simple celebration of scholarly departures, attending instead to the tensions that are formative of them, which is itself in tune with the broader emphases of this introductory piece.

120. White, 'Foreword', p. xi. Rancière, *Names of History*.

121. According to Braudel, the history of mountainous regions, as worlds far removed from civilization proper, is to have no history. Braudel, *The Mediterranean and the Mediterranean World in the Age of Philip II: Vol I*; Medick, '"Missionaries in the Rowboat"?, pp. 42–4.

122. E.P. Thompson, 'Patrician Society, Plebian Culture', *Journal of Social History*, 7

(1974), pp. 382–405; E.P. Thompson, 'Eighteenth-century English Society: Class Struggle without Class', *Social History*, 3 (1978), pp. 133–65; E.P. Thompson, 'Time, Work-discipline and Industrial Capitalism', *Past and Present*, 38 (1967), pp. 56–97; E.P. Thompson, 'The Moral Economy of the English Crowd in the Eighteenth Century', *Past and Present*, 50 (1971), pp. 76–136.

123. On such questions see, Hans Medick, 'Plebian Culture in the Transition to Capitalism', in Raphael Samuel and Gareth Stedman Jones (eds), *Culture, Ideology and Politics* (London, Routledge and Kegan Paul, 1983), pp. 84–113.

124. Thompson, 'Time, Work-discipline and Industrial Capitalism'.

125. I explore such issues in Dube, *Stitches on Time*, esp. pp. 133–7.

126. Ranajit Guha (ed.), *Subaltern Studies I-VI: Writings on South Asian History and Society* (New Delhi, Oxford University Press, 1982–1989); Partha Chatterjee and Gyanendra Pandey (eds), *Subaltern Studies VII: Writings on South Asian History and Society* (New Delhi, Oxford University Press, 1992); Arnold and Hardiman (eds), *Subaltern Studies VIII*; Shahid Amin and Dipesh Chakrabarty (eds), *Subaltern Studies IX: Writings on South Asian History and Society* (New Delhi, Oxford University Press, 1996); Gautam Bhadra, Gyan Prakash and Susie Tharu (eds), *Subaltern Studies X: Writings on South Asian History and Society* (New Delhi, Oxford University Press, 1999).

127. See here the discussions between history and anthropology as represented in Keith Thomas, *Religion and the Decline of Magic: Studies in Popular Beliefs in Sixteenth- and Seventeenth-Century England* (London, Weidenfeld and Nicolson, 1971); E.P. Thompson, 'Anthropology and the Discipline of Historical Context', *Midland History*, 1 (1972), pp. 45–53; E.P. Thompson, 'Folklore, Anthropology, and Social History', *Indian Historical Review*, 3 (1977), pp. 247–66; and Keith Thomas, 'History and Anthropology', *Past and Present*, 24 (1963), pp. 3–24.

128. This becomes clear from the preceding discussions concerning the place of culture within the earlier subaltern studies scholarship and the dispositions toward tradition and time in the work of E.P. Thompson.

129. Hill, *The World Turned Upside Down*; Thompson, *Customs in Common*.

130. Genovese, *Roll Jordan Roll*; Levine, *Black Culture and Consciousness*.

131. Ranajit Guha, 'On Some Aspects of the Historiography of Colonial India', in Guha (ed.), *Subaltern Studies I*, p. 7. Emphasis in the original. For a wider discussion of such questions, see Dube, *Stitches on Time*, chapter 5.

132. Concerning the influence of the linguistic turn on history-writing, such developments had their antecedents within the discipline in, for example, works by Paul Veyne and Hayden White, which, respectively, emphasized the importance of the 'plot' and of the 'trope'. Paul Veyne, *Writing History*, translated by Mina Moore-Rinvolucri (Middletown, Wesleyan University Press, 1984), a work first published in French in 1971; Hayden White, *Metahistory: The Historical Imagination in Nineteenth-Century Europe* (Baltimore, Johns Hopkins University Press, 1973).

133. See the discussion in the sections titled 'Genealogies', 'Communities', and 'Empire and Nation' below, which elaborate such developments in scholarship on South Asia.

134. For example, Madan, *Pathways*; Sarkar, *Writing Social History*; Ramchandra

Guha, *Savaging the Civilized: Verrier Elwin, His Tribals, and India* (New Delhi, Oxford University Press, 1999); Jain, 'Social anthropology of India'; Uberoi, Deshpande and Sundar (eds), *Disciplinary Biographies*. Here, I am excluding numerous literature surveys of Indian anthropology/sociology and history that may constitute valuable contributions in other respects.

135. A shorter, somewhat different version of the arguments presented in this section has appeared as 'Historical Anthropology of Modern India', *History Compass*, 5 (2007), and I am grateful for permission to reproduce the materials here.

136. Interestingly, some of the most significant ethnographers associated with Sri Lanka have shown a key interest in history for a long time now. Gananath Obeyesekere, *Land Tenure in Village Ceylon: A Sociological and Historical Study* (Cambridge, Cambridge University Press, 1967); Gananath Obeyesekere, *The Cult of the Goddess Pattini* (Chicago, University of Chicago Press, 1984); Stanley J. Tambiah, *World Conqueror and World Renouncer: A Study of Buddhism and Polity in Thailand against a Historical Background* (Cambridge, Cambridge University Press, 1976); David Scott, *Formations of Ritual: Colonial and Anthropological Discourses on the Sinhala Yaktovil* (Minneapolis, University of Minnesota Press, 1994): and Gananath Obeyesekere, *The Apotheosis of Captain Cook: European Mythmaking in the Pacific* (Princeton, Princeton University Press, 1992). Concerning the historical anthropology of Nepal, see, for instance, Sherry B. Ortner, *High Religion: A Cultural and Political History of Sherpa Buddhism* (Princeton, Princeton University Press, 1989); and Sherry B. Ortner, *Life and Death on Mt. Everest: Sherpas and Himalayan Mountaineering* (Princeton, Princeton University Press, 1999).

137. Redfield, *Peasant, Society, and Culture.*

138. Mckim Marriot, 'Village Structure and the Punjab Government: A Restatement', *American Anthropologist*, 55 (1953), pp. 137–43.

139. A.M. Shah and R.G. Shroff, 'The Vahivancha Barots of Gujarat: A Caste of Genealogists and Mythograpers', in Milton Singer (ed.), *Traditional India: Structure and Change* (Philadelphia: American Folklore Society, 1959), pp. 40–70.

140. A.M. Shah, *Exploring India's Rural Past: A Gujarat Village in the Early Nineteenth Century* (New Delhi, Oxford University Press, 2002). Much of the work for— and writing of—this monograph was carried out in the late 1950s and early 1960s.

141. Surajit Sinha, 'State Formation and Rajput Myth in Tribal Central India', *Man in India*, 42 (1962), pp. 25–80.

142. See, for example, K.S. Singh (ed.), *Tribal Situation in India* (Shimla, Indian Institute of Advanced Study, 1972); Ravindra K. Jain, this volume; and Ravindra K. Jain, *Between History and Legend: Status and Power in Bundelkhand* (Hyderabad, Orient Longman), which contains several essays written in the 1970s. On other earlier writings in Indian anthropology/sociology variously oriented to history and temporality, see Ramkrishna Mukherjee, *The Rise and Fall of the East India Company: A Sociological Appraisal* (New York, Monthly Review Press, 1974); Saberwal, 'Sociologists and Inequality in India'; and Satish Saberwal,

Mobile Men: Limits to Social Change in Urban Punjab (Delhi, Vikas, 1976). See also Bailey, *Caste and the Economic Frontier;* Adrian Mayer, *Caste and Kinship in Central India: A Village and its Region* (Berkeley, University of California Press, 1966); and A.R. Desai, *Social Background of Indian Nationalism* (Bombay, Popular Prakashan, 1959).

143. For a survey, see Sarkar, *Writing Social History,* chapter 1; see also Partha Chatterjee, 'Introduction: History and the Present', in Partha Chatterjee and Anjan Ghosh (eds), *History and the Present* (Delhi, Permanent Black, 2002), pp. 1–23. In different ways, Sarkar and Chatterjee both point to the existence of social histories in vernacular idioms that have for at least a century now existed outside of the canons of professional history-writing. Such issues require further examination.

144. For example, D.D. Kosambi, *An Introduction to the Study of Indian History* (Bombay, Popular Prakashan, 1975); D.D. Kosambi, *The Culture and Civilisation of Ancient India in Historical Outline* (London, Routledge and Kegan Paul, 1965); Romila Thapar, *Cultural Pasts: Essays in Early Indian History* (New Delhi, Oxford University Press, 2000); Kunal Chakrabarti, *Religious Process: The Puranas and the Making of a Regional Tradition* (New Delhi, Oxford University Press, 2001); Phillip B. Wagoner, *Tidings of the King: A Translation and Ethnohistorical Analysis of the Rayavacakamu* (Honolulu, University of Hawaii Press, 1993). See also, Norbert Peabody, *Hindu Kingship and Polity in Precolonial India* (Cambridge, Cambridge University Press, 2002); Burton Stein, *Peasant State and Society in Medieval South India* (New Delhi, Oxford University Press, 1986); Velcheru Narayan Rao, David Shulman and Sanjay Subrahmanyam, *Symbols of Substance: Court and State in Nayaka Period Tamil Nadu* (New Delhi, Oxford University Press, 1992); Romila Thapar, *Time as a Metaphor of History: Early India* (New Delhi, Oxford University Press, 1996); S.C. Malik, *Indian Civilization: The Formative Period: A Study of Archaeology as Anthropology* (Shimla, Indian Institute of Advanced Study, 1968); Ronald Inden, Jonathan Walters, and Daud Ali, *Querying the Medieval: Texts and the History of Practices in South Asia* (New York, Oxford University Press, 2000); and Richard M. Eaton, *The Rise of Islam and the Bengal Frontier, 1204–1760* (Berkeley, University of California Press, 1993).

145. Indeed, social scientists could turn toward the historical record to explicate considerations of peasant societies and movements. See, for example, Kathleen Gough, *Rural Society in Southeast India* (Cambridge, Cambridge University Press, 1981); D.N. Dhanagre, *Peasant Movements in India, 1920–1950* (New Delhi, Oxford University Press, 1983); and Hetukar Jha, *Social Structures of Indian Villages: A Study of Rural Bihar* (New Delhi, Sage, 1991). See also Jan Breman, *Patronage and Exploitation: Changing Agrarian Relations in South Gujarat, India* (Berkeley, University of California Press, 1974); and A.R. Desai (ed.), *Peasant Struggles in India* (Bombay, Oxford University Press, 1979).

146. For example, Ravinder Kumar (ed.), *Essays on Gandhian Politics: The Rowlatt Satyagraha of 1919* (Oxford, Clarendon Press, 1971); Gyanendra Pandey, *The Ascendancy of the Congress in Uttar Pradesh, 1926–1934: A Study in Imperfect Mobilization* (Oxford, Clarendon Press, 1978); David Hardiman, *Peasant*

Nationalists of Gujarat: Kheda District 1917–1934 (New Delhi, Oxford University Press, 1981); and Majid Siddiqi, *Agrarian Unrest in North India: The United Provinces, 1918–22* (New Delhi, Vikas, 1978).

147. K. Suresh Singh, *The Dust Storm and the Hanging Mist: A Study of Birsa Munda and his Movement, 1874–1901* (Calcutta, Firma KLM, 1966); K. Suresh Singh, 'Colonial Transformations of the Tribal Society in Middle India', *Economic and Political Weekly*, 13 (1978), pp. 1221–32; and K. Suresh Singh, *Tribal Society in India: An Anthropo-historical Perspective* (New Delhi, Manohar, 1985). See also K. Suresh Singh, *Birsa Munda and His Movement, 1874–1901: A Study of a Millenarian Movement in Chotanagpur* (Delhi, Oxford University Press, 1982).

148. For different assessments of Cohn's work see, Nicholas Dirks, 'Foreword', in Bernard Cohn, *Colonialism and its Forms of Knowledge: The British in India* (Princeton, Princeton University Press, 1996), pp. ix–xvii; Axel, 'Introduction: Historical Anthropology', esp. pp. 7–9; and Ranajit Guha, 'Introduction', in Cohn, *Anthropologist among the Historians*, pp. vii–xxvi.

149. Cohn, *Anthropologist among the Historians*, chapters 11 and 12.

150. Bernard Cohn, *India: The Social Anthropology of a Civilization* (Englewood Cliffs, NJ: Prentice-Hall, 1971).

151. Cohn, *Anthropologist among Historians*.

152. Dirks, 'Foreword', p. xii.

153. Some among Cohn's anthropologist colleagues working on South Asia at the University of Chicago also addressed questions of temporality and history in distinct ways. See, for instance, Ronald B. Inden, *Marriage and Rank in Bengali Culture: A History of Caste and Clan in Middle Period Bengal* (Berkeley, University of California Press, 1976); Milton B. Singer, *When a Great Tradition Modernizes: An Anthropological Approach to Indian Civilization* (New York, Praeger, 1972). See also, Milton Singer and Bernard Cohn (eds), *Structure and Change in Indian Society* (Chicago, Aldine, 1968).

154. Cohn, *Anthropologist among Historians*, chapter 23.

155. Cohn, this volume; Cohn, *Colonialism and its Forms of Knowledge*.

156. Cohn, 'History and Anthropology'; Bernard Cohn, 'Anthropology and History in the 1980s: Towards a Rapprochement', *The Journal of Interdisciplinary History*, 12 (1981), pp. 227–52.

157. It is important to note that the impact of Cohn's work was equally felt in the world of historiography. Such impact can be traced from the manner in which his writings—on the census, for example—could open up specific fields of research through to the ways they served to orient wider terms of historical enquiry. Cohn, *Anthropologist among Historians*, chapter 10; Frank F. Conlon, *A Caste in a Changing World: The Chitrapur Saraswat Brahmans, 1700–1935* (Berkeley, University of California Press, 1977); and David Lelyveld, *Aligarh's First Generation: Muslim Solidarity in British India* (Princeton, Princeton University Press, 1978).

158. Tom G. Kessinger, *Vilyatpur 1848–1968: Social and Economic Change in a North Indian Village* (Berkeley, University of California Press, 1974); Richard G. Fox, *Kin, Clan, Raja and Rule* (Berkeley, University of California Press, 1971). See

also Richard G. Fox (ed.), *Realm and Region in Traditional India* (Durham, Duke University Press, 1977).

159. Appadurai, *Worship and Conflict*; Arjun Appadurai and Carol Breckenridge, 'The South Indian Temple: Authority, Honour, and Redistribution', *Contributions to Indian Sociology* (n.s.), 10 (1976), pp. 187–211; Dirks, *The Hollow Crown*. This is, of course, an indicative list. Other writings intimating distinct emphases and arenas include Paul Greenough, *Prosperity and Misery in Modern Bengal* (New York, Oxford University Press, 1982); Richard G. Fox, *Lions of the Punjab: Culture in the Making* (Berkeley, University of California Press, 1985); and Nita Kumar, *The Artisans of Banaras: Popular Culture and Identity, 1880–1986* (Princeton, Princeton University Press, 1988).

160. Burghart, *Conditions of Listening*; van der Veer, *Gods on Earth*; Susan Bayly, *Saints, Goddesses and Kings: Muslims and Christians in South Indian Society 1700–1900* (Cambridge, Cambridge University Press, 1989); and D.H.A Kolff, *Naukar, Rajput, and Sepoy: The Ethnohistory of the Military Labour Market of Hindustan, 1450–1850* (Cambridge, Cambridge University Press, 1990).

161. Thomas Trautmann, *Dravidian Kinship* (Cambridge, Cambridge University Press, 1982).

162. Ronald Inden, *Imagining India* (Oxford, Basil Blackwell, 1990).

163. On these questions, see Sarkar, *Modern India*.

164. Ranajit Guha, 'The Prose of Counter-Insurgency', in Guha (ed.), *Subaltern Studies II*, pp. 1–42; Guha, *Elementary Aspects*; Gayatri Chakravorty Spivak, 'Subaltern Studies: Deconstructing Historiography', in Guha (ed.), *Subaltern Studies IV*, pp. 330–63; and Rosalind O'Hanlon, 'Recovering the Subject: *Subaltern Studies* and Histories of Resistance in Colonial South Asia', *Modern Asian Studies*, 22 (1988), pp. 189–224.

165. Bernard Cohn, 'The Command of Language and the Language of Command', in Guha (ed.), *Subaltern Studies IV*, pp. 276–329; Veena Das, 'Subaltern as Perspective', in Guha (ed.), *Subaltern Studies VI*, pp. 310–24; Upendra Baxi, ''The State's Emissary': The Place of Law in Subaltern Studies', in Chatterjee and Pandey (eds), *Subaltern Studies VII*, pp. 257–64. See also, Sherry Ortner, 'Resistance and the Problem of Ethnographic Refusal', *Comparative Studies in Society and History*, 37 (1995), pp. 173–93.

166. Ravindra K. Jain, this volume; Saurabh Dube, this volume; Susan Visvanathan; this volume; Ishita Banerjee-Dube, this volume; Shail Mayaram, *Against History, Against State: Counterperspectives from the Margins* (New Delhi, Permanent Black, 2004); and Yasmin Saikia, *Fragmented Memories: Struggling to Be Tai-Ahom in India* (Durham, Duke University Press, 2004). See also Wendy Singer, *Creating Histories: Oral Narratives and the Politics of History-Making* (Delhi, Oxford University Press, 1997); Ajay Skaria, this volume; Ann Gold and Bhoju Ram Gujar, this volume; Paul Greenough, this volume; and Velcheru Narayana Rao, David Shulman and Sanjay Subrahmanyam, *Textures of Time: Writing History in South India* (Delhi, Permanent Black, 2001).

167. Shahid Amin, *Event, Metaphor, Memory: Chauri Chaura 1922–1992* (Berkeley, University of California Press, 1996); Ann Gold and Bhoju Ram Gujar, *In the*

Time of Trees and Sorrows: Nature, Power, and Memory in Rajasthan (Durham, Duke University Press, 2002); Ajay Skaria, *Hybrid Histories: Forest, Frontiers and Wildness in Western India* (New Delhi, Oxford University Press, 1999); Dube, *Untouchable Pasts*; Prathama Banerjee, 'Re-presenting Pasts: Santals in Nineteenth-century Bengal', in Chatterjee and Ghosh (eds), *History and the Present*, pp. 242–73; Ishita Banerjee-Dube, *Religion, Law and Power: Tales of Time in Eastern India, 1860–2000* (London, Anthem Press, 2007).

168. Banerjee-Dube, this volume; Ajay Skaria, 'Writing, Orality, and Power in the Dangs, Western India, 1800s–1920s', in Amin and Chakrabarty (eds), *Subaltern Studies IX*, pp. 13–58; and Dube, *Untouchable Pasts*. See also, Daud Ali (ed.), *Invoking the Past: The Uses of History in South Asia* (New Delhi, Oxford University Press, 1999).

169. Michel-Rolph Trouillot, *Silencing the Past: Power and the Production of History* (Boston, Beacon Press, 1995); Saikia, *Fragmented Memories*; Shahid Amin, 'On Retelling the Muslim Conquest of North India', in Chatterjee and Ghosh (eds), *History and the Present*, pp. 24–43; Skaria, *Hybrid Histories*; Ishita Banerjee-Dube, 'Taming Traditions: Legalities and Histories in Eastern India', in Bhadra, Prakash, and Tharu (eds), *Subaltern Studies X*, pp. 98–125.

170. Gyanendra Pandey, *Routine Violence: Nations, Fragments, Histories* (Stanford, Stanford University Press, 2005); Amin, *Event, Metaphor, Memory*; Chakrabarty, *Provincializing Europe*; and Dube (ed.), *Postcolonial Passages*. See also Ashis Nandy, 'History's Forgotten Doubles', *History and Theory*, 34 (1995), pp. 44–66; and Vinay Lal, *The History of History: Politics and Scholarship in Modern India* (New Delhi, Oxford University Press, 2003).

171. For instance, Chakrabarty, *Provincializing Europe*; Dipesh Chakrabarty, *Habitations of Modernity: Essays in the Wake of Subaltern Studies* (Chicago, University of Chicago Press, 2002); Dube, *Stitches on Time*; and Dube (ed.), *Enduring Enchantments*.

172. Peter Redfield, *Space in the Tropics: From Convicts to Rockets in French Guiana* (Berkeley, University of California Press, 2000); Dube, *Stitches on Time*.

173. Anthony Cohen, *The Symbolic Construction of Community* (London, Routledge, 1989), p. 14.

174. Nandini Sundar, this volume; Gyanendra Pandey, this volume; Malavika Kasturi, this volume; Visvanatahan, this volume; Skaria, this volume; Dube, this volume; Mayaram, this volume; Harjot Oberoi, *The Construction of Religious Boundaries: Culture, Identity, and Diversity in the Sikh Tradition* (Chicago, University of Chicago Press, 1994); Rowena Robinson, *Conversion, Continuity, and Change: Lived Christianity in Southern Goa* (New Delhi, Sage, 1998); Das, *Critical Events*; Prem Chowdhry, *The Veiled Woman: Shifting Gender Equations in Rural Haryana 1880–1980* (New Delhi, Oxford University Press, 1994); Piya Chatterjee, *A Time for Tea: Women, Labor, and Post/Colonial Politics on an Indian Plantation* (Durham, Duke University Press, 2001); Dube (ed.), *Postcolonial Passages*; Malavika Kasturi, *Embattled Identities: Rajput Lineages and the Colonial State in Nineteenth-Century North India* (New Delhi, Oxford University Press, 2002); Charu Gupta, *Sexuality, Obscenity, and Community: Women, Muslims, and the Hindu Public in Colonial India* (Delhi, Permanent Black, 2002); and Sandra

Freitag, *Collective Action and Community: Public Arenas and the Emergence of Communalism in North India* (Berkeley, University of California Press, 1990).

175. Ranajit Guha, this volume; Dube, this volume; Shail Mayaram, *Resisting Regimes: Myth, Memory and the Shaping of a Muslim Identity* (New Delhi, Oxford University Press, 1997); David Hardiman, *The Coming of the Devi: Adivasi Assertion in Western India* (New Delhi, Oxford University Press, 1987); and Anand Pandian, 'Securing the Rural Citizen: The Anti-Kallar Movement of 1896', *The Indian Economic and Social History Review*, 42 (2005), pp. 1–39.

176. Partha Chatterjee, *The Nation and its Fragments: Colonial and Postcolonial Histories* (Princeton, Princeton University Press, 1993); Partha Chatterjee, *The Politics of the Governed: Reflections on Popular Politics in Most of the World* (New York, Columbia University Press, 2004).

177. Saurabh Dube, 'Presence of Europe: A Cyber-conversation with Dipesh Chakrabarty', in Dube (ed.), *Postcolonial Passages*, pp. 254–62; Amin, *Event, Metaphor, Memory*.

178. For instance, Skaria, *Hybrid Histories*; Banerjee-Dube, *Religion, Law and Power*; Dube, *Untouchable Pasts*; and Chakrabarty, *Provincializing Europe*.

179. See Dube, 'Terms that Bind', pp. 6–8.

180. For discussions of such prior understandings of colony and empire, see, for example, Sarkar, *Writing Social History*, pp. 24–49; and Prakash, 'Writing Post-Orientalist Histories of the Third World'.

181. Wider conceptual elaborations of these two tendencies—based on relevant writings from different parts of the world—include Stoler and Cooper, 'Between Metropole and Colony'; and Dube, 'Terms that Bind', pp. 8–12.

182. The arguments of this paragraph draw on Dube, *Stitches on Time*.

183. van der Veer, this volume; Cohn, this volume; Sudipta Sen, *Distant Sovereignty: National Imperialism and the Origins of British India* (New York, Routledge, 2002); Sumathi Ramaswamy, *The Lost Land of Lemuria: Fabulous Geographies, Catastrophic Histories* (Berkeley, University of California Press, 2004); Michael H. Fisher, *Counterflows to Colonialism: Indian Travellers and Settlers in Britain, 1600–1857* (Delhi, Permanent Black, 2004); Uday Singh Mehta, *Liberalism and Empire: A Study in Nineteenth-Century British Liberal Thought* (Chicago, University of Chicago Press, 1999); and Antoinette M. Burton, *At the Heart of the Empire: Indians and the Colonial Encounter in Late-Victorian Britain* (Berkeley, University of California Press, 1998).

184. John Kelly, this volume; Nicholas Dirks, this volume; Cohn, *Colonialism and its Forms of Knowledge*; Piya Chatterjee, *Time for Tea*; Guha, 'Not at Home in Empire'; E.M. Collingham, *Imperial Bodies: The Physical Experience of the Raj, c. 1800–1947* (Cambridge, Polity Press, 2001); Dane Kennedy, *The Magic Mountains: Hill Stations and the British Raj* (Berkeley, University of California Press, 1996); Dube, *Stitches on Time*, esp. chapter 1; and Dirks, *Castes of Mind*. See also, Thomas Metcalf, *Ideologies of the Raj* (Cambridge, Cambridge University Press, 1995).

185. Pamela Price, *Kingship and Political Practice in Colonial India* (Cambridge, Cambridge University Press, 1996); Ishita Banerjee-Dube, *Divine Affairs: Pilgrimage, Law and the State in Colonial and Postcolonial India* (Shimla, Indian

Institute of Advanced Study, 2001); David W. Rudner, *Caste and Capitalism in Colonial India: The Nattukottai Chettiars* (Berkeley, University of California Press, 1994); G. Arunima, *There Comes Papa: Colonialism and the Transformation of Matriliny in Kerala, Malabar, c. 1850–1940* (Hyderabad, Orient Longman, 2003); and Veena Naregal, *Language Politics, Elites and the Public Sphere: Western India under Colonialism* (London, Anthem Press, 2002).

186. Ramachandra Guha, *The Unquiet Woods: Ecological Change and Peasant Resistance in the Himalaya* (Berkeley, University of California Press, 1990); K. Sivaramakrishnan, *Modern Forests: Statemaking and Environmental Change in Colonial Eastern India* (New Delhi, Oxford University Press, 1999); Skaria, *Hybrid Histories*; and Gold and Gujar, *In the Time of Trees and Sorrows*. See also Sumit Guha, *Environment and Ethnicity in India, 1200–1991* (Cambridge, Cambridge University Press, 1999).

187. Kelly, this volume; Sivaramakrishnan, this volume; Paul Greenough, this volume; Martha Kaplan, 'Panoptican in Poona: An Essay on Foucault and Colonialism', *Cultural Anthropology*, 10 (1995), pp. 85–98; Scott, *Formations of Ritual*; Gyan Prakash, *Another Reason: Science and the Imagination of Modern India* (Princeton, Princeton University Press, 1999); Richard S. Smith, *Rule by Records: Land Registration and Village Custom in Early British Panjab* (New Delhi, Oxford University Press, 1996); Carol Breckenridge and Peter van der Veer (eds), *Orientalism and the Postcolonial Predicament: Perspectives on South Asia* (Philadelphia, University of Pennsylvania Press, 1993); and Metcalf, *Ideologies of the Raj*.

188. Manu Goswami, *Producing India: From Colonial Economy to National Space* (Chicago, University of Chicago Press, 2004); Mathew H. Edney, *Mapping an Empire: The Geographical Construction of British India, 1765–1843* (Chicago, University of Chicago Press, 1997); Ian Barrow, *Making History, Drawing Territory: British Mapping in India, c. 1756–1905* (New Delhi, Oxford University Press, 2003); David Arnold, *Colonizing the Body: State Medicine and Epidemic Disease in Nineteenth-Century India* (Berkeley, University of California Press, 1993); Collingham, *Imperial Bodies*; Satadru Sen, *Disciplining Punishment: Colonialism and Convict Society in the Andaman Islands* (New Delhi, Oxford University Press, 2000); and Meena Radhakrishna, *Dishonoured by History: 'Criminal Tribes' and British Colonial Policy* (Hyderabad, Orient Longman, 2001).

189. Carol Breckenridge, 'The Aesthetics and Politics of Colonial Collecting: India at World Fairs', *Comparative Studies in Society and History*, 39 (1989), pp. 195–221; Tapati Guha-Thakurta, *Monuments, Objects, Histories: Art in Colonial and Post-Colonial India* (New York, Columbia University Press, 2004); Metcalf, *An Imperial Vision*; Christopher Pinney, *Camera Indica: The Social Life of Indian Photographs* (Chicago, University of Chicago Press, 1997); Daniel J. Rycroft, *Representing Rebellion: Visual Aspects of Counter-Insurgency in Colonial India* (New Delhi, Oxford University Press, 2005); A.R. Venkatachalapathy, *In Those Days there was No Coffee: Writings on Cultural History* (New Delhi, Yoda Press, 2006); Emma Tarlo, *Clothing Matters: Dress and Identity in India* (Chicago, University of Chicago Press, 1996).

190. Mrinalini Sinha, *Colonial Masculinity: The 'Manly Englishman' and the 'Effeminate*

Bengali' in the Late Nineteenth Century (Manchester, Manchester University Press, 1995); Lata Mani, *Contentious Traditions: The Debate on Sati in Colonial India* (Berkeley, University of California Press, 1998); Indrani Chatterjee, *Gender, Slavery and Law in Colonial India* (New Delhi, Oxford University Press, 1999); and Kumkum Sangari and Sudesh Vaid (eds), *Recasting Women: Essays in Indian Colonial History* (New Brunswick, Rutgers University Press, 1990).

191. An important role has been played here by the probing of the links of the disciplines with the colonial archive. Axel, 'Introduction: Historical Anthropology', p. 15; and Tony Ballantyne, 'Rereading the Archive and Opening up the Nation-state: Colonial Knowledge of South Asia', in Antoinette M. Burton (ed.), *After the Imperial Turn: Thinking With and Through the Nation* (Durham, Duke University Press, 2003), pp. 102–21.

192. Benedict Anderson, *Imagined Communities: Reflections on the Origin and Spread of Nationalism* (London, Verso, 1983).

193. Tarlo, this volume; Mayaram, this volume; Pandey, *Remembering Partition*; Peter van der Veer, *Religious Nationalism: Hindus and Muslims in India* (Berkeley, University of California Press, 1994); Sumathi Ramaswamy, *Passions of the Tongue: Language Devotion in Tamil India, 1891–1970* (Berkeley, University of California Press, 2001); Joseph S. Alter, *Gandhi's Body: Sex, Diet, and the Politics of Nationalism* (Philadelphia, University of Pennsylvania Press, 2000). See also Vasudha Dalmia, *The Nationalization of Hindu Traditions: Bharatendu Harishchandra and Nineteenth-Century Banaras* (New Delhi, Oxford University Press, 1999).

194. Consider, for instance, the emphases of Mayaram, this volume; Tarlo, this volume; Christopher Pinney, *Photos of the Gods: The Printed Image and Political Struggle in India* (London, Reaktion Books, 2004); Amin, *Event, Metaphor, Memory*; and Butalia, *Other Side of Silence*.

195. I elaborate these issues in Dube, *Stitches on Time*.

196. Kamala Viswesaran, 'Small Speeches, Subaltern Gender: Nationalist Ideology and its Historiography', in Amin and Chakrabarty (eds), *Subaltern Studies IX*, pp. 83–125; Tanika Sarkar, *Hindu Wife, Hindu Nation: Community, Religion, and Cultural Nationalism* (Delhi, Permanent Black, 2001); Menon and Bhasin, *Borders and Boundaries*; and Anupama Roy, *Gendered Citizenship: Historical and Conceptual Explorations* (Hyderabad, Orient Longman, 2005).

197. Brian K. Axel, *The Nation's Tortured Body: Violence, Representation, and the Formation of the Sikh 'Diaspora'* (Durham, Duke University Press, 2001); and van der Veer, this volume.

198. Thomas Blom Hansen and Finn Stepputat, 'Introduction: States of Imagination', in Thomas Blom Hansen and Finn Stepputat (eds), *States of Imagination: Ethnographic Explorations of the Postcolonial State* (Durham, Duke University Press, 2001), pp. 7–9.

199. Tarlo, *Unsettling Memories*; C.J. Fuller and Véronique Bénéï (eds), *The Everyday State and Society in Modern India* (New Delhi, Social Science Press, 2000); Hansen, *Wages of Violence*.

200. For wider discussions of these questions see Dube, *Stitches on Time*; and Dube, 'Introduction: Enchantments of Modernity'.

Formations

This section contains writings that intimate the first formations of the historical anthropology of the subcontinent. The readings were chosen not so much on grounds of simple chronology—that is, when they initially appeared in print—but more on account of what they reveal of the wider concerns and critical emphases of their authors, which carry key implications for the volume as a whole.

Bernard Cohn has been one the founding figures of historical anthropology, the influence of his work reaching far beyond writings on South Asia. Appropriately, our considerations open with an essay that bears the trademark style and substance of Cohn's seminal scholarship. Focusing on the most quotidian of cultural commodities, that truly routine among diverse embodied objects, Cohn imaginatively unfolds the place and the presence of cloth and clothes as expressive of the interplay between meaning and power under imperial rule.

The essay begins with a poignant vignette concerning a Sikh's turban in postcolonial Britain, which captures the formidable entanglements between the past and the present as stitched into the fabrics of social worlds.[1] The stage skilfully set, Cohn presciently reads archival materials through ethnographic sensibilities in order to critically consider: first, the 'orientalization' of clothes, especially for the Indian army and the 'native' royalty, in the post-1857 era as emphasizing the basic racial divide between the Britons and their subjects; second, the seeming sedition caused by an offending accessory and an associated gesture in the comportment of the Maharaja Gaekwar of Baroda in front of the King and Queen of Britain; and, finally, the poetics and politics of order and transgression as encoded in the 'breast cloth' controversies surrounding women of the lower-caste Nadars of southern India following missionary intervention in the community. All this highlights the salience of attire and its accompaniments, understood as symbol and practice, as woven into historical textures in ways that together suture and unravel the colonizer and the colonized, the metropolis and the margins, and the dominant and the subaltern.

The designs of the dominant and the subversions of the subaltern have long constituted focal forms of critical enquiry in Ranajit Guha's extraordinary oeuvre, which has contributed immensely to the making of historical anthropology. The piece in this volume derives from his magisterial *Elementary Aspects of Peasant Insurgency in Colonial India*, a pioneering work that remains one of the most significant achievements of scholarship of the subcontinent.[2] In *Elementary Aspects*, Guha's aim is to situate the peasant as a conscious and political subject–agent of history. To this end, he examines peasant rebellions in nineteenth-century India, identifying the 'elementary aspects' of the common forms and the general ideas of insurgency, the consciousness that informed the activities of rebellious peasants.

The starting point of Guha's enquiry is the principle of negation: 'the peasant learnt to recognize himself not by the properties and attributes of his own social being but by a diminution, if not a negation, of those of his superiors.'[3] The peasants' revolt against authority derived much of its strength from the same awareness, intimating a project constituted negatively. The 'negation' characteristic of insurgency followed two sets of principles: discrimination and inversion. The peasants used discrimination in selectively directing violence against particular targets, and negative consciousness of this type extended its domain by a process of analogy and transference. Inversion involved the peasants in turning the world upside down by violating the basic codes that governed relations of domination and subordination. Here norms of verbal deference and their corresponding structures of authority stood demolished through direct abuse toward superiors and the adoption of their modes of speech. The written word—a sign of the peasant's enemy and an exploitative device—was usually destroyed, and appropriated symbolically in certain cases. Other non-verbal sign systems of authority—forms of body movements, gestures, and uses of space—were challenged intimately. The palpable symbols of the dominant groups' authority, status, and power—clothes, homes, and means of transport—were chosen as objects of attack. The rebel peasants destroyed and/or appropriated the signs of domination. In doing so, they sought to abolish the marks of their own subalternity. In the excerpt reproduced in this volume, Guha's deft explorations among the subaltern of articulations of authority as encoded in graphic verbal forms and as embodied in diverse non-verbal modalities—temporal and spatial distances, corporeal movements and gestures, and bodily dress and adornments—carry wide implications. They not only reveal imaginative possibilities of critical re-readings of the archival record, including of earlier ethnographies as historical sources, but underscore the importance of careful understandings of the incessant interchange between culture and power in everyday arenas, in the past and the present.

The bringing to life of the past in the present acutely marks the sensibilities of the next chapter, K.S. Singh's discussion of the transformation of a rebel leader into a subaltern prophet at the end of the nineteenth century. Derived from his book, *The Dust Storm and the Hanging Mist*, the simple style and the straightforward story line of the account bear immense import.[4] Singh weaves a rich tapestry by drawing together oral testimonies, colonial records, and missionary writings concerning Birsa Munda. Here, Birsa emerges as something of a *bricoleur*, innovatively combining elements of a rudimentary learning in school, basics of an evangelical Christianity, and concerns of the times of *adivasi* communities, altering each in a new matrix. Furthermore, in Singh's account Birsa passes from being a mere Munda *sardar* to becoming a healer, then a preacher, and finally a prophet; yet each of these steps emerges as being intimately entwined with the other. It is in this way that the analysis can point toward structures of authority among the Mundas, while implicitly evoking the construal of pasts and the making of history as shored up by the incessant interplay of heterogeneous yet coeval temporalities.

Distinctive dynamics of historical practice find critical consideration in the last chapter of the section, Paul Greenough's discussion of the famine of 1943–44, derived from his important book on the subject.[5] Combining explorations of political economy with those of cultural formations—and representing the conjunctions between anthropology and history in the US academy that followed Cohn's pioneering endeavours there—the chapter raises wide-ranging questions regarding the place of meaningful action in the unravelling of historical processes. To begin with, far from crop failure or military activities, it was practices of state and governance—based on a belief in the Midas of the market as axiomatically carrying rice into a grain-deprived area 'whenever the local price or level of demand made such shipments profitable'—which played a crucial role in the beginning and development of the devastating famine. At the same time, such 'man-made' dimensions of the famine equally extended to the cultural choices in colonial Bengal underlying the human responses to this historical horror. On the one hand, it was intrinsically culturally patterned purposeful human conduct that governed the decisions of rulers, land-controllers, and 'masters' to abandon their subjects, clients, and dependents. These actions that turned violence 'downwards' and 'inwards' in the social and familial order shaped thereby the onset, crisis, and denouement of the famine. On the other hand, militating against imperial official, Bengali middle-class, and contemporary scholarly expectations of collective violence from the lower orders as a 'natural' response to utter deprivation and fatal hunger, the Bengali peasants found their own culturally moulded active adaptations to the famine. These adaptations extended from varieties of dramatizations of their helplessness by the victims in the hope of re-stimulating a flow of benevolence on the part of possible providers through to designs of 'fatalism' that were yet no empty surrender to death but which endorsed instead distinctive, prior values—entailing the metonymies of 'prosperity' and 'misery'—in the midst of a deadly, ongoing crisis.

In the critical tradition of historical anthropology, Greenough's provocative arguments bid us to examine the place of 'culture' in 'history': to cautiously reconsider issues of sameness and difference—and of the universal and the particular—in the articulation of varieties of histories. They provide a link to the next section, which explores the plurality and mutability of expressions and experiences of the past.

NOTES

1. Indeed, the vignette presented by Cohn no less evokes the fierce controversies surrounding clothes and accessories—the 'head-scarf' to be worn by Muslim women, for instance—in wide varieties of contemporary arenas. These are too well known to require recounting here.
2. Ranajit Guha, *Elementary Aspects of Peasant Insurgency in Colonial India* (New Delhi, Oxford University Press, 1983).
3. Ibid., p. 18.
4. K. Suresh Singh, *Birsa Munda and His Movement, 1874–1901: A Study of the Millenarian Movement in Chotanagpur* (Calcutta: Oxford University Press, 1983).
5. Paul Greenough, *Prosperity and Misery in Modern Bengal: The Famine of 1943–1944* (New York, Oxford University Press, 1982).

Cloth, Clothes, and Colonialism*

BERNARD COHN

In 1959, Mr G.S. Sagar, a Sikh, applied for a position as a bus conductor with Manchester Transport. His application was rejected because he insisted that he wanted to wear his turban rather than the uniform cap prescribed by the municipality for all its transport workers. Sagar argued that the wearing of the turban was an essential part of his religious beliefs. He didn't understand why, if thousands of Sikhs who had fought and died for the empire in the two World Wars could wear their turbans, he could not do so. The transport authorities argued that 'if an exception to the rules of wearing the proper uniform were allowed there was no telling where the process would end. The uniform could only be maintained if there were no exceptions.'

At its most obvious level, this was a dispute about an employer's power to impose rules concerning employee's dress and appearance, and the employee's right to follow the injunctions of his religion. Early in the dispute, which was to last seven years, a distinction was made between such items of attire as the kilt of a Scotsman, which were expressions of national identities—a 'national costume' that could be legally prescribed for workers—and those items of dress that were worn

* Originally published in Bernard Cohn, *Colonialism and its Forms of Knowledge: The British in India*, Princeton: Princeton University Press, 1996, pp. 106–43, as 'Cloth, Clothes, and Colonialism: India in the Nineteenth Century'. In the present version, all notes and references have been deleted. For the complete text, see the original version.

as the result of a religious injunction. The advocates of allowing the
Sikhs to wear their turbans on the job said that to prevent them from
doing so was an act of religious discrimination. The transport worker's
union supported management in the dispute, on the grounds that an
individual worker could not set the terms of his own employment,
which they saw as a matter of union–management negotiation.

At another level the dispute was about working-class whites' resentment of dark-skinned, exotically dressed strangers, whom they saw as
'cheap' labour allowed into their country, to drive down wages and take
pay packets out of the hands of honest English workingmen. The fact
that many of these British workers preferred easier, cleaner, or higher-
paying jobs did not lessen their xenophobic reactions. Similarly, some
members of the middle class saw the immigrants from the 'new'
commonwealth as a threat to an assumed homogeneity of British culture.
The turban, the dark skin, and the sari of Indian and Pakistani women
were simply outward manifestations of this threat.

In short, the dispute over the Sikh's turban can be seen as a symbolic
displacement of economic, political, and cultural issues, rooted in two
hundred years of tangled relationships between Indians and their British
conquerors. [...]

'ORIENTALIZING' INDIA

[...] Britain had a feudal past, and so did India, particularly the India of
the princes and the great mass of the Indian peasantry. The application
of social evolutionary theories to India by a wide range of British officials
and scholars yielded a crucial ruling paradigm: the Indian present was
the European past. This construction of a universal history enabled the
British to control the Indian past, as they too had been feudal but were
now advanced out of this stage. But since the British were still in a
position through their own history to direct the future course for India,
it made the British part of India in their role as rulers.

India was seen as being capable of being changed through British
beneficence. They had created the conditions for the Indians' advance
up the social evolutionary ladder by introducing the ideas of private
property and modern education, the English language and its thought
and literature, railroads, irrigation systems, modern sanitation and
medicine, and authoritarian yet rational bureaucratic government, and
the form of British justice. The British also knew the dangers of too
rapid a move out of the feudal stage—the unleashing of disorder, dislocation, and potentially dangerous revolutionary forces that, if not
controlled and checked, could lead to anarchy. To prevent this dangerous

outcome, Indians had to be controlled, made to conform to the British conception of appropriate thought and action, for their own future good. India had a future, but its present had to be an 'oriental' one to prevent a too rapid and hence disruptive entry into the modern world. What might be thought of as the orientalization of the clothes of British rule in India began, as did the Westernization of clothing in the army.

During the Great Uprising, the British quickly shed their heavy, tight, redcoated uniforms. [...] With the re-establishment of social order in upper India, the army was reorganized. What had been the Bengal Army was in effect dissolved. European soldiers who had enlisted in the Company service were pensioned off and/or repatriated to Great Britain, and henceforth all the European troops serving in the Indian army would be from regular royal battalions, which were rotated through India. The British officers of the Indian army were now commissioned by the king and would be permanently assigned to units made up of Indians, who were recruited from 'the martial races': Sikhs, who accounted for 20 per cent of the army in 1912; Punjabi Muslims (16 per cent); Gurkhas (12 per cent); Rajputs, mainly from Rajasthan (8 per cent); Dogras and Garhwalis (7.5 per cent); Pathans (8 per cent); and Jats (6 per cent). The remaining soldiers in the army were made up of Marathas, Brahmins, Hindustani Muslims, and 'other Hindus', of whom the only significant number were Telugus and Tamils.

In addition to the 'class composition' of the new army, its dress was transformed as well, for both Indian soldiers and British officers. Over the second half of the nineteenth century, the service uniform for Europeans and Indians was much the same—cotton khaki trousers and shirt, with a jacket added in cold weather. Indians were given 'exotic' headgear: the Sikhs turban as previously discussed, and each of the other major martial races had their distinctive turbans in terms of wrapping and colour. The Gurkhas began to be recruited after the Gurkha wars of 1814–15 and took readily to European-style uniforms, which they have continued to wear in the British and Indian army to the present. Their distinctive head-dress in the second half of the nineteenth century was the Kilmarnock cap, a visorless, brimless pillbox. For service in the Boxer Rebellion they were issued broad-brimmed felt hats, which they wore up to World War I in the Australian style with one side turned up. Subsequently they have worn it with the brim down and at a 'jaunty angle'. Their uniforms, with jacket and trousers, have been dark blue or green.

Vansittart, the author of the handbook on the Gurkhas for use by their officers, described them as having a strong aversion to wearing a turban, as they associate it with the plainsmen whom they 'despise'.

Vansittart goes on to eulogize the Gurkhas 'as delighting in all manly sports, shooting, fishing...and as bold, enduring, faithful, frank, independent and self reliant...they look up to and fraternise with the British whom they admire for their superior knowledge, strength and courage, and whom they imitate in dress and habits.' The Gurkhas had a 'traditional' weapon, the *kukri*, a twenty-inch curved knife carried in the waistband which became their trademark.

It was in designing the dress uniforms for the officers and men that the British exercised their fantasy of what an 'oriental' warrior should look like. As was common in the second half of the nineteenth century, the cavalry units got the most colourful and dramatic uniforms. [...] during the Mutiny the British began to add cummerbunds and *pagris* (linen covers wrapped around their wicker helmets or cloth caps and hats). A few Britishers went all the way and began to wear full turbans, which were recognized as having some protective function. A full turban could be made up of thirty or forty feet of cloth, and, when thickly wrapped over the whole head and down the ears, could protect the head from a glancing sabre blow. General Hearsey, who commanded a division of the Bengal army, came from a family which had long provided officers, and many British thought he had Indian 'blood'. After the Mutiny, Hearsey had his portrait painted in a long black oriental-style robe, wearing a richly brocaded cummerbund and holding a scimitar. Could he have been seeking to appropriate part of his enemies' powers through using their clothes?

By the end of the nineteenth century, the dress uniform of the British officers of the cavalry had become fully 'orientalized'; it included a knee-length tunic in bright colours, breeches and high boots, and a fully wrapped colourful turban. The Indian non-commissioned officers and troopers were similarly attired for dress parades and the increasing number of ceremonial functions.

The change in uniform for both European and Indian emphasized a basic conceptual change. One of the results of the Mutiny was to rigidify the already considerable differences between Indians and British. The Indians, seen by the British in the first half of the nineteenth century as misguided children, had been revealed by their actions in 1857–9 to be treacherous and unchangeable. Outwardly they might conform to the sahib's expectations, but they could never be trusted. At any time their deep-seated, irrational superstitions could break forth in violence and overturn all the painful efforts of the conquerors to lead them in proper directions. Policies based on an assumption of change were proven wrong, so what was required was a strong hand capable of smashing any 'sedition' or disloyalty, combined with an acceptance of Indians.

Henceforth, the British should rule in an 'oriental manner', with strength and with the expectation of instant obedience.

For this reason, Indians more than ever should look like Indians; those the British most depended on to provide the strength to keep India, the soldiers, should appear as the British idea of what Mughal troopers looked like, with their officers dressed as Mughal grandees. Another characteristic believed to be quintessentially Indian or oriental was a love of show, of pageantry, of occasions to dress up in beautiful or gaudy clothes. Indians, it was believed, were susceptible to show and drama, and hence more occasions were found where rulers and subjects could play their appointed parts and could act their 'traditions' through costume. Hence the insistence that the chiefs and their retinues should always appear in their most colourful (if outmoded) clothes. The first major demonstration of this new ruling paradigm was during the visit of the Prince of Wales to India in 1876.

The prince and his large suite travelled widely throughout India, arriving in Bombay, then proceeding to Ceylon and Madras, and reaching Calcutta in November of 1876. There he was treated to a month-long round of entertainments, balls, and levees, culminating in a large investiture ceremony for the Star of India. The trip was well reported in England, with correspondents from the local newspapers. The *Graphic* and the *Illustrated London Weekly* sent artists who recorded all the events for the home audience. In their drawings, the artists dwelt upon the exotic quality of Indian life and dress, such as the 'wild' Naga tribesmen and women brought down to Calcutta to entertain the prince and British high society with their barbarous dances. The prince was also treated to a nautch—a dance by young women which was a popular entertainment for eighteenth-century *nabobs*. The dancers' beautiful and colourful dresses and their sensuous movements were anything but Victorian.

At centre-stage throughout the Prince of Wales' visit were the princes of India, in all their splendour. Neither the pen of the journalists nor the black-and-white line drawings of the artists could adequately capture the variety and colour of the clothes, nor the extraordinary display of precious stones and jewellery with which the figures of the Indian rulers were decked. The intent of the whole visit was to inspire the princes' loyalty by the presence of the eldest son of their English queen, and to affirm their central role in the maintenance of the empire.

Everywhere he went, the Prince of Wales was showered with valuable gifts by his mother's loyal Indian feudatories. Princes vied to outdo their competitors with the value, ingenuity, and brilliance of the jewels, paintings, antique weapons, live animals, richly embroidered brocades, and other artworks which they presented to him. What he collected in six months of touring in India literally filled the large converted troop ship, the *Serapis*. When he returned, his trophies and gifts went on travelling exhibition throughout England and eventually wound up in a quasi-museum in London at the Lambeth Palace. In return for their gifts, the Prince of Wales presented the princes with copies of Max Müller's English translation of the *Rig-Veda*.

It was not only the princes themselves who enthralled the prince and his suite as they travelled, but also their exotic retainers, dressed in a dazzling variety of costumes.

[...] Through the first half of the nineteenth century, the British seemed to eschew competing with the splendours of Indian royal clothes. Unlike their eighteenth-century counterparts who wore vividly coloured silks and satins, they wore fairly informal coats, dark or muted in colour, straight and at times baggy trousers, and plain shirtwaists and vests. Until the middle of the nineteenth century, when the *sola topi* (pith helmet) became ubiquitous, their headgear was a beaver stovepipe hat or a cap. The white ruling elite must have appeared dowdy in comparison with their Indian underlings, who dressed in a version of Mughal court dress while carrying out their official functions. The British appeared to have given up the sartorial struggle of trying to out-dress the pageant of oriental splendour they sought to control.

It was Queen Victoria herself who suggested that civil servants in India should have an official dress uniform, as did their counterparts in the Colonial Service. The administration of India was completely separate from the ruling of the other colonies, one being run through the India Office and the other through the Colonial Office. Although the question of a special uniform was raised several times after the Queen expressed interest, the Council of India decided that prescribing a dress uniform would be an undue expense for their officials.

Lord Lytton, viceroy from 1876 to 1880 and a great believer in the power of ceremony and display as an integral part of ruling India, complained to his queen that 'official functions' in India looked like 'fancy dress balls', because there was no check on the 'sartorial fancies of the civil service'. Although no uniform was prescribed for the Indian Civil Service until the early twentieth century, 'some civil officers had provided themselves with one which was similar...to the levee dress of the 3rd and 5th class civil servants at home and in the colonies.' The only civilians allowed a 'dress uniform' by regulations were those who had 'distinct duties of a political kind to perform, and who are thereby brought into frequent and direct personal intercourse with native princes.' This uniform included a blue coat with gold embroidery, a black velvet lining, collar and cuffs, blue cloth trousers with gold and lace two inches wide, a beaver cocked hat with black silk cockade and ostrich leathers, and a sword.

THE GAEKWAR AND THE KING

An incident occurred during the imperial *darbar* of 1911 that illustrates the official British concern with conformity of dress and manners expected of the Indian princes. In 1911, King George V and his queen travelled to India for his formal crowning as the king–emperor of India. This was to be the only time that a reigning monarch of Great Britain was to visit India before Independence. All three imperial darbars took place at the same site. In the first two, the structure marking the ritual centre was a dais on which the viceroy proclaimed the new titles of the emperor. In 1911 the focal point of the event was a large platform, covered by velvet awnings and drapery and dubbed the 'homage pavilion', on which the king and his princess sat on thrones. In previous darbars, the Indian royalty and nobles had been more or less passive bystanders; this time, it was decided that the leading princes would individually offer 'homage' as an expression of fealty and respect to their imperial majesties.

The Gaekwar of Baroda was highly Westernized, and generally considered by the British to be a 'progressive' ruler, but too friendly with a number of prominent Indian nationalists. Baroda was ranked second behind Hyderabad in the official order of precedence at the imperial darbar established by the Government of India for Indian states. Therefore, the Gaekwar was to follow the Nizam of Hyderabad in offering homage. The day before the actual ceremony a rehearsal was held to instruct the princes in the proper form of offering homage to the king-emperor and his consort. They were told to walk up the steps of the platform, bow low before each of their majesties, and then walk backwards down the steps in such a fashion as never to show their backs to the royal couple. The Gaekwar of Baroda was unable to attend the rehearsal and sent his brother to take notes for him.

On the day of the offering of homage, the Gaekwar was dressed in a plain white knee-length jacket and his 'traditional' red turban. He wore white European trousers and carried an English-style walking-stick. He did not wear, as was expected, the sash of the Order of the Star of India. The Gaekwar approached the king, bowed once, omitting any obeisance to the princess, took several steps backward, then turned and walked down the steps swinging his cane. It appears that at the time nothing was said about his behaviour; subsequently however, led by the *Times* reporter, his behaviour was interpreted as seditious. A major row ensued in the English-language press of India as well as in England itself over what was defined as a studied, purposeful, and seditious insult. The storm was revived three weeks after the event, when the newsreels taken at the darbar reached England. The *Illustrated London News* of 29 January reproduced a page of sequential stills from the film showing 'very clearly the way in which the Gaekwar of Baroda, carrying a stick, entered the Presence, bowed curtly, and walked off with his back to the King-Emperor.' In addition to the pictures of the Gaekwar, they printed pictures of two other ruling chiefs paying homage with deep bows of reverence. The Gaekwar and members of his court protested that, for personal reasons, the Gaekwar was distressed on the day of the ritual, was confused as to what was proper behaviour, and intended no insult or lack of manners by what had happened.

The intentions of the Gaekwar are less relevant than his failure to maintain the dress code expected of Indian princes. The most seditious touch of all would seem to have been the Gaekwar's use of a walking-stick, an accoutrement of the white sahibs, military and civilian, which marked the insouciance they displayed in the presence of the Indian masses. It was also used on occasion to thrash Indians whose actions, manners, or appearance irritated them.

In India, the military 'orientalized' to overawe the Indian princes and the heathen masses; at home, the ruling classes archaized their ceremonial dress to overawe the new middle classes and the potentially dangerous lower orders of society. From the middle of the nineteenth century, the British at home increasingly invented or re-invented civic rituals at all levels of the polity. These rituals called for the creation of costumes, regalia, and accoutrements to mark them as special and hallowed by tradition. They were designed to evoke in participants and audience—from the lord mayors of small cities to wealthy merchants and bankers in London, to the royal family, to union officials—a collective conception of the past. The use of costumes and accoutrements developed for such civic rituals were transported to India by the British to hierarchize the grandeur of their Indian princes. As a writer in the *Illustrated London News*, summing up what for him was the success of the imperial darbar of 1911, explained:

Despite the oft-repeated statement that this age is a very drab one sartorially so far as the West is concerned, there are various occasions on which Europe is able to show the Orient that it, too, can display itself in brilliant plumage. Such instances as the Coronation of King George and Queen Mary and that of King Edward VII and Queen Alexandra jump to the mind at once; and to these memories of glittering kaleidoscopic state pageantry must now be added those of the Great Darbar held so recently at Delhi. There Europeans vied with Asiatics with excellent effect. [...]

INDIAN WOMEN'S DRESS AND EUROPEAN CONCEPTIONS OF MODESTY

[...] Official British India did not concern themselves with women's attire as it did with that of its Indian employees and allied princes. Until the later part of the nineteenth century, women did not often appear on those public occasions when the Raj was on display. The Begum of Bhopal, her face entirely veiled and her body fully draped in her mantle of the Star of India, was a curiosity much commented on and a mainstay of the illustrated periodicals of the later nineteenth century. When women did appear in public, as at the visit of the Prince of Wales to Gwalior in 1876, the British artist sketching the scene depicted many of the women with heads bowed and hands covering their faces.

Although officially the Raj was little concerned with the 'decency' or indecency of women's attire, there were some Europeans—the Protestant missionaries—who were very much concerned with how Indian women were dressed. During the first half of the nineteenth century in Travancore, a princely state on the southwest coast of India, Protestant missionaries had been successful in converting a substantial number of low-caste Shanars, or Nadars as they came to term themselves. The southwest coast is sociologically and culturally one of the most complex regions in the subcontinent, with a significant population of Muslims, Moplahs (also Muslims), a community of Syrian Christians, and even Jews who date from the first or second century CE. In addition, there was a large and highly stratified Hindu community. European observers of the nineteenth century regarded the caste system of Malabar in general and Travancore in particular as the most rigid in the subcontinent.

[...] The Nadars, among whom the missionaries were to have so much success, are usually described as palmyra tappers, the sap being used to make jaggery, a form of sugar which when distilled becomes toddy. Some Nadars were also carters and semi-nomadic; others were agricultural labourers and tenants of Nair landlords. They were concentrated in the southwestern tip of India, some in the Tinnevelly district of Madras, and others across the border in the southernmost part of Travancore. The Nadars were ranked below *shudra* Nairs, who were the military and landholding caste in the state, and the untouchable 'slave castes', who were bound to upper-caste landholders and the state.

The highest-ranking caste, the Nambudri Brahmins, were priests, landlords, and state officials.

There was a highly specified code of respect and avoidance behaviour enforced by the state. Caste status was marked by fixed distances to which a low-caste person could approach a Brahmin: the Nadars were supposed to remain 36 paces from the person of a Nambudri Brahmin. They were also prohibited from carrying umbrellas, and wearing shoes or golden ornaments. Their houses had to be only one storey high, and they could not milk cows. Nadar women could not carry pots on their hips nor could they cover the upper part of their bodies. Nair women were allowed to wear a light scarf around their shoulders, which at times would be draped over their breasts. However, they were expected to be bare-breasted in the presence of Brahmins and other high-status people, as a sign of respect. In addition, all castes below the rank of Nair could wear only a single cloth of rough texture, which was worn by both men and women and which could come no lower than the knee nor higher than the waist.

Syrian Christian and Moplah women were permitted to wear a short, tight-fitting jacket, the *kuppayam*. The Syrian Christians were in a relatively privileged position in the state and were, like the Nairs, warriors and landholders. The Moplahs also supplied troops and were merchants.

The conversion to Christianity of the Nadars began in the Company's Tinnevelly district. Here the Nadar women began wearing 'long clothes' at the request of the missionaries; as conversion spread across the border into Travancore, the Nadar women began to wear the Nair breast cloth. Colonel John Munro, who was both the British Resident and *dewan* (prime minister) at the Travancore court in 1813, issued an order granting permission to 'women converted to Christianity to cover their bosoms as obtain among Christians in other countries.' This order was quickly rescinded when the *pidakakars*, members of the Raja's ruling council, complained that such an order would eliminate the differences among castes and everything would become polluted in the state. Munro modified his orders by forbidding the Nadar women to wear the Nair loose scarf but allowing them to wear the kuppayam, the jacket worn by Syrian Christians and Moplahs.

In the next ten years the missionaries followed a policy of vigorous proselytizing with an educational and economic programme aimed at changing the economic and legal position of dependence of their low-caste followers. One of their first acts was to establish a school for Nadar girls in which they were trained in European-style lace making. Earnings from lace making and other cash-producing activities were used to buy their 'freedom' from their landlords, who had extracted various forms of labour from them. The Nadars, somewhat ironically, also profited from their traditional trade of toddy tapping, as the Company's government here and everywhere in India controlled and encouraged the use of alcohol. Establishing a system of shops for its sale, the government taxed its use and collected fees from the licenses granted to the sellers.

The missionary agenda, in addition to conversion of the Nadars, was to free them from what they saw as the thraldom of 'the heathen caste system'. To do this meant establishing communities, centred on chapels, churches, and schools, and to enhance their sense of worth and separate them from other subjects of the Travancore kings. The missionaries, directly and through the British Resident, established a position of influence with the king and his immediate court as representatives of a culture and political order whose power was clearly growing throughout India. In doing this they attempted to bypass the king's local and regional officials, usually drawn from or with close connection to the dominant landed caste of the Nairs and Nambudris, who resented what they took to be the pretensions to higher status within the caste system being demonstrated by their inferiors, the Nadars.

Although the wives of the missionaries had designed and were producing a loose jacket that met their criteria for modest clothing that befitted Christian women, the Nadar women continued, with or without the jacket, to prefer to wear the Nair-style breast cloth. In the 1820s there were an increasing number of incidents in markets and other public places, when Nadar women wearing the Nair breast cloth were attacked, stripped, and beaten; chapels and schools were also burned. The government of Travancore acted in 1828 to prevent further violence by restating the previous policy of forbidding the Nadar women to wear the Nair-style cloth, but allowing the jacket. The king reaffirmed the requirement that the Nadars, like other low castes, were still required to perform *ooliam* service—corvee labour—and that Nadars were enjoined to act in relation to upper castes according to 'usage before conversion'.

In 1859, trouble broke out in Travancore. General Cullen, the British Resident, reported to the governor of Madras 'that the wearing of the cloth by Shanar women, like that of the Shudras [Nairs] had led gradually to violent outrages and quarrels and almost to an insurrection.' Cullen explained that many of the Nairs had misinterpreted Queen Victoria's proclamation of 1858, which ended the Company's rule and established direct rule of India under the Crown of Great Britain. In the proclamation she stated that 'we shall respect the rights, dignities and honour of Native Princes as our own' and then went on to state, 'in framing and administering the law due regard' would 'be paid to the ancient rights, usages and customs of India.' The proclamation was widely read and disseminated in all the languages of India. The Nairs and the officials interpreted the proclamation to mean that it not only prohibited all future interference with caste, 'but annulled all previous interventions.'

Although Cullen leaned toward enforcing the right of the Travancore state to enforce rules forbidding the wearing of the Nair cloth by Nadar and other low-caste women, the government of Madras, under pressure from missionaries in England and in India, instructed Cullen in no uncertain terms that they were a Christian government and 'the whole civilized world would cry shame on us, if we did not take a firm stand' against the King of Travancore.

The Maharaja did not completely yield to the pressure of the Madras government, but seemed to satisfy them that 'he was desirous to put an end to the barbarous and indecent restrictions previously existing on the dress of Shanar women.' In his proclamation of 26 July 1859, he agreed to extend the privileges previously granted to Nadar Christians to all Nadars, as he did not want any of his subjects to 'feel aggrieved'; all could wear jackets like Christian Nadars, and they could all dress in 'coarse-cloth, and tying themselves round with it as the Mukkavattigal [low-caste fisherwomen] and they could cover their bosoms in any manner whatever; but not like the women of higher caste.' These 'rights' were further extended to *Iravars*, another low caste that was rapidly being converted to Christianity.

The solution was far from satisfactory as far as the missionaries were concerned. The proclamation was seen as, if anything, retrograde. Christian Protestant women occupied a good position in Travancore life 'socially and morally', wrote the Reverend Samuel Mateer of the London Mission Society. They were educated and 'trained in the habits of refinement and comfort'; they were accomplished in the work of producing 'embroidery or beautiful lace, for which medals have been given at some of the great Exhibitions.' Yet they were still forced to wear coarse cloth, which although tied across the breasts left the shoulders bare, as in the dress of fisherwomen, whom the Nadars considered beneath them. Mateer found this attempt to legislate dress counter to the spirit of 'advancing civilization', and the prescribing of the coarse, that is, handwoven, cloth was a 'suicidal policy in respect to the development of commerce and manufactures'.

It appears that the Nadars continued to ignore the restrictions, and evolved a costume that imitated the costume 'of the higher class Hindus'.

P.S. Menon, who was dewan, a *peishcar* (high revenue official), and who had been personally involved in the events of 1859, wrote 'that this style of costume adopted by the Shanar converts was with the express object of annoying the Hindu section of the population.' Menon believed that it was the missionaries who were directly behind what could only be thought of as a direct insult, not only to Nairs but to all Hindus. He conceived of the dress as part of a concerted plan on the part of the missionaries, who used their colour and nationality to influence the Madras government, 'to create in the Hindus a spirit antagonistic to the Christian religion,' and by implication to draw the British government into supporting the Christian converts in Travancore. He may have been right, as Mateer states, that not until 'all classes of the community are allowed, as in Tinnevelly [a part of British India] full liberty to follow their own inclinations and tastes in matters of dress, personal adornment and comfort' would the issue be settled.

The controversy over the breast cloth lives on in the works of the historian R.N. Yesudas. The analysis and discourse which Yesudas adopts translates the battle into part of a wider class struggle, and the missionaries are credited with providing the conditions for a Marxist-style social revolution. T.K. Ravindran, in the foreword to Yesudas' *People's Revolt*, considers the battle waged by the Nadar women as a victory in the march of progress against entrenched habits, customs, and privileges of orthodox Hindus, who are the representatives of a 'licentious, degenerate, pleasure loving feudal caste-culture'. These Hindus have dominated an 'oozy, slavish and meek underprivileged class' until, through 'the conscious and voluntary efforts' of the lower classes, they overthrew the outmoded social and political order and showed the way towards 'the social regeneration of Travancore'.

Whether the breast cloth controversy was part of an epic struggle to free the lower classes from feudal domination, as Yesudas and Ravindran would have it, or part of a wider movement within the caste order of south India for the Nadars to raise their status in the social hierarchy, as [Robert] Hardgrave would have it, or the triumph of decency and Christian values, as Mateer would have it, would seem paradigmatic of the relationship between clothes and colonialism. Changes in dress become the tokens of much wider social, economic, and political changes that refracted in unpredictable ways, from the point of view of the principal actors in the events. For the missionaries, as part of their civilizing package, Indian women had to be modestly dressed, taught useful skills, and be freed from the domination of—in this case —Brahmins and Nairs who were sexually as well as economically exploitative. A bare-breasted woman was, by definition, the object of male lust. Significantly, it was the wives of the missionaries who seemed to have taken the lead in designing a properly demure clothing style.

The Nadars utilized the position and influence of the missionaries to directly attack their superiors in the state hierarchy; throughout the controversy they were much more concerned with wearing the Nair woman's scarf or adopting the dress of upper-caste women than appearing to meet the missionaries' concern with decent dress per se. The controversies became crucial in the formation of a wider caste or group identity, which fit with the capacity to take advantage of new economic opportunities created by the conditions of foreign colonial rule, through the government's encouragement of the use of alcohol to increase revenue. As Hardgrave has traced, some of the Nadars moved from being toddy tappers and makers to being sellers and transporters of the toddy, and from these activities into other lucrative occupations. In the twentieth century, the Nadars in Madras utilized their religious, caste, and economic networks to become a political force. By trying to overthrow the prescriptive rules imposed by the Travancore state, a wider market for machine-manufactured cloth would be created, Mateer argued, so that decency and proper dress would be linked with the expansion of the markets for British industrialists, and all this could be done in the name of the advancement of civilization. [...]

Negation*

RANAJIT GUHA

[...]

The inversion of verbal authority brought about by rebellion was
not limited to spoken utterance alone but extended to its graphic
form as well. There was hardly a peasant uprising on any significant scale in colonial India that did not cause the destruction of large
quantities of written or printed material including rent rolls, deeds and
bonds, and public records of all kinds. When in the course of the *dhing*
[rebellion] against Deby Sinha, the *ryots* of Dinajpur attacked his *kachari*
[landlord's office] at Dihi Jumtah, they made it a point to take away the
papers they found there, and this was the fate common to landlords'
estate offices wherever these lay in the path of a jacquerie. Again, popular
violence was often astutely selective about all written evidence of peasant
debts. Even the semi-official *Calcutta Gazette* noticed how during the
Barasat insurrection led by Titu Mir, a raid on an indigo factory in the
neighbourhood did not lead to 'mere wanton destruction', for apart
from a little damage done to some furniture only its 'papers were
destroyed [and done so] most probably by the villagers for the purpose
of destroying the record of their own debts.' In much the same way, the

* Originally published in Ranajit Guha, *Elementary Aspects of Peasant Insurgency
in Colonial India*, New Delhi: Oxford University Press, 1983, pp. 51–66, as 'Negation'.
In the present version, all notes and references have been deleted. For the complete
text, see the original version.

revolt of the Kunbi peasantry in Poona and Ahmadnagar districts in 1875 was distinguished by its singular concentration on the instruments of usury. 'The object of the rioters was in every case to obtain and destroy the bonds, decrees, etc., in their creditors' possession,' according to the Commission set up to inquire into these disturbances. Indeed it was led to believe that this 'was not so much [a] rebellion against the oppressor as an attempt to accomplish a definite and practical object, namely, the disarming of the enemy by taking his weapons (bonds and accounts).' Large deposits of official documentation too were often wrecked by insurgent crowds. The *levée en masse* triggered off by the Mutiny ended up by destroying 'all records of every kind' in Hamirpur district of Uttar Pradesh, as its magistrate was ruefully to observe soon after the event. In Muzaffarnagar, again, the records of the Civil, Criminal and Collectorate *Duftars* were burnt by the local population on the night of 14 May 1857, an incident regarded by the irate local officer as by no means 'a solitary instance' but as part of a pattern seen 'throughout this rebellion' of the burning of government offices by *budmashes*.

Regarded from a less hostile perspective, however, one could see in all this a rather different pattern—that of the objectification of the peasants' hatred for the written word. He had learnt, at his own cost, that the rent roll could deceive; that the bond could keep him and his family in almost perpetual servitude; that official papers could be used by clerks, judges, lawyers, and landlords to rob him of his land and livelihood. Writing was thus, to him, the sign of his enemy, and 'favoured the exploitation of human beings rather than their enlightenment.' The sense of these words was dyed into his soul by his everyday experience. On Lévi-Strauss, to whom we owe this formulation, its truth dawned in a flash as he witnessed the very first attempts at a crude mimicry of writing (inspired unintentionally by the anthropologist himself) and the uses made of it by a Nambikwara chief fraudulently to retain his authority over his illiterate people living in conditions of a Stone Age culture in the Brazilian jungles.

The reaction of the Nambikwara to writing was as forthright as it was negative. Having 'felt in some obscure way that writing and deceit had penetrated simultaneously into their midst' they deserted their chief and their village and retreated to a remote area of the bush. In an equally negative gesture the Indian peasant, who had nowhere to hide when driven to desperation, burnt down the graphic instruments of *zamindari*, *sahukari*, and *sarkari* dominance: the deeds, bonds, *khatas* and files, and their repositories—the *kachari*, the *gadi*, and the government office. This by itself contributed significantly enough to turning things upside down in the countryside [...] But the process was taken a step further in some instances by the rebel trying, positively, to appropriate the sign of writing for himself.

Ideally such appropriation should have been no problem at all. The peasant could avail himself of the institutional means which were there precisely for this purpose. He could go to school, at least to its lowest denomination at the village *pathsala* [village primary school] and acquire the three Rs. Unfortunately, however, he lived in no ideal world. The colonial government, keen on educating the middle classes in order to ensure manpower for its administration, was hardly interested in bringing literacy to the tillers of the soil. Primary education for the latter was left to the mercy and munificence of local landlords who took pride in setting up schools on their estates but were careful not to encourage too much literacy among the *ryots*. When Govinda Samanta, the hero of Lal Behari Day's well-known story about rural Bengal, pleads his inability to pay an arbitrary feudal levy (*mathot*), this is immediately seen as insolence bred by primary education. For he had indeed attended the village pathsala for some years when he was a child. 'So you have become a *pandita* [man of learning],' shouts the zamindar at him, 'and your eyes have got opened, therefore you refuse to pay the mathot. I must forbid Rama Rupa [the schoolmaster] to teach any peasants' sons.' This was fairly representative of the attitude of the rural elite towards education for the peasantry under the Raj. Teach the *chasha* [peasant] the three Rs and he will 'have his eyes opened' and learn to resist!

In no way therefore was the peasant in a position to appropriate writing as it really was, that is, as the graphic representation of a natural language. Want of literacy barred him access to it as a secular, intellectual aid to remembering, learning, and understanding. In order therefore to use it for insurgency, for purposes of reversing the world, he appropriated it symbolically. He had been conditioned by his own subalternity and the elite monopoly of culture to look upon writing as a symbol of dominance. Lévi-Strauss noticed how in some of the villages of what is now Bangladesh, the moneylender also functioned as the local scribe and this combination gave him a 'hold over others'. Indeed all who had a hold over the peasant, whether as rentiers, usurers, or officials, used writing as a direct instrument of authority in one form or another. He regarded this, as he did many other expressions of power in a semi-feudal society, not as a social, empirical phenomenon, but as something that was quasi-religious and magical: to write was not a matter of skill but of inspiration. The written word was endowed with the same sort of mediatory, occult quality as he customarily attributed to the spoken utterances of an oracle possessed by the spirit of the dead during a propitiatory ceremony. The popular Hindu association of writing, with priesthood on the one hand and with deities like Ganesa and Saraswati on the other, enhanced this sense of sanctity about it. It was this sacred and magical power of writing which Sido and Kanhu appropriated for themselves as they declared war on the sahib and the *diku*.

Writing figures so prominently indeed in the Santal leaders' own perception of the *hool* that it is not possible for the historian to ignore it [...] What concerns us here is the authority they derived from it in the conduct of the hostilities. Both the *Subahs* acknowledged, in retrospect, that their decision to launch the insurrection had been directly prompted by writing. But this was writing seen as divine intervention. As Sido explained at the interrogation following his arrest,

half a piece of paper fell on my head before the Thacoor came & half fell afterwards. I could not read but Chand & Seheree & a Dhome read it, they said 'The Thacoor has *written* to you to fight the Mahajens & then you will have justice.'

This, he said, was 'the Thacoor's order'—an order given *in writing*. Kanhu was to confirm this later on when he, in his turn, was captured and related the circumstances leading to the revolt. Asked, 'What was the Thacoor like?' he replied:

Ishwar [God] was a white man with only a dootee & chudder he sat on the ground like a Sahib he wrote on this bit of paper. He gave me 4 papers but afterwards presented 16 more.

Thus the authority of the graphic form was further reinforced by fusing together the images of a supernatural being, a white official, and a native scribe sitting cross-legged on the floor and scribbling away. In what was clearly a case of overdetermination, the power of the colonialist sahib and that of the pen-pushing *dhoti*-clad *babu* were telescoped here in a composite vision and raised to divine power. The apotheosis of writing could not be more explicit nor indeed its use by the insurgents to justify turning the world upside down in the Thakur's name.

Of the non-verbal expressions of authority which come under attack in all uprisings, there are those which are paralinguistic in character and operate as kinesic and proxemic systems under the sign respectively of gestures and body movements and that of distances in space and time. Every society treats the body as a memory in which to store the basic principles of its culture 'in abbreviated and practical, that is, mnemonic form', as Bourdieu has observed. This is particularly true of pre-literate societies 'which lack any other recording and objectifying instrument' so that 'inherited knowledge can survive only in its embodied state.' It is quite in order therefore that gestures of obeisance should figure so prominently in the Hindu Dharmasastras as the key to a better life. Why, for instance, must a youth leave his seat and greet an older man? 'For,' says Manu, 'the vital airs of a young man mount upwards to leave his body when an elder approaches; but by rising to meet him and saluting he recovers them.' There are many other verses in that text devoted to the virtues of rising, prostrating, clasping of feet, and so on, as indicative of subordinate status. And the authority of this language of the body derived not only from sacerdotal prescriptions but also from the power of the state. Thus according to Abul Fazl, kings 'made regulations for the manner in which people are to show their obedience.' This was meant to promote 'true humility'. For instance, *kornish*, an approved mode of salutation at the Mughal court, signified that the saluter 'placed his head...(the seat of the senses and the mind) into the hand of humility, giving it to the royal assembly as a present', and another, known as *taslim*, that he was 'ready to give himself as an offering'.

The substitution of Mughal royalty by the British made little difference to such feudal kinesics. They continued to operate as status markers in colonial India too. 'When a Coorg meets an elder on a ritual occasion,' wrote Srinivas, 'he has to salute the latter by bending the upper half of his body and touching the elder's feet thrice with both hands. After each touch the younger man takes his hands to his forehead, where he folds them together.' This, he remarked, was not very different from the form of salutation one adopted towards a deity. In fact, variations of 'bodily automatism' of this kind featured in all homologous relations—between father and son, husband and wife, landlord and tenant, high caste and low caste. In Madhya Pradesh, for instance, it was customary for the wife to demonstrate her fidelity by bending down before her husband at a distance and touching the earth with her fingers. A Balahi, ranked as one of the lowliest in rural society in this region, would replicate this movement on meeting a Brahmin, bending forward to touch the ground and lifting his hands, palms folded to his forehead. Elsewhere, in Orissa, a Bauri untouchable had to adopt much the same self-debasing posture under similar circumstances. 'When we passed by higher-caste people,' said Muli to the visiting anthropologist, 'we crouched so that one hand touched the ground; we walked by in that position, so that our faces were toward the ground.'

It was not the rise and fall of empires but the violence of the masses which alone interrupted from time to time this age-old avowal of subservience by gestures. Yet another index of the world turned upside down, this might have been the reversal feared by the dominant Brahmanical culture when among the many topsy-turvy features of the mythical 'epoch's end' (*yuganta*) it counted *Sudras* who were 'controlled in the movement of their eyes' (*jitakshah*), not unlike, presumably, their superiors in the *varna* hierarchy. Less fantastically, however, and indeed in our own epoch, there have been occasions in the course of agrarian disturbances when insulting gestures appeared to have hurt the peasants' enemies no less than acts of physical assault. A detail of the Birsaite *ulgulan* should make this clear. On 16 August 1895, the villagers of Chalkad drove out a police party which had camped out there for about a week in an attempt to seize the Munda chief but had failed to do so. As the posse began to withdraw in the face of superior insurgent forces, this was how it felt to the Head Constable of Tamar to be, for once, at the receiving end:

We then moved off by the Birbanki road towards Tamar followed by some 800 to 900 men who were having [*sic*] winnowing fans, beating toms and waving bows as insults to us. They were also carrying the three bedsteads (*khatia*) on which we had lain. These latter they flung into the river which we reached about one mile from Chalkad...In throwing the khatias in the river the crowd exclaimed, 'The Sarkar's Raj is at an end and their servants are dead, hence we throw their beds into the river'. They were beating the toms and the fans not only as insulting signs but as a very inauspicious thing, as they consider Birsa was preaching to the people not to attend to the *bhooth* or make sacrifice but to obey him.

There are references in this account to physical violence, too—to the guardians of the law being pushed and hustled and pricked with spears by the pursuing Mundas. What however sticks out in the Head Constable's memory of this ordeal is the rebels' use of the 'insulting signs'. Far from being treated as the august representatives of the sarkar to the accompaniment of obsequious body movements, they were treated as *bhut*, dead souls fit only to be exorcised by the whiff of winnowing fans and the noise of drums. Far from being regarded as distinguished guests who brought prestige to a village by visiting it, they were unceremoniously rejected as polluting agents so that even the beds they had slept in had to be thrown away in a simulation of funerary rites. Far from being feared as the strong arm of the state they were mocked and defied by the Mundas flaunting their bows at them. In other words, what shocked the Head Constable was that these downtrodden and docile people had 'now audaciously *lifted up their heads*' (as Mao was to say of the Hunan peasantry)—a figure of speech signifying the very opposite of what bending and prostrating stood for.

There is yet another class of paralinguistic signs which represents social rank and grade in terms of distances. Thus temporal distances indicating degrees of authority were often expressed as rights of precedence. In nineteenth-century Calcutta, clan leaders used to fight over precedence during the ceremonial distribution of sandal paste and flowers at sacred recitals and funeral banquets. Again in Malwa, according to Mayer, a wife's standing in her husband's family varied according to whether she was allowed to have her meal at the same time as the other women of the household or afterwards. Among the Coorgs, the headman was traditionally called the *mupayanda*, which means 'having precedence', and, as Srinivas observes, 'the sense of precedence is ubiquitous.' It was the headman who took the first shot at target-shooting contests on ritual occasions, it was he who led the village dance at harvest festivals, and it was his pack-bullocks which had the right to lead a caravan. Precedence such as this governed relations between castes as well. In Nimar district, a high-caste villager's bullock-cart had the right of way over a Balahi's, and in agricultural operations high-caste farmers had the right to help themselves first to the local supplies of labour: 'Only after they are satisfied will field servants go to work on the fields of their Balahi creditors.'

Foil to these were distances in space used both laterally and vertically as status markers. 'The regulation of the difference among men in rank' at Akbar's court was quite clearly a matter of seating and standing arrangements: the nearer a royal prince or nobleman was to the throne, the more important he was supposed to be. Centuries later, distance was still very much in evidence as an index of seniority in age and caste in rural society. It was a part of Coorg etiquette that a youth did not walk with an elder side by side but a few respectful paces behind him. Informal gatherings around a cot in a UP village often conformed to the same pattern. 'If all are members of one caste, the oldest person sits at the head of the cot...others sit next in order of prestige ranking. If a Brahmin is present he will be offered the head seat. Lower caste persons and sometimes also poor Rajputs will sit on the floor and untouchables at a slight distance from the group.' Notice how the inferiority of the poorer Rajputs and untouchables is indicated by the fact of their having to squat on the floor while the Brahmin has his seat on the cot. This constitutes yet another aspect of proxemics, that is, the expression of hierarchical differences in terms of levels of seating. The subordinate must not be seated above the superordinate. An unmistakably feudal notion, this too has an ancestry stretching back to the Smrtis. 'When his teacher is nigh,' said Manu, a pupil must 'let his bed or seat be low.' The principle worked with the followers of Islam as well. When the Pir Pagaro was taken out in a ceremonial procession, a devout *Hur*, we are

told, left her perch on the roof of a nearby house so that she would not
be situated higher than her spiritual leader when the latter passed along
that road. Secular authority also operated by the same sign. Beals observed that in Gopalpur even the more important men of the village
would, when they called on the landlord, sit on the ground beneath the
platform occupied by the latter.

Distance was thus a measure of prestige. No wonder that the followers
of Birsa remembered this when in explaining to their people how they
'had lost their honour and were biting dust,' they mentioned that the
Mundas were, among other humiliations, barred by the Raja and the
zamindars from using chairs and high seats. Indeed their revolt, like all
others of its kind, was made up of the peasant's urge to recover his self-
respect by eliminating or turning against his oppressors the apparently
innocuous, because traditionally tolerated, signs of subalternity, such
as those of prescribed distances, which had been imposed on them.
Inversions of this order occur frequently and on a large scale in the
course of all such massive explosions of violence. The rule of differential
heights is broken whenever the peasants ride past a landlord's or an
upper-caste man's house on horseback during a riot in defiance of customary prohibitions. The calculated and otherwise inviolable margins
of avoidance in a caste-ridden society sensitive to pollution are necessarily infringed whenever they raid a zamindar's or a *bania's* residence,
or lay their hands on the person of anyone in authority. Violations of
this kind are indeed so numerous that these are almost taken for granted
in reporting or commenting on rural disturbances, so that what catches
the observer's eye and survives the levelling influence of redundancy in
his narrative is the destruction by the rebel of the more obvious symbols
of his enemy's power.

Such symbols constitute the staple of peasant grievances. The rural
masses everywhere use these both as a measure of their own deprivation
and as objectives worth fighting for when roused to do so. These figure,
therefore, conspicuously in all rebel discourse—in that ancestral voice
of insurgency, John Ball's Sunday exhortations, as well as in the Birsaite
propaganda on the eve of the ulgulan. 'They are clad in velvet and
camlet lined with squirrel and ermine, while we go dressed in coarse
cloth,' said the 'crack-brained priest of Kent', contrasting the lords' way
of life with the serfs':

They have the wines, the spices and the good bread: we have the rye, the husks and
the straw, and we drink water. They have shelter and ease in their fine manors, and
we have hardship and toil, the wind and the rain in the fields. And from us must
come, from our labour, the things which keep them in luxury.

Dress, food, mansions—these and other 'things which keep them in luxury' crowd into all *cahiers de doléances* wherever they originate. Adapted to Indian conditions, hence with some variation of detail, the same sort of contrast is implied in the Munda *pracharaks'* enumeration of the wrongs (some elements of which have been noticed above) suffered by their tribe.

The Raja and zamindars exploited them and reduced them to a position of carriers (forced and unpaid labourers) and depend[e]nts, deprived them 'of their clothes, their dhoti and garments, turban and footwear'; they could not use even an umbrella. They were not allowed to sit on chairs and high seat, to enter a temple or to eat from golden or silver or brass plates ...

The list could of course be longer. For the authority the elite had over the peasantry was nearly all-pervasive and symbolized by many objects and attitudes. Indeed the struggle for any significant change in existing power relations in the countryside often appears as a contest between those who are determined to retain their traditional monopoly of such status symbols and others who are keen on appropriating them—that is, as a cultural conflict. This is why all dominant cultures are particularly sensitive to anything which even remotely looks like usurpation and quick to discipline offenders.

Take, for instance, the set of symbols which related directly to the body, either as its parts or as ornament and garment. Physical characteristics were often regarded as indicative of rank both by peasants and their enemies. The leaders of the rebel Tuchin movement of central France in the fourteenth century suspected courtliness or elegance in all who had smooth uncalloused hands, and rather than recruiting them to their bands, marked them out for killing. Conversely, the Brahmanical nightmare of a cataclysmic upheaval, as evoked by the *Vayupuranam*, had in it the image of Sudras with teeth as white as those of members of the higher varnas. Even under less mythical circumstances the rural elite have been known for their aversion to sharing any of their own distinctive physical styles with their social inferiors. The curled, upturned moustache represents one such style for upper-caste, upper-class males in many parts of India. When a member of the traditionally labouring community of Bareias was found sporting such a moustache in a Gujarat village dominated by rich and politically powerful Patidars, he was forcibly shaved, beaten up, and driven out beyond its boundaries. This anecdote was recorded by an anthropologist as evidence of 'greater concern with caste order in the past', presumably in colonial times and before. However, in the light of the facts published by the Elayaperumal Committee's report, it seems that the ban on the upturned moustache continues to be a feature of the outcaste's subalternity even in India today.

Objects of wear too were seen as status markers. It was 'out of respect to the higher castes' that no woman of the Bharia caste of farm-servants and agricultural labourers in Madhya Pradesh would wear a nose-ring, as Russell and Lal had noticed. Many decades later, social inferiority still continued to be denoted in much the same way in Uttar Pradesh by means of sanctions against the use of jewellery by outcastes: 'Shoe-maker women, for example, report having been prevented by Rajputs from wearing ornaments and clothes similar to those of the Rajput women.' Umbrellas and shoes too have been jealously guarded symbols. A part of the insignia of feudal monarchies, the umbrella retained some of its importance as an exclusive 'sign of noble rank...not permitted to the commonalty', even after it had ceased to be an appanage of kings. Throughout the colonial period it continued to operate as a general index of dominance and subordination, sorting out, especially in the rural areas, the rulers and the ruled, high caste and low caste, and so on: in Champaran, no Indian 'whatever his status', could hold an umbrella on his head in the presence of a white planter, nor could a Bania do so while passing by a Bundela Rajput's house in Saugor. Shoes, too, could offend if worn in the presence of one's superiors. Members of the lower castes, particularly if they were women, had to take these off on meeting a high-caste man and in some villages even while going past an upper-caste residence or through caste-Hindu wards. Indeed, umbrellas or shoes could be so suggestive of power that under conditions of growing antagonism between the peasant and his enemies both sides often regarded these as symbolic sites of conflict. The ban imposed on their use by the diku landlords was felt to be an unbearable tyranny by the Mundas as they became increasingly politicized. Conversely, the Tamil Nadu landlord who identified shod feet as the symptom of rebellious-ness among agricultural labourers at the time of the Kilvenmani massacre, spoke up against what was, to his class, a real affront: 'Things used to be very peaceful here some years ago. The labourers were very hard-working and respectful. But now...the fellow who used to stand in the backyard of my house to talk to me comes straight to the verandah wearing slippers and all....These fellows have become lazy and arrogant, thanks to the Communists. They have no fear in them any more.'

However, of all things worn on the person it is clothes which are the most semioticized. For the body 'as purely sensuous, is without signifi-cance,' and it is clothing, writes Barthes, following this Hegelian dictum, which 'ensures the passage from the sensuous to the meaningful: it is, one could say, the signified par excellence.' Nowhere is this more explicit

than in the countryside, where the distinction between peasants and
others—townsmen, officials, gentry, etc.—is often perceived as one of
dress in the first instance. 'Dress is a fundamental element of distinction,'
said Gramsci about Italy. Indeed, this was true of most societies, especially
of those vegetating for long under colonial and semi-feudal conditions.
It is known, for instance, that in Bolivia under Spanish rule dress was 'a
means of publicly manifesting the status of the *persona*' and of 'social
control in favour of the estamental order'. In India too, castes, classes,
and ethnic groups were often differentiated by the clothes their members
wore and the manner of wearing them. The Bengali *bhadralok* was
utterly self-conscious about his dress, for 'no self-respecting person
could go about his business in society wrapping himself up in a dirty
knee-length *gamcha*,' wrote the *Sadhana* in a clear reference to a typically
lower-class garment. In south India it was obligatory for a low-caste
man to approach anyone of the upper castes or indeed for a servant his
master by first stripping himself to the waist as a mark of respect. In
Gujarat, the so-called impure Mahars 'were not allowed to tuck up
their loin-cloth but had to trail it along the ground,' while in central
India among the Kurmi the difference in length between the peasant's
jacket (*bandi*), covering the trunk only up to the hips and the landlord's
long coat (*angrakha*), reaching down to the knees, was indicative of the
difference in their social standing. And among the Santals the word
deko referred not only to alien Hindu landlords, but also, according to
Bödding, 'any Indian in good clothing'.

It is not surprising therefore that in societies so sensitive to dress
differentials any serious crisis of authority should be expressed in
sartorial terms as well. Dress has indeed a way of insinuating itself into
the history of all of the more widespread and militant agrarian movements. It is at such times that distinctions of this order tend to generate
the utmost animosity and many of the reversals characteristic of these
conflicts are acted out symbolically by the reallocation of garments
and styles of wear between peasants and their enemies. Zimmermann
recorded a number of such incidents in his account of the German
Peasant War of 1525: an insurgent snatching away a nobleman's hat
and putting it on himself, some of the counts forced to take off their
gloves by the peasants while the latter keep theirs on in defiance of all
rules of etiquette, and so on. During the Bolivian peasants' revolt of
1899, all who wore trousers (*pantalones*), or rather were not clad in
coarse rustic homespuns, were marked out by the rebels as their
enemies. Willka, their leader, had it as one of his aims to try and abolish
distinctions of dress between the estaments by introducing the use of
homespun for all; and following a tradition of insurgency going back

to the eighteenth century, they forced homespun peasant clothes on townsfolk in some instances. And in Tanzania during the Mau Mau rebellion, the Christian missionaries feared that the Ngoni would kill all who wore European clothes.

In rural India, too, dress, which discriminated so clearly between the elite and the subaltern as a matter of course, acquired an added signifi-cance in the eyes of both the parties in periods of serious confrontation between them. The Rangpur dhing of 1783, for instance, broke out at a time when widespread disturbances were not uncommon in that part of Bengal, thanks to gang robberies and incursions of *fakirs*, *sanyasis* and predatory soldiers of the East India Company's army. When, there-fore, a large gathering was reported from Kadagaon and Magurrah, its character as a mass of rebel peasantry was identified, among other things, by the dress worn by the members of the crowd. 'Each of these peasants has a stick or bamboo in his hand,' reported an official witness, 'their dress is like that of the ryots or villagers, they are neither sepahis, fakirs or night robbers.' In yet another historic struggle, that of the tenant cultivators of Pabna in 1873, the manner of dress was recognized by all concerned—landlords, their *proja* [subject], and the administra-tion—as an index of class divisions made explicit by antagonism over the rent question. The officer in charge of the sub-division most affected by the *bidroha* [rebellion] put it in unmistakable terms in a report to the higher authorities:

This class feeling was so universal that the opinion of any native on the agrarian question may be told to a certainty by looking at his dress. If he wore a light chadar on his shoulder, used shoes on his feet and carried an umbrella, one could make sure that he was a zamindar's man. If merely clad in the dhoti and gamcha he was at heart an unionist.

Dress had a place in the Santal hool, too, as an element of the idiom of that revolt. At the battle of Maheshpur, said Sido after his capture, 'many of the Manjees were dressed in red clothes.' Neither he nor his brothers had taken to wearing red until then. However, it appears that after his death, when the insurrection was at its peak, Kanhu, Chand, and Bhairab adopted this rather conspicuous garment as an assertion of authority, as indeed a gesture of turning things upside down, just as 'Giuliano's solitaire ring, the bunches of chains and decorations with which the anti-French bandits of the 1790s festooned themselves in Southern Italy, would be regarded by the peasants,' according to Hobsbawm, 'as symbols of triumph over the rich and powerful.' There was yet another striking instance of the use of dress—the turban (*pagri*), to be precise— as a means of reversal during this rebellion. This form of headgear carries much weight in many regions of rural India. With some local communities, such as the Balahi, it is only the headmen who have the right to wear this. In Gujarat this used to be an exclusive privilege of the dominant caste of Patidars, so that anyone of a lower caste risked being severely punished if he was tempted publicly to try it on. The Mundas, as noticed above, held it against the dikus that the latter denied them the right to put on a turban. And if it was a matter of prestige to wear a pagri, to confer it was all the more so. This is precisely what Kanhu, the supreme commander of the Santals, did at the very height of the insurrection. As stated in a report from Major-General Lloyd on 19 November 1855, 'Kanoo Manjhee with his Brothers and Followers had visited on Bechoo Raout[,] a gwallah[,] the head of the village of Sooria Haut...Kanoo had created him a Soobah and as a Symbol of the rank conferred, had bound a turban on his head.' The turban came thus to stand for a historic inversion, for nothing turns the world upside down more radically than when the subaltern feel bold enough to delegate power seized in an act of rebellion. [...]

CHAPTER
4

The Making of a Prophet*

K.S. SINGH

[...]

Birsa's career so far except for his sensitivity to religious influence was typical of a *Sardar*'s. Thereafter he rapidly evolved through a sequence of interesting events; the agitator grew into a prophet in 1895.

While chopping a piece of wood Sardar Birsa sustained an injury in the leg. He went to a *bhagat* who declared that it was caused by a spirit who could be propitiated by the sacrifice of a goat. He offered the sacrifice and after the committal he recovered, though at the time of the offering, Birsa and others were frightened to the extreme. Through this experience his religion was born: his prayers poured forth of themselves. This account attempts to explain his reversion to the original faith, and also, paradoxical though it would appear, his revulsion against *bonga* [deity] worship.

Birsa also fell foul of other cherished beliefs. Once his family starved for days and lived off forest produce. He could not support his family. Not long before this time a pregnant woman had died of labour pains

* Originally published in K.S. Singh, *Birsa Munda and His Movement, 1874–1901: A Study of the Millenarian Movement in Chotanagpur*, Calcutta: Oxford University Press, 1983, pp. 45–56, as 'The Making of a Prophet: June 1894–July 1895'. In the present version, all notes and references have been deleted. For the complete text, see the original version.

and been buried with her jewels and some money at a solitary place in accordance with Munda practice. Driven by hunger, Birsa went to the burial place in the dead of night, dug up the corpse and took out the jewels and the money buried with it. Then he proceeded to the bazaar at Birbanki which was held on Saturday, sold the jewels and bought provisions for his family. He was caught at the market by some men from Chalkad and soon the news got around. When interrogated he admitted what he had done. His parents refused to take food from him and he was excommunicated. This earned him the opprobrium of *balu* Birsa, Birsa the mad man. It was, however, not long before he rehabilitated himself.

Then came the consummation of his experiences: on a cleared and burnt upland the Supreme God of the Mundas is said to have entered his heart, in May–June 1895. There are two versions of how this came about.

He dreamt one day of a grey-haired old man who sat on a chair with a spear in his hand. He planted a *mahua* tree on the fallow land and smeared it with oil and butter to make it smooth and slippery, and left a valuable object on top of it. There were four persons there: the bonga or spirit, a Raja, a judge, and Birsa himself. The old man called upon all of them to climb the tree and bring down the valuable object. At first the bonga tried but he slipped down. The judge and the Raja shared the same fate. Birsa went up and brought down the valuable thing. He then woke up. The dream was a subconscious projection of his conflicts, his confrontation with the three enemies of his race: the judge representing the authorities, the Raja, the *zamindar*, and the bonga, the old religion. The old man was the *Singbonga* himself. Thus, out of this contest over which the Supreme God presided, he emerged triumphant. He took it as the Divine sanction of his mission and was completely changed within a few days. Such inexplicable words as *owal, dol, pot, dol, pait, dend, mend, sat, ser*, etc. poured out of him. He claimed that he had got back for his people their lost kingdom.

Another day Birsa had been to the jungle with a friend of his, inferior to him in intelligence, in the early monsoon of May or June. There was a thunderstorm; a bolt of lightning struck him and he was transfigured: his face appeared not black but red and white to the astonishment of his friend. Though he exclaimed at the marvel, Birsa remained undisturbed. He, however, gave out that he had received the Divine word. The precise nature of the revelation was not disclosed immediately, though it related to the deliverance of his people. The news of Birsa's transfiguration was announced in the village by his companion who had preceded him.

THE HEALER

On his return Birsa found scores of people of his village waiting for him and eying him in amazement. A fond Munda came to him with her sick child. He touched it, recited the *mantra*, blew at it, and laid his hand on its head. It actually recovered, though not immediately, and the mother declared that it was cured by Birsa's prayer.

After the incident Birsa talked of strange things and shut himself up a good deal in his house. It was given out that he ate only once in eight days, being sustained miraculously from heaven, and that he was going up to heaven and would not be seen on earth for many days. He told Bir Singh Munda, a Sardar of the village, that he had been entrusted with everything in the world by God himself. He would cure the sick; they [the people] would not have to pay rent, etc. Bir Singh, a clever man, went to the Birbanki bazaar and gave out the news to the people. The people of Katui (a village near Birbanki) decided to see Birsa on the following day. They saw him wearing the sacred thread and the wooden sandal. He started talking to them, but they could not follow what he said. Then he talked to them in their language, and intelligibly. He claimed that he had all the powers in the world. They should bring the sick to him or they should send for him. The people of Katui submitted that an epidemic had broken out in their village. Birsa went to the village and ordered the diseases to leave the village by the main lane. He asked the diseased persons to fall in a line and sit one behind another. He looked towards the sky and uttered certain words. Then he recited the mantra, and shook his sacred thread. He visited another village and repeated the ceremony. The people were cured. The people of Katui eulogized Birsa and spread the tales of his miraculous powers. This was the beginning of his reputation as a healer. This won him a number of disciples in Longa, Kuria, Naranga, Tubil, Muchia, Banapiri, Gopala, Birbanki, and Bondo Bamba.

When a smallpox epidemic broke out, an *ojha* [witch-doctor] declared that Birsa was responsible for it as he had offended the deity of the village. He was compelled to leave the village, but the epidemic did not abate. He returned and served the sick and the suffering. This won him a reputation for selfless service among his people. He declared his faith in the efficacy of prayer as the cure of all diseases; he advised the people to bear their sickness, disease, and suffering cheerfully. When the diseased were brought to him, he prayed with folded hands with them. Then he clapped. Those who had faith were cured.

A report mentioned only one instance of Birsa's success in reducing to silence a half-crazy, garrulous old woman, whose sharp tongue was the plague of the village. That he could do this without resort to decapitation was counted a miracle. He gave no medicines but used to say, 'Go, you are cured,' or 'Go after such and such a time, you will be cured.' A Mohammadan of Khunti brought to him the dead body of a relative to get it restored to life. Looking at it after dusk from his doorway in the glare of a fire, he flew into a rage, and declared that the visitor was trying to impose on him, that what he had brought was not a dead body at all but clay, and that if a real body was brought he would restore it to life. His followers turned the man and the 'clay' body out on his orders.

There were two different accounts of Birsa's methods of curing the sick of their ailments. According to Rev. G.H. Lusty of the Murhu mission, he healed them by repeating a charm over them in the heavenly language, one of which was '*pulter pewter walter*' and the other '*steel store stare stale*', which was all that had remained of his knowledge of English obtained from elementary English books at the Chaibasa school. According to the other and the more reliable account which was in consonance with Birsa's and the Birsaites' faith in God, the recitation of prayers was the secret of the cure of all diseases. Those who had no faith in the Messenger of God were not cured. As Rev. Hoffmann, a contemporary witness, reported:

My mission station (Sarwada) being but nine miles from Chalkad, I saw day after day endless files of people from all parts of the country winding their way towards that village to hear the new gospel and be healed. Failures did not seem to discourage them, for they were attributed, not to a want of power in the *Dharti Aba*, but to a lack of faith and confidence in him.

THE PREACHER

Though Birsa's reputation as a healer was the first to win him popularity, the people flocked to him to listen to his words; he started preaching his religion. In the beginning he preached sitting on his bed placed on the verandah of his house. When the number of the people increased he shifted his seat to the field under a *neem* tree. The four poles of the platform were tied with sacred threads. He himself wore the sacred thread, a pair of wooden sandals, and a *dhoti* dyed in turmeric, a characteristic Vaishnav outfit. He would bathe thrice during the day and wore dhotis of three different colours, yellow in the morning, white in the afternoon, and blue in the evening. This gave him the reputation that he changed colours.

The people went to him from all over the Munda country and even beyond. Banapiri was one of the early villages to join the fold of Birsaism.

Rokan Munda, along with Budhua Munda and Guhal Lohar and one Sado Munda of Silda, heard of Birsa and proceeded to Chalkad. On their way they met Bir Singh and requested him to introduce them to Birsa. They were asked to pay six annas for the *darshan* of Birsa and to bow to him with folded hands. If Birsa recognized a man of pure heart, he turned the right hand in the right direction and made a circular sign. If he did not want to speak to a man, he moved his right hand in the left direction and made a sign. He had, being a Sardar, obviously expanded on what was being done by the simple folk. When they were introduced to Birsa, no payment was asked for. He exhorted them to pray thrice a day; the people should be clean, live in love with one another, and organize collective prayers. He accepted his visitors as his disciples and called upon them to attend his prayer meetings everyday.

Birsa's method of preaching was modelled on that followed in the missions. He cited parables; the people were called upon to be industrious like ants, and live together in love. The lazy, the cowardly, and the selfish were compared to the pathway, the rocky place, and the land covered with thorns. Good people, like good lands, were rare.

He claimed to be the Father of the Earth, *Dharti Aba*; he was also called so by his followers. One day when his mother, sitting with the audience listening to her son, addressed him as her son, Birsa reminded her that he was Dharti Aba and that from then on he should be addressed as such. He also called himself a messenger of God:

I have been sent on behalf of God to show you the way. Having imparted the message in a few days, I shall be leaving you. Afterwards, I shall have to go to the *diku*s to convey the message to them. If you so wish, follow what I say.

He launched a bitter attack on the bongas—the priesthood of bhagats, *sokha*s, and *deonra*s. One day he told the *Pahan* that his wooden sandals would turn golden. The Pahan called him a madman. He thereupon replied that the world would go mad and attacked his system of the propitiation of demons.

His activities caused a flutter in mission dovecotes. He often entered into disputations with *pracharak*s of different missions—Daud of Dolda, John of Parasu, Abhiram of Chalkad (who had baptized him), and Paulus of Birbanki. They also kept in touch with the police stations. The initial reaction of the missions was described by Rev. Lusty of the Murhu Anglican mission:

At the commencement, hearing that these crowds were gathering, I had sent three of my readers there, hoping that they might do some little good by preaching, especially as the tendency of the movement seemed to be in the direction of Christianity. I soon discovered, however, that this was useless. The people's faith in Birsa was too implicit; and they had eyes and ears for no one beside him. One of my readers, Nehemia of Kander, was so unfortunate as to receive his curse, and it was solemnly announced that it was possible—it would not quite be said for certain, but it was just possible that he would fall down dead before he reached home. The curse was not fulfilled, but on Nehemia's account and on account of the fact that the Kander people (of whom many are Christians) did not believe God's messenger, that village was to have the unenviable distinction of being the first to be destroyed.

According to the missionaries, Birsa considered Christianity the best religion extant, but there were two or three things against it: the padres held collections in church, and so took money from the people, which was not right. Second, the people went to church with their boots on, which also was not right. Birsa's claim to be a messenger of God and the founder of a new religion sounded preposterous to the missions. There were also within his sect converts from Christianity, mostly Sardars. His simple system of offerings was directed against the church which levied a tax, and the concept of one God appealed to his people who found his religion an economical religion saving them the expense of sacrifices. A strict code of conduct was laid down: theft, lying, and murder were anathema; begging was prohibited.

Slowly, the messenger of God began to be identified with God himself. The people approached him as their Singbonga or the Sun god, the good spirit who watches over them and can do no ill. He was looked upon as an incarnation of Khasra Kora, who had destroyed the Asurs. They said that the Sun (which they worship) was above and Birsa was below; in June, it was given out that he was *Bhagwan* himself. Later Birsaites formed themselves into a sect worshipping him as such.

The messenger from God was not only a preacher; he was a miracle worker too. The stories of the miracles, apparently influenced by the rudimentary knowledge of the Bible, spread far and wide. While sowing one day, Birsa found a small quantity of seeds adequate for the entire field. His brother and the servant were astonished. When questioned about it, he replied that he had been so blessed by God. There was an instance of the multiplication of rice. One day when the people were in a hurry to return from a prayer meeting, Birsa reminded them that if they had faith in God, a handful of rice would be found sufficient for their family. In the house of one Sugana Munda (not the father of Birsa), a handful of rice was found sufficient for eight persons and a dog. There was also the story of the bullock-king: his message was understood even by animals; on a Tuesday morning a sheep came up to him, and knelt before him thrice; on a Wednesday his bullock came and saluted him. Further, in a meeting something like lightning fell from the sky and entered his body which turned yellow like the yellow-ish part of the egg; afterwards it became white like cotton. It attracted wider notice and consequently bigger crowds. Then it was said that he walked on water and his soles were not wet, even though he remained standing in it, praying to God. He could identify the eyes of the witches and read others' thoughts. Once when a Pahan went to him, he was told that he had sacrificed a boar the day before and was asked to accept the new faith. The same day he told another woman that she had buried a brass pot full of money; she should dig it out and spend it usefully.

The stories of Birsa as a healer, a miracle-worker, and a preacher spread, exaggerated out of all proportion to the facts. The Mundas, Oraons, and Kharias flocked to Chalkad to see the new prophet and to be cured of their ills. The Oraon and Munda population up to Barwari and Chechari in Palamau became convinced Birsaites. There were very few Christians who did not openly side with the new redeemer. During this period, 'Have you been to Chalkad?' became the ordinary form of greeting when two persons met.

Contemporary and later folk songs commemorate the tremendous impact of Birsa on his people, their joy and expectations at his advent. The name of Dharti Aba was on everybody's lips. A folk song in *Sadani* showed that the first impact cut across the lines of caste or tribe and the Banias, Hindus, and Muslims also flocked to the new Sun of religion. All roads led to Chalkad:

O, pray, tell me, how far is Chalkad? I shall go slowly.
Some, say, it is eastward, others say it is southward.
O, I shall go to the South slowly,
The wild forest is infested with leopards and bears, and they make terrible sounds,
O, I shall go, together or slowly?
Birsa's words are pleasing, I too shall go and listen to them.

There is a graphic contemporary description of the exodus:

In the meantime, the sick, the lame,...the blind, began to flock to him from scores of miles around. His village is in a very remote spot, right away in the jungle, where it was impossible to obtain any kind of shelter. This, however, proved no obstacle, in spite of the fact that it was the rainy season, and that both travelling and camping out were consequently in the highest degree unpleasant, to say the least. The pilgrims brought with them their bamboo umbrellas, and with these as their only shelter they remained out in the jungle there night and day until the food they had brought was exhausted and then...they went home for fresh supplies.

A comet had risen in the sky; Birsa was the new king. He had come down by a thread from heaven and spoken the new word. There was suspense; he might disappear:

O friend, let us go to Chalkad amid forests,
Let us go to see him,
Our friends are going, we (too) shall go to see him for ourselves.
From the sky he has come down by a thread.
He speaks the new word
We shall carry a pumpkin-pot full of water,
We shall fulfil our hearts' desire.
He has risen like the sun, he has come up like the full moon,
He does not rise every day, he will suddenly disappear one day.
Then we may not see him, let us see him one of these days.
He will not rise every day, he may leave the land in the dark.

THE PROPHET OF CHALKAD

Slowly, the healer, the miracle-worker and the preacher grew into a prophet. A fiat went forth: white pigs and white fowls, being unclean, were to be destroyed. This was obeyed in the Munda households all over the district. He also announced through John Munda, son of Bir Singh of Chalkad, that fire and brimstone would be sent from heaven and would destroy all men of earth except those who were at Chalkad and with him on that day, wearing new clothes for the occasion. This accelerated the rush to Chalkad. In the coming deluge, crops and the cattle would hardly be of any use; so thousands of cattle were turned loose to feed on the crop. This injunction was obeyed in hundreds of cases. Not much damage to rice followed from it as the sapling was only about a foot or so high and consequently not in ear; but other crops were totally destroyed. In the event of total destruction, money would melt into water and be useless; it could be profitably spent in buying new clothes in which visitors were to appear before their redeemer:

Then there began to be a run on the clothes market, and the cloth vendors, who were almost exclusively Hindus, suddenly found themselves doing a roaring trade. In fact, the demand for cloth became so great that it considerably exceeded the supply. Two traders' men in Murhu cleared Rs 100 each in three days owing to this.

On the appointed day, Chalkad swarmed with people from all over this land: there were six to seven thousand of them. But the deluge did not occur:

The crowd waited in breathless anxiety for 12 o'clock to strike, the time announced for the catastrophe, but as the morning wore on, Birsa intimated that there was some doubt as to whether it would not be postponed for a time, after all. He tied a piece of string between two trees, and forbade anyone to touch it. The whole thing depended, he told them, upon whether that string broke or not. Naturally enough, the string did not break, and consequently the world didn't come to an end that day. One thing which prevented it was that the Sahebs had not come to take shelter under his wing. The padres were to come first, then the Government officials, and last of all, the *Maharani* (Queen Victoria).

Whoever might have been responsible for the announcement, Birsa did nothing to counteract it. The damage to crops was a factor at the root of the famine of 1896–7, which Birsa had foreseen and pre-announced, if not done his best to produce. He, in turn, prescribed the recipe of faith: those who believed in him would only harvest a very small amount of rice—the amount he indicated would be perhaps half a hundredweight —yet this would be marvellously increased in using, and would be found to supply all their wants for the year. He cited the example of his family which lived in a miraculous way on as much rice as he could hold in one hand, as a daily allowance.

The incident, however, highlighted the role of the Sardars, the new elements in the situation. A Sardar, Bir Singh's son, had made the announcement; another Sardar, Eliazar, the treasurer, made money. Later, Birsa probably had this incident in mind when he said that if he fixed a date like the Sardars, he would only disappoint his people. The Sardars obviously wanted a crowd to propagate their ideas and cashed in on Birsa's popularity to this end. The countryside was in ferment. Birsa had prophesied that the sun and the moon would fall: fire would rain from the sun and the earth would be destroyed. When on the dark night the moon was not visible, people took it that the prophecy had come true. In one house at Chandragutu they ate up all their fowls, let out their cattle to graze on their *gora* paddy land, and left with all their belongings for Chalkad. The same thing happened at Buruma. Rumours spread of the arrival of the *bargis*, the Marathas who had overrun Chotanagpur towards the end of the eighteenth century.

The movement so far was on purely reformative lines and showed the range of Christian influence on the Mundas. In his roles of a healer, preacher, miracle-worker, and prophet, Birsa demonstrated what he had learnt from Christian literature at mission schools, and, to a lesser extent, exemplified the Vaishnav influence on him. There was an undertone of protest against the missionaries, at their disapproval of Birsa's heretical religion, which was slowly evolving into a popular independent movement. [...]

Famine[*]

PAUL GREENOUGH

The 1943–4 famine stands distinctly apart from a historical pattern for the onset of famines in Bengal, indeed in all of India. In this pattern, starvation begins after one or more seasons of widespread, weather-induced crop failure. Widespread crop failure did not occur in 1942, and there is little reason to think there was an absolute scarcity of rice in Bengal on the eve of the famine. Significant exports of grain by rail and sea had not taken place, while rice imports from Burma, cut off in March 1942, had previously supplied only a small part of the province's consumption needs. Further, despite refugee influxes and the presence of Allied military units, the rice-consuming population in Bengal in 1943 was only fractionally larger than before the famine. Worse rice deficits had been weathered in preceding years. It is thus difficult to maintain that the supply and demand for rice were so far out of balance in early 1943 as to make a famine inevitable.

It is also implausible to maintain that military activities directly precipitated the famine. Bengal was never invaded. No enemy starved the cities, as the Germans had the Russians at Leningrad in 1941 and the Dutch at Amsterdam in 1944. Nor did the Allied military authorities in Bengal precipitate famine by scouring the countryside and seizing

* Originally published in Paul Greenough, *Prosperity and Misery in Modern Bengal*, New York: Oxford University Press, 1982, pp. 261–75, as 'Conclusion'. In the present version, all notes and references have been deleted. For the complete text, see the original version.

rice, as Vichy and Japanese forces were to do in North Vietnam in late 1943. British, American, and Indian troops in any case did not consume rice in quantity, and what requisitioning there was took place only in coastal sub-divisions under civil officers during the 'rice denial' episode in April–May 1942. True, the military presence was disruptive, the removal of 66,000 boats and 35,000 peasant households for military reasons produced great hardship, and the bombing of targets in urban areas had serious psychological effects, but these were not on such a scale as to cause province-wide famine.

There is abundant evidence that the famine began with a serious disruption of the wholesale rice market. The Civil Supplies Department's attempts after mid-1942 to control wholesale prices, to garner large supplies through novel means, to favour a privileged urban workforce, and to manipulate inter-provincial grain-flows—these steps provoked and enhanced a market crisis, which led to balkiness among the primary sellers, hostility from grain traders at all levels, unbridled speculation and black-marketing, rapidly rising prices, and the spasmodic constriction or 'freezing up' of wholesale and retail trade alike. Starvation—already evident in war-torn Chittagong and cyclone-stricken Midnapur—was inconceivable as a general prospect at the beginning of 1943. Yet after six months of further official efforts to influence the price, movement, and distribution of marketed rice, overt famine broke out in nearly every district in Bengal.

The fact that an interrupted supply, or the complete disappearance, of rice in the markets would severely distress millions of rural consumers should not have come as a surprise. The Bengal census had recorded, decade by decade, the growth of a landless, market-dependent agricultural wage-labour force, while sporadic investigations had shown that the dietary level of peasants was low and declining. What could not have been anticipated was that the familiar mechanism for meeting rural distress—relief operations as set out in the famine code—would fail in 1943.

The long interval of freedom from serious famine in Bengal was in itself a contributing factor to famine's reappearance, for officials and politicians largely ignored the warning signs worked out by nineteenth-century authors of the famine code. To be sure, the settled conviction had spread through India since the beginning of the twentieth century that serious famines were no longer possible. The public had been taught to regard famine as a 'bogey' from the past.

[...] It is true that an integrated transport network combined with fiscal and administrative measures had succeeded in minimizing the effects of food shortages everywhere in India. In Bengal, the mainstays of famine relief, as laid out in the *Bengal Famine Code*, included gratuitous doles for the infirm, employment of able-bodied destitutes for cash on 'test relief' works, and cash advances or remissions of revenue for cultivators. Since 1900, these measures had largely served to suppress starvation and need. Yet implicit in the working of 'test relief', the most important of these remedies, was the assumption that the grain marketing system would carry rice into an area of famine whenever the local price or level of demand made such shipments profitable. It was this assumption that dictated paying cash wages rather than wages in kind on relief works. The government was the paymaster but stayed aloof from the grain trade, intervening only to stimulate traders, if need be, by subsidizing the transport costs between surplus and deficit districts. What was never contemplated was the complete inability of the trade to move and distribute rice despite the liberal provision of relief wages; yet this was the very situation that developed in early 1943 wherever district officers organized 'test relief' works. The price of rice everywhere in Bengal was shooting up, but little or no rice was moving into or being offered in the marketplaces. Not just the poor but all who lacked direct access to land and paddy—including portions of the 'middle class'—experienced great difficulty in purchasing rice. By March 1943, the government of Bengal had abandoned its traditional stand-offishness and plunged deeply into the buying and selling of grain, all of which was earmarked for Calcutta. District officers, unable to secure imports, began to improvise relief and turned to methods of coercion and expropriation never contemplated by the famine code. These methods increased the reluctance of cultivators and traders—already alienated by dacoits, official buyers, and price controls—to resume normal patterns of trade and further restricted market supplies. In the meantime, responsible ministers in the capital were banking on the timely arrival of large rice shipments from outside Bengal. Unfortunately, these shipments did not arrive in quantity until June and were not distributed in rural areas until late November. The opening of thousands of gruel kitchens, a stop-gap relief measure offering small quantities of exotic foodstuffs with limited nutritional value, did little to halt starvation. Mortality rose steadily after June, reaching a peak around December.

The failure of official relief meant that popular responses to starvation could no longer be inhibited by administrative procedures. Rural Bengal had not experienced anything like severe, widespread famine since 1866, and in some ways the survival strategies adopted in 1943 reached back even further to the great famine of 1770. It was a commonplace at the time to say that *pancaser manvantar* (the famine of the

Bengali year 1350 or AD 1943 was a recapitulation of *chiyattarer manvantar* (the famine of the Bengali year 1176 or AD 1770). The comparison was not entirely apt, for 170 years of British rule had transformed the economic and public life of Bengal. Yet the 1943 famine revealed the importance of certain perduring cultural values and of latent choices, the realization of which was the responsibility of males and adults. In fact, the most useful framework for understanding responses to the famine is provided by the notion of cultural choice.

Faced with a clear threat of starvation, authority figures in peasant households implacably abandoned numerous dependents deemed inessential for the reconstitution of family and society in the post-crisis period. In these acts of abandonment, it should be noted, 'masters' were paralleling unusual behaviour already in evidence—the abandonment of 'market', 'casual', and in some cases 'fixed' clients by land-controllers. Nor did the parallel end there: on the broadest scale the government of Bengal had initiated the famine by abandoning the rural needy. Thus at three levels—the household, the land-holding, and the province—Bengal's 'destined providers of subsistence' openly declined to fulfil the chief obligation of the *annadata*, which was to feed 'dependent persons requiring nurture' (*posyas*). This pattern of abandonment was the consequence of another equally evident pattern— the protection and feeding of persons whose survival was held essential for the future. At the provincial level those favoured above all were the 'priority classes', whose well-being was desired by officials and military officers, that is, by those who ruled. At the level of the land-holding, *zamindars* and large tenant-farmers sought to preserve above all those clients with whom they had 'fixed' relationships, while at the household level 'masters' strove to subsist themselves and, where possible, their spouses. Rulers, the 'priority classes', landlords, *jotdars*, 'fixed' clients, 'masters' and their spouses—these were the persons and groups conceded to be most capable of restoring the full complement of roles and institutions which subsequently would make up prosperous Bengal.

Admittedly, the rulers, land-controllers, and 'masters' who took the decisions to abandon their subjects, clients, and dependents were actuated by motives of self-interest; yet in Bengal the self-interest of authoritative, resource-commanding males in a crisis is not absolutely in contradiction with morality. In saving themselves and their closest dependents, clients, and subjects, they ensured the maintenance of their patrilineages, their estates, and the realm itself. Again, this is not to deny that the abandonment of posyas was contrary to an ingrained duty to feed and protect the helpless, and bitter complaints that the 1943 famine was 'man-made' were evidence of the distress abandonment aroused. In a direct, political sense, the epithet 'man-made' was an accusation, a shaft directed at the officials, politicians, and merchants popularly held responsible for the famine. But the fuller implications of calling the famine 'man-made' were that it was not a result of natural disasters or organic pathologies, that it was shaped by purposeful human conduct, and that the chief actors were—literally—Bengali men, whose actions reflected Bengali values and Bengali conceptions of what was ultimately at risk. In short, the 'man-made' famine was culturally patterned in its onset, crisis, and denouement.

One of the more characteristic features of the famine—a feature that many observers considered uniquely Bengali—was that the victims accepted, virtually without protest, their victimization. The separation of husbands from wives seems to have occurred without rancour, and there is little evidence that abandoned peasants resisted their fate. Famine victims were said to be 'fatalistic', an oft-repeated term. The principal evidence for their 'fatalism' was their general lack of violence. While there were instances of unusual violence during the famine [...] neither food rioting nor insurrection seems to have been a typical accompaniment of starvation. Senior police officials, who were in a position to take a comprehensive view, reported a significant rise in professional gang-robberies in 1943 but gave no suggestion that attacks on zamindars' granaries, government storehouses, or merchants' stocks were common. This fact struck observers with force. Speaking of Calcutta, anthropologist T.C. Das observed:

We did not hear of any organised attempt at robbery by the destitutes.... Food of all sorts lay before their eyes, arranged in heaps, in shops all over the city. But no one attempted to seize it by force, though we definitely know that men and women were dying of starvation on those very streets...The attitude of the people themselves was that of complete resignation: they attributed their misery to fate or *karma* alone, which afforded poor consolation to them in their miserable plight.

An English medical officer, Lt. Col. E. Cotter, made similar remarks in testimony before the famine commission:

...What I felt in Bengal was that if such a state of affairs had arisen in the United Provinces or in the Punjab, you would have had terrific riots. The husbands and brothers would have had those food shops opened, but in Bengal they died in front of bulging food shops.
Q: Bulging with grain?
A: Yes, they died in the streets in front of shops bulging with grain.
Q: Because they could not buy?
A: Yes, and it was due to the passive, fatalistic attitude of those people that there were no riots and they were dying.

Implicit in these observations is the assumption that turning to violence to feed oneself—especially looting food shops—is somehow natural, predictable behaviour. The absence of violence in Bengal has thus to be explained by invoking an extraordinary failure of will or a powerful religious inhibition—'fatalism', 'resignation', 'karma'. It is noteworthy that educated Bengalis who witnessed the passive behaviour of famine destitutes were as perplexed by it as Europeans; it seems likely their conviction that violence was somehow expectable, derived from schooling and books rather than from personal experience. Jnananjan Niyogi, an official of the Calcutta Relief Committee, pointed out that

...from our boyhood we have been told repeatedly that hunger breeds revolution. But that aphorism proved false in the case of this tragic Bengal famine. It is really difficult to say anything conclusively why there was no rising worth the name nor any sensational looting or the rush of hunger-marchers like a northwester [spring storm] making for their target a government store or private stock or any mobile foodstuff transportation. Indeed, it is most amazing and surprising to observe how millions of people struggled and died in abject docility. The lessons and evidence of history have been nullified by the [...] fatalism of a people who have been kept for decades in a state of chronic poverty and helplessness under fettered conditions....

Niyogi's puzzlement here is patent; like other educated Indians, he suggests that colonial oppression might help to explain Bengali passivity, but neither he nor others developed the theme. Of more interest is Niyogi's appeal to 'the lessons and evidence of history', which were 'nullified' by the failure of victims to resist starvation with violence. But *whose* historical experience was Niyogi appealing to?

In the great Bengal famine of 1770—a famine in which nearly 10 million peasants are thought to have died in one year—observers had similarly been struck by Bengali 'fatalism'. The remarks of Abbé Raynal, who had access to an eyewitness account, are notable:

But it is still more remarkable...that amidst this terrible distress, such a multitude of human creatures, pressed by the most urgent of all necessities, remained in absolute inactivity, and made no attempts whatever for their self preservation. All the Europeans, especially the English, were possessed of magazines [that is, stores of grain]. These were ever respected, as well as private houses; no revolt, no massacre, not the least violence prevailed. The unhappy Indians, resigned to despair, confined themselves to the request of succour they did not obtain, and peaceably awaited the release of death. Let us now represent to ourselves any part of Europe afflicted by a similar calamity. What disorder! What fury! What atrocious acts! What crimes would ensue! How should we have seen among us Europeans, some contending for their food with their dagger in their hand, some pursuing, some flying, and without remorse massacring each other! How should we have seen [them] at last turn their rage on themselves, tearing and devouring their own limbs, and in the blindness of despair, trampling underfoot all authority, as well as every sentiment of nature and reason!

Raynal's excessive language aside, the essential point is that Bengali famine responses in the eighteenth century seem to have been no more violent than in the twentieth.

Both Congress and Communist organizers in 1943 were forced to concede a lack of revolutionary potential among the famished population. Bhowani Sen, secretary of the provincial committee of the Communist Party of India, succinctly evoked the situation when he spoke of destitutes 'standing in the queue of death'. He observed:

...had this vast army started looting, then in one moment the whole of Bengal would have been turned into a jungle infested with ferocious beasts. It was not that there was nothing to loot in the country—rather the rich have enriched themselves in this very period. But these destitutes came from the villages, saturated with the love of peace and honesty, characteristic of rural society. They are the inheritors of a great and ancient civilisation, and standing even in the queue of death, they kept up within themselves the last streak of civilisation; the unbounded fortitude of our village civilisation kept them away from the path of looting.

The Communists, in loose alliance with the Calcutta ministry during the famine, made no particular effort to organize peasants around the food issue. The Congress rebels in Midnapur had no such political inhibitions and pushed hard to mobilize antagonism against the government and landlords. In July 1943 the editor of *Biplabi*, the underground newspaper of the rebel Congress in Midnapur, cried out in a typical exhortation:

Hindu and Muslim brothers and sisters of Bengal! Will you put up with such enormous insults and then lie down like dogs and jackals in a famine created by devils or will you die as heroes, uttering a menacing cry and seizing the throat of this devilish administration in your hands? Does anyone not realize today that without full freedom there is no escape from this disgraceful death and insults more unbearable than death?

Two months later, in September, *Biplabi* openly advocated attacks on landlords and big tenants, a culmination of the gradually more radical stance the Midnapur Congress had been led to adopt as the famine reached a climax:

In the name of the country, seize the surplus paddy of those among the rich who attempt to sell it in disregard of the pleas of the villagers; then arrange for free distribution of the paddy among the destitutes of the village. Such acts cannot be equated with dacoity nor with anti-social or religiously sinful behaviour. On the contrary, in the present circumstances, this alone is the prime obligation, the highest righteousness, the ultimate pious act for each and every human being.

The results of such exhortation, however, were disappointing; there were neither popular risings nor grain seizures. It seems evident that educated Bengalis could not in practice elicit the violence they presumed starvation would spontaneously inspire.

What are we to make of the fact that Bengali 'fatalism' was a more characteristic feature of famine than violence? Will anyone seriously argue that it resulted from some character defect, perhaps an effeminate Bengali spirit, as certain nineteenth-century British writers were wont to allege? A more fruitful line would be to re-examine the assumption that hungry men necessarily rebel, for this is the standard from which all observers assumed Bengali behaviour had departed.

The most recent statement of the position is given by James C. Scott, who argues axiomatically that peasant violence and rebellion can arise directly from the loss of subsistence:

There is a naive notion, current among social scientists, that really hungry people do not rebel because they lack the energy.... At some point in the process of starvation, it is undoubtedly true that lassitude sets in. Well before that point is reached, however, one may expect reasonable men to do whatever they can to lay their hands on food. In anything less than a concentration camp context, the coincidence of severe hunger with available stocks of food in the possession of landlords or the state is a call to action. There are instances, to be sure, where a collective famine exhausts the food resources of the society as a whole and in which the issue of hunger is thus not joined with the issue of injustice and the right of the poor to a subsistence from the means of the relatively well-to-do. But the onset of hunger in most societies, whether in Annam [in the 20th century] or 17th-century England, leads not to listlessness but to rage.

This argument is nothing if not bold. It sets out a sequence of linked responses at various levels—starvation of the organism, assertion of rights in the legal–ethical structure, and revolt in the social sphere—and it does so in nearly universalistic terms. In support of his argument, Scott mostly relies on the numerous food riots in England and France from the seventeenth through the nineteenth century. And indeed, the researches of E.P. Thompson, George Rudé, and Eric Hobsbawm leave little room for doubt that when Europeans were deprived of their usual subsistence, they turned to time-honoured tactics of violent expropriation to satisfy their hunger and dramatize their grievances. What is doubtful is that these responses were ever common outside western Europe. In contrast to Scott's sweeping assertions about what 'reasonable men' will do, Thompson has been particularly cautious about the notion of any 'spasmodic' relation between hunger and collective violence. Rather, he asks, 'being hungry...what do people do? How is their behaviour modified by custom, culture, and reason?' In famine-stricken Bengal it seems evident that hungry men did not resort to collective violence, which 'custom, culture, and reason' alike eschewed. With this said, it must be pointed out immediately that eschewing violence is not the same thing as 'fatalism', however confused these may have been in the minds of educated Bengali and European observers.

It is absurd to think that Bengali peasants were unresponsive in the face of famine. 'Fatalism', the uncomplaining surrender to death by starving victims, is in fact the most obvious piece of evidence we have for an active Bengali adaptation to the famine. This was an adaptation, however, which succeeded only by imposing mortality upon some persons in order to secure the survival of others. In the European tradition, famine violence was turned 'outward' and 'upward' against offending landlords, merchants, and officials; in Bengal the tradition was to turn violence 'inward' and 'downward' against clients and dependents. This was the cold violence of abandonment, of ceasing to nourish, rather than of bloodshed and tumult. The quasi-legal notions in western Europe of subsistence 'rights', of a 'just price', and of the duty of the state to uphold the 'commonweal' gave legitimacy to the hot violence of food disturbances, a legitimacy sometimes conceded by officials who refused to punish enraged looters and leaders of hungry crowds. In Bengal such notions were entirely absent, and the cold violence of 'masters', land-holders, and officials was morally justified only by the need to salvage those who would construct a subsequent prosperity. Since the demands that 'persons requiring nurture' made on their 'destined providers of subsistence' were not legal but moral, abandoned victims could do no more than to dramatize their helplessness in the hope of re-stimulating a flow of benevolence. Mendicancy, cries and wails, imploring gestures, the exhibition of dead or dying children—all were part of the destitutes' attempts to evoke charity and to transfer responsibility for their nurture to new 'destined providers'. While the sources tell us that many victims lay down in front of 'bulging' food shops, they also tell us that such sights created great anxiety among privileged Bengali and European witnesses. Throwing themselves in the path of those who visited these shops, starving victims ensnared well-to-do strangers in nets of reproach.

When begging proved inadequate for subsistence, 'fatalism' ensued. If we portray to ourselves the situation of Euro-Americans who consent to remain aboard a sinking ship, who acquiesce in the order given by a responsible authority that the lifeboats must only be filled with those

who all concede are most deserving of survival—if we can imagine this
situation and the mental stale of the victims, we see at once that Bengali
'fatalism' was no empty surrender to death. It represented instead the
continued acceptance in a crisis of the very values which hitherto had
sustained the victims: that submission to authority is the essence of
order, and that men and women, adults and children, patrons and
clients, rulers and ruled stand in different relations of necessity to the
establishment of prosperity.

[...] The conduct of authoritative males—kings, officials, landlords,
fathers, and husbands—is a crucial matter to attend to if one wants to
understand how Indian paternalism has functioned in an environment
of periodic subsistence crises. In evaluating such conduct, however,
one wears double lenses, for patently immoral acts can be viewed in a
time of crisis as necessary steps toward ensuring the survival of cherished
institutions and valued roles. Famine behaviour in Bengal confronted
observers with innumerable violations of 'the way things should be',
yet this same behaviour formed its own pattern of necessity: 'the way
things *must* be'. The famine is therefore best expressed as a silent clash
between two patterns of need. Whereas the distinctive tropes of Bengali
prosperity are metonymies, linked symbols of abundance and gen-
erosity—rice, gold, Mother Lakshmi—the distinctive tropes of Bengali
misery are all oxymorons—cold violence, active fatalism, parental
abandonment—which symbolize the struggle to salvage order from
chaos. [...]

Genealogies

The chapters in this section address two overlapping yet distinct issues in the recent rethinking of history at the heart of historical anthropology. On the one hand we have the manner in which forms of historical consciousness vary in their degree of symbolic elaboration, their ability to pervade multiple contexts, and their capacity to capture the imaginations of social subjects. On the other we have the ways in which history exists as a negotiated resource at the core of shifting configurations of social worlds, in the past and the present. In taking up these themes, the chapters in this section further raise critical questions concerning the overarching oppositions between myth and history, and tradition and modernity, as well as regarding the pervasive presence of notions of progress and nation in history-writing. Together, the chapters emphasize—at the very least, in practical and implicit ways—the importance of approaching the writing of history in critical and ethnographic modes.

To start off, Ravindra Jain discusses the modalities of historical consciousness as these assume form and acquire substance in a royal genealogy or *vamsavali*.[1] The locus of his enquiries is Bundelkhand, the area of the former Bundela Rajput kingdoms that also constitutes a distinct linguistic region in central India. Here, Jain explores the *vamsavali*, 'a record of the strictly exogamous patriline' and the 'most comprehensive charter for the Bundela past', as at once conjoining and separating 'legendary', dynastic histories and their 'mythological', sacred geographies. His effort is to clarify, on the basis of 'the Bundela's view of their past', the terms of juxtaposition between two interpenetrating structures: the 'martial' (or 'political') on the one hand, and the 'marital' (or 'descent alliance') on the other.

The essay initially charts the typical character of the 'mythical beginning' of the royal Bundelas: their origin from the stem of the lotus flower and from the sun, which carries symbolic salience 'at all levels of royal descent ideology and for Bundela ideology as a whole'. Next, Jain considers oral and written narratives of the 'legend' of Bundela origin. These reveal that 'the conjunction between the principle of descent and territory in the Bundela ideology of kingship is expressed in the metaphor of divine intervention in human affairs.' Specifically, the divine intervention of Vindhyavasini Devi who embodies 'multi-vocal symbolic significance'—as the female principle, the territory, and the giver and nourisher (through her milk) of princes—brings together unilineal descent (blood) and territory (milk) to 'complete the picture of Bundela royal agnation in the idiom of clanship.' Finally, the essay explores the legend of Bundela expansion as marked by two simultaneous processes: on the one hand, those of caste segmentation that emphasize the relative hierarchy of statuses among the (Bundela) Rajputs; and, on the other, those of 'dispersed clanship and merging lineage segmentation' that function as a charter for social and political inclusion.

All this allows Jain to undertake distinct tasks: to distinguish between the political function of clanship and the ritual function of caste as idioms of hierarchical social distinctions; to question a simplified equation between hierarchy, caste segmentation, and hypergamy of indigenous ruling groups as not only founded on the exclusion of historical time but as hindering the understanding of key variables in the social organization of dominance; and to elaborate political processes of the expansion of Bundela rule in middle India, entailing dynamics where 'exclusion from a confirmed *jati* status was the means of gaining power and creating a new framework of statuses and offices.' Here are to be found critical questions concerning caste and power and hierarchy and dominance as part of the past's wider existence as a reworked resource and of the inherent diversity that characterizes forms of historical consciousness.

The formative plurality and constitutive malleability of the past find distinct configurations in the next chapter. Ishita Banerjee-Dube focuses on *Bhima Bhoi Malika ba Padmakalpa*, an apocryphal text, which was produced within the interstices of a subaltern religious formation— and as part of popular orientations to time and history—in Orissa in eastern India. Highlighting the presence of the concept–metaphor of *kaliyuga*—the era of evil—in everyday imagination, the chapter explores the innovative expressions—and the profound polyphony—of the notion of kaliyuga as engendering distinct and novel understandings of the past, present, and future.

Bhima Bhoi Malika ba Padmakalpa was shaped as a hybrid blend of oral forms and written modalities, of 'modern–linear' orderings of history and 'mythical–cyclical' notions of time. Banerjee-Dube's unravelling of the text showcases the surfeit of meanings generated by popular modes of envisioning and articulating time and the past, temporality and the here-and-now. On the one hand, such a surplus of denotations within shared stocks of knowledge puts a question mark on influential, hermetical divisions between orality and writing, myth and history, and linear and cyclical time. On the other, the chapter underscores the critical place of experience and appropriation in construing and elaborating texts and temporalities, and history and time.

Everyday articulations of the past come alive further in Susan Visvanathan's discussion of 'people's history' among the Syrian Christian community of Kerala. Approaching people's history as a heuristic reconstruction based on anthropological analysis, Visvanathan highlights the importance of the construct for the exploration of chronological events. At the same time, she underscores the problematic nature of the notion of 'remembrance', underlining that it is 'a social fact constrained by official ideologies and diversities of interpretation born of uncertain situations'.

The essay charts its course by interweaving narrative levels of people's history with units of anthropological analysis: general history–church; local history–neighbourhood; genealogy–family; biography– individual. This further allows Visvanathan to attend to how the physical, spatial, and symbolic geographies of neighbourhood, house, and church remain critical 'props' in narratives and descriptions concerning the past and the present.

My own chapter focuses on the myths of the Satnampanth, a large untouchable and heretical community of Chhattisgarh. The myths have been marked by a high degree of symbolic elaboration and form part of the ongoing oral traditions of the community. They suggest the need to explore the relationship between myth and representations of the past. Now, the counter-posing of history and myth as opposing categories reinforces the distinction between societies with a dynamic past and other people with unchanging mythic orders. Indeed, as we have seen, this distinction is itself a part of a wider set of overarching oppositions between modernity and magicality, rationality and ritual, and West and East. Clearly, we need to think through these oppositions, and my chapter takes a small step in this direction. Two points stand out. To begin with, myth can be a form of the ordering of historical consciousness and embody specific cultural conceptions of the past. A corollary to this is the fact that the stratification of myth and ritual in temporally layered religious cults and movements underscores the importance of attending to the internal order and the structure of meanings of myths and rituals.

My reading of Satnami myths combines these emphases and concerns. As I have shown elsewhere, the writing down of Satnami myths by Baba Ramchandra, an upper-caste outsider, in a curious manuscript called *Ghasidasji ki Vanshavali* (the genealogy of Ghasidas), in the 1920s remained bound within an oral logic. Even as Ramchandra sought to frame a continuously performed oral tradition in writing in the *Vanshavali*, the devices of literacy could not compromise the internal order of myth, and the written text actually derived its meaning from oral and mythic categories.[2] These myths ordered the past of Satnampanth. The Satnami gurus underwent trials, overcame obstacles, and negotiated and displaced figures of authority to define the boundary and orchestrate the symbolic construction of Satnampanth. The rehearsal of the myths in the performance of oral traditions reaffirmed the identity of the Satnamis as a bounded group, a community. At the same time, the principles of feminine sexuality governed the construction of women in Satnami myths, and the unbridled and untamed desire of wives of the gurus evoked disruption and disorder within Satnampanth. Satnami myths allow us to trace, at once, the group's cultural conception of its past, the creation of a new mythic tradition, and the interplay of community and gender. All this further forms a bridge to the next section discussing communities.

NOTES

1. See also, Ravindra K. Jain, 'Bundela Genealogy and Legends', in J.H.M. Beattie and R.G. Lienhardt (eds), *Studies in Social Anthropology: Essays in Memory of E.E. Evans-Pritchard* (Oxford, Clarendon Press, 1975), pp. 239–72. It is poignant that Jain's chapter combining anthropology and history first appeared in a volume of essays in honour of E.E. Evans-Pritchard, the scholar who, as we have seen, wrote so passionately about the interchanges between these 'sister disciplines'. As such, the essay could well have found place in the earlier section on 'Formations', and forms a bridge, as it were, between the preceding and the present section.

2. Saurabh Dube, *Untouchable Pasts: Religion, Identity, and Power among a Central Indian Community, 1780–1950* (Albany, State University of New York Press, 1998).

Genealogy and Legend[*]

RAVINDRA JAIN

Until a year after the independence of India in August 1947, the northern districts of Madhya Pradesh formed the territories of native states ruled over by the scions of Rajput (literally 'kingly sons' from the Sanskrit *Raja-putra*) families. From the beginning of the nineteenth century, the British had established their paramountcy over the native states. This chapter deals with the traditional history of these native kingdoms (*rajya* or *raj*) as rendered in the oral narratives and endogenously written sources of this area. More specifically, my concern here is to demonstrate the value of these sources in defining the region of dominance and salient social institutions of a ruling group known as the Bundela. The area of the former Bundela kingdoms is still known by its indigenous name 'Bundelkhand' (literally, 'the domain of the Bundelas'). It might also be mentioned that besides designating the territory of former Bundela rule, Bundelkhand is the name of a linguistic region of India. The great majority of the people of four southern districts of Uttar Pradesh and eight northern districts of Madhya Pradesh speak Bundeli, a dialect of western Hindi. The Bundeli linguistic region is much larger (43,452.4 sq km) than the area of the former Bundela kingdoms and domains (22,180.7 sq km).

* Originally published in Ravindra K. Jain, *Between History and Legend: Status and Power in Bundelkhand,* Hyderabad: Orient Longman, 2002, pp. 1–33, as 'Bundela Genealogy and Legends: The Past of an Indigenous Ruling Group'. In the present version, all notes and references have been deleted. For the complete text, see the original version.

The data was collected in the course of intermittent fieldwork, from 1969 to 1971, in several villages and towns of Chhatarpur district in northern Madhya Pradesh. [...]

BUNDELA GENEALOGY

The most comprehensive charter for the Bundela past is their genealogy (*vamsavali*). It is a record of a strictly exogamous patriline. When put into diagrammatic form, it shows only males descending from males. The women are not represented.

Histories compiled from primary or secondary sources—in Hindi and English—provide succession lists of the ruling dynasties. The ruling line is the main or senior line. These sources also contain lists of subsidiary or junior lines, since all descendants of the ruling stock (*rajya vamsa*) were normatively included among the right-holders (*haqdar*) in the kingdom. Since such lists could become unwieldy, only those agnates from junior lines that possessed large hereditary appanages (*jagir*) in the kingdom have been selected. Those marital allies that held appanages in the kingdom are also listed. A typical example is the compilation in the series *Rulers, Leading Families and Officials in the States of Central India*.

At present, the most senior living member of a Bundela patrilineage in one village or a group of nearby villages usually possesses an up-to-date genealogical extract of his own residential unit (*patti*). This local group corresponds to a minimal segment of the Bundela patriline. The apical ancestor for this segment would be the Bundela founder of the patti. Nevertheless, the term patti denotes a share. It implies division from a larger entity and segmentation of the group from a higher level. The definition and scale of customary rights to a share are validated at this higher pre-patti level of segmentation with reference to those areas of the genealogy where a local Bundela patrlineage is linked by descent to a particular ruling house. This indigenous procedure of tracing rights among rural Bundela landholders was imperfectly understood by the British, who intervened in their land disputes throughout the nineteenth century. The discrepancy between Bundela custom and the alien juridical framework that the British attempted to enforce on local Bundela dominants (*thakurs*) is epitomized in the repeated assertion by the latter that they were co-sharers (*hissedar*), and not merely right-holders (*haqdar*), in certain Bundela kingdoms. This does not deny the existence of customary law by which the distribution of rights, offices, and titles over territory in the indigenous kingdoms was regulated. It merely establishes a strong linkage between Bundela customary law and

Bundela rules of descent, succession, and inheritance—the sphere of 'family law' as Maine saw it—and the problems in attempting to align it with substantive law through a 'double institutionalisation of custom'.

The Bundelas had a vested interest in emphasizing their common descent from their rulers. This is reflected in the ability of Bundelas in rural areas to trace, beyond the patti level, their patrilineal links with the ruling dynasty of the kingdom where they are located. Since all Bundela kingdoms grew by a process of political fission in the patriline, the links between various ruling dynasties are also contained in Bundela genealogy. As mentioned earlier, historically the Bundela dynasty of Orchha was the parent ruling house from which the other Bundela kingdoms subsequently separated. The last Bundela kingdom thus formed was Charkhari. The patti level of Bundela patrilineal segmentation, designated here as the dominance level of Bundela genealogy, is thus subsumed by the dynastic level which spans—socially and politically—the time and space of kingdom formation in Bundela history.

However, in the genealogy itself, the origin of the Bundelas and their kingship (as distinct from historical kingdoms) belongs to a legendary and mythical past. The legendary and mythical levels of the genealogy are an invaluable repository for the anthropologist and can be explored for the unconscious structure of Bundela ideology of descent-based rule. The view of their past depicted at these levels exercises a powerful hold on the popular imagination of the people of this area. This is expressed in a variety of media—stories, songs, poems, and anecdotes. The Bundelas themselves enact their legendary origin in the annual ritual worship of the Devi (the female principle in divine creation). The categories of Bundela rule—the boundaries of socially legitimate exercise of power by the ruling group—are constituted by the formal and sensory properties of symbolic statements and enactments associated with this legendary and mythological past. An analysis of the myths and legends of Bundela origin and kingship in the next section of this chapter demonstrates that these levels of Bundela genealogy (like the dominance and dynastic levels) do not stand in isolation. They form an integral part of the encapsulated history of the ruling group represented as a hierarchical series. Before the analysis, however, two clarifications are necessitated.

The myths and legends of Bundela origin have a dual aspect. The legends trace Bundela descent from an eponymous apical ancestor and, at the same time, describe the origin of Bundela kingship in the present territory—the region of the Vindhya mountains. With regard to the specificity of geographical information, the legends of Bundela territory identifying it with the Vindhya mountains, stand between the much clearer geopolitical boundaries of the kingdoms described by dynastic histories and the elemental and transitive sacred geography of their mythology. The association of the group with a more or less specific territory is one criterion for distinguishing the legendary from the mythological. The latter, in the absence of an unequivocal territorial specification, should be viewed as the standard 'great tradition' prolegomenon to Hindu royal genealogies.

The second clarification concerns the analytical vocabulary adopted in discerning the patterns of descent at various levels of Bundela genealogy. So far the terms 'patriliny' for the genealogy as a whole, and 'local patrilineage' and 'royal house' for territorially identifiable groups corresponding to the dominance and dynastic levels of Bundela genealogy, have been used. The term 'patriline' is a translation of the indigenous *vamsa*. Owing to the segmentary structure of Bundela unilineal descent groups, however, the same term, vamsa, may occasionally be used to denote a smaller unit, for example, a 'local patrilineage' and a 'royal house'. But in a context where the smaller units need to be distinguished from more inclusive descent constructs (for example, the patriline as a whole), the terms *kula* and *khandan* are used interchangeably. Among the terms denoting a more inclusive descent construct for the Bundelas, the indigenous *kuri* and *bans* belong to the same semantic set as vamsa. Lexically, *bans* is a corruption of the Sanskrit vamsa. In the written genealogies of Bundelkhand, the Sanskrit word vamsa is invariably employed to designate the record as a whole (genealogy—vamsavali), and the mythological aspect of the genealogy, for example, to designate the two main branches—solar (*surya vamsa*) and lunar (*chandra vamsa*) of the ruling (kshatriya) clans. However, from the legendary level downwards, the unilineal descent segments (not only of the Bundelas but of their 'Rajput' marital allies as well) are designated as bans. In spoken Bundeli, moreover, the term bans is uniformly employed to designate Bundela genealogy as a whole (*bansavali*), the mythological branches, and the 'Rajput' clans (for example, the Bundela bans). The most common designation for Bundela corporate identity and the last of the preceding meanings is inherent in the speech of the Bundelas in the expression 'The Bundela clan is not a friend of brothers' (*Bundela bans bhaiyya ka mit nahin hota*). I locate the meaning of bans as clan at the legendary level of Bundela genealogy. In my definition, the Bundela bans is a clan in that all Bundelas trace their mythical descent, through males, from an eponymous ancestor; through him they identify themselves with a more or less specific territory; and they practice bans exogamy. It corresponds to the maximal level of segmentation of the Bundela patriline.

Closely allied to the ideas of vamsa and bans (but much more complex) is the term kuri. The most frequent local usage of this term suggests a classification of Rajput bans into two categories along an East–West territorial axis. Each category is endogenously known by the number of clans composing it. There are, therefore, the 'three-kuri Rajputs' (*tin kuri ke Rajput*) and the 'thirty-six-kuri Rajputs' (*chattis kuri ke Rajput*), belonging to the eastern region (Bundelkhand) and the western region (Malwa and Rajasthan), respectively. Here, the term kuri is being used in its meaning of 'kind', 'type', or 'variety' (Hindi—*prakara*). The translation is provided by the informants themselves. But the term kuri, as used this way, does not by itself suggest a basis for classifying Rajput clans into these two categories. Nor does an ancillary usage which sorts individual Rajput men of families as belonging 'either to the three or the thirty-six' (*tin me ke, ya chattis me ke*) tell us any more than that, being different from one another, each category represents a unity of some kind.

A second meaning of the term kuri is more explicit. A Hindi lexicon (*Nalanda Visal Sabdasagar*) gives the following meanings: '[noun, masculine gender] (In Sanskrit), i. a grain, bean sprout, (In poetry), vamsa, gharana, khandan, (In Desaja), a plough, [noun, feminine gender]; (in Hindi), a subdivision, a part, a portion.'

Undoubtedly the term kuri is a derivative from the Sanskrit *ankura* which means 'sprout', 'blade', 'hair', 'water', 'blood'. In this semantic set the term kuri is a metaphor for the segmentary ideology of Bundela descent. The Bundelas themselves express the idea of fission and fusion of their patriline in a statement about the process of the formation of segments (for example, a local patrilineage): 'Formerly all were one, subsequently different kuri sprouted' (*pahle sab ek the; bad me alag alag kuri phut gayin*). Kuri in this statement, and in many similar statements, is associated with 'sprouting'. Similarly, with reference to a particular apical ancestor or brothers, it is said that from him or them 'the branching-out commenced' (*phutan chali*). Here the apical ancestor—always male—is likened to a seed. An apt graph of the collective representation of the Bundela patriline in the metaphor of sowing and sprouting is the genealogical extract, characteristically drawn in the form of a creeper or a plant, with the male descendants only being shown as leaves on several veins and the leaves again sprouting more leaves on more veins. The orientation is always bottom upwards.

As handled in speech by my Bundela informants, the term kuri connotes both the fission and fusion aspects of Bundela patrilineal descent ideology. Yet, the principle of patrilineal segmentation cannot be extended to the classification of Rajput clans (including the Bundela clan), into the 'three-kuri' and 'thirty-six-kuri' categories without further exploration of the internal structure of each category. I hope that in this exploration the identification of the exogamous 'clan' segment at the legendary level of Bundela genealogy will prove serviceable. The grounds for an experiment in Bundelkhand ethnology are provided by the fact that the eastern or Bundelkhandi category (the 'three-kuri Rajput') can be identified with three exogamous clans, namely, the Bundela, the Panwar, and the Dhandhera. Intermarriage among the three follows a rule of non-hypergamous circulating connubium. However, in one legend, the Bundela conquerors are depicted as having consciously formed a league of intermarriage with the other two groups, following help rendered by them in their victory against an out-group, the non-Kshatriya Khangar. Thus martial alliance preceded marital alliance. Here is a perfect case of two structures which, as comparative social anthropology tells us, interpenetrate each other—on the one hand 'political', and, on the other, 'descent and alliance'. My limited purpose here is to clarify the terms of this juxtaposition on the basis of the Bundelas' view of their past.

THE MYTH OF ROYAL ORIGIN

The mythical beginning of royal Bundelas has a typically Hindu character. The account starts with Lord Visnu (Narayan, reclining on the serpent, Sesa who holds the universe). From Visnu's placenta, in the form of the stem of the lotus flower, issues Brahma. From Brahma issues Marichi. From Marichi is brought forth Kasyapa. By Kasyapa's wife, Aditi, are born the eldest son, Surya (the sun), and the gods (*devata*); of his twelve other wives, by Diti are born the demons (*daitya*). The descendants of Surya (*Suryavamsi*) are Iksvaku, Dilip, Raghu, Aja, Dasaratha, Ramachandra, and the two brothers, Lava and Kusa. Lava becomes the ruler of Punjab. Kusa succeeds to the throne (*gaddi*) of Ayodhya. The descendants of Kusa are Haribrahma and Vihagaraja. In the seventh generation, Vihagaraja's descendant is Kiratdeva. A few generations after Kiratdeva, Virabhadra, the raja of Kasi (Benaras), is descended. The Bundelas, in this version, are the descendants of Virabhadra through the line of his younger son, Hem Karan, alias Pancham, alias Jagdas.

This mythical prologue contains elements which carry a symbolic significance at all levels of royal-descent ideology and for Bundela genealogy as a whole. The origin of the rulers from the stem of the lotus flower is one such element. On account of its free-floating roots, the lotus flower is a persistent cosmological Hindu motif for depicting the exalted origins of royalty. It symbolizes the special creation and inherent legitimacy of kingship, investing royal descendants with the spiritual authority which they must possess as lords and protectors of 'land-cum-people'.

Second, in the oral tradition, Bundela kings are descended from the sun (Surya) and belong to the solar pedigree (Suryavamsa). The conjunction of the sun and the lotus is regarded by the Hindus as auspicious. Both these, and their related attributes, have occupied a significant place in Bundela symbolism of kingship, for example, in royal architecture. Third, demons and gods are brothers as Kasyapa's sons. While the idea of brothers as potential enemies permeates Bundela royal agnation, the principle of succession by primogeniture is clearly expressed in specifying that Rama's elder son, Kusa, succeeds to the throne of Ayodhya. Finally, kingship is associated with sacred geography. Only two capitals, Ayodhya and Kasi, are identifiable places. Both have multiple associations with the Hindu sacred tradition. Along with three other pilgrim centres they belong to a quintet of sacred Hindu locales. As a 'great tradition' mode of classification this quintet, rather like the four-fold varna scheme, serves to legitimize kingship in the idiom of descent.

The flexibility inherent in associating royalty with sacred locales has been exploited by genealogists to insert fictions of glorious antecedents for their Bundela patrons and by priests and poets to align the royal pedigree with their own priestly pedigree. A good example of the latter is an early seventeenth-century poetic biography of the Bundela ruler of Orchha, composed by his Brahmin priest and poet Kesava Das. Kesava Das, whose own ancestors came from Kasi, constantly refers to his Bundela royal patron by the honorific 'Kasi Raja' (the Ruler of Kasi). The title did not conform to the historically known boundaries of the kingdom of Orchha, which never included Kasi (Benaras or Varanasi in modern Uttar Pradesh). The point here is not that Kesava Das was fabricating Bundela history; rather, on account of its sacredness in Hindu ideas, Kasi, like Ayodhya, is a good place to think of as the seat of royalty.

THE LEGEND OF BUNDELA ORIGIN

The legend of Bundela origin narrated to me in Sendpa village is as follows. Virabhadra, the king of Kasi, had two queens. From the senior queen (*patrani*) there were four sons: Raj Singh, Hansaraj, Mohan, and Man. The son of the second queen (*lahuri rani*; literally, junior queen) was Jagdas, alias Hemkaran. Following Virabhadra's death, the half-brothers of Jagdas refused to give him a portion (*hissa*) in the kingdom of Kasi and banished him. Jagdas wandered away to the shrine of Vindhyavasini Devi (literally, 'the Devi who dwells in the Vindhya ranges') to do penance under her protection. ('Devi' is the manifestation of the female principle in divine creation; when not regarded as a deity localized in the Vindhya mountain ranges she is known either by her generalized name 'Devi', or by any of her other manifestations such as 'Bhawani', 'Durga', 'Kali', etc.). Despite the most arduous penance, he received no sign of blessing from the Devi. Dejected, Jagdas decided to offer his life in sacrifice to the Devi by beheading himself with his sword. No sooner had a drop (*bund*) of blood dripped onto the floor from a cut in his throat, than the Devi appeared and held the hand of her devotee. She blessed him with the boon that from that drop of blood a brave son who would conquer large territories to be known the world over as Bundelkhand would be born.

With a few variations and additions of detail the same legend appears in an eighteenth-century poetic biography of Maharaja Chhatrasal, the Bundela ruler of Panna, composed in his lifetime by the poet (*bhat*) Lal Kavi or Gorelal. In this text, the name of Virabhadra's son from the second queen alone is mentioned. He is called Pancham or Devadasa. Both these names are formulaic in the sense that they refer to the attributes of the person being designated; Pancham means 'the Fifth' (his place in the sibling birth-order) and Devadasa, 'the deity's servant' (his disposition for acquiring a boon from the goddess). Although the text is far from explicit, it seems to indicate that Virabhadra, in his own lifetime, partitioned his estate (*puhumi* meaning 'land'; it might also stand for 'kingdom') among his sons. Pancham being a minor, Virabhadra, as father and king, became the trustee of his share of inheritance. Following Virabhadra's death, Pancham's four older brothers grew covetous, took advantage of his minority, and appropriated his portion of the estate 'partitioning it among themselves in four shares'. There is no mention of Virabhadra's successor to the seat of Kasi. This makes sense if we bear in mind the mythical character of this 'seat', and my view that the story of Pancham marks the point of transition from a mythological to a legendary level of Bundela past.

The forward-looking facet of the legend, which enables us to view Pancham as the founder of the Bundela clan, is his gaining a kingdom and a patriline of royal descent after being gifted a heroic son by Vindhya-vasini Devi. Pancham's son was created from a drop of Pancham's own blood and appropriately called 'Bundela' (from bund—drop). Details of the boon, given in the gift (*varadan*) of a son to Pancham, and the son's 'special creation' by divine interposition, are vividly portrayed in the poem. The mental process by which Pancham, the unhappy prince, is drawn towards Vindhyavasini Devi is known as 'yoganidra' [...]'the tranquil repose of the mind from an abstraction of ideas'. Pancham practices penances and austerities at her shrine in Vindhyachal, the hills near Mirzapur in Uttar Pradesh, and a neighbouring religious resort on the Ganga. The episode is narrated as follows in the text:

After the first seven days Pancham heard a voice from the sky say to him, 'Your land will be restored to you.' He replied, 'I have practiced these austerities to win your [Devi's] favour.' Whereupon, the voice returned to the sky. Somewhat heartened by this, he devoted the next seven days to even stricter penances and gradually lost all hope that his wish would be fulfilled. He took out his sword and poised it to behead himself in sacrifice to the Devi. However, by now his perseverance, piety, and devotion had won her affection. She appeared in person and wrested the sword from his hand. Drops of blood oozed out from a few gashes on his head, 'like stars shooting from the sky'. The sight filled her heart with pity. She instantly conveyed to the wound some *amrita*, or water of immortality, inherent in every *devta*. At the same time *amrita* rained from the sky. A drop of Pancham's blood which fell on the ground assumed the form of a child, a replica of Pancham. On beholding the infant, she [Devi] was filled with maternal affection and put it to her breast, which supplied a copious flood of nourishment. Then, blessing Pancham and the baby, she, with prophetic spirit, revealed that the sword should always help him in war, and be the prop of his prosperity, by which the sovereignty should continue from one generation to another...'Thou, O favoured mortal,' she added, 'shall repossess thy estate, increase them to the full extent of thy wishes and conquer all against whom thou wagest war.' Then placing her hand on his head, she said, in commemoration of the drop [*bund*] of blood, 'Thine descendants shall be called Bundelas.'

In this version, the conjunction between the principle of descent and territory in the Bundela ideology of kingship is expressed in the metaphor of divine intervention in human affairs (the *pauranic* device). In reality the Vindhyas are a mountain range. The territory and the female principle dwelling there take their name from it. In the metaphorical structure of the legend, Vindhyavasini Devi represents 'territory-for-kingdom'. She is actually designated puhumi or 'land' (fem.) in the course of the poem. Bundela, the son created from a drop of Pancham's blood on the earth, is nourished by Vindhyavasini Devi—the divine female principle—and blessed by her with a line of brave royal descendants; and is gifted away to Pancham. This son incarnate is to be distinguished from Pancham's other, 'real', son Bir Bundela. The former never again makes an appearance in the book. What remains of him is only the name 'Bundela' assumed by Pancham himself after the incident, and passed on to his descendants. The son incarnate is, therefore, a ritual apotheosis of the principle of clanship at the legendary level of Bundela genealogy. All Bundela royal houses worshipped Vindhyavasini Devi as their clan goddess (kula devi), although the members of Bundela lineal segments, localized in rural areas, worship their clan goddess in her generalized form, Devi. What is significant about the legend of Bundela origin is its representation of territory in the form of Vindhyavasini Devi endowed with multi-vocal symbolic significance—the female principle, the territory, and the giver and nourisher of princes. Through her divine intervention, unilineal descent (blood) and territory (milk) complete the picture of Bundela royal agnation in the idiom of clanship (bans).

A LEGEND OF BUNDELA EXPANSION

The expansion of the Bundela clan following the boon to Pancham is closely associated with the legendary martial exploits of his royal descendants in the Vindhya region. One particular event, again the founding by conquest of a separate kingdom by one of the royal siblings, is repeated extensively in all oral narratives and receives significant mention in literary works as well. The following summary is based mainly on the latter set of sources: Arjanpal, ruler of Mahoni had three sons: Birpal, Sohanpal, and Dayapal. Sohanpal was a most capable warrior. He reduced the forts of Garhkundar and Kateragarh. Sohanpal undertook the successful expedition to Kateragarh on behalf of his father. His victory at Garhkundar followed the death of his father and his elder brother's succession to the throne of Mahoni. The cause of this expedition was Sohanpal's dissatisfaction with his share of inheritance. With 45 *sepoys* and 13 *sowars*, Sohanpal went to Naga (alias Hurmat Singh), the Khangar raja of Kundar, seeking his help in taking his share from his brother.

Naga promised to help him, on condition that Sohanpal eat, drink, and intermarry with him. Sohanpal was enraged at this suggestion, and was about to leave Kurar [Kundar], but hearing of his intention, Naga formed a plot to forcibly detain him and compel him to accede to his proposal. Sohanpal hearing thereof, fled from the court, and went to Mukatman Chauhan, a descendant of Dhandhera Deva who commanded 4,000 men on behalf of Naga. He requested his assistance against his brother, but Mukatman refused, saying that he would remain neutral. After this, Sohanpal, leaving his small force behind, went alone successively to the Salingars, Chauhans, and Kachwahas, and told them his story. But none of them offered to assist him. However, a Panwar Thakur named Panpal (Punyapal), Jagirdar of Karhara, offered assistance, and together they conspired to remove Raja Naga from his kingdom, the revenue of which was worth [Rupees] 13 lakhs. It was agreed that Sohanpal should go to Kurar and pretend to accept Raja Naga's conditions of intermarriage, etc., and invite the raja and his relations to his house. Sohanpal went to Kurar and, after a time, Raja Naga, his brothers, and ministers came to Sohanpal's house, whereupon Panpal arrived with 300 Kshatris. As soon as Raja Naga and his followers sat down to eat, Panpal Panwar and Sohanpal Bundela fell upon and slaughtered all the Khangar chiefs, and immediately seized the fort of Kurar. In this way, on Wednesday, the 2nd of Kartik Sambat 1354 (AD 1288), Sohanpal became raja of Kurar and appointed Panpal and Mukatman as his ministers. He said to them, 'As no Kshatri in my time of distress gave me help except you, no other save yourselves shall marry into my family.' Accordingly, he gave his daughter in marriage to Panpal and as dowry a village named Itaura, and to Panpal's younger brother a jagir of one lakh. From this time the Kshatris were divided into three different classes of Bundelas, Panwar, and Dhandheras. The total revenue of the whole Bundela territory was 26 lakhs, of which half Birpal possessed and the rest was Sohanpal's.

This is the most secular of early Bundela legends. It depicts two social processes, which must be kept conceptually distinct in order to understand the political expansion of Bundela rule in the Vindhya region. The first is a process of caste segmentation [...] before the capture of Garh Kundar, the Bundelas intermarried exogamously with a large number of Rajput clans. The marriages of Sohanpal's immediate descendants, on the other hand, take place with the Panwar and Dhandhera clans only. [...] the narrowing of the Bundela endogamous circle involved their exclusion from commensal relations with the other Rajput clans. Similarly, there is evidence that the Panwar and the Dhandhera had also experienced exclusion from a more inclusive Rajput category. The views of nineteenth-century amateur historians, attributing inferior or impure Rajput status to the Bundela on account of miscegenation with the non-Aryan Khangar, could also be seen to describe a process of caste segmentation by exclusion. Whatever the specific terms under which this process is perceived, the concept of caste segmentation emphasizes the relative hierarchy of statuses among the Rajput. In this particular case an endogamous segment of the main body of Rajput caste, formed by a process of exclusion, had a definitely lower ritual status vis-à-vis the rest.

What is excluded from the main body of Rajputs constitutes the inclusive category, the 'three-kuri Rajput'. The constituent units of this category are three intermarrying exogamous clans. The discrete groups belonging to the three clans are localized lineage segments. The principle of inclusion, I submit, cannot be elucidated by the process of caste segmentation, but only through the complementary processes of dispersed clanship and merging lineage segmentation.

In our exploration of these processes, we encounter the Bundela legend of expansion not in its function as a cover for social and ritual exclusion, but as a charter of social and political inclusion. The contextual information in our sources elucidates this function.

Rajput territorial organization in much of insular central India during the pre-Bundela period was based on dispersed clanship. Each named clan (bans) was an exogamous unit. Its constituent patrilineages at various levels of segmentation were designated, in addition to the clan name, by the locality (a village, or cluster of villages) where the relevant apical ancestor is supposed to have created rights in land and its produce either by conquest or political alliance. These rights tended to become presumptive. Thus, even when they were overlaid by superior rights, say through conquest by another clan or by a foreign power, or during the protracted absence from the locality of members of the original descent-group, they could still be revived if the occasion warranted. Their non-recognition by the authorities became a frequent cause of rebellion. [...] This customary claim (whatever be its historical character), by deep patrilineages to particular territories, formed the basis of their local identification. Legends of former rule by the concerned clans, which still abound in these localities, are probably not without some historical foundation, as long as alleged dynastic succession is distinguished from agnatic inheritance of presumptive rights in land and its produce, and a fully fledged state political system is distinguished from a combination of feudal and acephalous political systems.

The various localized patrilineal segments of Rajput clans referred to in the legend of Bundela expansion can be set against the background of social and political organization delineated above. They were located in the Gwalior-Jalaun-Jhansi region, roughly the same area as Arjunpal's seat of Mahoni. The various chiefs who exchanged women in marriage appear to have been *primi inter pares* as dominants (thakurs) in their localities. The diversity of titles assumed by them either emanated from their position in the segmentary lineage structure stratified into senior and junior branches (for example, *rao, diman,* and *sawai diman*) or they referred to offices held currently or in the past in a local patrilineage as feudatories to a superior power (for example, raja, *rai,* and *diwan*). [...]

In order to gain political advantage through territorial expansion, the local lineage segments of Rajput clans arranged and rearranged themselves into patterns of marital and martial alliance.

Interpreting the formation of the 'three-kuri Rajput' from the legend of Bundela expansion, one must distinguish between martial-cum-marital alliance in the context of the regional, social, and political structure and the message concerning the superiority of the Kshatriya ruler vis-à-vis that of the non-Kshatriya Khangar. The former cannot be wholly understood from merging lineage segmentation, nor the latter merely as caste segmentation in the idiom of ritual hierarchy. What is the middle ground left, in historical fact and conceptualization, between these dominant modes of interpretation? The answer suggested by a contextual interpretation of this Bundela legend has, as I shall point out in conclusion, wider implications.

The lineage organization of ruling clans at this time had an important political function. The Khangar ruled over the wild tracts of southeastern Bundelkhand by allocating political authority to localized lineage segments, where each segment was identified with a fortress serving as a military garrison. Fortresses assigned to rulers' sons as secondary capitals continually figure in Bundela legends and in traditional history as well. Conflict between half-siblings in the Bundela ruling lineage of Mahoni is presaged by a military expedition commanded by Sohanpal to capture the fort of Kateragarh. According to Bundela annals, besides being overlooked in the succession, Sohanpal was disinherited of this fort. It is conceivable that this disinheritance was the main cause of the quarrel between him and Birpal. In later Bundela history it became a standard tactic for a ruler to assign a fort far away from the capital to a troublesome younger brother.

[...] However, the agnatic factionalism in the ruling lineage, which was an important cause of Sohanpal's expedition against the Khangar, does not, even according to the legend, lead to permanent fission. The fate of the senior branch (Birpal-Dayapal), after Sohanpal's capture of Garhkundar, is not passed over. The breach between the half-siblings is healed, but on terms dictated by Sohanpal. There is an equal division of territory between him and Birpal, while Dayapal is assigned an appanage (jagir) of one lakh. This is an early example of the process of merging lineage segmentation in the Bundela ruling group. The idiom in which this merger is expressed is that of kingdom (rajya or *raj*), but we have no need to assume that it refers in this case to a centralized state political system.

The legend tells us that a connubial league of the Bundela, the Panwar, and the Dhandhera was formed following their martial alliance to defeat the Khangar. But it is not clear why this inclusive category, the 'three-kuri Rajput' covers all Bundela and not merely Sohanpal and his descendants? There is no indication whatever (either in Bundela history or in present-day practice) that some Bundela, namely, the descendants of Birpal and Dayapal against whom the martial league was partly directed, were excluded from the marital league. Conversely, no section of the Bundelas has shown consistent normative preference for marriage with the Rajput of thirty-six kuri and a corresponding disinclination to intermarry with the Panwar and the Dhandhera. It would be easy to 'explain' the exhaustive inclusion of the Bundela into the 'three-kuri' category by evoking the superior and contagious efficacy of ritual exclusion over political alliance: the well-known phenomenon of the formation of sub-castes. This precisely would be the argument of those analysts who assume that the dynamics of inclusion and exclusion in Indian social structure has to be based on the ritual hierarchy of purity and impurity. In this case, however, it is the historical and contextual facts of changes in the distribution of political power that explain the dynamics of social structure. To be more precise, we move away from a model of caste-based dynamics to one based on the clanship of Rajput groups in this region. Thus, to the extent, however, that there are deep localized patrilineages of the Bundela Rajputs in the Bundelkhand region, a long history of kingdom formation and rule by Rajput branches from the mid-fifteenth century to the mid-twentieth century, and the lack of a consistent hypergamous pattern of marriage in the three-kuri Rajput 'caste', the framework of intra-caste ritual hierarchy is by no means self-evident. Correspondingly, explanations of socio-political organization in terms of ritual hierarchy, or inclusion and exclusion (for example, caste segmentation), do not work automatically, that is, outside time. These social facts demand that analysis take a different direction. The internal dynamics of lineage organization bears a structural relationship to its external political function. In the case of Bundela lineages, during the period of their expansion, the organizational framework of their external political functioning is dispersed clanship.

The political implication of this dispersed clanship are better understood by specifying the internal and external functioning of patrilineages in clans allied to them by marital and martial bonds during the capture of Garhkundar. The clans directly involved are the Panwar and the Dhandhera, but the Chauhan, the Tonwar, and other clans belonging to the category of the 'thirty-six-kuri Rajput' also enter the picture. Punyapal, to whom Sohanpal gave his daughter in marriage, belonged to a Panwar patrilineage in Gwalior. The Panwar of Gwalior enjoyed a high rank among the regional Rajputs, taking brides from the eastern Chauhan dominants and the Tonwar rulers. Punyapal's father had received the appanage of Panwaya in dowry from the Tonwar ruler of

Gwalior, whose daughter he had married. We have no comparable data for appanages and offices held by the affines of Bundela rulers at Mahoni. From the fact that during this period the Bundela are constantly shifting their capitals southwards, it is possible to speculate that the quest of Bundela heroes, of 'territory for kingdom', pervades the entire legendary phase culminating only in the founding of their first dynastic capital at Orchha in *c.* AD 1531. With their victory at Garhkundar, however, we begin to hear about appanages and offices granted by Bundela rulers to their affines. In developmental terms, the Bundelas at this juncture enter the cycle of kingdom-formation in which the Tonwars of Gwalior had already attained maturity.

The story of Punyapal Panwar strikingly reveals the link between marital and political alliance in the Rajput cycle of kingdom formation. At the same time it throws up certain geopolitically conditioned contrasts between the social organization of dominance between the 'three-kuri Rajput'(the eastern division) and the 'thirty-six-kuri Rajput' (the western division). According to a legend, Punyapal Panwar had a horse which his uncle (mother's brother) coveted. This horse he agreed to give to his uncle in exchange for a beautiful dancing-girl. On the appointed day he went to his uncle's house mounted on the horse. As he rode up he saw the dancing-girl standing among the people surrounding his uncle. Without waiting to make a salutation even, Punyapal rode up to the girl, swung her onto his saddle, and, followed by his people, galloped home. Insulted, his uncle, it is said, persuaded all the Rajputs to have nothing to do with Punyapal's family.

The broken exchange between the mother's brother (the Tonwar ruler) and the sister's son (the Panwar 'vassal') expresses a political conflict in the kin-feudated Rajput polity of Gwalior. In Rajput legends of Bundelkhand, the gift of a concubine's daughter frequently symbolized the value given in exchange by the ruler to a political ally. Translated into quasi-jural terms, the gifted woman represented some kind of subordinate territorial rights granted to an ally by the ruler. The horse, on the other hand, represented the oath of martial fealty by a Rajput 'vassal' (*jagirdar*) to his politically superior kinsman. An exchange that involved a Rajput's parting with his favourite horse might seal a political alliance between kinsmen or ritual kinsmen; such a transaction did not extend to non-kin, even though the party proposing the transaction was the paramount ruler himself.

According to the legend, as a consequence of the broken exchange, not only the Tonwar, but also other Rajput clans that had marital and political links with the Panwar, stopped inter-dining and intermarrying with the 'family' of Punyapal Panwar. Unlike the Bundela, this exclusion applies only to the Panwar patrilineage of Panwaya; the western Panwar patrilineages (such as of Malwa) continued to intermarry with the 'thirty-six-kuri Rajput'. Punyapal Panwar of Panwaya, the head of the excluded family, married the daughter of Sohanpal Bundela, who gave him the appanage of Karera in dowry. Thus included among the eastern or Bundelkhandi 'three-kuri Rajput', Punyapal Panwar becomes the apical ancestor for localized segments of Panwar patrilineage of Bundelkhand. In political terms, Punyapal replicates the career of his father; he establishes the same kind of political-cum-affinal link with Sohanpal Bundela as his father did with the Tonwar ruler of Gwalior.

In relation to the exogamous Panwar, then, the process of exclusion (of a section from the 'thirty-six-kuri') is marked by asymmetry of ritual status, but that of inclusion (of a section into the 'three-kuri') is characterized by the symmetry of political forms. The former process lends itself to conceptualization, both by the observer and the observed, as an occurrence in mythical time. The latter process is remembered in legends of territorial expansion and political incorporation.

Just as Panwar and Tonwar constituted a special alliance in the regional set of intermarrying Rajput before the Bundela capture of Garhkundar, so also the Dhandhera and Chauhan are depicted as special allies. The Dhandhera claim to be the descendants of Dhandhu, an officer in the army of Prithviraja Chauhan. This is the martial link. The marital link with the Chauhan can be inferred from the description of Mukutman Chauhan, master of an appanage of the Khangar of Garhkundar, as 'a descendant of Dhandhera deva ... which probably means that he was Dhandhera on his mother's side.' Mukutman Chauhan has also been depicted as *matul* (classificatory mother's brother) of Sohanpal Bundela. He chose to remain neutral in the quarrel between the Bundela brothers. It is likely that Sohanpal's avuncular relationship with Mukutman derived from 'linked affinity' between the regional Bundela, Dhandhera, and Chauhan patrilineages. Insufficient information is available on the local identification of intermarrying lineages, but there is enough to indicate that the Dhandhera only *gave* their daughters to the Chauhan and Bundela.

Does this suggest the ranking of these intermarrying patrilineages in a hypergamous pattern? [...] The lack of internal status gradations regulated by hypergamy in these branches indicates the strength of clanship among them.

The clanship of the Mahoni Bundela, which provided leadership for the capture of Garhkundar, clearly constitutes the pivot for the political incorporation of their martial and marital allies into the 'three-kuri Rajput' division. Unlike their Panwar and Dhandhera allies, the principle of Bundela clanship emerges untrammelled by any claims to a previous connection with the clan-caste configuration of the 'thirty-six-kuri Rajput' division. As constituted in the ideology and traditional history of Bundelkhand, the 'three-kuri Rajput' division has shown no tendency for internal hierarchical segmentation. The western Rajput tendency to transform the exogamous clan into caste, converts in the east into territorial expansion and political consolidation by kin-feudated kingdom formation.

It is vital to distinguish between the political function of clanship and the ritual function of caste (*jati*) as an idiom of hierarchical status distinctions. The typification of hypergamy as characteristically 'Rajput' in Indian sociological literature rests on a confusion between these two functions. It will not do to simply state that the ritual function of jati subsumes the political function of clan. What I am contending in the context of Bundelkhand is the absence of a necessary and sufficient interdependence between the attribution of ritual status by jati segment-ation and the processes of political power which in the cases of the 'three-kuri Rajput' category, developed, changed, and atrophied by the principle of clanship. The reason why a distinction has not been main-tained between the two functions and why, in discussions of Rajput hypergamy, the political functions of descent have been reduced to manifestations of ritual status hierarchy is not hard to seek. The cul-tural premise, 'Rajput hypergamy par excellence', is based on one variant of the conscious model, that provided by the western-Rajput division, which has so far been studied to the exclusion of other regional modalities.

[...] A more serious deficiency in Indian sociological literature emanates from the elaboration of an 'unconscious' model from one variant of the conscious model. The 'truth' of this partly observer, partly observed model of hypergamy as an entailment of hierarchy is beyond doubt, but the model takes account only of mythical time. To the extent that historical time is excluded from it, a simplified equation between hierarchy, caste segmentation, and hypergamy of the indigenous ruling groups hinders, rather than helps, the perception of key variables in the social organization of dominance. This, in any case, holds good for the Bundelkhand region during the pre-British period. I seek to do more than just putting the historical record straight. It would seem that the residue of institutionalized conflict in nineteenth-century central India leading up to the currently publicized contemporary menace of 'dacoity' (brigandage) in Gwalior and Bundelkhand cannot be under-stood without restoring to their legitimate place the ideology and processes of clanship in the traditional ruling groups.

THE CLANSHIP OF THE RULING GROUP

We can see how the regional Rajput ideology of kingship contributes to kingdom formation by transforming the Bundela martial alliance with the Panwar and Dhandhera into a marital alliance. The symbolic equivalence of 'territory for kingdom' with the female principle, as contained in the legend of Bundela origin, is conducive to the formation of a territorial state based on a confederation of three Rajput clans that exchange women. For the dynastic and dominance phases of the Bundela past there is much evidence to suggest that the form of their polity was defined by processes of kin (including affinal) dispersal and merger. The legendary phase enables us to view these processes delimited by the symbolic constraints of exogamy and alliance as aspects of the ideology of clanship in the ruling group.

Clearly the principle of clan exogamy alone is insufficient to explain all the available facts of political and affinal incorporation involved in Bundela expansion and kingdom formation. Why should the connubial league of the ruling group be confined to three 'Rajput' clans? What prevented the Bundela from intermarrying with the non-Rajput Khangar, as amateur anthropologist-historians speculate they actually did? The answer would seem to lie in the operation of the ideology of legitimate rule derived from the attributional category of Kshatriya. Indigenous sources consistently oppose the Kshatriya Bundela and other 'Rajput' clans to the Khangar as non-Kshatriya. As the myth of royal origin specifies, the appurtenances of legitimate rule belong only to those who are born Kshatriya. Nevertheless, as noted earlier, the same myth also sacralizes territory. It serves as a cover for the uncertain possession of actual territory by the 'kingly-sons'. Now, the insertion of the territorial equation into the attributional category, Kshatriya, is manipulated by the notion of royal clanship. In accordance with the rule of royal-clan exogamy, a Kshatriya clan might give and take daughters (or have political agreements over territory) with the other Kshatriya clans, but not with the non-Kshatriya. Hence the absolute refusal of Sohanpal Bundela to have connubial and commensal relations with the Khangar.

In relation to the vanquished Khangar, the Bundelas' Kshatriya role, as rulers protecting 'territory-cum-people', is narrated in an oral version of the legend of Garhkundar:

Maharaja Sonhanpal led an expedition to Garhkundar and killed all the Khangar men who had gathered in the fort. He spared their women, since it is forbidden for the kshatriya to kill women. One Khangar woman hurled her new-born son at

Sohanpal's feet and begged for mercy. Her wish was granted and the baby was spared. But from then on it became the bounden duty of the Khangar to be the 'shoe-bearing servants' (*naquib*) of Bundela rulers [narrative from Sendpa village].

The descendants of the Khangar boy were incorporated into Bundela polity. They functioned under the general title of *khasbardar* as aides-de-camps to Bundela rulers. The Khangar tradition [...] corroborates the story of their political incorporation as khasbardar. [...] Furthermore, the nature of this conflict between the Kshatriya and non-Kshatriya is underscored by the symbolic significance of a set of restrictions imposed on the Khangar by the Bundela victors. The Khangars were not permitted (1) to wear red turbans; (2) to touch *kathris* (swords); (3) to drink liquor; (4) to put red lead on their hair-parting; (5) to eat *rotis* (baked bread) sold in public; (6) to eat *kachchi* (boiled food) touched by a Kshatriya, Vaishya, or Shudra. These restrictions cannot be understood simply as defining a low ritual status for the Khangar in the caste hierarchy; they are precise ritual diacritics confirming the loss of political power and pretensions to royal prerogatives now legitimately wrested from the Khangar by the victorious Bundela as Kshatriya. Again the system of social stratification of the ruling groups of the 'three-kuri Rajput' category seems supported by rituals which do not fit neatly into a theory of caste-segmentation operating in mythical time. They appear rather as creations conjoint with political developments in historical time. [...]

CONCLUSION

An unfortunate consequence of using caste as a blanket term for all hierarchical status distinctions has been to obliterate the perception of other contextually meaningful schemes of classifying political and social relations. Thus if we do not freeze the ruling groups' descent in a caste framework but examine it in the context of the expansion of indigenous rule, we can discern at least three bases of political relations between the ruling groups and their allies in Bundelkhand: intermarriage (Bundela–Panwar–Dhandhera), pseudo-agnation (Bundela–Dauwa), and dispensation (Bundela–Khangar).

In the phase of kingdom formation in Bundelkhand, unilineal descent was significant as the basis of group formation, in the assignment of status, and struggles for power. The primary identities of the ruling group and of its allies and adversaries were based on clanship rather than on caste as generally understood in north Indian ethnography. Among the 'three-kuri Rajput' of eastern Bundelkhand, clan exogamy

combined with circulating connubium of the three clans provided the
principle for inclusion and exclusion.

[...] At a more general level, I have to reverse the hypothesis of
Sanskritization to understand the dynamics of political processes in
pre-industrial middle India as exemplified by the case at hand. Far
from political power being converted into jati status to become legitimate and meaningful, the expansion of Bundela rule shows that under
certain geopolitical conditions throughout middle India, exclusion
from a confirmed jati status was the means of gaining power and creating
a new framework of statuses and offices.

Reading Time*

ISHITA BANERJEE-DUBE

Kalikala riti dekhi made bhiti hrudaya channa katara
Thaya heunahin panchabhuta atma Sriguru karibe para

[The ways of *kaliyuga* make the heart tremble—terror holds sway
My soul of five elements finds no peace—Sriguru will show the way]

The opening couplet of *Bhima Bhoi Malika ba Padmakalpa*, an early twentieth-century Oriya text published as late as 1971, authoritatively asserts the lingering presence of the idea of *kaliyuga*, the era of evil. In the classical conception of time in Hinduism, kaliyuga constitutes the last of the four progressively deteriorating epochs that complete the time cycle before a return to the pristine *satya/kreta* age. Kaliyuga has enjoyed great prominence in Brahminical literature since the time of the early Puranas. General disorder characterizes the era: the different castes do not perform their assigned functions, rituals are disregarded, heretical sects prevail, and non-Brahmin and foreign rulers reign. *Dharma* (right ritual and conduct, often conceived as a superior being personifying these qualities), who measured four feet in *satyayuga* (the age of truth) at the beginning of the universe, is reduced to just one

* Originally published in *Studies in History*, 19 (1), 2003, pp. 1–17, Sage Publications, as 'Reading Time: Texts and Pasts in Colonial Eastern India'. In the present version, all notes and references have been deleted. For the complete text, see the original version.

foot in kaliyuga. Kaliyuga is finally brought to an end by the tenth and final incarnation of Vishnu who re-establishes *satya* dharma (true faith). This last incarnation is yet to appear; kaliyuga continues its long sway. It is a ready source of an appropriable past that lives on and gives meaning to the present. Through an analysis of *Bhima Bhoi Malika*, this chapter underscores the significance of the persistence of kaliyuga in popular time reckoning. It highlights the multiplicity of meanings the idea of kaliyuga generates and the myriad uses to which it is put. Kaliyuga occasions novel understandings of the past that make the present meaningful and envisage the future. These perceptions often find expression in a diverse range of texts that appear and circulate in different regions at different times.

Bhima Bhoi Malika ba Padmakalpa forms a part of a particular genre of literature of Orissa: the *malikas*. Cast in the mode of the Puranas, malikas are apocryphal texts that deal with the theme of kaliyuga, and prophesy its dissolution through the appearance of a redeemer and the establishment of true faith. A close reading of malikas reveals the changing dimensions of the recurrent reference to Kali that form the basis for varied understandings and multiple appropriations of these texts. These appropriations, again, give the contents of the malikas specific slants at particular times. This amenability to manifold render-ings accounts for the continued popularity of the malikas. They serve as vehicles through which changing notions of time and history, good and evil, the enemy and the saviour find expression, and cyclical time and linear historical time exist in perfect harmony to portray a glorious past and a difficult present that pave the way for a promising future. In the malikas, mythical and legendary heroes join hands with ordinary human beings to fight the evil forces of Kali, who often embody 'real' enemies.

'Reading' lies at the heart of the numerous appropriations of the malikas. I do not use 'reading' here in the narrow sense of its mech-anics—of the decoding of written words into spoken words—but as an inventive and creative exercise, a process of understanding meaning that often governs the social uses to which it is put. Indeed, in India, where traditions of reading aloud and recitation of texts in a collectivity still continue, understanding and appropriation inhere in the very act of reading. This kind of reading presupposes a 'pre-knowledge' of the content of the text to be read out and expects the reader to be in a proper frame of mind for the 'reading', factors that facilitate both understanding and appropriation. The imaginative and creative uses of reading, in turn, stem from the very nature of the texts whose contents are flexible.

The Puranas provide the classical example of texts of this genre. Proclaimed as oral 'texts' uttered originally by Brahma, spoken by Vyasa, and narrated by his several disciples, the written versions of the Puranas lack any reference to a definite author. Their stories have been told and retold, and new materials added. While this underlines the popularity of the Puranas, these texts have not found much favour with both scholars of Sanskrit and religious reformers, who have bemoaned their lack of authenticity and decried their role in promoting 'superstition'. At the same time, they have been commended as important historical and cultural documents, and as representing the assimilative powers of Hinduism.

My purpose is not to attempt an assessment of the Puranas. Rather, I wish to highlight the interesting issues that these texts raise. The 'performers' of Puranas emphasize the orality of the texts. This orality, however, is totally different from the European notion of orality, which is, in most cases, equated with illiteracy. The performers of the Puranas are literate. They are proud of their knowledge of grammar and of their ability to correctly recite texts that were initially uttered. Indeed, they often carry written versions of the texts to display their skills in deciphering the written, although they place greater stress on the spoken. 'Literate thinking' and 'literacy' thus form integral parts of this oral tradition. Moreover, oral tradition comes out as both rigid and flexible in that emphasis is placed on 'correct' renderings, while texts are 'composed' through recitations. The binary division between the oral and written loses its meaning and viability.

The malikas of Orissa closely follow the Puranas. While these texts are ascribed to authors, their contents narrate dialogues between divinities regarding the future of the cosmos. If at all, the authors make short appearances to emphasize the significance of the prophecies. This absence of the strong imprint of a definite author and the general nature of the prophecies facilitate different readings of the malikas. This is reinforced by the recurrence of the theme of kaliyuga that serves to constitute a 'pre-knowledge' that is easily evoked during reading or listening. This pre-knowledge does not only help in the comprehension of what is read; it engenders the creation and construction of an entire range of new texts in times of difficulty, which are then ascribed to acclaimed 'authors'. As we will see later in this chapter, the process of composition of malikas underscores the interactive relation between the spoken and the written, in which the domains of 'orality' and writing, the reader and the author, get fused. In this form of reading what is learnt is so inextricably bound to what is understood that knowledge gets transformed in the very act of transmission.

Malikas have constituted an important part of Oriya literary tradition since the sixteenth century. Malikas are widely held to be creations of the *Panchasakhas*, Five Friends—Achyutananda Das, Balaram Das, Jagannath Das, Ananta Das and Yasovanta Das—all eminent medieval mystics. This belief grants credibility and legitimacy to the prophecies of the malikas, while the ascription of woes to the evil kaliyuga, the assurance of an eventual dissolution of sufferings and the ultimate triumph of good over evil explain the continued presence and popularity of these texts. Their success lies in their capacity to transform and metamorphose complex theological principles and esoteric religious ideas into an idiom grounded in the familiar and in everyday life through the invocation of kaliyuga. At the same time, as stated before, the overwhelming and constant presence of kaliyuga, an inherently evil era whose constituent elements can vary, and the vague and general nature of the prophecies make the malikas responsive to multiple workings and reworkings. This process generates new readings and creates new 'texts' as it helps communities in distress to negotiate and cope with situations of difficulty, and emerging religious sects to establish themselves.

Mahima Dharma, of which Bhima Bhoi was a key adherent, was initiated by Mahima Swami in the 1860s in Orissa. It advocated a belief in an all-pervasive, formless, indescribable Absolute who had created the world out of his *mahima* (radiance/glory). The Absolute was accessible to all through *bhakti*, devotion. Members of all castes could be initiated into the sect: but its constituency lay primarily among low-caste untouchable and tribal groups, particularly in the *garhjats*, the tributary states under Oriya rulers. The new faith discarded the deities of the Hindu pantheon, did away with the Brahmin's role as the mediator between god and human beings, and disregarded rules of caste and commensality. It questioned thereby the close connections between divine, ritual, and social hierarchies, and challenged the authority of the king and the Brahmin by allowing renouncers of the faith to accept food from all except the households of kings and Brahmins. This challenge to power exercised through and encoded within religion made Mahima Swami appear as a genuine benefactor to those groups of Orissa whose subordination had been secured through the close intermeshing of religion and power. He became deified in his lifetime as the incarnation of the Absolute he spoke about.

Several factors contributed to Mahima Swami's deification; the use of and belief in a malika by his followers played a crucial role. The malika served a dual purpose: trust in its prophecy, believed to have been made by one of the five medieval mystics, served to highlight the inevitability of the appearance of an *avatar* (incarnation) and the founding of true faith by him. It also established Mahima Swami as that avatar and Mahima Dharma as the *satya dharma* that was to bring kaliyuga to an end. Official reports on Mahima Dharma drawn up in the 1880s mention the followers of the sect to be in possession of a book of predictions. This book treated 'the incarnation of Alakh in the shape of Mahima Swami to save the world from the burden of sin and to pave the way towards salvation.' In the first decade of the twentieth century, N.N. Vasu, a scholar serving in an official capacity in the feudatory state of Mayurbhanj, chanced upon *Yasomati Malika*. Vasu based his description of Mahima Dharma primarily on *Yasomati Malika*, which he declared to be one of the major scriptures of the sect. In the 1930s, the works of Biswanath Baba, a leading renouncer of the sect, quoted extensively from not one but several malikas and other works of the Panchasakhas to identify Mahima Swami with '*prabuddha narayan*' (the enlightened one) and '*iswar purush*' (god personified).

Mahima Dharma suffered a setback after the death of Mahima Swami. Belief in his divinity had become so strong that his death shocked his followers. The crisis was aggravated by the fact that Mahima Swami had made no arrangements for the continuation of the faith after his death. He had not nominated a successor. He had not allowed permanent structures to be built, nor acquired any property during his lifetime. He had initiated *gruhi*s (lay disciples) and *sanyasi*s (renouncers) into his faith. He differentiated two groups of ascetics by giving *balkal* (bark of the *kumbhi* tree) to some and *kaupin* (waistcloth) to others, but he did not specify the relative position of the two orders. Mahima Swami had also not left any written records of his own. Instead, he had endowed Bhima Bhoi, a blind tribal of western Orissa with the gift of poetry, and left it to him to spread the message of Mahima Dharma through *stuti*s, *janan*s, and *bhajan*s (prayers in praise of the Lord). Organization became crucial to the survival of the faith after the death of the founder. The ascetics convened a meeting of followers at Joranda in Dhenkanal, where Mahima Swami had come to reside before his death. The decision to construct a memorial for the Guru at Joranda was taken at this meeting. Bhima Bhoi, however, dissociated himself from the sanyasis at Joranda, set up his own *ashram* at Khaliapali near Sonepur, and started to initiate new followers into Mahima Dharma.

From the 1870s till his death in the mid-1890s, Bhima Bhoi was a key player in the propagation of the faith in western Orissa. His stutis, janans, and bhajans were recited and sung at religious gatherings, and the message of the Absolute spread. In fact, in this part of Orissa, Bhima Bhoi came to rival and finally adopt the role of Mahima Swami. The

deep devotion of his disciples cemented the gap between the master
and the devotee; in their eyes the *bhakta* (disciple) became *bhagaban*
(god). Legends and stories began to gather around Bhima Bhoi, stories
that drew directly from the legends about Mahima Swami and often
conflated the identities of the two. The malikas that had established
Mahima Swami as the incarnation of the Absolute now identified
Bhima Bhoi as his divine devotee. Indeed, N.N. Vasu, who wrote his
account of Mahima Dharma 'only ten years' after Bhima Bhoi died,
categorically identified Bhima Bhoi as the leader of the sect. He further
claimed that Bhima Bhoi's sons were in possession of the *gadi* (seat/
headquarters of Mahima Dharma) 'at Juranda near the Dhenkanl state',
where Bhima Bhoi 'used to sit'. The feudatory state of Mayurbhanj was
the site of Vasu's excavations and explorations. This is where he found
Yasomati Malika and *Alekh Leela*, and spoke to renouncers and lay
followers of Mahima Dharma. His account reveals the remarkable
importance acquired by Bhima Bhoi after the death of Mahima Swami,
an importance that baffled followers into jumbling the identities of
Mahima Swami and Bhima Bhoi, the guru (preceptor) and the *sishya*
(disciple). Indeed, Vasu claims, on the basis of *Yasomati Malika*, that the
'revival of Buddhism in the name of Mahima Dharma took place in
the twenty-first year of the reign of Divya-Simha, late King of Puri, that
is in 1875.' 1875 is when Mahima Swami 'left his mortal remains'. By
the first decade of the twentieth century then, Mahima Swami had
become the incarnation whose only purpose in coming down to earth
was to bless the blind Bhima Bhoi with 'the eye of knowledge'. The task
of propagation of true faith was left entirely to Bhima Bhoi. And that
Bhima Bhoi had achieved sensational success in his task was evident
in the way his name and works had spread.

Geographically Mayurbhanj is located at the northeastern part of the
province of Orissa, virtually at the other end from the Sonepur region
in the west where Bhima Bhoi lived and preached. It is also far from
Joranda in Dhenkanal, which probably accounts for Vasu's ignorance
of what was happening there. But his claim that Bhima Bhoi's sons
were at the helm of affairs in Joranda reflects the mixed-up nature in
which the message of Mahima Swami had spread through Bhima Bhoi's
creations. Ambiguity inhered in the very way Bhima Bhoi's works came
into being. The blind poet is said to have uttered his inspired creations,
which were then written down by scribes devoted to him. Thereafter,
they were sung and recited by large groups of devotees and the message
of the true faith spread. Collective recitation and singing rather than
individual, private reading, helped the adherents of Mahima Dharma,
a vast majority of whom were non-literate, to gain knowledge of the

'scriptures' of Mahima Dharma. This flux and fluidity, in turn, set in
motion novel interpretations of Bhima Bhoi's works and teachings,
and, from the early years of the twentieth century, spurred the composition of new texts, notably malikas in the name of Bhima Bhoi.

Before analysing the contents of one such malika, let me give a brief
idea of the works and ideas of Bhima Bhoi. The works of Bhima Bhoi
reflect the rich heritage of religious traditions that flourished in Orissa:
they display elements of Hinduism, Buddhism, *tantra*, mysticism, and
bhakti. Apart from speaking of a formless, indescribable Absolute, who
was accessible to all through devotion, as the only object of worship,
Bhima Bhoi decried rituals and the practice of going on pilgrimages.
All pilgrim sites, he asserted, were located in the body; the body (*pinda*)
was a replica of the universe (*brahmanda*). These ideas are neither novel
nor original, what is new is their use and significance in the context of
late-nineteenth century Orissa. However, the currency of these ideas
before Bhima Bhoi has led discussions of his works in the direction of
an obsession to hunt for possible ideological lineages and genealogies.
The details are not pertinent here. I need only to outline the links with
the writings of the Panchasakhas, to whose tradition Bhima Bhoi's
works owe their largest debt. This also possibly explains the creation of
malikas in Bhima Bhoi's name.

The Panchasakhas have been described as the exponents of a
sixteenth-century 'revival' of Vaishnavism in Orissa. Although they were
disciples of Sri Chaitanya, in their writings they advocated a theology
distinct from Chaitanya's Gaudiya Vaishnavism. After his arrival in
Puri, Chaitanya had identified Sri Krishna/Vishnu with Jagannath, the
Lord of the Universe and the state deity of Orissa for centuries. Jagannath
symbolized the personification of the Supreme Being, who is 'full of all
powers', the 'personal Godhead manifested in the transcendental plane'.
The Panchasakhas also accepted Jagannath as their supreme lord, but
they conceived of him as the ultimate reality who is *nirakar* (formless)
and *sunya* (void). This sunya was not the nothingness of Buddhism, but
the highest, indescribable (*alekh*) Absolute, whose glory (mahima) was
to be preached. The Five Friends combined *saguni* and *nirguni* traditions in conceptualizing the Lord, and rendered this high philosophy
accessible by declaring that Sunya Brahma himself will become incarnate to spread the message of the Supreme Being. Knowledge of the
Brahman will destroy ignorance, and save humanity from the clutches
of the evil Kali. The works of Bhima Bhoi not only speak of the
indescribable Absolute, they throb with the anguished cries of the
poet to his Lord to save him and his fellow beings from the sufferings
of kaliyuga.

In her search for the genealogy of Mahima Dharma, Anncharlott Eschmann came upon three doctrines that, according to her, Bhima Bhoi had taken directly from the Panchasakhas. These were: 'the worship of the sunya, the theory of Pinda Brahmanda, and the idea of a future redeemer who will come and openly establish what is for the time being a secret docrine.' This future redeemer, who according to the Vaishnava tradition is Kalki, the last avatar of Vishnu, 'becomes Niranjana or Sunya Brahman or Adi Jagannatha in the literature of Oriya Vaishnavism.'

My purpose in outlining the connections between the works of Bhima Bhoi and the medieval mystics has not been to place Bhima Bhoi in a literary tradition. Rather, I stress the continued presence over centuries of the idea of kaliyuga, and of the appearance of the divine in a human form to destroy Kali, in order to underscore the existence of a common stock of 'knowledge' (a pre-knowledge in Roger Chartier's terms), a social 'memory', and a live tradition that unites the past, present, and future into a composite whole and restructures the past as a 'living precedent' of the present. In such a situation, the past, a usable and negotiable resource, is easily drawn upon at different times and in distinct contexts to express the anxieties and uncertainties of the present, and to point to a way of dealing with them.

Let us return to the story of Mahima Dharma. The faith struggled for survival after the death of the founder. Bhima Bhoi, who played a key role in the propagation of Mahima Dharma after Mahima Swami, was shunned by the renouncers who were in command at Joranda, which gradually grew into the gadi, the seat (headquarters) of the sect. These sanyasis fought amongst themselves over the interpretation of the Guru's teachings and for control over the memorial of Mahima Swami. Disagreements centred on the relative position of the two groups of renouncers: the Balkaldharis, wearers of the bark of the kumbhi tree, and Kaupindharis, wearers of waistcloth. Matters came to a head in the early 1920s when a Balkaldhari sanyasi granted balkal to a few Kaupindharis, emphasizing thereby the higher position of the wearers of balkal. Disagreements turned to dissension and the ascetics became entangled in a never-ending struggle that led to the intervention of the law courts and effected a final breach between the two groups.

As the leaders fought, the lay disciples strove to grapple with the situation, to find ways of holding fast to their faith. Soon after Mahima Swami's death, in 1881, a small group of men and women from a village in western Orissa, inspired by a divine command communicated through a dream, marched to Puri to take out the images of Jagannath, his brother, and sister from the temple and to burn them. This effort to pave the way for the spread of the 'true faith' did not succeed; but memories of the incident lingered in rhymes and tales in western Orissa. Mahima Dharma survived the death of Mahima Swami. But now crisis came in the shape of division among the adherents. At this stage, Bhima Bhoi's malikas made their appearance. They prophesied the reappearance of Mahima Swami in the new incarnation of a warrior. He was to lead the battle against the forces of Kali and cause their destruction.

Bhima Bhoi Malika ba Padmakalpa published by the Cuttack Dharma Grantha Store in 1971 is widely accepted by the followers as a creation of Bhima Bhoi. It has, however, not been given a place in *Bhima Bhoi Granthabali* (collected works of Bhima Bhoi), published by the same store, as the sanyasis of Mahima Dharma in charge at Joranda doubt its 'authenticity'. *Padmakalpa* was preceded by another short *malika* of Bhima Bhoi, which expressed Bhima Bhoi's anguish and confusion at the disappearance of the preceptor. How could the Lord forget his devotees and leave them? What were the bhaktas to do? Whose commands were they to follow? Surely the Lord could not abandon his followers. He was to come back again, in the form of Kalki, the warrior, destroy kaliyuga, and end the sufferings of the true devotees for all time to come. This belief is given greater finesse and flourish in *Padmakalpa*.

True to the tradition of the malikas, the text dwells on the miseries engendered by the evil era, foresees its destruction through a devastating war led by an avatar, and describes the beginning of satyayuga following the establishment of satya dharma. The tract consists of thirty-seven chapters, each made up of a varying number of *padas* (verses). The padas are two-line and three-line verses in which the number of words varies significantly. As in other malikas, the text is composed in the form of a dialogue, in this case between Anadi (the eternal one) and Adi (*mata*), mother of the world, who is also called Sati. It is to satisfy Adi and to clear away her doubts that the Absolute unravels the mysteries of his *leela* (divine play) and the events of kaliyuga. Bhima Bhoi figures as the narrator of this dialogue. From time to time, he interjects his own comments, addressing the reader directly. The text is composed in a language of time and timelessness. There is a constant change of tense as the dialogue moves back and forth between what has happened, what is happening, and what will happen.

The text opens with Bhima Bhoi expressing his fear and helplessness at being surrounded by the evil ways of Kali and calling upon Sri Guru (the master), at whose feet he has taken shelter, to save him. This is followed by an account of kaliyuga which has a long life of four hundred and thirty-two thousand years and which, in the end, gets destroyed by

its own sins. But before its destruction, the evil ways of the era and the
sinful deeds of human beings living in it cause mother earth to suffer
immensely, prompting her to send anguished cries of help to the Lord.
The injustice of kings and Brahmins disgusts Jagannath so much that
he leaves his abode to dwell in secret for sixteen thousand years.

The activities of several dynasties of rulers form an integral part of
the account. The *soma* (lunar) dynasty reigns over the world at the
beginning of the age; the British, who follow the Gurkhas and Turks,
come to power toward the end of the era. All rulers of this age are
oppressive. There is, however, a progressive degeneration in the nature
of the rulers and in the condition of the earth. Hence the British are the
worst. Their duplicity makes them particularly dangerous: with an
outward show of speaking the truth they secretly oppress their subjects
and destroy them gradually but thoroughly, in the manner of white
ants destroying wood. This wile goes hand in hand with their dirty
habits—they eat the flesh of cows and buffaloes and drink liquor
everyday. Is it surprising that they do not wash themselves after
defecating?

Carisa panchanabe barasa rajuta karibe se adhikara
Satya kali tunde dandiba jenhe paidara nira

[For 495 years will they be the rulers
Like coconut water acting on plants they will utter truths and be secret oppressors]

Uikita jenhe mukhejal thai kasthaku kariba lina
*Temanta prai*re paraja kulaku karibe se chinnabhinna*

[Like white ants that survive on wood and eat through it gradually,
They will bring about the ruin of subjects completely]

Prakriti karina na ghenibe nira mlechha acarana kari
Garu chagal je mahisa madira ahar se nityekari

[Like extreme outcastes they will not use water after attending to nature's call
Every day will they eat cows, goats, buffaloes, and drink alcohol]

Exploitation by these *mlechhas* (extreme outcastes) robs *prithvi devi*
(mother earth) of her beauty and compels Lakshmi (goddess of wealth
and prosperity) to seek shelter in *patal* (the nether world). Scarcity is a
constant feature; floods, droughts, and famines regular happenings.

Sinfulness comes to characterize humanity in general. Brahmins
give up the study of the Vedas, start eating flesh, cohabit with other
men's wives, forget the *gayatri mantra* and adopt the tantric *garedi mantra*.
Members of other castes follow suit: caste distinctions disappear, leading
to a situation of anarchy and chaos. Each man cheats the other and

acquires wealth through lies. Even true devotees waver. They fail to recognize the redeemer, the Brahma avatar (incarnation of the Absolute), when he appears and refuse to pay heed to his precepts. Under the influence of Kali they behave like 'a host of blind men.' The Guru leaves the earth. Kaliyuga holds sway. Fear and despair prompt the gods to come together and pray to the Absolute in a gesture of abject surrender. In response to their prayers Anadi comes to *yogaghara* (a place for meditation), sends his devotees to earth, compels *Brahmarshis*, *Rajarshis*, and *Devarshis* (saints who have attained self-realization) to sit in meditation, and finally saves the earth by destroying Kali, lighting the Brahma *dhuni* (eternal flame), and establishing true faith.

A fierce battle has to be fought and great sufferings undergone before Kali is annihilated. Bhima trembles and his heart fills with sorrow as he narrates the events of the future. Kalki will play the game of non-violence in the era of evil. He will be called Gandhi-Sankarsana. A bhakta called Madana Malabya will always be with Gandhi. Motilal Nehru, a very powerful man, will be born in the Chudanga dynasty. Narendra Natha (Vivekananda?), who had been imprisoned in *dwaparayuga* (the era that immediately preceeds Kali), will come and join these men and will be imprisoned again. Some other bhaktas, both men and women, will start an agitation. They will disobey the king and preach truth. A river of blood will flow during the seventh and eighth years of the reign of Ram Chandra Dev. Sunya Guru will be fighting then, flying his sunya *bana* (flag).

This agitation is a part of the war that paves the way for the beginning of a novel world and a new era by rooting out evil and effecting a complete break with the past. References to the war abound in the text, references which by virtue of their frequency, magnitude, and detail create an intimidating picture of anarchy, destruction, devastation, and death.

The description is neither clear nor consistent. At times it approximates to a fight between Gandhi and his followers on the one hand and the British on the other, at times it assumes the massive proportions of the 'Kuruksetra' war of kaliyuga. An uncertainty lingers. Is there one war or several battles? At the same time, the uncertainty adds to the picture of anarchy. The confusion in narration becomes a tool in the generation of the picture of total chaos, where the several descriptions function as building blocks to construct the whole.

The human form of Anadi leads the forces of truth against the forces of kaliyuga in the Kuruksetra war. In course of his dialogue with Adi, he declares with remarkable clarity that he will appear during the reign of Ram Chandra Dev, in the year 1941. He is Mahima Swami, Gandhi, and Kalki. His soldiers are many: the gods and goddesses, *nagantis*, *yogantis*, and *risis* (super humans and saints), the great heroes of the past, the present, and the future—Ramchandra and Hanuman, the five Pandava brothers, Gandhi and his followers, the followers of Anadi, troops from all over India and abroad. The forces of the evil age, which include the British, are powerful both in terms of numbers and the sophisticated arms and ammunition they command. It requires the combined strength of gods and men, of mythical, legendary, and historical figures, to overpower and destroy them.

The fierceness of the battle is difficult to convey in words. The earth trembles under the pressure of 700,000 marching soldiers, 400,000 horses, and a million elephants. The battle continues for twelve years and devastates the world thoroughly. Humanity faces destruction; countries disappear from the face of the earth.

Dvadasa barsa jana
Prithvi heba rana bhana
Ghodankara padaghate dharani nasa
Rana bhana hoibe nara
Desaman nasajiba bujha satvara

[For twelve years
will a battle rage on earth
The world will be devastated by the hooves of marching horses
Humanity will face destruction
Listen to this: nations will face annihilation]

Mughals come to rule again in the newly engendered world and are assisted by brave men from the families of Dhruba and Prahlada, the favoured devotees of Vishnu. People prosper under able rule, famines and scarcity are erased from memory. Anadi Brahma returns to his own abode, after establishing satya dharma on earth.

Padmakalpa is a richly flavoured concoction. It is a novel text that draws upon a tradition that goes back to the Puranas, and uses a language that is at once simple and esoteric. There is a remarkable similarity to the general motifs that characterize kaliyuga in the Puranas. Exploitative foreign rulers feature prominently in the description. At the same time, the analysis of their cunning and culpability is ingenious. It reveals a familiarity with the rhetoric of the nationalist movement that finds easy expression through the language of the everyday. British rulers are dangerous because they are deceptive; they rob their subjects secretly but steadily like white ants destroying wood. Their habits cannot but be strange and dirty; they form an integral part of the picture of the vile mlechha who is immensely powerful.

Such a strong enemy requires a mighty saviour. He is one and many at the same time, a combination of mythical and national leaders, legendary and real characters. He is Mahima Swami, Gandhi, and Kalki. This mix-up and inconsistency again displays a drawing upon of diverse 'traditions' that are understood, used, and combined in novel ways to churn out unique constructions. On the one hand, Mahima Swami's identification with Kalki, in establishing him as the divine incarnation who appeared on earth to root out Kali and bring back satya dharma, indicates the place he had secured for himself in the minds of his adherents. On the other, the prominence accorded to Gandhi is a good example of the hold of the 'Mahatma' in popular imagination in a region that was never in the forefront of the nationalist struggle. This combination of Puranic and nationalist ideas turns the war against kaliyuga into a battle against the British. Remarkably, the memory of the revolt of 1857 is portrayed in a return to the rule of the Mughals after the destruction of kaliyuga. The Mughals, however, have Dhruva and Prahlada—the devotees of Vishnu—as their lieutenants, symbolizing the harmony and amity that is to prevail at the end of the era of evil.

A similar coupling of the 'mythic' and the 'modern' characterizes the use of time in *Bhima Bhoi Malika*. This malika, as stated before, does not merely prophesy the future; it records what happened in the past to make sense of the present. And in this process the past is recreated as the present acquires new significance. The emotive and existential force of kaliyuga jumbles up events and epochs, eternal truths and temporal contingents, mythical characters and legendary heroes. Time is at once eternal, cyclical, and linear. The events occur during the reigns of the four kings of Puri—Mukunda Dev, Ram Chandra Dev, Birakishor Dev and Dibya Singha Dev. These are titles adopted by the kings of Puri when they ascend the throne. Temporally, then, their rule can cover centuries. At the same time, the year of appearance of Kalki is announced with remarkable precision. Moreover, Ram Chandra Dev's rule features prominently in the discussion along with the activities of Mahima Swami, Gandhi, and their followers. This seems to suggest that the text was composed in the early twentieth century when Ram Chandra Dev was the king of Puri.

This also points to the fact that the text must have been constructed after Bhima Bhoi's death or parts of it were interpolated. This accounts for the reluctance of Mahima Dharmi ascetics to include it in Bhima Bhoi's collected works. Indeed, the expressed concern with the disappearance of caste distinctions during the age of evil—another dominant motif of kaliyuga in the Puranas and the Mahabharata—

stands in direct contrast to Bhima Bhoi's ideas. Yet, the fact that the *Malika* is ascribed to Bhima Bhoi and its particular style of composition are proofs of Bhima Bhoi's enormous appeal to the adherents of Mahima Dharma, and of his rootedness in the rich popular tradition of Orissa, a tradition he drew upon and enriched. The text's resemblance to *Yasomati Malika* is striking. *Yasomati Malika* had announced the appearance of the incarnation in the shape of Mahima Swami and his divine disciple Bhima Bhoi. *Padmakalpa* announces the reappearance of the redeemer. The first appearance of Mahima Swami had not brought about the end of suffering. Under the influence of kaliyuga the bhaktas had failed to recognize the redeemer and had behaved like 'a host of blind men'. The immoral era had gained in strength. Its miseries continued. Evil rulers had become specially powerful and dangerous. The fight against them— not imagined but real in the early decades of the twentieth century— thus came to assume the proportion of the Mahabharata war. On another front, 'fake' *yogis* posing as the disciples of Mahima Swami had started to create dissension among the few faithful followers. The situation was ominous indeed. But all was not lost. In *Padmakalpa*, Bhima Bhoi calls upon the 'true' devotees to take shelter in the Guru without further delay. The Guru is to appear again. He will take on the form of a warrior to deal with the massively mighty Kali and his soldiers, the British. He will be Kalki, the tenth incarnation of Vishnu. Gandhi will be his foremost follower. He will lead the war along with numerous other followers. These 'true' bhaktas will be victorious in the battle against the wicked era. The corrupt ones will perish. Kaliyuga will stand completely annihilated; truth will prevail.

Padmakalpa is a remarkable text in several respects. Its very existence and the process of its coming into being interrogate and problematize durable dichotomies: myth and history, orality and writing (read literacy), the primitive and the modern. These dichotomies, it bears pointing out, have been questioned by a host of important studies within history and anthropology. Such work has exposed the arrogance that underlies the separation of myth from history, which makes history a feature and product of the 'modern'. This goes hand in hand with a reification of writing as a sign of the modern, something that marks out the 'west' from the rest of the world as superior and 'civilized'. By emphasizing that oral and written should be associated with altered social and institutional practices rather than with distinct mentalities, these studies have not only challenged dichotomies, they have underlined the myth-making that went into their construction.

And yet, more needs to be done. As Ajay Skaria has argued, it is not enough to have a 'new and inoffensively correct consensus' regarding the interpenetration of orality and literacy. The picture has to be muddied to an extent that the dichotomies lose meaning. *Padmakalpa* is a concrete illustration of the inefficacy of such binaries. The text is rooted in a 'religious' tradition. It constantly invokes kaliyuga symbolizing a use of mythic, cyclical time. At the same time it is written. And its construction draws upon both oral and written traditions. Indeed, *Padmakalpa* results from a fluid interaction of myth and history, orality and writing, and it gives rise to further fluidities. *Padmakalpa* provides a striking example of the surplus of meanings that reading and writing generate: it offers a rare insight into the ways texts are perceived and apprehended by the community of readers.

In a recent essay Sumit Sarkar has dealt with kaliyuga texts of late-nineteenth and early twentieth-century Bengal to explore the confused impact of innovations of colonial rule—clock time and print culture on the colonized, particularly the urban lower middle class. The kaliyuga texts, in Sarkar's opinion, are proofs that the changeover from cyclical Hindu time to linear 'western' time was neither 'total' nor 'painless'. While this is a valuable point to make, Sarkar admits in the end that except for a spectacular but apparently unconnected event in a village in Dacca in 1904, his exploration of the texts is constrained by the unavailability of evidence on how these texts were read and understood. Also, in a somewhat dismissive manner, Sarkar remarks that in general the message of the 'traditional' kaliyuga texts is one of resignation, since the evils were inevitable, and the apocalypse lay in a very distant future.

In *Padmakalpa* we have a 'traditional' kaliyuga text that speaks in a language of hope. It also allows an entry into the world of reading, hearing, understanding, and perception of texts by their 'interpretive community'. With an ease that bespeaks familiarity, *Padmakalpa* blends history and myth, cyclical and linear notions of time to effect a narration that unifies the past, present, and future into a comprehensive whole. In doing so, a text rooted in a Hindu religious tradition comes close to the use of time in Christian eschatology. Time in this tradition is 'salvational'. It is 'not something to be transcended but embraced as the medium in which salvation occurs.' Salvation, again, is not a superhuman process unrelated to time but a part of the order 'expressed in human choices and enacted in human action and its results.' In *Padmakalpa* too, salvation results from human action conducted under divine guidance. It is true that the difficulties that humanity is undergoing at present occur because of the pervasive presence of the evil kaliyuga. But the real devotees of the saviour have it in them to bring this epoch to an end and to herald a bright future. That the age will come to an end is premised upon events that happened in the past—in classical ways in which epochs are dissolved and renewed periodically. At the same time, when it will come to an end is consequent upon human action. After all, the redeemer has made his appearance and the people have failed to recognize him. They have been divided amongst themselves. Their sufferings are, in a large measure, due to this failure on their part. But the signs of the present are promising. There are hints that a struggle against the British, the forces of kaliyuga, is underway. The adherents of the true faith are getting ready to unite in the fight against vice. Their efforts will be crowned with success and dissension amongst them will disappear with the re-appearance of the redeemer. In a graphic use of linear time and its markers, *Padmakalpa* declares the year 1941 to be the exact year in which the redeemer is to reappear. Is it only coincidence that this year coincides with a very important phase in the nationalist struggle for India's independence from British rule? The sufferings of kaliyuga will end in a very near future, and *Padmakalpa* urges its community of readers to strive for and spread the word of that bright foreseeable future. An organic combination of faith and reason, myth and history, contributes to the creation and continuation of a modern 'tradition'.

Reconstructions of the Past*

Susan Visvanathan

This chapter attempts to show the importance of 'people's history' in the reconstruction of chronological events. It argues that the category of 'remembrance' is a problematic one, and that it is a social fact constrained by official ideologies and diversities of interpretation born of uncertain situations. [...]

SYRIAN CHRISTIANS: AN INTRODUCTION

[...] The Syrian Christians of Kerala believe that they are descendants of Brahmins converted by Thomas, the Apostle of Christ. He is said to have arrived in Malabar on his apostolic missions in AD 52.

The relationship between the St Thomas Christians and the Church of Persia crystallized in the fourth century AD. A Christian, Thomas of Cana, set out in AD 345 with the permission of the Catholicos of the East, taking with him a number of Christians, both lay and ecclesiastical, from Jerusalem, Baghdad, and Nineveh to provide succour to the Thomas Christians, who were by now spiritually impoverished. The immigrant Syrians merged with the indigenous Christians in both the economic and spiritual spheres. But according to tradition they

* Originally published in *Contributions to Indian Sociology*, 20 (2), 1986, pp. 241–60, Sage Publications, as 'Reconstructions of the Past among the Syrian Christians of Kerala'. In the present version, all notes and references have been deleted. For the complete text, see the original version.

remained separate and endogamous groups. This link was, however, reinforced by the arrival of Syrian prelates through the centuries.

In the last decade of the sixteenth century, the ritual control of the Persian Church over the St Thomas Christians slipped, and the latter came under Portuguese Latin jurisdiction. The culmination of Portuguese ecclesiastical domination came in 1599 when the Synod of Dramper began its proceedings. Here the Portuguese laid down the rules of ritual conduct and religious belief that the Christians were to follow. In 1653, the Christians broke free from Portuguese ecclesiastical domination, though not all of them did so; there were those who preferred the rites and celebrations of Rome. Those who revolted against the Portuguese ecclesiasts came to be known as the *Puthencoor* (New Group), those who remained under the Latin rite as *Pazhecoor* (Old Group).

In 1664, with the coming of the Jacobite bishop Mar Gregorious, the West Syrian Church became established in Kerala, a relationship which continues, though rather tempestuously, till today. The revolt of 1653 signalled the first schisms in a community that had been united under the name of Thomas the Apostle. By this time, the Portuguese had lost control of the sea and the arrival of the Dutch was welcomed by the Syrians, signalling the end of Portuguese control. The Dutch, though sympathetic to Syrian interests, left no lasting impact on the history of the Thomas Christians.

In 1800, a British resident was appointed to the Court of Travancore. The ecclesiastical interest of the British began as early as 1806 with the effort to bring to the Syrians a vernacular Bible. Following Anglican ecclesiastical intervention, the Syrians were to enter a period of internal dissension involving even litigation, which would continue for more than a century and a half, and remains unsettled today. The Puthencoor Syrians are severally divided having different denominational identities. [...]

PEOPLE'S HISTORY AS REINTERPRETATIONS OF FORMAL HISTORY

In my analysis, 'people's history' is a reconstruction, borrowing elements from the 'academic' and 'official' versions of the general history of the Syrian Christian community, weaving into it elements which are local, genealogical, and biographical. The narrative levels of people's history and the units of anthropological analysis interweave in the following way: general history–Church; local history–neighbourhood; genealogy–family; biography–individual.

Moreover, the physical, spatial and symbolic geography of neighbourhood, house, and church remain the constant units at the level of description. This is because narration and narrators are to be seen here more in the context of dramatic enactment, of personal involvement, than as mere storytellers in the folktale tradition. Necessarily, then, neighbourhood, church, and house in their spatial and architectural dimensions are like stage props which the narrators and actors live with and take for granted as essential accessories of the parts which they narrate or play, but which have in themselves an essential symbolic significance.

[...] the Christians in Puthenangadi are divided according to their ecclesiastical differences. Predominantly Yakoba (Jacobite), they are divided into two feuding sections: those who owe loyalty lo the Patriarch of Antioch (*Bawa Katshi*) and those who owe allegiance to the Indian Catholics (*Metran Katshi*). The nature of rifts and peace-making between the two halves of this Church is extremely complicated. Informants, though able to keep up with general trends, important personages, and some specific events, tend to give chronologically irregular descriptions of the events. Most accounts of a quarrel are prefaced by the phrase *Korrae varshangal numbil* (some years ago).

These quarrels, with their divisions of loyalty, are deeply regretted, particularly by the women of both parties. An old woman said:

It is we who feel the impact of these quarrels and divisions. It is for us that the quarrels between churches are difficult to expect. For every quarrel a new church is spawned, churches grow out of quarrels, not out of faith. At every corner we have a new church, and each of these is a living memory of bitterness.

When the quarrel in the Church is probed into, quite often narratives follow which show a concern for detail, for names, dates, and an identification with the characters and events of this chronicled past, which is asserted in statements like, 'Then in 1663 we came together and revolted against Portuguese rule'. Differences in narrative depend upon the social position of the narrator. I offer below two excerpts from *metran* and Patriarch party supporters respectively.

The problem for our people began with the coming of the Portuguese. In 1599, the rulings of the Synod of Udeyemperoor were imposed on us. One hundred and eight churches were summoned. For 165 years the Papists ruled us. In 1656 the Koonen Kurisu episode occurred where at Mattancheri the Thomas Christians gathered and vowed not to be oppressed by the Romans. From Antioch came Gregorious, and Pakalomattam Thoma was ordained as Mar Thoma I.

This rendering of general history continues almost by rote. From the same narrative:

> However, Gregorious from Antioch insisted on changing the liturgical language from Chaldean Syriac to Moronite saying that this was the language in which Christ spoke. Out of 108 churches, 36 under the leadership of Itti Thomas Kattanar, complied with Gregorious, in the change of ritual language. Seventy-two churches objected to the change and retained Chaldean. The 36 who came to Mar Gregorious were called the *Puthencoor* (new people) by local people, and the 72 who remained with the Chaldean language into which the Roman liturgy had been translated were called the *Pazhecoor* (the old group) and are what we call the Romo Syrian denomination.

The remembrance of numbers is symbolic of the effort to be accurate (not entirely successful since the Koonen Kurisu episode is placed in 1663 by one informant and 1656 by another, while it actually took place in 1653). Nevertheless, it symbolizes the effort to be objective and like the academic historian.

The objective format of *sabha charitram* (church history) constantly slips, exposing the emotion of ecclesiastical cleavages. Talking of the early nineteenth century, when the Puthencoor were to become divided by the intervention of Anglican theologians, a Metran Katshi supporter said:

> It so happened that the educated among the priests and the people received the faith of the CMS. Abraham Malpan, the strongest among them, manipulated a scheme for getting ordination from Antioch. He sent his nephew at the age of 21 to the Patriarch. At 22 he was ordained a Bishop. The person who sends a young boy to be bishop, and the person who ordains him are both rogues.

In his narrative, a Patriarch supporter said:

> Whatever I tell you, the Orthodox, if they hear it, will say 'All lies, nothing but lies'! In fact, if you mention my name they will say 'liar' at once! But I stick by my story, for it is the truth. You may say there are different sides to it, and that you want to look at both. There can be no two truths, that much is my belief, but I shall tell you the truth as I know it.

Sabha charitram exposes the trauma of the law courts, and the recurring problem of what is truth, and perhaps tentatively posed, the problem of the hierarchies of truth. The domain of truth relevant to the law courts was one where logical consistency rather than ethical consistency was in focus. The people admit that the truths in the court of law may be of a different order from the moral truth formulated by Christian precepts. Some way to win had to be found. The result was the false canons (*Kolla*

Canon). 'Our forefathers came together and produced a document which was a forgery.'

According to the narrative, the document was dropped in tea to make it look old, and later, after the case was won, the additions were scraped off from the palm leaf manuscripts with a kitchen knife.

The following narrative, from the point of view of legal defeat, expresses the tension born of the crisis of ecclesiastical identity and its effect on family history and individual biography. It begins with the polemics of official history:

The quarrels began because the Metropolitan Gevarghese Dionysius tampered with the democratic constitution as it existed and manipulated things so that all power came to himself. [It then breaks into biography.]

The land where Alleppey Zilla Court now stands was sold by the metran without consulting the other two trustees. It was church property gifted by our family. My grandfather was extremely angry and said that as lay trustee, he would resign.

A metran party version of the same episode is deliberately vague:

There was some quarrel about the felling of some coconuts and their disposal— something to do with the income (*varumanam*) of the church. The metran was isolated on the matter, while the priest trustee and the lay trustee stood together.

The next subject of discussion in both narratives is that of a murder. The Patriarch party representative said, referring to the court case in progress:

To make sure that the records at the old seminary would not be lost both parties posted guards. The metran party had a man called Anna Papi in their pay, a known drunk. One day, Anna Papi went to the toddy shop near the Seminary and was stabbed. The metran people say that my family was involved in the stabbing.

The metran party version mentions the murder, and then says:

Eapen Thomas' family was suspected and everyone says that there is a curse on the Eapen family. It is true, from being an extremely well placed and honoured family they have become ordinary. No one makes any progress among them now.

All popular expressions of sabha charitram constantly reveal the levels of neighbourhood, family, and individual existence. The economic depression of the Eapen family who were active respondents in litigation; the 'strange' case where one individual in a dominantly Patriarch loyalist family goes over to the Orthodox side; the marriage of a member of the Kadappra family to the famous priest's daughter—all these contribute to those narratives we call sabha charitram, describing the general history of the Church.

While narratives describing the general history of the community for
the last hundred years have a staccato quality about them, echoing the
formal and constrained language of the courts and circulars, the
subjectivization of this general history through the events of personal
history brings about a change, expressing the emotional context of
narration.

The language used in these formal expositions of general history
was frequently English or an equivalently technological Malayalam.
Most of the narratives of this type were offered to me by male informants,
who uniformly have an interest in church affairs and are for the most
part well versed in the major movements of church history. The women,
when asked about even the most dominant details of such a community
history, will say '*Kettu ittva ondu. Achayen odu choyichel parinjutharrum.*'
[I have heard of this. If you ask Father he will tell you.]

When general history becomes subjectively oriented, that is, when
it becomes part of an informant's biography, the narratives are then
offered by women both extensively and in depth. We saw through very
brief examples that even general history had a strong core of the personal
and the subjective, as when family members were involved in its
making. Here the narratives still exhibited a formal structure, because
the uncle or the grandfather who played a dominant part in the court
cases was an actor on an official stage, a representative of one party or
another, playing a part that was demarcated, not as kinsman but as
lawyer or as unswerving follower. The fact that the behaviour of such
an actor resulted in the impoverishment of the family or its increasing
fame or notoriety is incidental to the narrative. These personal details
are brought in by narrators parenthetically, as it were. The important
focus of the narrative is the telling of the story about the Church and its
problems, that story having a historical format and thus called by the
informant sabha charitram.

BIOGRAPHY, NEIGHBOURHOOD LIFE, AND THE CHURCH QUARREL

Reconstructions of the past often include narratives which emphasize
biography. Such accounts weave together the three strands of community, neighbourhood, and individual life. These are not merely biographical, for the events also reflect a moment in the general history of the
Syrian community and the particular history of neighbourhood life.

These narratives, to a great extent, express the pathologies of neighbourhood life. They are accounts of events which express the deviation

from the ethic of neighbourliness undisputed in times of harmony. Many of the narratives also express the fact that the women bear the consequences of divided loyalties most, because at the time of marriage they must accept the loyalties of their husbands' affiliation and abide by them. They must teach their children to stand by the ecclesiastical affiliation of the patriline. The women must suppress their own sympathies, and it is often painful to betray the loyalties inculcated in childhood. The most evocative pleas for union between the estranged groups come from such women:

The quarrel is like that between the Pandavas and the Kauravus: what need is there for it? Is the issue one that will lead us to salvation? Because I am married into an Orthodox family, I do not have the fortune to see the Patriarch when he comes to visit his people. Whatever we have regarding the customs of our faith we have got from Antioch, we did not make them up ourselves. Why should we not then give honour to the Patriarch, and the Patriarchs before him, who since the time of the Apostles have made and blessed the laws of the church?

When two women in a Patriarch-loyal family are by birth followers of the Catholicos, they are able to say things more easily and openly in defence of the latter. In one such case, however, the head of the household, staunchly Patriarch, said to a neighbour, 'Two Catholicos' party women in my house and I am ruined!' The tension between the loyalties of the natal and conjugal homes expressed through differing affiliations is thus most apparent in the women. However, constant intermarriage between members of the two parties has tended to blur the issues at the everyday level.

Biographical narratives express the nature of ecclesiastical cleavages most commonly at the time of crucial neighbourhood events such as the visit of some important but controversial ecclesiastic or the celebration of some saints' day not shared by both parties.

At the time of death, however, pathological situations have arisen which are not limited to the contained vehemence of verbal insults, but break into physical fights and abuse. The focus of difference here lies in the question of property—who 'owns' the cemetery, or rather, which party has jurisdiction over it.

When my father died we wished access to our *taravad* (ancestral home) church. But we, as Patriarch's people, were not allowed to use the church since our priests were not given permission to enter churches controlled by the Catholicos' party. We said the last prayers in the house and only when these were completed could we take the body to the cemetery. When we reached there they would not let us in and finally after much argument they allowed a few members to enter the cemetery with the body, but not the priests, and the body was lowered without ceremony into the grave.

Just as death in its dual dimension of the biographical and collective can mark off the nature of neighbourhood relations, so also narratives describing prelatial visits are to be seen as the representations mediating collective and individual experience. In themselves they are the specific speech acts of the individual Christian, who is yet, simultaneously, a representative of some group with which he identifies himself at a particular moment.

Again, the oral reflections on events occurring in the very recent past do not have the same quality as narratives which describe events of a century or so ago. The narrator infuses into his account a subjectivity that can be born only of direct participation. In such cases, the subjects of the narrative are not merely characters or personages on a public stage, but also persons for whom the narrator has certain strongly defined and closely articulated feelings. So, when the Patriarch or a Syrian Metropolitan visits the neighbourhood, or when the Catholicos choose to celebrate his birthday at the local parish church, the Christians relate to a person rather than a personage.

Narratives about the general history of the community relating to the distant past indicate that the narrators' conception of the chief actors was based on hearsay or on what they had read. These were men taken out of the pages of history, line drawings from newspapers and history books, distilled in narrators' accounts with the tales told to them by an older generation, and produced as a kind of 'bricoleurian' history by each narrator. Accounts of the recent past lack any claim to objectivity, being dominantly and vividly biographical and personal. In such instances the attitude of the narrator to the subject of his account is not directed merely to a character outlined in the clear sharp lines of brief newspaper articles and official histories of the Church, but to a person whose actuality lies in his vulnerabilities constantly exposed to a watchful people. In this case, the narrator has actually participated in a drama that took place in his own lifetime and scenes of which continue to unfold before him. The earlier scenes were narrated to him; the knowledge of that past is essential for understanding what he presently experiences. The continuity of the story told depends upon each Christian having in himself two simultaneous and interdependent functions: as listener (or reader) and as narrator. [...]

A Contested Past[*]

SAURABH DUBE

The repertoire of Satnami myths, part of a vigorous oral tradition, provided the group with a powerful statement of its past. The myths were written down in the late 1920s by Baba Ramchandra, the leader of the Kisan Sabha movement in Awadh in north India between 1918 and 1920, in a manuscript called *Ghasidasji ki Vanshavali*. [...] The myths in the *Vanshavali* had developed over a hundred years, a creative cultural process which involved accretions and, within limits, deletions and improvisation. [...] [T]his makes it very difficult to construct a chronological account of the development of Satnami myths over the course of the nineteenth century and through to the period they were written down by Baba Ramchandra.

These limits suggest other possibilities. First, the corpus of Satnami myths tells a full story that elaborates the group's cultural construction of its past and embodies its representations of history. Indeed, the Satnami rehearsal of myths in multiple contexts [...] ordered the past of Satnampanth. Second, the internal order and structure of the myths reveal the symbolic constitution of Satnampanth. The specific symbols within the myths were implicated in the definition of boundary of

* Originally published in Saurabh Dube, *Untouchable Pasts: Religion, Identity, and Power among a Central Indian Community, 1780–1850*, Albany: State University of New York Press, 1998, pp. 115–39, as 'A Contested Past'. In the present version, all notes and references have been deleted. For the complete text, see the original version.

Satnampanth. Third, Ghasidas and Balakdas, the major mythic figures of Satnampanth, effected resolutions and negotiated figures of authority that populated the cosmic and social order, in order to define the boundary and orchestrate the construction of Satnampanth. The three movements served to reaffirm Satnami identity, reinforce their solidarity, and interrogate the relationships of power constituted by the ritual hierarchy of purity and pollution, the culturally and ritually constituted centrality of kingship and dominant caste(s), and colonial authority within Chhattisgarh. But the death of Balakdas also signaled the end of the bold narrative of Satnami myths, which were now replaced by more fragmentary and tendentious tales. Among the later gurus weakness replaced resolve and they did not command the truth of Satnam. The mediation of feminine guile and desire led to disputes. The guru *gaddi* (seat) was divided. Untamed female sexuality manifested principles of disorder. The work of gender brought to a close the heroic history of the myths of Satnampanth.

THE INITIATION OF GHASIDAS

The *Vanshavali* opens with Ghasidas's encounter with his landed master, a critical step in the constitution of the mythic status of the guru.

Ghasidas made his *tapsthan* [place of worship] in Girodpuri. After performing *tap* (worship), he took up the work of ploughing in the field of a Marar [a caste which traditionally grows vegetables]. Ghasidas picked up the plough on his shoulder. His master started walking behind him. The master saw that the plough was suspended in the air, above Ghasidas's shoulder. When they reached the field the master joined the plough to the bullocks. Once again, he saw that Ghasidas's hand was above the handle of the plough which was moving on its own.

[...] [U]ntil the revenue settlement operations carried out by the colonial regime in the 1860s, the plough was the basis of assessment of land revenue in Chhattisgarh. A *nagar* or a 'plough' of land was an elastic measure intended to represent the area which one plough and four oxen could cultivate. The plough was the basis both for the apportioning of land and the state's revenue demand within the village. In a land-surplus situation, within a social order in which the plough was charged with cultural significance, the nagar was a critical metaphor of power within the work process and in everyday village life. The plough was, in a manner at once substantive and symbolic, constitutive of the relationship between a ploughman and his master. Ghasidas worked for his Marar master: but he did not carry the burden of his master's plough on his shoulder, and his hand remained above the handle of the plough. Ghasidas had made a move to transform his relationship, mediated by the plough, with his agricultural master.

The myth emphasizes that the master became worried since he could not ascertain if Ghasidas was holy man or a trickster. But the Marar master's uncertainty about Ghasidas was to end soon. It only had to await Ghasidas's meeting with *satnampurush*:

Ghasidas ploughed the field and left the bullocks to graze. The field was next to a mountain and the bullocks went there. When Ghasidas went there to bring back the bullocks, *satnam* emerged. It was there that Ghasidas met the pure white form of satnam. Satnampurush said to Ghasidas, 'I had sent you to reform the lineage, but you forgot and have started working for others. This entire Chamar lineage has got spoilt. Have you forgotten this? Intoxicated by meat and liquor, these holy men have got ruined. You spread the name of satnam. I am satnampurush, know me.' So Ghasidas said, 'Who will believe my word since in order to look after my wife and two children I work for other people?' Satnampurush answered, 'I shall bring all the Chamars to you. You give them betel leaf and make them repeat the name of satnam.' Ghasidas, once again, refused. But Satnampurush tied two pieces of coconut to Ghasidas's clothes.

Ghasidas is the person who had been sent by satnampurush to reform the Chamars. The Chamars, in turn, are a *vansh*, a lineage. The use of a metaphor of kinship emphasizes the boundedness of Chamars as a community; a collectivity whose destiny could be orchestrated by its mythic figures. Ghasidas had forgotten to reform his own people, his lineage, and was working for others. The Chamars, as a result, had taken to *mas madira* (meat and liquor) and had been ruined. Second, it was of essence that the Chamars, who were holy men, be restored to a state of purity. They had to be reformed through their coming to know satnam. The name of satnam had to be spread. Satnampurush was to bring the Chamars to a reluctant Ghasidas. Finally, Ghasidas's refusal to follow the orders of satnampurush was a consequence of his working for other people. He had to accept the apparent subordination that followed this labour in order to support his wife and children.

Ghasidas took the plough and the bullocks to the master. The master said, 'Ghasidas I shall not have you work because your body appears peculiar to me. It seems as though you have a crown, four arms, and a conch shell. I have never seen your body like this.' The master, overwhelmed by the form, cried 'Jai Guru Ghasidas'. He fell on Ghasidas's feet.

The reversal that had begun with the change in the relation of Ghasidas's body to the plough had been completed by the submission of the Marar master. The master's act was brought about by the change in Ghasidas's form, directed by satnam. It occurred after Ghasidas's encounter with satnampurush. Indeed, the crown, the four arms, the conch-shell—signs of the deity Vishnu—had fleetingly transfigured the lowly Ghasidas into a supremely divine being, on par with the greatest of gods, where the signs of a particular deity were metonymically extended to refer to wider distinctions of divinity, the embodiment of satnam. This proved the final step in effecting a resolution of the contradiction between the authority of Ghasidas—a low-caste labourer and ploughman—and his higher-caste agricultural master.

Yet, much more was to happen before Ghasidas was initiated into his new status as a guru. For what lay ahead were trials, ordeals, and obstacles, and all these had to be overcome by Ghasidas.

When Ghasidas returned from the Marar's house his children ran up to him and ate the pieces of coconut [that had been tied to his clothes by satnampurush]. Ghasidas's wife gave him water and food. After eating, when he sat down, the children died. His wife and neighbours were bewildered and anguished. The children were buried with the advice of the *jati* [caste]. After three days Ghasidas took the ritual bath, finished other jati rituals, and slept with his wife who died. She too was buried.

What is striking is the very ordinariness of the acts of Ghasidas, of eating and of sleeping with his wife, which led to the deaths. The acts spoke of routine domesticity and of ties within the family. With the death of his children and his wife the ties were broken, the domesticity was no more.

Ghasidas was left alone, a mood of renunciation set in. He went to a mountain in Sonakhan. There satnampurush assumed the form of a tiger and ran towards him. So Ghasidas said, 'Yes, you have eaten three; eat me as well.' The tiger bowed his head. Then satnampurush assumed the form of a python. Ghasidas went up to him and asked to be eaten. The python bowed his head. When night fell, Ghasidas climbed a Tendu tree and put a noose around his neck. The noose left him and he sat down. Ghasidas thought that he had not tied the noose properly. A second time he tied his neck tightly to the Tendu tree. The branch of the tree bent down and reached the ground. Satnampurush assumed the four-armed form and stood aside. He then said to Ghasidas that he had again forgotten to worship satnam. He was asked to spread the name of satnam and make the place into a site of pilgrimage and get it worshipped: 'You worship here for six months and the Chamars nearby will come to this holy place. You feed them betel leaf, get them to worship the name of satnam; the idols of gods and goddesses in their houses should be thrown out.' Ghasidas replied that his wife and children had died and he was being asked to get a name worshipped. He could not do it. So satnampurush said to Ghasidas, 'I will make everyone alive, but the name of satnam should be spread. I am telling you to worship here. After six months I will make your son and daughter alive.' After saying this satnampurush disappeared and Ghasidas started worshipping there. In the meanwhile, people of the caste and family tried to find Ghasidas. When they could not find him, they gave the funeral feast. For six months Ghasidas purified his body. For six months he left all food and drink. After six months satnam emerged in the same form. Ghasidas recognized that form and touched the feet of satnam. A pond emerged at the place where satnam had kept his feet. From that pond *amrit* [nectar] was obtained. In that water satnam made Ghasidas have a bath and then gave him the amrit. Satnampurush then asked Ghasidas, 'Now have you experienced satnam?' Ghasidas answered, 'Maharaj, I have experienced your form' ... Telling him the rule of making disciples satnampurush brought Ghasidas to the real/original place of worship and asked him to give coconuts and betel leaves and spread the name of satnam. Satnampurush said, 'I shall give all the Chamars the dream of this name and send them to this place,' and then went back to his world.

This can be read as the story of the initiation of Ghasidas that was directed by satnampurush. Satnampurush, in various guises, put Ghasidas through the ordeal of death. The revelation by satnampurush of his true form, after Ghasidas failed to see that it was he who held the noose, was a statement of the power of satnampurush. Ghasidas's mistake was that he still did not know satnampurush. He had not worshipped and spread the name of satnam. Satnampurush instructed him on what had to be done for the creation of Satnampanth. But Ghasidas refused. It was the assurance that he would make Ghasidas's wife and children alive which resolved the problem. In their first meeting satnampurush had emphasized, '*Mein khud Satnampurush hoon, mujhe pahchan* [I am satnampurush, recognize/know me].' The later events resulted from Ghasidas's inadequate recognition of satnam. It was after he carried out the instructions of satnampurush and cleansed his body by renouncing food and drink and performing worship that full recognition followed. To know/recognize satnampurush was to accept satnam; satnampurush created the *kund* (pond), gave Ghasidas *amrit* (nectar), and purified him. In brief, he conducted Ghasidas's rite of initiation. Satnampurush also provided that little extra—the rule for creating disciples, a vision to the Chamars—that gurus need. The conditions of possibility of Ghasidas becoming the guru of a reformed vansh of Chamars, of the creation of Satnampanth, had been fulfilled.

Obeyesekere has discussed the classic pattern in which a figure new to a mythic tradition passes through ordeals and trials set up by the supreme deity till the final moment when the mythic figure recognizes the deity's powers and is simultaneously incorporated into the existent pantheon and the mythic tradition. What we find in Satnami myths is a play on the familiar theme. The relationship between satnampurush and Ghasidas is ridden with tension. The tension, I suggest, is linked to the specific character of the myths of Satnampanth. The Satnami mythic order was a new construct. Both Ghasidas and satnampurush, unknown in their specific form, had to be established within this mythic tradition. This involved a double movement: Ghasidas had to pass through trials and ordeals set up by satnampurush before he was initiated as a guru; and Ghasidas, in turn, put satnampurush through tests. From the moment of their first encounter, at each step, satnampurush had to counter the resistance offered by Ghasidas. In the trials which Ghasidas underwent with the tiger and the python, the tables were turned. Ghasidas recognized that it was satnampurush who had come in the form of the tiger and the python. When he addressed satnampurush he offered a challenge, 'Yes, you have eaten three, eat me as well.' The tiger, the python, and the branch of the tree bowed down before Ghasidas. The note of resistance was struck, once again, when Ghasidas refused to follow the orders of satnampurush because his wife and children had been taken away from him. All this is related to the fact that Ghasidas, in spite of a mood of renunciation, is not quite a 'world renouncer'. [...] My point here is that Ghasidas's resistance bore the mark of, and carried forward the ambiguity in, the relationship between these two mythic figures. It was by tying the pieces of coconut to Ghasidas's clothes, effecting a separation between Ghasidas and his wife and children, setting up ordeals, and providing the assurance that his wife and children would be made alive that satnampurush was recognized in his true form by Ghasidas. Two new mythic figures were established within a new mythic tradition.

The constitution of Ghasidas as a guru was premised upon diverse attributes of asceticism, which at once combined features of the 'individual-outside-the-world' and the 'man-in-the-world', and elements drawn from popular traditions. Ghasidas had to 'renounce' his wife and children, be dead to the world, and cleanse his body. He was a novice who was purified by satnampurush through amrit before he was initiated into his new status. At the same time, Ghasidas went through the exercise only after satnampurush gave him his word that the wife and children would be brought back to life. To a significant degree, Ghasidas's renunciation was framed by his desire to go back to being a householder. Moreover, after his initiation, Ghasidas did not come back as a 'renouncer'. He was brought to the world, reclaimed by his jati people, who had presumed him to be dead and had gone through the motions of a symbolic burial. In the mythic tradition of Satnampanth, Ghasidas's wife had been both sleeping and dead for six months. It was only after Ghasidas woke her up, brought her back to life, and fixed her broken arm that Chamars started becoming Satnamis in large numbers. Finally, Ghasidas possessed the characteristics of a saint, a shaman, and a healer in popular traditions. He fulfilled his followers' desire for the birth of a child, gave a blind *banjara* (gypsy) the gift of sight, cured snake bites, and repaired bodies. Ghasidas healed the bodies of members of Satnampanth.

GURU GHASIDAS, A GOND RAJA, *ANGREZ SARKAR*, AND DANTESHWARI DEVI

The establishment of the authority of Ghasidas required him to displace other figures of authority within the social and cosmic order. The classic manner of displacement within a mythic tradition takes the form of a mythic figure totally eclipsing the other mythic figures. This was the fate of village gods and goddesses who were thrown on the rubbish heap by Ghasidas and the Satnamis. At the same time, in Satnami myths the gurus also effected displacements by demarcating their separate sphere of authority. The exercise, once again, served to constitute the boundary of Satnampanth. To illustrate this process I shall take three examples: Ghasidas's encounters with a tribal Gond raja, with the *angrez sarkar* (British government), and his relationship with Danteshwari devi, the tribal goddess whose propitiation required human sacrifice.

The first of these encounters took place very soon after the establishment of Satnampanth.

The Gond raja of Sonakhan [an estate north of Raipur] got the news that a Chamar by the name of Ghasidas was accumulating money and coconuts in his kingdom. The raja told Ghasidas that he wanted half the money and coconuts as his share. Ghasidas replied that he had only betel leaves and coconuts and no money, and agreed to give a share of the betel leaves and the coconuts if the king desired. The king took half the coconuts and then said. 'I am in debt; help me pay the debt of fifty thousand rupees or I will kill the moneylender.' When the king killed the money-lender Ghasidas knew that *pap* [sin] had entered the place and it would be better for him to move out. On the day of *maghipuno* [the day and night of the full moon in the month of *magh*, January–February] the king sent soldiers to Ghasidas's house. There were a few of Ghasidas's men among the soldiers. It struck them that they had surrounded the guru's house, but if they were to catch him it would be a grave insult to Satnampanth. They began to sing *bhajans* [devotional songs]. All the soldiers then became devotees of Ghasidas, broke open the door to the house, and prepared the way for Ghasidas to escape. Ghasidas reached a village; the villagers started celebrating maghipuno; the king of Sonakhan attacked; Ghasidas had to leave. This happened again and again as Ghasidas went from one village to another.

Each celebration of the festival of maghipuno led to attacks by the raja and his soldiers. Maghipuno, established as a sacred date in the Satnami calendar by Ghasidas, marked the boundary of Satnampanth as the community came under attack for its distinctive celebration of the power of Ghasidas. The numerous attacks on Ghasidas at various places on the day of maghipuno are possibly a form of collective remembering of the hostility faced by the Satnamis.

There is also, however, an important sub-plot in this story: the relationship between Ghasidas and the king of Sonakhan. Ghasidas's response to the king's demand for money and coconuts served to demarcate their respective spheres of authority. Ghasidas said that he had only betel leaves and coconuts and no money. The betel leaves and coconut—offered to the guru by his disciples and an important medium in the rituals and practices of Satnampanth—were comprehensive icons of Ghasidas's authority. Similarly, Ghasidas did not dismiss the authority of the king and readily agreed to part with a share of the betel leaves and the coconuts. The difficulty was that the king was unjust and had been visited by pap (sin). The soldiers, the instruments of the king's unjust authority, were won over by the just and moral authority of Ghasidas, who had, in any case, made up his mind to leave. The soldiers now provided him with a way out of a place contaminated by sin. Ghasidas's move from one village to another, all of them celebrating maghipuno, was a statement of his authority and of the spread of Satnampanth.

Ghasidas's second key encounter, now with the angrez sarkar, was equally charged with the interplay of meaning and power.

Ghasidas had built a house in Bhandar which he had to abandon because of the attacks by the raja of Sonakhan. After rule had been established by the British, he returned to Bhandar. Ghasidas had lived there for ten years when the angrez raja [English king] received the news about the guru. Soldiers carrying the orders of Agnew saheb and Mulki saheb came from Raipur. Ghasidas had been summoned to the capital. Ghasidas went to Raipur sitting in a *doli* [palanquin].

In a characteristic move, the doli, reserved for their use by the upper castes, a signifier of status and rank within the caste hierarchy, stood appropriated by Ghasidas. The act of appropriation was an expropriation of the dominant. The upper caste expropriators had been divested of their monopoly over a symbol that was constitutive of their domination. Ghasidas had adequately answered the summons of the saheb.

And so it was that very soon,

Ghasidas arrived in Raipur. His authority in the capital was awesome. Tens of thousands of Satnamis reached there. As a result, Ghasidas had to sit on a *chaupai* [a small cot], high up on a tree, where he could be visible to all. The *chaprasi* [peon] gave the news of Ghasidas's arrival. The saheb demanded Ghasidas's immediate presence, but Ghasidas's response was to delay.

To see and to be seen by Ghasidas was *darshan*, a spectacle, which affected thousands of Satnami devotees. The substance of Ghasidas's authority, in the seat of the angrez raja, was transmitted through sight. Moreover, to wait upon a superior is an aspect of subordination. Ghasidas obeyed the saheb, but deliberately took his time, arriving with dignity in the evening. It is barely surprising then that the saheb subjected Ghasidas to tests and trials.

The saheb got the peon to give Ghasidas a *lota* [a small vessel] of *sharbat* [a sweet drink] which contained poison. Ghasidas drank it. He returned to his *aasan* [seat] on the tree. When the night was over the colonial authorities sent the peon to see whether Ghasidas was alive or dead. They were informed that he was alive. Ghasidas had passed the trial. The saheb called Ghasidas again, and both the saheb and the memsaheb did salaam [saluted him]. Ghasidas said satnam and put both his hands on their heads.

Ghasidas's authority as a guru had been recognized by the angrez saheb. But the saheb still considered him a *kachha* (weak) guru who had to be tested further. He wrote down the name of Danteshwari, the man-eating goddess, on a piece of paper. The saheb's command was not merely expressed in but was also shaped by writing. Indeed, the written form bore the mark and was constitutive of the saheb's command, which was a concrete form of colonial authority.

Ghasidas was sent with a chaprasi to Danteshwari devi in the chiefdom of Bastar.

It was an eight-day journey to the devi's shrine. After being taken there, Ghasidas was put inside the devi's temple and the doors were locked. The devi emerged from water. The doors of the temple opened.

The encounter between Danteshwari and Ghasidas demarcated the separate but complementary spheres of authority and the different spaces inhabited by the two mythic figures. Danteshwari lived in water, and Ghasidas on land. The goddess addressed Ghasidas as *bade*. In Chhattisgarhi this is a mode of address reserved for the *kurra sasur*—the husband's elder brother—a relationship characterized by mutual avoidance. In the kinship network of the Satnami cosmic order the relationship between Ghasidas and Danteshwari bound them through mutual avoidance.

Danteshwari asked him, 'Why have you come here?' Ghasidas answered that he was there because he was obeying the king, and insisted that Danteshwari should eat him. The goddess replied that she ate all jatis [castes/communities] except Satnamis, and asked Ghasidas to spread the name of satnam. Ghasidas pledged that he would not betray Danteshwari and tempt her by allowing *mas* [meat] and *madira* [liquor], the substances she devoured, in Satnampanth. The goddess instructed Ghasidas further that if he spread the use of [...] substances that carried purity among his devotees she will never trouble the beings in his *teerth* [place of pilgrimage].

It was the purity of Satnampanth, the avoidance of meat and liquor, which made Danteshwari encourage Ghasidas's endeavour. The space inhabited by Satnampanth was a teerth, a holy place. The reinforcement of the boundary of this space, through a continuous purification of the body, maintained the distance between Danteshwari and Ghasidas. In Satnami myths, the maintenance of distance was the mutual acceptance by Danteshwari and Ghasidas of each other's authority and of the relationship of avoidance which bound the devi and the guru. Once more, Ghasidas negotiated and displaced the purchase commanded by a key player within the social and cosmic order by demarcating his own sphere of authority. In all three cases, this served to establish Satnampanth.

BALAKDAS, *JANEU*, AND CONQUEST

After Ghasidas's death—which I discuss later—his son Balakdas took over as guru. In Satnami myths Ghasidas had initiated the challenge both to caste hierarchy and to colonial authority. Balakdas also took this up, although in rather different ways. This emerges in the myth about Balakdas and the *janeu*.

It was on the day of Ghasidas's funeral feast that Balakdas told the Satnamis who had assembled, that Ghasidas had appeared in a dream and told him, 'I had given the *kanthi*; you spread the janeu.' Now, there is complicity between the writing of British administrators and the upper caste people to whom I talked about the incident. Both depict it as an act born of the inordinate vanity of Balakdas. This fits well with their shared stereotype of the Satnamis as an arrogant people. The Satnami version, on the other hand, emphasizes the continuity with the past. The wearing of the sacred thread by the Satnamis was the last wish of Ghasidas. It was conveyed on the day of the funeral feast—the last life cycle ritual—of Ghasidas. Balakdas was to honour Ghasidas's word and build upon the beginning that had been made with the kanthi through the spread of the sacred thread. The janeu was to become a principle of Satnami faith. According to the myth, the enterprise had the critical support of members of the guru family and key members within Satnampanth. When they went to Balakdas wearing the janeu, the guru was pleased, 'Our *kul* is fortunate.' [...] the appropriation of the sacred thread by a low caste is often subsumed within the 'master discourse' of Sanskritization. Here I find several problems with such an approach. First, if Satnampanth appropriated the signs afforded by the ritual hierarchy of purity and pollution, it also drew upon popular traditions which had negotiated and challenged the caste order in different ways. Second, it rejected and overturned key elements of the divine and social hierarchies within caste society. Finally, the janeu was an addition to Satnampanth, a part of a process of symbolic construction which situated the sign in a new context and questioned the caste system. The concept, it seems to me, can prove to be much too facile. It circumvents an analysis of the processes and the logic of the symbolic construction of a low-caste endeavour. It follows that placing the Satnami appropriation of the sacred thread within the framework of Sanskritization would miss out on the simultaneity of the critique of caste society and a questioning of British rule under Balakdas. The wearing of the sacred thread by the Satnamis, an oppositional step, led to a conflict with the upper castes and brought colonial law into play. Thus,

The news about the janeu spread from one village to another. The ignorant Hindus created an organization which resolved to kill Balakdas. But the Hindus were worried. Balakdas had to be found alone for their plan to succeed. Once, Balakdas was travelling with a few companions. The Hindus initiated a quarrel but could not harm Balakdas. The Satnamis appealed to colonial authorities. There was an enquiry. The Raipur *kutcherry* [court] asked Balakdas if he had distributed the janeu among Satnamis. The guru, of course, did not lie. He won the case. The officials were given a bribe of a thousand rupees by the Hindus. They arrested five Satnamis who were kept in a *hawalat* [jail]. The *sarkar* in order to test the Satnamis and to get more money from the Hindus went 'against its law' and gave each of them five large measures of grain to grind. The Satnamis said that they would perform the evening purificatory practice and then grind. They prepared themselves by defecating and taking a bath in the evening. The Satnamis then put the grain in the *chakki*, the mill, in front of soldiers. As soon as they said Satnam and moved the handle, the mill burst. The peon informed the officials who thought that the Satnamis had deliberately, as an act of mischief, broken the mill. The officers called the five Satnamis and in front of the Hindus asked, 'What is your caste?' The answer, 'Satnami. The decision about food and drink was taken by Ghasidas. When he heard about the janeu, Balakdas has made us wear it. Satnam is *sancha* [true/pure], any other name is *asancha* [false/impure]. This is all we know'. In front of the Hindus the officers wrote on small pieces of paper. The papers contained orders. Wear the janeu; put on a tilak [ash mark on the forehead], keep a *choti* [or *shikha*, tuft of hair allowed to grow long at the back of the head]. After this the janeu started being worn in many villages.

There are two closely linked themes in this story: the truth of satnam and the legitimacy of the Satnami endeavour; and the relationship of

the Satnamis with colonial authority. It was critical for the Hindus to
find Balakdas alone. The point is that in Satnami self-perception they
are defeated only when there is a division within their ranks or when
they are disunited. Balakdas had only a few companions, which was an
invitation for the Hindus to attack. But the few Satnamis were united.
Balakdas could not be killed. The Satnamis were also loyal subjects.
After the quarrel it was they who appealed to the sarkar. In the court it
was the straightforward answer of Balakdas, the power of his word that
carried the truth of satnam, which won him the lawsuit. The government was, however, corruptible. The five Satnamis were jailed because
the officials had been bribed. Moreover, the sarkar went against its own
law when the Satnamis were given five measures of grain to grind. The
Satnami mythic tradition drew upon the language of colonial law and
used it to criticize the sarkar, the power that defined its lexical rules. At
the same time, the Satnamis once again obeyed the king's orders. They
first created the conditions in which satnam could operate. It was after
they had purified themselves that they faced the ordeal of grinding five
measures of grain in the mill within the confines of the jail. In Hindi
the phrase *chakki peesna* commonly refers to the practice of prisoners
grinding grain in a mill. It evokes subjection within the disciplinary
institution of the prison. The power of satnam burst the chakki. The
sarkar did not recognize what lay behind the breaking of the mill which
was understood as a deliberate act of Satnami mischief. It was, in fact,
after the Satnamis stated the truth of satnam in a brief and simple
fashion that recognition came to the sarkar. At each step, the loyalty
and obedience of the Satnamis to the sarkar was accompanied by the
questioning of colonial law. The truth, legitimacy, and power of
satnam—a glimmer, perhaps, of an alternative legality—had triumphed
over the sarkar that had at different points shown itself to be corrupt
and ignorant, unjust and unlawful. At the same time, once the sarkar
had been compelled to act as a properly constituted moral authority,
the Satnami claim over the janeu, tilak, and choti—the symbols of upper-
caste domination—was established through the orders of government
officers, which were, characteristically, inscribed in writing on small
pieces of paper.

In Satnami myths Balakdas is cast in the mould of a conqueror.
The myths engaged with the patterns and properties of ritually constituted kingship to fashion the guru as a figure who possessed regal
attributes and, significantly, was on par with the king. Ghasidas's
encounter with the Gond raja had demarcated the separate sphere of
authority of the Satnami guru. Balakdas built upon and consolidated
this move but also added a royal dimension to the seat of the guru. It

bears pointing out that, Balakdas had formalized an organizational hierarchy which extended from the guru at the top to *mahants, diwans,* and, finally, *bhandaris,* and *sathidars.* The organizational structure of Satnampanth constituted an alternative ritual and symbolic centre of power to kings and dominant caste groups. Now,

Balakdas called his men and asked them to get ready to go to villages. The Satnami population had to be acquainted with the holy men and the members of the organizational hierarchy. Balakdas was [on the one hand] accompanied by Sarha and Judai—two warriors of Satnampanth who were adept at using swords and guns—and four thousand other brave men, and [on the other] by hundreds of pious Satnamis. The guru [embodying the attributes of purity and royalty] put on a janeu and tilak and carried a spear, a sword, and a gun and rode on a decorated elephant. The impressive cavalcade moved from one village to another. Satnamis came in droves and thronged the guru. Their joy was unbounded and the sound of *panthi geet* [songs of Satnampanth] rent the air. After the guru's darshan they showered Balakdas with gold, silver, and clothes.

Clearly, Balakdas had begun his dramatic conquest.

In the course of his tour Balakdas encountered figures of royal authority. The king of Nandgaon took a horse from a Satnami and broke the kanthi of a few others. Balakdas got the news. He made it clear that as a guru he did not fight with anyone. Instead he cursed the raja that the throne of Nandgaon could never have a legitimate heir. According to the myth, the curse has continued to this date. The raja of Khairagarh decided to test Balakdas. He had meat put in a *katori* (a small round vessel) which was then covered with a piece of cloth. The king asked Balakdas what the vessel contained. Balakdas said that that it had pieces of coconut. When the vessel was uncovered the ritually polluting meat had, indeed, turned into pure bits of coconut. The raja gave Balakdas a prize and declared that he was a true guru. The raja then got a letter from the Hindu king of Bilaspur to kill Balakdas. The letter was returned with the reply that the one who kills shall be put to death. An order was passed against the killing of Balakdas in the kingdom of Khairagarh. Balakdas was called by the raja of Kawardha who asked the guru to sit next to him. The raja had heard that Balakdas's body had the imprint of the ten incarnations of the god Vishnu and wanted to see it. Balakdas took off his clothes and showed the signs on his body. The raja was happy. He worshipped the guru and gave him money from his treasury. The spheres inhabited by the king and Balakdas were complementary: the raja, as the ruler, rewarded Balakdas with money; and the king was the supplicant who worshipped Balakdas, the guru. The final measure of Balakdas's triumph in Kawardha was his entry into the inner space, the female and feminine domain, of the house of the raja. The raja's sister called him inside and made him her guru. Balakdas's spectacular success was also the triumph of his community. [...]

DEEDS OF DEATH

The death of a guru was the disruption of the cosmic order of Satnam-panth. The critical event occurred in situations of disorder, and it was characterized by patterns of betrayal. We find then that towards the end of Ghasidas's life, Satnampanth was in a bad way. The Satnamis had forgotten to worship satnam. Satnampurush had assured Ghasidas that he would take a human incarnation and sort out the problems of Satnampanth. When Ghasidas's daughter-in-law became pregnant, he asked his associates within Satnampanth if the child would be a boy or a girl. The guru was told that it would be a girl. But Ghasidas was expecting a boy, the incarnation of satnampurush. The prophecy of the birth of a girl meant that he had now to take on the responsibilities of Satnam-panth all over again. The guru verbally chastised satnampurush and once more appealed to his mentor to take a human incarnation, yet to no avail. Ghasidas had withdrawn from the world but had now to go into it again.

Ghasidas started building a house. When the workmen ran short of wood for the beams of the roof, he gave an order to look for a tree. The only tree to be found was a bel under which someone had buried a *trishul* (trident) long ago. Bel and trishul are the marks of Mahadeo, the god Shiva. Ghasidas remembered satnam and struck the tree five times with his *tangiya* (axe). Truly it was an awesome conspiracy of circum-stances within the divine order. The tree fell and Ghasidas sat down. The branches of the tree spread all over the guru's body. His entire body became extremely hot. Ghasidas asked the servants to bring the tree and went home. The guru, racked by pain, had food and went off to sleep. After this unfortunate encounter with Mahadeo, Balakdas's wife gave birth to a girl. Balakdas and other Satnamis were called at night. Ghasidas told them that satnampurush had betrayed them. He had promised a boy but a girl was born. Ghasidas announced, 'I shall go to satnampurush...and ask him that you were going to take *avatar*, why has the opposite happened?' Ghasidas left his body with the Satnamis for two-and-a-half days during his sojourn to meet satnampurush. It was another betrayal at this stage which established the finality of Ghasidas's death. On discovering that Ghasidas's body was being guarded, his son Balakdas stated that the dead do not return. When Ghasidas came back after two and a half days he found that his last rites had been performed. The guru had to go back to the other world.

It was the combination of disorder and betrayal that, once again, lay behind the death of Balakdas. In the course of his tour Balakdas reached Bilaspur. The raja of Bilaspur wanted Balakdas dead. Balakdas made matters worse by camping in the village of Amara Bandha, which was the heart of enemy territory. The Rajput Kshatriyas held a meeting and passed a written resolution. 'The *shikar* (prey) has come into our house. We should not delay. He must be killed tonight.' The night was ominous. It was cold and dark. The full moon of *pus* (December–January) had been eclipsed by a cloud cover and torrential rain. The right eyes of Sarha and Judai, the two legendary Satnami warriors, were fluttering. The constellation of stars spoke of a battle that night. Balakdas and his group were to eat the evening meal at the house of Kariya Chamar. Kariya had taken money from the Kshatriyas and was on their side. A Satnami had betrayed Satnampanth.

Balakdas tempted fate. He decided not to go to eat and sent off his group. There was only one Satnami with Balakdas in his tent. The Hindus attacked. They could identify Balakdas because he was sitting on a chair wearing gold ornaments. The first blow of the sword hit the chair. The second claimed the life of Kodu Bahiya. In a dim light from a fire burning outside, the Hindus thought that they had killed Balakdas. Yet the terror of the night was not over. Sarha and Judai were returning after the meal. They took the enemy to be their companions. The warriors were killed. The Hindus, convinced that they had completed their task, were going back when they heard the guru's companions shouting, 'Balakdasji come this way?' The Hindus started looking for Balakdas. The dark night was suddenly illuminated by a flash of lightning. The Hindus saw Balakdas in his gold ornaments; they asked him who he was; the guru did not lie. A major fight broke out. Balakdas was killed amidst chaos. Horses and elephants left their places and ran, people ran helter-skelter and fought and killed not recognizing each other. In death too Balakdas had lived a belief of Satnampanth: Satnamis can be defeated only when they are disunited.

SEXUALITY, DESIRE, AND THE DIVISION OF THE GURU GADDI

[...] The death of Balakdas signaled a change in the relationship between the guru and the women within the family. In Satnami myths, woman's sexuality forms the overriding concern, the key trope, in the construction of the figure of the guru *mata*, the wife of the guru. Wives— ever the outsiders in male perspectives within patrlineal kinship—rather than mothers and sisters, were the principal players. Sexuality invested the women with agency. For a guru to be in control was to master his wife's sexuality and divest her of agency. Where the early gurus had succeeded, the later ones failed.

[...] Let us turn to the chequered career of Partappurin *mata* (who, over time, married the three sons of Ghasidas), which illustrates this pattern.

After his encounter with Danteshwari devi, Ghasidas returned to Bhandar and arranged the marriage of his eldest son Amardas with the daughter of the *malguzar* of Partappur in Bilaspur district. The wedding took place in Partappur. The bride and the groom came back to Bhandar. On the first night, when Partappurin mata came to sleep with Amardas she found him meditating sitting in the yogic lotus posture. Partappurin returned saying that she would come back soon. Partappurin's lust remained unfulfilled. One afternoon when Amardas was lying in bed Partappurin caught him off guard and in a lascivious move started rubbing his feet. Amardas was equal to the occasion and drew upon his inner reserves to frighten off his wife with yogic illumination. Partappurin ran off screaming loudly. Amardas set off, a spear in his hand, in hot pursuit. The guru followed the mata from one village to another. Before he could catch up with her Amardas reached the village of Chattua. It was *janmashtami*. The villagers worshipped Amardas and invited him to dance the *panthi naach*. Amardas, immersed in the *panthi*, died in Chattua.

[...] the very name of Partappurin mata invoked her alien, natal home; her father as the *malguzar* of Partappur was something of a rival figure to the gurus within configurations of local kingship; and left untamed her sexuality was unbounded, all too capable of overwhelming her husbands, the Satnami gurus.

Amardas had curbed his sexual instincts and countered Partappurin's desire through celibacy and meditation. At the same time, it was the unfulfilled lust and desire of Partappurin which broke Amardas's meditation and led him to Chattua, unto his death. If Amardas's death on janmashtami, as he danced the panthi naach—both marks of distinction within Satnampanth—conjoined the critical event of a guru's end with signs defining the boundary of the community, it was Partappurin's sexuality that ordered this past.

Balakdas, ever the masculine hero, could not be similarly undone by concerns of celibacy. He was in complete charge in his dealings with Partappurin, whom he married after the death of Neerabai, his first wife. Partappurin's obedience to Balakdas was total. She was the first member of the guru family to make sacred threads when Balakdas embarked on the enterprise of distributing janeu among the Satnamis. The mata was happy at Balakdas's decision to marry Radha, the girl

who had seduced Balakdas but who afterwards had remained under
his control. And then Balakdas died young.

Partappurin stood transformed after the death of Balakdas. Now
implicit obedience was replaced by the assertion of a dominant sexuality, and the mata acquired the aspect of a devi through the mediation
of desire.

At the feast for Balakdas's last rites the matas performed worship. The time unto
midnight was spent in this work. Agardas went to sleep in this place. The mata
[Partappurin] dressed up and went to Agardas to make love. The woman said to
Agardas, 'See what form I have taken and come. Look at me carefully.' At that
moment that woman's being had eight arms and seemed full of [the attributes of]
many different kinds of characters. Seeing this otherworldly form, Agardas became
worried. He thought to himself, where can I run. Agardas started pleading with his
woman with folded hands. Then she said to Agardas, 'Do *keli* [make love] or I will
turn you to ashes.' To this Agardas replied, 'Whatever you say I am willing to do, just
don't kill me.' Mata Partappurin told him, 'Listen to me and make me your *patrani*'
[most prominent wife, literally queen who sits on the thigh].

The time and the place set the stage for the encounter between Partappurin mata and Agardas. Balakdas's last rites had been performed, and
the matas had paid their respects and worshipped the dead guru. It was
just after midnight. Agardas had gone to sleep at the site of the feast.
Partappurin mata struck swiftly, at the first opportune moment, after
Agardas became the new incumbent to the gaddi. Agardas was caught
unawares and off guard. At any rate, he did not stand a chance. Partappurin, dressed for the occasion and driven by her desire for Agardas,
had been transformed into a figure of another *lok* (world). The guru
recognized that there was no escape. Partappurin's form had eight hands
and was full of aspects of 'many different kinds of characters'. The tale
emphasizes Agardas's total submission to Partappurin mata: he pleaded
before her with folded hands, agreed to satisfy her desire so that she
spared him his life, and no sooner had she expressed the command
married her so that she became his patrani .

Clearly, the legendary acts of Ghasidas and Balakdas, cast on a grand
and epic scale, did not find a sequel among the later gurus of Satnampanth. The transformation in the figure of the guru was worked through
the motive force of sexuality of the women who had been incorporated
into Ghasidas's lineage through marriage. Sexuality invested Partappurin with agency and, indeed, imbued her with the aspect of a devi.
Agardas was putty in the hands of this mata. It followed that Partappurin
quickly moved into a dominant position within Satnampanth. [...]

Communities

The chapters in this section at once index and take forward the rethinking in historical anthropology of the concept–entity of community, reconsiderations that were discussed in the introduction. First, communities appear in these pages as critical players in the historical unravelling of colony, modernity, and nation-state, as actors that imbue these processes with their own terms and textures. Second, this further involves the tracking of communities as accessing and articulating, reproducing and resisting diverse and wide-ranging relationships of meaning and power at the core of social worlds. Third and finally, here are to be found not only explorations of the contending connotations of community as construed by its members but considerations of the internal divisions of communities as expressed along lines of class, status, and gender.

Our deliberations open with Gyanendra Pandey's path-breaking discussion of the forging of the stereotype of the 'bigoted Julaha' within a colonial sociology of knowledge.[1] The reputation for 'bigotry' of the Muslim Julahas, a large and internally differentiated 'community' of weavers, in the United Provinces in north India was well established by the end of the nineteenth century. It was related to their participation in sectarian strife between Muslims and Hindus in the preceding period. At the same time, Pandey shows how such involvement of the Julahas in Hindu–Muslim strife, 'only a part of the history even of their role in public agitations in the nineteenth century', was intimately bound to

their existing conditions, from the unpredictable and rapid transformations in economic, social, and political conditions across
northern India under colonial rule through to the low social standing
of the Julahas—born of their relatively recent conversion to Islam as
well as their position as generally non-literate and poor manual labourers
—in the eyes of both Hindus and Muslims of the upper classes and
castes.

In this situation, the Muslim weavers sought to 'purify' themselves
and advance their social position. The endeavours were undertaken
within the interstices both of wider efforts launched by religious reformers
and revivalists against 'syncretistic, un-Islamic' popular practices and
of broader emphases of the colonial government to rigidly classify social
groups. Here, an important role was played by 'the mystic quality of the
weaving process and the close interconnection between work and
worship in the weavers' lives' as well as the heritage and self-image of
sections of the community. Together, Julaha solidarity was worked upon
and arrived at 'gradually and imperfectly through struggles against
concrete disabilities, for concrete ends.'

It is ahead of the unravelling of these contending and contradictory
processes that Pandey presciently tracks the framing of the image of
Julaha bigotry in colonialist writings. He shows how this persistent
representation actually derived from a mere few instances of 'Hindu–
Muslim riots in one small part of the Gangetic plain in which [only]
sections of the north Indian weaving community were involved.' On
the one hand, in tune with the one-sided character of stereotypes, the
image of the 'bigoted Julaha' reveals much more about colonial knowledge itself than about the particular pasts of the community. On the
other hand, in tenor with the nature of stereotypes as forms of condensed
knowledge, the ready representation became an enduring trope and
palpable staple of the historical record.

In the next chapter, Malavika Kasturi takes us back to the pre- and
early-colonial period in order to explore the anatomy of collective
violence among Rajput lineages in northern and central India.[2] Her
principal focus is on *bhumeawat*, a political and cultural process entailing
struggles for 'identity, status, and power by elite Rajputs, arising out of a
commitment and attachment to territory, and, more specifically, to the
homeland, or *bhum*', and the rebellions of the community. At the same
time, in Kasturi's hands, cultural and historical understandings of
collective violence open a window to the contingent and contentious,
differentiated and gendered processes at the core of the affirmation
and articulation of the (masculine) identity and solidarity of the Rajputs
as a community. By recognizing the central role of collective violence

in projections of Rajput selfhood and pride and the acute embedding of these processes in socio-economic and political structures, Kasturi also reveals the limitations of colonial representations of this multi-layered phenomenon, which links her arguments—albeit with discrete emphases—with those of Gyanendra Pandey in the preceding chapter.

In the pre-colonial period, bhumeawat was undertaken for a range of reasons involving the rights either of an entire lineage or of a particular individual. On the one hand, bhumeawat was successful as a strategy on account of the ability of elite Rajput lineages to recruit in their ranks kin, clansmen, and other men. Bearing strong linkages with state-building and propelled by prosperity (as much as by deprivation), it provided a framework for the operation of bonds of clan, lineage, and dependence, further feeding into more generalized movements. On the other hand, bhumeawat reveals the contending and contested characteristics of the Rajputs as a community. Taking place both between lineages as well as inside them, its ever-changing processes consisted of inherently contradictory strains, simultaneously cementing ties and widening factions and reshaping the identities and boundaries of lineages. Together, all this was expressed in the variety of responses subsumed by Rajput collective violence, from rebellion and feuding to banditry and plunder. But with the advent of colonial rule, Kasturi goes on to argue, bhumeawat underwent critical mutations and key transformations as it became a struggle for survival, increasingly more defensive than offensive, under new regimes of territoriality and sovereignty and in-formation and empire. It now informed diverse rebellions and responses to the British assumption of authority, while being expressed anew as part of separate situations and shifting strategies.

Questions of politics, masculinity, and kingship receive another spin in the imaginative take on community and its contradictions offered by Ajay Skaria. The setting is the distant Dangs district of Gujarat in western India, a place populated principally by *adivasi* communities of Bhils, Koknis, and Girasias, although much of Skaria's chapter is concerned with the first of these social groups.[3] The discussion is based on a formidable range of written records as well as on thickly textured oral narratives that abound among the Dangis. These oral traditions that exist as *goth* (stories) bring into play distinct yet overlapping epochs of the *moglai* (a time of freedom, or broadly the extra-colonial) and the *mandini* (a time of restraint, or broadly the colonial), epochs that are not simply chronological but are defined in opposition to each other in ways that the former traverses the latter and both extend into the present.[4] The central concern running through the chapter turns on issues of wildness—its aesthetics and anxieties, its desires and ambivalences, its politics and contentions. The issues allow Skaria to explore the concept-entity of the community through historically and ethnographically layered discussions of livelihood and pleasure, gender and witchcraft, and kingship and kinship.

In the chapter, Skaria's starting point is the ways in which practices of livelihood among the Dangis entail a distinctive aesthetics of wildness marked by anxiety and pleasure, running through activities of shifting cultivation, hunting, fishing, gathering, and the collection of flowers of the mahua (*Bassia latifolia*) tree that were used to distil liquor and also eaten. Against the grain of colonial and postcolonial representations of the lazy native and the happy-go-lucky tribal and commonplace and scholarly projections equating pleasure with nature, Skaria suggests that the affirmation of wildness and pleasure among the Dangis—and, especially, the Bhils—is better understood 'not as natural but as constructed through an agonistic relationship to a discourse centred around the upper-caste ideals of rightful work and living.' He elaborates these emphases not only by deftly rendering Dangi practices of livelihood in terms of their dense significations—an imaginative envisioning of activities, often considered as merely economic, as actions that are nothing but profoundly meaningful—but by presciently probing the ambivalences of gender in the construal of female wildness.

The gender of wildness also provides the thread that ties in the ensuing discussion of the politics of shared kingship and its critical lacks, especially those centring on witchcraft and masculinity, among the Dangi Bhils. Reflecting on the ramifications of the wide sharing and contestation of political power—so that 'every Dangi man, and certainly every Bhil man, was a raja'—Skaria engages and extends authoritative theories of kingship and caste in South and Southeast Asia. Zeroing in on the enactment of kingship in the Dangs, he makes an elegant case for how the widespread participation and inclusion of all men in Bhil kingship was associated with a politics of lack, a lack of self-sufficient loci of kingship. This meant that 'kingship resided in no one place, and there were multiple hierarchies of kingly authority.' At the same time, there was 'an even more pervasive lack involved in nineteenth-century Bhil kingship—a lack in the authority of Bhil men because of what was perceived as the power of Bhil women.' The lack involved its own ambivalences. On the one hand, practices of bride-wealth and men's inability to control female labour made for the relatively powerful status of Dangi women. On the other hand, this power was deeply resented and contested, and often considered as illegitimate. Skaria explicates this tension by focusing on the figure of the *dakan* or the witch, further linking the discussion with how Dangi chiefs enacted their rule by laying claim to an accentuated masculinity that was meant to control the presumed power of women

Once more, however, there are no ready resolutions in Skaria's analysis. It follows that the chapter ends by asking us to stay longer with the ways in which the masculine kingship of Bhil rule 'continued to be haunted by the apprehensions of its prosthetic nature', stalked, that is to say, by the formative prevalence of witches and the productive power of women, including Bhil queens. All this is related to the fact that Bhil kingship and kinship were not only about masculine power but about critical enactments of a distinctive wildness and particular politics of Bhil women. In these ways, Skaria foregrounds expressions of community as embedded in and constitutive of wide-ranging relationships and dense networks of meaning and authority, shot through with ambivalence and anxiety, defined by contention and contradiction, and subject to displacement and dissonance.

In the final chapter of the section, Veena Das constructs an imaginative ethnography of a critical event of contemporary history, the formation of the Sikh militant discourse in the Punjab and its intonations—of community and history and Self and Other—in the first half of the 1980s.[5] Das's key concerns revolve around the efforts of this discourse to forge an effective and unified political agency of the Sikhs out of a heterogeneous community, its assertions of and incitements to violence, and its reliance on rigorous dualisms—between masculine and feminine, Hindu and Sikh, and state and community —that yet operate upon different registers of nature and culture. All these elements form part of an unstable, emergent political language, crucially stamped with the impress of contemporaneity. Indeed, 'while the militant discourse sees the sacred and the eternal as an essential element, it emphasizes those aspects of the eternal which break their way into modern political events,' entirely a characteristic of the new language that is at once grounded in current political cultures in India and seeks to create historical self-recognition among the Sikhs as a community.

Das analyses crucial constituents of the written and oral discourse produced by Sikh militants beginning in 1981 through to the end of 1984. Insightfully working her way through incendiary materials, her wide-ranging explorations touch upon several key questions in the contemporary practice of historical anthropology. Tying these overlapping concerns is the formidable dynamic between history and the here-and-now in the imagination, invention, and instantiation of community, where the validity of the past and the inequity of the present are secured through the ways the former is made to break upon the

latter in Sikh militant discourse. If this present is the very site of the
militant movement, containing the possibility of a resplendent future,
it exactly follows that normal rules of morality toward violence, murder,
and terror do not apply here.

Together, Das highlights the central place of the dualisms between
the (Sikh–communitarian–masculine) Self and the (Hindu–state–
feminine) Other that turn on particular procedures and palpable patterns
in this discourse.[6] The motifs and modalities include: counter-posed
chronologies of the heroic Sikh community/past and the treacherous
Hindu nation/history; the martial masculinity of the martyred Sikh
and the seductive femininity of the weak Hindu; an incessant, current
recalling of Sikh history as repetition of past events and return of prior
protagonists—rendering non-contemporary events into coeval ones—
that is ever accompanied by a systematic, selective forgetting of shared
bonds between Hindus and Sikhs; 'the weaving of individual biography
into social text through the use of local knowledge'; and the validation
of violence in terms of ongoing mythological motifs and contemporary
political practices. Das closes the chapter by raising intriguing issues
regarding the relationship between Sikh and Hindu militancy, myth
and history, gender and state, community and violence, and suffering
and modernity, which not only ties up her contribution with the
preceding ones but also links it with the essays to follow, including
especially the considerations of culture and power in the next section.

NOTES

1. These explorations form part of Pandey's broader excursus into the relationships
    between sectarian strife, colonial power, and nationalist knowledge. Gyanendra
    Pandey, *The Construction of Communalism in Colonial North India* (New Delhi,
    Oxford University Press, 1990).
2. These issues are elaborated in Malavika Kasturi, *Embattled Identities: Rajput
    Lineages and the Colonial State in the Nineteenth-Century North India* (New
    Delhi, Oxford University Press, 2002).
3. For wider discussions of these communities, the region, and their pasts, see
    Ajay Skaria, *Hybrid Histories: Forests, Frontiers and Wildness in Western India*
    (New Delhi, Oxford University Press, 1999), the work from which the present
    chapter is derived.
4. Ibid.
5. The analyses and the chapter derive from Veena Das, *Critical Events: An
    Anthropological Perspective on Contemporary India* (New Delhi, Oxford University
    Press, 1995).

6. Simultaneously, Das shows in the chapter how the tangible figure of the (prior-ruler, ever-masculine, now-minority) Muslim Other has been gradually neutralized, mapped anew, and rendered somewhat spectral in this discursive terrain.

The Bigoted Julaha*

GYANENDRA PANDEY

[...]

The Julaha reputation for bigotry, which was well established in colonial sociology by the end of the nineteenth century, was clearly related to Julaha involvement in sectarian strife in the preceding period. [...] The occasions for strife were many and varied. In Banaras in 1809, the quarrel broke out over the 'neutral' space between a Muslim mosque and an older Hindu structure. In Ayodhya (Faizabad), where another much-talked-about riot occurred in 1855, the issue was a similar contention over the domination of a site where a Muslim mosque stood adjacent to an old Hindu temple. In Bareilly the coincidence of the Muharram and Ramnaumi festivals in 1837 and 1871 is said to have been the occasion for Hindu–Muslim rioting. In smaller towns, too, like the two major cloth-producing centres of Azamgarh district (Mubarakpur and Mau), violence broke out time and again during the nineteenth century: in 1813, 1834, and 1842 in Mubarakpur on account of the defilement of a mosque, an *imam-barah*, [and] a temple; and on the issue of cow slaughter in Mau in 1806 and on several occasions from the early 1860s onwards.

* Originally published in Gyanendra Pandey, *The Construction of Communalism in Colonial North India*, New Delhi: Oxford University Press, 1990, pp. 69–107, as 'The Bigoted Julaha'. In the present version, all notes and references have been deleted. For the complete text, see the original version.

In most of these instances, and in many others, large numbers of Julahas were actively involved in the quarrel on the Muslim side. As early as 1837, then, Thomason wrote in his report on the settlement of Azamgarh district that the Julahas of Mubarakpur, Mau, Kopaganj, and other such places in that region were 'a weak and sickly-looking people, but mostly possessing firearms, and very liable to be excited to riot by anything which affects their religious prejudices. They have of late years been particularly turbulent, in consequence of the spread amongst them of the tenets of Syed Uhmud [Saiyid Ahmad].' Muslim weavers were prominent again in the Baqr'Id riots of 1893 in eastern UP and western Bihar, as the following comment in the Ghazipur *District Gazetteer* testifies: 'The Julahas are the most bigoted of all Musalmans and...a turbulent and lawless race, as was amply illustrated during the conflicts between Hindus and Muhammedans in 1893 and on other occasions.'

One scarcely needs to point out the extreme one-sidedness of this statement. The Muslim weavers' involvement in Hindu–Muslim strife is obviously only a part of the history even of their role in public agitations in the nineteenth century; and their participation in Hindu–Muslim quarrels, when such quarrels occurred, was hardly surprising, given the fact that they constituted the largest segment of the numerically small Muslim community of the region and that they were concentrated in towns where the possibilities of serious and violent conflict were always greater. One could add that when riots have occurred in any urban concentration anywhere in the world, the densely populated, ill-serviced, and poorer localities of the lower classes have generally burned most fiercely. It is remarkable, in this context, that the extract from the Ghazipur *Gazetteer* quoted above takes the mere involvement of Julahas in the violent conflicts of 1893 as evidence of their 'turbulence' and 'lawlessness', although then, as on many other occasions, the weavers were not the attackers but the besieged.

It is also the case that, because of the nature of their occupation, weavers everywhere have been commonly dependent on moneylenders and other middlemen and vulnerable to the play of market forces.

[...] One point that needs particular emphasis is that the struggle for power and status, which in colonial India often took the form of a contest over the boundaries of ritual space and 'traditional' authority, was reinforced by the rapid and unpredictable shifts that took place during the nineteenth century in the general social, economic, and political condition of the people of northern India.

[...] The evidence regarding north-Indian weavers in the nineteenth century gives us a picture of a community that was cruelly tossed about as their dependence on a whole range of intermediaries—moneylenders, lawyers, recruiting *sardars*—significantly increased. The beneficiaries of the new conditions in the cloth trade included, prominently, a large group of Hindu merchants and moneylenders who came to attain a perhaps unprecedented hold not only on the trade but on the weavers themselves. There can be no doubt that this heightened strength of the merchants/moneylenders, their powerful position in law under the new colonial dispensation, and their increasing arrogance, as the lower classes often saw it, caused much annoyance to the 'losers'—not only to lower classes like the weavers, but also to the declining class of small *zamindars* and service gentry who claimed a 'traditional' authority and status. It is but a small step from there to saying that weaver/moneylender (or weaver-merchant) conflict inevitably followed, and, since the weavers were mainly Muslims and the moneylenders mainly Hindus, this took the form of Hindu–Muslim strife. But it may be well to take this small step slowly.

[...] There was much, apart from economic hardship, in the existing conditions of the Julahas to encourage them to wage a struggle to upgrade their status as a 'community'. Widely scattered and internally differentiated as they were, one obvious feature that the Muslim weavers had in common, apart from their occupation, was their lowly social standing in the eyes of both Muslims and Hindus of the upper castes and classes. This was the result, evidently, of their comparatively recent conversion to Islam and their position as manual labourers who were generally poor and illiterate.

One of the more obvious status-markers in northern India in the nineteenth and twentieth centuries, as perceived by the locally dominant classes and by outside observers, was the distinction between the *sharif* (plural *ashraf*, the respectable classes) and the *razil* (or labouring people). The former category appears to have included all those who did not soil their hands with the messy business of labour: the Brahmins, Rajputs, and Bhumihars (that is, the 'zamindari castes' of the region), together with the 'true' Saiyids and Sheikhs (that is, those who could demonstrate some sort of descent from 'noble' Arabic ancestors), Pathan converts from Rajput clans, and some smaller Hindu castes like the Kayasthas who were prominent in the bureaucracy and the 'learned' professions. All the rest, from the 'clean' cultivating castes like the Kurmis, Koeris, and Ahirs, and equivalent Muslim castes like the Zamindaras (or Rautaras) of Azamgarh, to the 'unclean' labouring and artisanal castes, Chamars, Dusadhs, Lohars, Julahas, and so on—were classified as razil.

Perhaps the most important indicator of a community's razil status thus was the performance of menial and other tasks for the upper castes and landowners. Orr exaggerated, but not wildly, when he wrote on *begari* in the mid-nineteenth century: 'The Chamar, Lodh, Kurmi, and all inferior castes are the prey of all, caught at every hour of the day or night, made use of as beasts, of burthen, beaten and abused, treated as if incapable of feeling pain or humiliation, never remunerated.' But there were other indicators too: the incidence of widow remarriage, for example, or the proportion of a group's womenfolk that went out to work, which was far greater among the lower castes than the higher. It was found in Bihar in 1911 that there were but 8 female workers to every 100 male workers among the Bhumihars, 10 to every 100 among Rajputs and 12 among Brahmins. By contrast, the statistics were 52 in every 100 for the Kurmis, 54 among the Ahirs and the Koeris, and as high as 69 and 71 among the Julahas and Dusadhs respectively. On this calculation, then, the Julahas emerged ranked with some of the lowest of the Hindu 'untouchable' castes. Several pronouncements of Muslim learned men in the nineteenth century also placed them on par with the Dabgars, a Muslim caste equivalent to the Chamars, and the Bhangis.

The division that existed between Julahas and other 'low-born' Muslims on the one hand, and the sharif or 'respectable' Muslims on the other, was reflected also in some of their religious practices. That popular Islam in India paralleled popular Hinduism in remarkable ways from very early days is now widely recognized. Kunwar Muhammad Ashraf wrote of pilgrimages to the graves of reputed saints that characterized popular religious practice among the Muslims of northern India in the period of the Sultanate. In Sindh, pilgrimages of this kind brought together such great crowds that 'there was hardly any room to stand.' The sexes mingled freely and the atmosphere was decidedly festive, a situation disliked by the orthodox, and especially the theologians. But, as the author of the contemporary *Tarikh-i-Tahiri* observed, 'the custom has so long prevailed among these people and what time has sanctioned, they never relinquish.'

[...] The powerful attacks launched against these syncretistic, un-Islamic practices by religious reformers and revivalists alike are certain to have reached most weaving towns and *qasba*s in the nineteenth century. Early in the century, officials reported the spread of Wahabi influence among the weavers of Mau, Mubarakpur, and Kopaganj. As the century advanced, and the debate between the new theologians and the orthodox deepened, the pressure to reform and become 'pure' Muslims is likely to have grown.

[...] To these kinds of pressure was added [...] the pressure of a colonial government out to classify *everything* and to fix the status, character, and administrative usefulness of one and all by means of a public record. Many groups of Muslims in northern India, too, were therefore moving quickly by the turn of the century to shed 'Hindu' names and establish for themselves a 'purer' Islamic status. As an important part of this trend, Muslim weavers came together in an endeavour to change their caste appellation, overthrow the derisive views about them which the upper classes (Hindu and Muslim) helped to promote, and gain an equal standing in the fraternity of Islam.

The word 'Julaha' was in all probability of Persian origin (*julah*—weaver, from *jula*, ball of thread). In India in the nineteenth century many observers sought to trace the name to the Arabic *juhala*, meaning the 'ignorant class', to bring it in line with their notions of the weavers' stupidity. Julaha spokesmen countered with the argument that the term in fact came from *jal* (net), *jils* (decorated), or *ujla* (lighted up, or white); hence also the name which local weaving communities sometimes used for themselves even in the early nineteenth century: *nurbaf* or 'weavers of light'. They claimed Adam as the founder of their craft—when Satan (or, in some versions, Eve, or a fairy) made him realize his nakedness, he learnt the art of weaving and later taught it to his sons—and declared that their ancestors came from Arabia. From the later decades of the nineteenth century Muslim weavers in many places came to reject the name Julaha altogether, and insisted that they be called 'Momin' ('the faithful', 'men of honour'), 'Ansari' (after a claimed Arabic ancestor who practised the art of weaving), 'Momin-Ansar' or 'Sheikh Momin'. By 1911 they had succeeded in having themselves recorded under these names in the census. Today, it is rare for anyone in Banaras or Patna, Mubarakpur or Mau, to use the name 'Julaha' to refer to any member of this community.

The Muslim weavers' efforts to 'purify' themselves and upgrade their social position were, of course, in line with social reform and protest movements among many other lower- and middle-ranking groups and castes at this time.

[...] In the preceding pages there have been more than a few references to the Julahas and the community of Muslim weavers in northern and central India. It is necessary to stress, however, [...] that this 'community' was far from being homogeneous or united for most of the period under study. Julaha solidarity was forged gradually and imperfectly through struggles against concrete disabilities, for concrete ends. The fact is of some importance if we are to fully appreciate the role of the weavers in the caste and community struggles of the nineteenth century, not to mention the extent to which they were successful in achieving proclaimed goals.

It is only to be expected that there would have been major differences in the economic well-being of different groups among the

Muslim weavers: between 'master-weavers' and ordinary 'independent' weavers, and weavers who worked on others' looms in Banaras, Mubarakpur, Mau, and elsewhere. Much more striking are the 'caste' (one would also have to say 'historical') distinctions that existed among Muslim weavers even at the end of the nineteenth century—distinctions that the colonial administration did everything to obliterate as it isolated the category of the Muslim Julaha with its supposedly fixed and identifiable caste characteristics. Ibbetson's *Punjab Ethnography* listed groups that styled themselves Koli Julahas, Chamar Julahas, Mochi Julahas, and Ramdasi Julahas. There was little doubt, Ibbetson remarked, that in time these groups would drop the prefixes that indicated their lowly Hindu origins and become 'Julahas pure and simple': that is to say, the pressure of the censuses, and other political and social demands of the time, would lead them to do so. In UP, at the time of the 1891 census, the Parsotiya Julaha of Rohilkhand was found to be a Hindu, related to the major Hindu weaving caste of Koris. The remaining Julahas in the province registered themselves under 244 divisions. There were Bais, Bania, Bhangi, Bisen, Chamar, Chauhan, Koli, Rajput, Teli, and Tomar Julahas, for example, some who derived their sectional identity from a geographical area (the Chaurasia, Faizabadi, Purabiya, Sarwariya, Shahabadi, etc.), and others who claimed a more or less 'pure' Muslim descent, calling themselves Madari, Muhammadi, Momin, Mughal, Pathan, Shaikh, Siddiqi or Sunni Julahas—evidence enough of their mixed origins and still ambiguous position in the fraternity of Indian Muslims.

Just as there were major differences in caste identification among the Muslim weavers of northern India, so there were differences in historical associations and historical memories. The weavers of Banaras, Mubarakpur, Mau, Tanda, Jais, and other such centres had developed and long maintained special links with the *nawab*s of Awadh, the kings of Nepal, and even more distant rulers like the Nizam of Hyderabad. Even a relatively undistinguished place like Mau, not noted in the colonial period for the production of any exceptional fabrics, could trace its distinct traditions and the special position of its manufacturing population back to the days of the great Mughals.

Mau was mentioned in the *Ain-i-Akbari*, along with Banaras and Jalalabad, as being famous for the production of certain 'beautiful' cloths. In the reign of Shah Jahan, the *pargana* of Maunath Bhanjan was assigned to the emperor's daughter, Jahanara Begum, 'for [her] supply with cloth and sugar, the two great staples of the place', and its chief town (Mau) appears to have been renamed Jahanabad. Under the patronage of the imperial house, then and in the reign of Aurangzeb, the town flourished.

'Substantial buildings were erected, a large market place [or *katra*] built, and every means employed to induce persons to resort to the town and take up their abode there.' Mau quickly grew to have as many as 84 *mohallas* and 360 mosques. Julahas, Katuas (a specialized caste of spinners who were Hindus), and traders constituted the major part of its population. A 'great manufacturing industry in cotton cloth' thus came into being, and the subsequent establishment of an imperial customs post in the town indicates the volume of traffic that passed through it.

It is among the weavers of such towns in eastern UP that Burn, Census Superintendent of UP in 1901, is likely to have found that small number of 'uneducated Musalmans' who, in his reckoning, still spoke Awadhi—the dialect that was used by the officials and army of the former nawabs of Awadh. 'These people,' wrote Burn, '[who] are almost entirely Muhammadans...believe that they speak Urdu, as their language differs considerably from that of the people round them.' The language—which they believed to be Urdu—was just one mark of the pride and 'independence' of the weaving populations of Mau and Mubarakpur, Lucknow and Tanda, Banaras and Sassaram.

By the later nineteenth century there were other marks too. The weavers of Mau, Kopaganj, and Mubarakpur Khas (this excludes, presumably, the weavers of the areas surrounding Mubarakpur) 'are not, like most other weavers, worshippers of Ghazi Mian and his flag,' Reid wrote in his report on the settlement of Azamgarh district in 1877. In other words, groups of Muslim weavers were by now making a point of standing aloof from those practices of their fellow weavers which consisted in joining lower-caste Hindus in propitiating the whole range of supernatural powers that could conceivably aid them or do them harm.

That this new mood was beginning to penetrate even beyond the weaving qasbas and towns that had attained something of a privileged position owing to their links with the courts in the past is made clear by Deepak Mehta's study of Muslim weavers in two villages of Bara Banki district. This scholar notes the intimate connection between work and worship in the lives of the weavers, and the centrality of the weavers' major religious text (or *kitab*), the *Mufid-ul-Mominin*, in the practice of both. While Mehta does not mention this, it is more than likely that the *Mufid-ul-Mominin* came to occupy this place as *the* 'book' of the weavers fairly recently—not before the late nineteenth or the early twentieth century in any case, for it is only from that time that the name 'Momin' (that is, the 'faithful') was claimed as their own by the weavers.

The *Mufid-ul-Mominin* relates how the practice of weaving came into the world, at its very beginning. The story, as recounted by Mehta, is as follows:

Adam [is] expelled from *Jannat* [heaven] as punishment for having eaten wheat. Adam feels hungry and prays to Allah for food. Allah orders Jabril [Gabriel] to give Adam a wood named Salim, and a goat, and to teach him the work of agriculture. Adam and Hawwa [Eve] slaughter the goat and eat its meat. Adam next complains about his nudity. (Some weavers said that Hawwa taunts Adam about his nudity, while others argued that a *houri* [fairy], and not Hawwa, offers to marry Adam if only he can clothe himself fully.) Adam feels ashamed and complains to Allah about his nakedness. Allah orders Jabril to give Adam a box full of weaving instruments and to teach him the craft of weaving....

Adam then asks Jabril to teach him how to weave. Jabril says that there are certain prayers to be recited in the process of weaving, equivalent to reciting the Holy Qoran one thousand times, or feeding two thousand needy people and setting free one thousand camels in God's name. In retaining these prayers in his memory the weaver is protected from calamity. If, however, he practices his craft without reciting such prayers and continues to call himself Momin (faithful Muslim) he is a liar, barred from entry into the Muslim community on the day of judgement.

The *Mufid-ul-Mominin* goes on to list the 19 supplicatory prayers to be uttered in the different stages of weaving. These are given in the form of answers to questions that Adam asks of Jabril. The prayers are notable for their extreme simplicity and their straightforward message of the greatness and grace of the one God and his Prophet, Mohammed: 'Allaho Akbar', 'La Ilaha Illa Allah', 'Mohammad: o Rasul-Allah'. As Jabril says in the story, the recitation of these prayers in the process of weaving is 'equivalent to reciting the Holy Qoran one thousand times, or feeding two thousand needy people and setting free one thousand camels in God's name.'

Mehta finds, from his close study of the life processes and work of the weavers, that four distinct practices are associated with the weaver's loom. The first, and most obvious, is commercial production. A second is cloth production for the dying, the weaving of the *kafan* or shroud. Unlike with the first, this practice is not thought of as a right but as 'an obligation that every Julaha is required to fulfil at some point in his or her life'. The third and fourth practices have to do with the reproduction of the weaving community—the initiation of male children, and the transmission of the loom. During the initiation of the novice, all the prayers associated with the loom are recited in their sequential order and also repeated. 'The male headweaver, in whose household this initiation takes place, reads out all of Adam's questions and Jabril's answers from the kitab during the first six days of the month when both the loom and the *karkhana* [workshop or work-room] are ritually cleaned.' When the loom is passed on from father to son, again, 'the entire conversation between Adam and Jabril is read out once by a holy man'.

I have dwelt at some length on the heritage and self-image of certain groups of weavers, as well as the mystic quality of the weaving process and the close interconnection between work and worship in the weavers' lives, because all this puts a rather different light on their reactions to the turns and twists of economic fortune in the nineteenth century. There can be no doubt that the weavers were involved in many struggles in which the conditions imposed on their trade, and the matter of the profits and losses to be made out of it not only by weavers but also by merchants and moneylenders (British and Indian), were of central if not exclusive importance. But, equally, there is little room for doubt that in many places the memories and pride of the weavers contributed substantially to the contemporary struggle to preserve the community's occupation and rights.

One of the first references to the north Indian weavers as a 'troublesome' community appears in the context of a struggle between local weavers and the East India Company to preserve, or extend, their rights over certain portions of the trade. The weavers concerned belonged to the region around Banaras and the quarrel arose over a new British regulation by which goods imported into the city of Banaras for personal use were exempted from duty only if they did not exceed Rs 10 in value. The government agents were soon complaining about the 'clandestine importation' of thread, cotton, and other goods for commercial purposes: this was apparently done by distributing the goods into several hands to take advantage of the 'ten-rupee system'. The amounts involved were sometimes pathetically small: thus, for example, Barlow, Deputy Collector at the Banaras customs house, detained three weavers for the possession of thread which he described as their 'aggregate joint property', but felt compelled to release them since the value of the thread was so small—no more than Rs 11–4 annas in all. Nevertheless the officials complained of a 'systematic fraud' being practised on the government and pointed at the same time to the aggressive tactics adopted by the weavers. As Barlow wrote,

This class of people who subsist by daily labour are becoming so formidable that not an individual case occurs in which a weaver is concerned—but hundreds immediately assemble. Every summary proceeding is laid before the Magistrate [that is, the Collector's decisions were challenged in the Magistrate's court] and whatever costs they [the weavers] may incur by the suit they are ready to pay.

And again:

> The Weavers come to the Chokey's [*chaukis*—checkpoints] sometimes singly but as frequently in a body [they have become] exceedingly troublesome.... Whether I immediately release the property [*sic*], or have occasion to detain it, the case is immediately submitted to the Magistrate, by all Weavers who can be mustered together.

Even here, there are indications of a larger concern than the simple profit and loss of the individual or a group of individuals. There is emphatic protest against arbitrary changes being introduced into the conditions of the trade; and there is, beyond that, the question of the rights of the community as a whole: 'whatever costs they may incur by the suit they are ready to pay.' In other cases, there is even less evidence of any overwhelming concern with economic profit and loss, and indeed at certain times striking indications of a willingness to suffer economic loss for the honour of the community and the preservation of its lifestyle.

One may cite here some observations made by the collector of Saharanpur on the 'rather remarkable change' that had occurred in the local weavers' position as a result of the rise in cotton prices at the beginning of the 1860s. 'Formerly', he wrote,

> the weavers in this district generally purchased the thread on their own account, ultimately realizing the profits from the sale of the manufactured article. Since the rise in the price of the raw material, it appears that the weavers have, as a general rule, been unable to do this, and that they have consequently now assumed the position of daily labourers ....

Their employers included not only the shopkeepers and merchants who supplied them with thread and took the profits on the sale of the cloth, but also zamindars and 'even cultivators' who now engaged them for the manufacture into cloth of at least a part of their cotton crop. 'The weavers naturally feel this change has rendered their position by no means so independent as was formerly the case. I generally found that *they viewed this as more serious than the loss of income* which has undoubtedly been considerable [emphasis added].' At the end of the nineteenth century, again, we have evidence of a little-known movement of resistance by weavers to the introduction of the factory system. When a Kayasth entrepreneur tried at this time to set up a factory for the production of cloth in Mau, he came up against a serious obstacle— the local weaver refused to take up employment in his factory 'even for double the wage that he earns outside'. Another Indian entrepreneur had encountered exactly the same difficulty a little earlier in Banaras.

What the weavers protested here was the attempt to reduce them from the position of proud, and to some extent 'independent', craftsmen into that of faceless wage-earners; what they resented was 'the indignity of being ordered about'. But there was perhaps more to it even than that. The weaver's loom was the symbol of the community, a means of offering prayers to the Almighty, a gift from God. Deepak Mehta observes that 'weavers often express the view that the mosque and the karkhana [workplace] are interchangeable spaces in the work of weaving [and, one should add, worship].' The loss of a loom was therefore much more than the loss of an individual's or a family's means of livelihood. It was the loss of one's place in the world. This was one reason why weavers sometimes continued to ply the loom even at times and in places where it was plainly uneconomical to do so. One such example comes from Ghazipur during the 'cotton famine' of the 1860s. Here, as the Collector's report tells us, while not 'one-half of the usual number of looms' were now being worked, even of the reduced number, many were 'kept up merely in order that the children may not forget how to weave.' The centrality of the loom as the most important signifier of the community and as the means of its reproduction is here underlined.

It is hardly surprising to find that as part of the weavers' fight to preserve (and improve) their economic and social status, a vigil was maintained by prominent groups of weavers in what they considered to be *their* towns, *their* mohallas, *their* mosques, to guard against any innovations that might go to reduce the importance of their religious festivals and places of worship. As Reid put it in writing about the Julahas of Mau, 'they are very touchy about anything that seems intended to hurt their religious feelings, and act as one man in anything that concerns them as a body.' It was on account of these diverse, sometimes desperate, and often long-drawn-out struggles by weavers in many different places that the north-Indian Muslim weaving community acquired the reputation of being uncompromising, easily aroused, violent Muslims: a community of 'fanatical', 'clannish' and 'bigoted' Julahas. What the stereotype did, of course, was to decimate the weavers' history. It erased at a stroke the very noticeable differences in the self-image and historical circumstances of different groups of Muslim weavers in northern India. And it flattened flesh-and-blood, emotional, labouring and thinking people into one-dimensional, unvarying and 'irrational' entities.

[...] It can be shown, I think, that the image of Julaha bigotry was drawn up in colonialist writings on the strength of a few examples of Hindu–Muslim riots in one small part of the Gangetic plain in which sections of the north-Indian weaving community were involved. If we set aside for the moment the special circumstances and traditions of the weavers involved in these conflicts, and overlook also the many contemporary examples of cross-communal struggle against acts and institutions that were perceived as a common threat by all the people of a locality in which these same weavers participated, it is still remarkable how the idea of the 'bigoted Julaha' makes its appearance in just a few official accounts of the nineteenth century close on the heels of, and in direct response to, outbreaks of Hindu–Muslim strife.

The Julaha stereotype as we know it appears to have been forged in UP. This fact is surely not unrelated to the recurrent conflicts over religious practice and ritual precedence in this region that we have noticed earlier, and the fact that exclusively Muslim political organizations of a modern kind found their earliest roots here. Yet, when the gazetteers for the different districts of UP were drawn up at the turn of the century, and the Muslim weavers came to be presented as a major factor in the explanation of 'communal riots', a striking contrast appeared between western and eastern UP. It was in a handful of eastern UP districts alone that the 'turbulent' and 'bigoted' character of the Julaha was highlighted. Everywhere else a rather different Julaha character appeared.

Let us take western UP first. In Bijnor, where the proportion of Julahas among the local population was the highest in all UP, the Julahas were said to be 'often working as cultivators and attaining a fair proficiency as husbandmen'. From Saharanpur it was reported that 'with their scanty beards and almost bare cheeks, the Julahas are readily distinguishable and are to be seen in almost every village. Most of them still follow their hereditary trade of weaving, but hard times have driven large numbers to agriculture in which they have achieved fair success.' The report from Bareilly was along much the same lines, the local Julahas being described as 'remarkably careful and industrious' cultivators. In the Aligarh Gazetteer nothing notable is said about the community, nor again in that of Moradabad—where the Julahas were simply weavers 'or else...tillers of the soil'.

In eastern UP, too, the 'bigoted' or 'fanatical' character of the community was not everywhere observed. For Jaunpur and Gorakhpur it was merely said that a great many of the Julahas still followed their traditional calling, some had migrated to Calcutta and other centres of the modern cloth industry, and others had become quite successful cultivators. The absence of any further comment in the Gorakhpur case is particularly noteworthy, not only because Gorakhpur was a fairly important centre of the Cow-Protection Movement but also because there was evidently considerable political unity among the local Julahas.

'Almost all...[Julahas] in this district describe themselves as Momins,' the *Gazetteer* noted in an observation that testified to the solidarity of the Muslim weavers of Gorakhpur.

Nor was any statement regarding Julaha 'bigotry' forthcoming from the districts of Awadh. The *Gazetteer* for Lucknow recorded only that most Julahas of the district lived in Lucknow city; for Bara Banki that 'in spite of their proverbial stupidity, they are careful and laborious cultivators'; for Faizabad that while many had taken to agriculture, the Julahas of the district were 'still very largely engaged in their peculiar occupation of weaving'. It was left to the *Gazetteers* of precisely four districts on the eastern border of the province—Banaras, Ghazipur, Ballia, and Azamgarh—to draw up the portrait of the 'bigoted' Muslim Julaha.

Here, as I have already suggested, the existence of many old centres of cloth production, the numerical strength of the weavers in these 'urban' localities, the self-image and pride of the weavers, combined with the economic, social, and political dislocation of the colonial period and the renewed struggles for power and prestige that came along with this, brought the Julahas out in numerous acts of resistance and repeated outbreaks of fighting over the prized symbols of Hinduism and Islam. Much the same applied of course to the district of Faizabad, with its major weaving centres of Tanda, Akbarpur, Jalalpur, Nagpur, and Iltifatganj, and also to Lucknow city. But there was one crucial difference: neither Lucknow nor Faizabad was affected, as the districts of Azamgarh, Ballia, and Ghazipur were, by the cow-protection riots that took place in 1893, a short while before the *District Gazetteers* came to be compiled. The inference of 'Julaha bigotry' was drawn directly from the experience of these riots (in which, as I have already remarked, the Julahas and other Muslims were, in fact, the besieged) and from another instance of strife in Banaras in 1891 (an agitation against the demolition of a Hindu temple in which large numbers of Muslims protested side by side with Hindus, but which was taken, once again, as representative of 'Hindu–Muslim' conflict). As the Banaras *Gazetteer* put it, 'though they are almost certainly of Hindu extraction the Julahas are the most bigoted and aggressive of all the Musalmans, and have always taken a prominent part in the religious quarrels that have from time to time arisen in Banaras.'

The causal equation that is at work here can be traced back a fairly long way in colonialist writings on some places in eastern UP. I have already cited Thomason's judgement in 1837 on the Julahas of Mubarakpur, Kopaganj, and Mau: that they were 'very liable to be excited to riot by anything which affects their religious prejudices'. This was written three years after a violent outbreak in Mubarakpur and in the midst of a growing dispute over the size of *tazia*s for the Muharram processions in the qasba. Forty years later, when the next settlement of Azamgarh district was made, the new Settlement Officer, J.R. Reid, reported, amidst gathering tension over the issue of cow slaughter in Mau, 'In former times, both before and after cession, the weaver population [of Mau] was inclined to be turbulent.' For Mubarakpur he added that 'like their caste fellows of Mau, the weavers of Mubarakpur are fanatical and clannish in the extreme.'

The structure of this argument persists in later writings. A riot indicates fanaticism, nothing more nor less. As a magistrate put it in regard to certain zamindars of village Husainabad who were implicated in a riot in Mubarakpur in 1904, 'the matter is still *sub judice*,' but there was 'strong reason to believe' that the zamindars were 'more or less fanatical Mohamedans [*sic*]'. In its turn, of course, fanaticism can only lead to riots. The Azamgarh *Gazetteer* compiled in 1909 merely follows this circular logic. The Julahas of the district were concentrated chiefly in the towns of Azamgarh, Mau, Mubarakpur and Kopaganj, it observed, 'and like their kinsmen *in other districts* [N.B.] they are a turbulent race, and it is to them that the conflicts between Hindus and Musalmans that have from time to time disturbed the peace of the district are generally attributed.'

The Ballia *Gazetteer*, compiled a few years earlier, was slightly more specific about the evidence on which this characterization of the Julahas was based: '*Like their kinsmen in Azamgarh and Ghazipur*, the Julahas [of Ballia] are a turbulent and lawless race, and it is to them that the conflicts between Musalmans and Hindus, which have from time to time disturbed the peace of *the eastern districts* may generally be attributed [emphasis added].' The Ghazipur volume admitted the source of its findings even more directly. 'The Julahas are the most bigoted of all Musalmans and...a turbulent and lawless race, *as was amply illustrated during the conflicts between Hindus and Muhammedans in 1893 and on other occasions* [emphasis added].'

By the same process, the image of the 'bigoted Julaha' passed into some of the more general writings on UP. As Crooke wrote of his 'cowardly, pretentious, factious and bigoted' Julahas in *The Tribes and Castes of the North-Western Provinces and Oudh* published in 1896, 'they took *a leading part in the recent Benares riots* and some of the worst outrages in the Mutiny were their work [emphasis added].' In a monograph on cotton fabrics produced in UP, published two years later, Silberrad considered it unnecessary to advance any reasons for his judgement that the Julahas were 'very zealous' and 'much inclined to fanaticism', but his language was reminiscent of that employed by Reid which I have quoted in an earlier paragraph: they 'display a strong clannish feeling, helping one another [!], and to a great extent settling disputes between members of their own caste among themselves.'

Thus the stereotype passed into the sociological record, and thence to the hands of the modern historian—for whom the Julahas became 'a most bigoted and turbulent community', 'renowned for their bigotry'. [...]

Rebellion*

Malavika Kasturi

In 1839, Umrao Singh of Jaklone (later in British Bundelkhand) and *jagirdar* of Pali rebelled against Gwalior state to agitate for the estates formerly controlled by him in the erstwhile state of Chanderi. To strengthen his struggle, he garnered the support of the Bundelas of Jhansi and the surrounding areas, many of whom were his relatives. Gathering reinforcements on the way, Umrao Singh kept up the pressure on the Gwalior *darbar*, resorting to plunder to subsist. Officials such as Sleeman feared that the impact of such 'malcontents' resorting to collective violence 'must unsettle men's minds and must to a greater degree disturb the peace of mind of our possessions and render highway robbery and other crimes against the public more easy to perpetrate.' To British officials, Umrao Singh represented the archetype of the 'wild' Rajput, whose unbridled masculinity led to chaotic behaviour; a stereotype in which these lineages were perceived as 'robbers and disturbers of the public peace'. State coercive power was continuously engaged in curbing the violence arising out of 'affrays' [...] while colonial criminal law sought to contain the occurrence of collective violence in various ways, civil law tried to propel all disputes to the *diwani adalats*.

* Originally published in Malavika Kasturi, *Embattled Identities: Rajput Lineages and the Colonial State in the Nineteenth-Century North India*, New Delhi: Oxford University Press, 2002, pp. 172–83, as '*Bhumeawat* and Rajput Rebellion'. In the present version, all notes and references have been deleted. For the complete text, see the original version.

In British perceptions, the existence of violence in agrarian society was used to define and separate the 'civilized' and the rational from the 'irrational' and 'criminal' communities over whom they ruled. After 1857, the colonial state made a case for itself as the repository of overarching order in order to legitimize its power and strengthen its coercive apparatus [...]. Colonial officials, who looked upon instances of collective violence as a 'primitive' aspect of Rajput martial culture, did not seek to understand the social, economic, and political structures within which it was embedded. Nor did they seek to understand the complexity of this seemingly 'unstructured' violence, or the multiplicity of its various strands. They used an ahistorical understanding of such 'disorders' to come to conclusions about Rajput identity and culture. However, the forms violent acts take need to be studied within a specific political and cultural context. In the case of Rajput *biradaris*, violence was intrinsic to the affirmation of their masculine identity and solidarity. The type and nature of collective violence perpetrated by Rajputs, was, I argue, élite at its core.

Collective violence had an important role to play in the projection of Rajput pride and sense of self, for, as Tapti Roy suggests, violence 'vindicated their claim to be addressed as *thakurs*' and reassert group solidarity. During the British period, even if Rajput landholdings and resource bases contracted, 'their traditional norms in the use of violence by means of a combined resistance remained.' However, more than that, I argue that for the Rajputs, collective violence and conflict as expressed through *bhumeawat* was central to the political process by which biradaris negotiated with and exercised authority, articulated identities, and redefined their position within the overlapping and multiple hierarchies of which they were a part. Through bhumeawat, boundaries were constantly re-drawn between various Rajput factions, biradaris, and other social groups.

Bhumeawat was a component of most forms of collective violence in which elite biradaris engaged. Rajputs embarking on bhumeawat collected armies to raid and ravage the *bhum* of the enemy. As a precursor to armed conflict, villages were burnt and a *dand* (fine) extracted. In 1842, Sleeman, the Commissioner in the Sagar and Narmada Territories, partly understood the nature of bhumeawat when he commented that 'the mode of levying indiscriminate war on the territory of the chief with whom the landholders of the military class are dissatisfied is called *bhoomeeawut* from *bhoom* land and *Bhoomea* landed proprietor.'

Though Sleeman saw bhumeawat as 'indiscriminate warfare', I will argue that it might be understood as a political and cultural process operating within a specific matrix of variables. Bhumeawat may be better defined as the fight for identity, status, and power by elite Rajputs at various levels, arising out of a sense of commitment and attachment to territory, and, more specifically, to the homeland, or bhum. James Franklin had come closer to the truth in 1820, when he pointed out that the Bundelas used the term *bhumiddae* (another term for bhumeawat) to 'express their exertions, either in defence of, or to recover their lands, [and] might not unaptly be rendered patriotism, but of a very rude kind.' In pre-colonial north India, lineages had taken to bhumeawat for a number of reasons, either when the rights of particular individuals or the whole biradari were at stake.

Bhumeawat was highly successful because of the ability of elite Rajput lineages to recruit many men into their ranks, including kindred and clansmen. Sleeman noted with dismay that a Rajput taking to bhumeawat had 'the sympathy of the very large class of men of his own rank whose tenure in their lands and offices is improved by the atrocities he may commit.' He cited the example of Umrao Singh of Jaklone in Lalitpur, who, feuding simultaneously with both the raja of Chanderi and the maharaja of Gwalior regarding his proprietary rights and honour in 1840, was supported by his father-in-law Zalim Singh, who provided him with both men and materials. Such movements also attracted the attention of men-at-arms, increasingly on the loose in a demilitarizing social milieu, and 'whose object is plunder, or service.' Thus, officials noted that whenever 'disturbances' broke out:

...adventurers, who have nothing but their swords, spears and firearms to depend on for subsistence flock in from all quarters...in the hope of finding employment either in the extra establishments of the constituted authorities of Government, or the leaders of predatory gangs.

Agrarian society, it appears, was fraught with tensions, ever ready to explode into armed conflict, as most villages were armed and full of persons ready to join the forces of dominant lineages to make lucrative gains. Ties of lineage, clan, and dependence worked within the framework of bhumeawat and fed into more generalized movements.

Bhumeawat had strong links with state-building before British rule. When princely polities were weak, lineage elites had often garnered economic and political power and broken free from central control. In the eighteenth century, such states were constantly threatened either by full-scale revolts of tributary chiefs and their allies, or smaller-scale rebellions ignited by one or more localized Rajput lineages. Before *nawabi* Awadh was annexed by the British in 1858, long-drawn-out contests frequently occurred between the Nawab and Rajput landholders (many of whom were revenue contractors) over claims to land revenue and questions relating to the extent of control they could exercise over their *ilakas* (areas). These struggles reached their peak at the time of the harvest, a period when both thakur cultivators and co-sharers began to 'sharpen their swords and burnish their spears'. Rajput lineages also took to bhumeawat when deprived of their land, power, and privileges. The Bundela lineages of Chanderi agitated against Scindia on more than one occasion, when the raja of Chanderi, who laid claims to rule on the basis of lineage and clan loyalties, was ousted from power, his title revoked, and the region subsumed within Gwalior state between 1813 and 1835. The Bundelas revolted against the administration in Gwalior, ravaging and plundering its territory, recruiting men from other parts of Bundelkhand to fight for their cause.

Rajput collective violence was a complex phenomenon and subsumed a range of responses from rebellion and feuding to banditry, which were inextricably linked to the struggle between and within lineages over power, status, and position. Bhumeawat [...] comprised contradictory strains, cementing bonds and widening factions within biradaris in different social and political contexts and levels. Ties of clientelism and group loyalty binding lineages together often clashed with individual ambitions, creating changes in the nature of bhumeawat and the identity of those defined by factions or biradaris as the 'enemy'. Clearly, then, bhumeawat also took place both between and *within* lineages seeking to contest and reshape the limits of the boundaries, separating them from the 'other' in an effort to assert their identities and power.

Feuding, very much part of bhumeawat, occurred at all levels over territory, claims to authority, and matters of revenge. It was viewed as a legitimate and honourable cultural expression of conflict and as a component of bhumeawat was accorded space within pre-colonial political culture at all levels of power. The more the territory and resources owned or coveted by powerful biradaris, the more intense the feuding. The beginnings of many feuds in pre-colonial Awadh, in which the Nawab interfered to little avail, lay in the battles between Rajput revenue farmers over land and competing claims to authority. Plunder and cattle raids all fed into the feuds between various factions, which in turn instigated banditry and rebellion.

[...] In pre-colonial kingdoms, Rajput bhumeawat was propelled as much by prosperity as by economic deprivation. The Bais Rajputs, whose rebellions rocked the stability of the Mughal empire more than once,

inhabited a fertile region at the centre of trade routes linking Lucknow
with Khairabad. The origins of many eighteenth-century regimes may
be traced to the rebellions of elites inhabiting oases of plenty. In Awadh,
the Rajputs opposing state power were prosperous. As the Nawab
commented wryly to the Resident at Lucknow:

the villages and estates of the talooqdars are as flourishing and as populous as they
can possibly be; and there are many estates among them which yield more than two
or three times the amount at which they have been assessed; and even if the troops
should be stationed there, to prevent the cultivation of the land till the balances are
liquidated, the talooqdars immediately come forward to give battle, and in spite of
everything, cultivating the lands of their estates so that their profits from the land are
even greater than those of the Government.

Likewise, in the Maratha state of Jhansi, the powerful Panwar biradaris
of Udgaon, who were fighting with the state over revenue collection
rights, went on plundering expeditions in the surrounding region.
Various settlements gained 'exemptions' from their visits upon payment
of blackmail called *takhi*. The levying of blackmail was so systematic
that a tract of country was assigned to each family of thakurs in which
other parties abstained from interfering.

In the British period, bhumeawat took place in a new historical
context. The colonial state, which itself changed its shape and priorities
as it gained power, was soon at odds with indigenous power structures.
Much of Rajput bhumeawat in the nineteenth century may be viewed
not as a residue from the past, but as a political and cultural expression
of protest and reaction against a changing order. Now, pre-existing power
networks were set aside and an unfamiliar and threatening state
structure, based on conceptions of an all-enveloping sovereignty and
territoriality, new knowledge systems, and ideologies, fought successfully for dominance. Outward territorial expansion was no longer
possible: erstwhile powerful Rajput biradaris took to bhumeawat in a
struggle for survival. Bhumeawat increasingly became more defensive
than offensive in nature as lineages sought to preserve their resource
base and their spheres of influence from each other and the colonial
state. Economic variables played an important role in these struggles,
many of which were dismissed as instances of banditry. [...] as a
consequence of the economic and political changes instituted by the
colonial state, feuding and its concomitant, litigation, rose in our period
as biradaris fought one another for power, status, and rank. However,
the British were especially threatened by a series of revolts by Rajput
magnates. This chapter seeks to document and analyse some of these
movements. [...]

THE 'TURBULENT' COMMUNITY: EARLY REBELLIONS

In the twilight of the Mughal empire in north India, the Company and the Marathas were amongst the many players, alongside the numerous rajas, zamindars, and adventurers, seeking to establish spheres of influence. The Company gradually overcame the dominant elites and sought to build a new state form in the region. Elite opposition to the Company began in the eighteenth century in the form of unconnected revolts. British regiments were sent out as early as 1777 against rebellious zamindars controlling the rich hinterland around their forts in the Doab, who refused to pay revenue to *nawabi amils*. The fact that much of the nawabi revenue was going into the hands of the Company necessitated immediate action. The allegiances of these magnates with the Marathas and their 'family connections' with neighbouring kingdoms also constituted a threat to the Company. Powerful lineages commanded military forces, largely recruited from the members of the same clan and mercenaries. They also controlled *garhi*s surrounded by high bastions manned by gunmen and huge moats, 'protected' villages, towns and *ganj*s over which they did not relinquish control lightly.

After the conquest of northern India, elite responses to the Company varied. Some zamindars and rajas were willing to recognize British suzerainty if they were reconfirmed in their rights as revenue farmers and their *sanad*s (contracts or treaties specifying rights and responsibilities) renewed. Others, such as Raja Ram Singh of Chakarnagar, sought to establish their 'independence' in defiance of British efforts to assert their supremacy, collect revenue, and impose the rule of law. In 1803, the raja refused to give up the persons confined in his fort to the magistrate. On being served with a *parwana* (notice) for their release, he fled into Gwalior, where he also had an estate. Further, powerful and status-conscious zamindars rebelled in numerous ways on an 'everyday' basis against the colonial state. Recent research has indicated that wealthy landholders in Gorakhpur embezzled the public revenue and stole crops. To protest against hikes in revenue demand, they abandoned their lands, bringing cultivation to a standstill. They also ganged up against revenue officials, refusing to pay more to the state than they wished. In 1815, the Palwar Rajputs of Atraulia attacked the *tahsildar*'s treasury and resisted the collector in his efforts to restore control over their ilaka. 'If such a course of conduct were to be allowed with impunity,' observed the agent to the Governor-General in Bundelkhand with disquietude, 'then a large proportion of the country would be withdrawn from our control.' Subsequently, such biradaris were subdued by force.

Local rebellion often took on overt political overtones. After a body of Maratha horse crossed the borders into British territory in 1803, inducing a number of thakurs to break off their allegiance to the Company, the raja of Fattea rebelled, creating disturbances in Etawa and Kanpur. In 1824, during a period of acute drought, Vijay Singh, a Gujar zamindar from the village of Kunju in Saharanpur, with his adherents plundered villages, prevented the collection of revenue, and declared himself raja. His supporters were encouraged by the notion that British rule was about to cease, after which the 'strongest parties were to seize the sword and possess themselves of the country and the throne of Delhi.' Such movements incited elites to challenge Company rule. The British sought compliance from the rebels, for whom surrender was tantamount to disgrace. Many elites refused to accede to the demands of the Company, avowing that razing their forts to the ground and disbanding their armies would lead to a reduction in rank and disgrace them in the eyes of their 'tribe'. Thus, in 1803, Adhkaran, a rebellious Rajput zamindar of Farrukhabad district resisted pressure to capitulate on the grounds that 'it was not the custom of a Rajpoot to surrender his Fort and Guns peaceably....' When negotiating with the Company, Rajput magnates sought to maintain their authority over their towns, ganjs, and men, usually with little success.

Military confrontations were useful in themselves, for they served as an excuse to strike at the bases of opposition. Company troops subdued recalcitrant groups, demolished their forts, disbanded their armies, and attached their estates. Allegations of 'contumacy' were used to cut pre-existing ties of community and loyalty posing a danger to British authority. Loyalists such as Bhagwant Curras of Shikhohabad and Dilip Singh of Mainpuri were invested with marks of honour such as *khilat*s, to distinguish them from the rebels. During the rebellion of the Rajput raja of Fattea in 1803, Curras removed several wounded *sipahi*s (soldiers) to his fort, while Raja Dilip Singh sent armed men to protect the collector of Etawa and returned the property looted from him by zamindars from the adjacent villages.

The contradictory principles guiding official policy, however, complicated the issue. If the state attempted to disengage pre-existing networks of control, its comparative weakness in the early nineteenth century helped soften its attitude towards the landed magnates, whom it needed as allies. In 1818, the school of thought recommending a conciliatory policy emphasized that the strict enforcement of the regulations would result in the most 'mischievous' and 'injurious' consequences, like the 'forcible and voluntary expulsion of the principal landowners of the country to an alarming degree'. Therefore, rebellious brotherhoods whose 'disobedience' was not of a very serious nature were given back their lands and allowed to retain certain privileges in the hopes that under the 'benefits' of a 'settled' rule they would move into a 'peaceable' way of life. Further, officials argued that many of the adherents of the rebels had been compelled to join their ranks, and discrimination was necessary before they were convicted wholesale. As regards those zamindars who had not joined the rebels, the state 'endeavoured by suitable representation to conciliate and give them confidence in the protection of Government as far as it may appear prudent...' in return for the disbandment of zamindari armies. However, the success of disarmament was partial and many Rajput forts and clan levies remained untouched until 1857.

In 1803, a district official in Kanpur argued that given the waning of economic distress in northern India, the 'spirit of discontent and disaffection that at one time prevailed, and, which...served to procure to the leaders of the late disturbances, many more adherents and partisans than they otherwise would have had, is vanished....' However, contrary to all expectations this was not to be. The scale, organizational modes, and nature of rebellion rapidly shifted and changed as the dissatisfaction of many social groups, elite and subaltern, with colonial rule intensified. Here lay the difference between the later 'post-pacification' revolts and early resistance. Further, subsistence resistance continued to take place during times of distress such as 1837–8, when grain riots, robberies, and river *dakaities* (dacoities) were rife. Bhumeawat was redefined anew in each context. [...]

CHAPTER
12

Wildness
Livelihood, Kinship, and Gender[*]

AJAY SKARIA

*M*oglai was the time of shifting cultivation, hunting, fishing, gathering, and *mahua* collection. The many cessations of that time lie scattered across the twentieth century. Largely as a result of state intervention, shifting cultivation in the older sense ground to a halt by the early twentieth century; hunting, fishing, and gathering more or less ceased as significant activities around thirty years back; and mahua collection is now in rapid decline. *Goth* [stories] of these activities are in some senses ruminations on what it was that ceased with their cessation, what it was that changed. And in thinking about or trying to characterize them, *vadils* [elders] resort not to a dense description, not to a piling of detail one upon the other, but rather to an evocation of the distinctive aesthetics that runs through all these activities. That aesthetics is one of a certain kind of wildness, a wildness shot through with pleasure and anxiety.

Nineteenth-century colonial officials thought that the only aesthetics involved in Dangi forms of livelihood was laziness. They returned repeatedly to the topoi of the lazy or happy-go-lucky nature of Dangis in general, which made them avoid work. Dangis, officials remarked,

* Originally published in Ajay Skaria, *Hybrid Histories: Forests, Frontiers and Wildness in Western India*, New Delhi: Oxford University Press, 1999, pp. 63–94, as 'Anxious Pleasures of Livelihood' and 'Shared Kinship and Loss'. In the present version, all notes and references have been deleted. For the complete text, see the original version.

'will take ever so much trouble in digging for a rat [hunting], but will not cultivate or do any other work.' The lazy native, as we know only too well, was a persistent colonial trope. That trope sometimes persists, now restated as an opposition between the hardworking castes of the plains and the more fun-loving tribals.

This evidently misleading understanding has been attacked in various ways. One tack has been to defend or celebrate this idleness, associating it with 'the original affluent society' or to argue that 'primitive societies ...are characterized by the rejection of work.' Yet this is not a very satisfactory approach, for it is often part of a deeply questionable 'search for authenticity', and ascribes to communities like Dangis a proximity with nature: they were 'lazy' because they were more 'natural'. Another tack could be to deny laziness altogether. It could be plausibly argued that though such groups were less involved in settled agriculture, they were involved heavily in other forms of producing food, and there was a considerable amount of hard work involved in these forms, as much as in agriculture. Besides, to the extent that there was no natural abundance that could be reaped, the notion of 'the tribal' making less effort certainly cannot be sustained. And if Bhils, Varlis, and poorer Koknis were less involved in settled cultivation, this might have been because it required cattle and large cattle-driven ploughs, neither of which they had easy access to. Furthermore, there were the cultural factors. The Bhil imagining of themselves was primarily as rajas or kings. Cultivation did not sit very well with this identity, and so they were relatively unenthusiastic about doing settled agriculture themselves.

While all such explanations are partially true, there is something dissatisfying about them. Their sub-text is often a privileging of both hard work, that lodestone of the bourgeois ethic, and of settled agri-culture. The paradigm remains the same as that of colonial officials; only, now extenuating circumstances have been found for the behaviour of groups like Dangis. Maybe we need to take a more radical stance, and consider the possibility that in their own uncomprehending way, the British were right in seeing Dangis as opposed to the norms they were committed to. That is to say, rather than getting lost in the question of whether Dangis were 'really' lazy, it is much more satisfying to focus on the aesthetics of livelihood, and to view Dangi and especially Bhil activities as part of an aesthetics that affirmed pleasure and wildness. Of course, I say this from a position very different from those involved in colonial or postcolonial invocations of the 'happy primitive', 'lazy native', or 'original affluent society'. All these are based on the assumption of proximity with nature, on the idea that it was because these com-munities were more natural that they were lazy.

In contrast, I here depend on a point that Žižek has made in a very different context: that enjoyment is not natural or spontaneous but is closely connected to, and impossible without, repression or prohibition. He suggests, 'enjoyment itself, which we experience as "transgression", is in its innermost status something imposed, ordered—when we enjoy, we never do it "spontaneously", we always follow a certain injunction'. This way of questioning the association between pleasure and the natural opens up the possibility of a more radical stance. Dangi, and especially Bhil, affirmations of pleasure and wildness are best understood not as natural but as constructed through an agonistic relationship to a discourse centred around the upper-caste ideals of rightful work and living. This discourse organized to a considerable extent the forms of livelihood in the plains of western India. It was influential in significant ways amongst Dangis too [....]

Of course, the prohibition that Dangis violated was not only a 'no-saying power', one that only legislated, censored, and prohibited. As Foucault has pointed out, it is inadequate and misleading to understand repression and power in a restrictive way, as 'poor in resources, sparing of its methods, monotonous in the tactics it utilizes, incapable of invention, and seemingly doomed always to repeat itself'. Rather, the prohibitions that Dangis violated were part of complex regimes of power which elicited and even produced wildness. Dangi violations were not only rejections of dominant values; they were also tied up with these values rather than being outside them or innocent of them.

THE DILEMMAS OF CULTIVATION

Agriculture was the principal source of livelihood for many Dangis. Usually, one crop was taken annually, and that was reaped in October and November. The principal crop was *nagli*, a hardy millet which did quite well on hillsides and with scanty water. Rice was also grown in the low-lying areas. The other crops in the region were the millets *kodra* and maize, as well as the lentil *urad*. The Dangi adoption of cultivation was an acknowledgement of affinity with upper-caste values, a significant corpus of which valorized settled agriculture. But this was a profoundly qualified acknowledgement. In many goth, the activities and work associated with cultivation are subsumed under metaphors of drudgery, of work that had to be avoided. This fits in well, from a very different perspective, with the complaints of nineteenth-century officials that Dangis considered cultivation 'infra dig', and did not wish to be involved with it. By refusing to privilege and celebrate cultivation the way surrounding plains societies did, Dangis were taking their distance from these societies, and stressing instead their own wildness.

The fact that most Dangis practised shifting cultivation may also have been related to this affirmation of wildness. After two to five years (or longer) on the same spot, cultivators would shift to a new spot; sometimes, it could be as much as a generation before the same spot was cultivated again. Now, it could be argued that the absence of settled agriculture had to do with Dangis being unfamiliar with it, lacking the resources for it, and with the terrain not being suitable for it; it could be argued that shifting cultivation was ecologically perfect for Dangs, since it prevented the exhaustion of thin topsoils, required less resources, and used technologies that Dangis were familiar with. It would be pointless to deny that such ideas carry some truth. Still, we should not be too quick to read economic, ecological, or technological necessity into social practices. Settled cultivation was easily possible in several tracts of Dangs. Many Koknis had spent time in plains areas, were familiar with settled agriculture, were reasonably prosperous, and did even very occasionally practice settled cultivation. Rather than being dictated by necessity, then, the adoption of shifting cultivation may have been part of a distinctive politics. While affinity with upper-caste values was acknowledged by according centrality to agriculture, distance from them, and wildness, was articulated by practising mainly shifting cultivation, by rejecting settled cultivation, and by regarding cultivation itself as drudgery.

The affirmation of wildness took many forms, as was evident in the two broad styles of cultivation, *dahi* (also called *adar*) and *khandad*. In khandad, preferred by Bhils, a reasonably well-wooded area was selected, and 'bamboos and saplings are all cut. Large trees are stripped of their branches. Round each large tree plenty of bamboos and branches are piled to kill them and prevent their injuring the crop by shading it.' The loppings, which were usually cut around March, were allowed to dry for a few months, and were burnt just before the monsoons, usually around June or July. After the loppings were burnt, a *pawada* or hand-plough was sometimes drawn across the field, and the seeds scattered or dibbled in. They were then left to grow, with occasional weedings.

Khandad was often less productive than dahi, but Bhils preferred it 'because they consider that the necessary labour required is less...and a saving of exertion in the Dangs is considered of more importance even than the production of a superior crop.' This was not an entirely accurate representation: goth indicate that khandad involved just as much work as dahi. But the work involved in khandad, narrators agree, was much less tedious and boring: dahi required far more repetitive and regular operations, and more tending of the fields, while khandad required intensive effort over short bursts of time. Also Bhils may have preferred it since khandad was considered more *jangli* or wild because of its radical mobility, its use of hand-ploughs, and dependence on dibbling.

For dahi, preferred by Koknis, a relatively flat area or *mal* was usually selected. Around the same time as for khandad, the trees in the field were lopped to their stems. Just before the monsoons, the 'loppings are laid neatly in the form of a square on the ground and eventually fired. Seed, most often nagli, is sown in the ashes; the seedlings, when large enough, are transplanted close by into the open land which has been ploughed.' Sometimes, instead of making one large seed-bed, several small seed-beds would be prepared across the field, so as to make the task of transplantation easier. Dahi usually required cattle-driven ploughs.

Maybe some Koknis were involved in dahi because they were not prosperous enough to rent cattle or ploughs. Still, that so many Koknis, including prosperous ones, practised dahi—not settled cultivation and not khandad—may also have been the articulation of a distinct politics. [...] while most Koknis affirmed wildness, they carefully distinguished their own wildness from that of Bhils, and cast it as having closer affinities with dominant plains values. Dahi, neither quite part of plains' values nor quite Bhil, nicely staged this politics.

WILDNESS AND PLEASURE

Cattle rearing, hunting, fishing, gathering, and mahua collection, the principal forms of livelihood for nearly two-thirds of the year, were occasions for the production and enactment of some very different kinds of wildness. Consider cattle rearing. There were around 24,039 cattle in 1891—more than the population of the Dangs. Most Koknis kept at least enough cattle for ploughing, and some of the better-off ones had well over a hundred head, selling milk products from the herd in the plains. Some activities associated with cattle rearing, such as grazing, were privileged sites for the articulation of a distinctive aesthetics. Grazing took place ideally in the open grasslands, a space ambiguously between the village and the forests. Cattle themselves were part of the complex of cultivation, being used as bullocks. In that sense, grazing connoted a kind of dalliance with wildness that could be affirmed from within upper-caste values as well. Some plains Indian traditions, such as in the romantic motifs around the god Krishna as a cowherd, saw grazing in these terms. In Dangs too, these motifs surround grazing [....]

Fishing was a crucial component of subsistence from around March till the end of summer, a period when stocks of foodgrains from cultivation would be running low even for the more prosperous Koknis. But more seems involved here than economic or ecological needs. For example, there was the mobility that was enacted in fishing, one which emphasized its wildness as a lifestyle. Bhils and many Koknis would, once summer really set in, shift to the riverside from the hilltop huts around which they cultivated. Fishing was also made into a wild activity by imbuing it with pleasure. It was reported in the 1850s that Kerulsinh, raja of Ghadvi, had around the time of the *Shimga* festival in March, gone as was usual every year to the Purna river to fish and 'take air', accompanied by around ten to twenty Bhils. Though we do not know the original Dangi phrase which was translated in this way, it would not be surprising if the phrase connoted, as the former activity of fishing does in many goth today, a pleasant change of surroundings. Such taking of air was not, of course, limited to chiefs: ordinary Dangis, both men and women, were involved in it. The pleasure of the occasion also had to do with the fact that it often involved working in large groups, usually of relatives and friends from other villages; for married women, it was often an occasion to meet agnates.

Another major form of livelihood was mahua collection, which started in March, just before the period when people shifted to the riverbanks for fishing, and continued for well over a month or two. The mahua crop, coming at a time when grain was running low or scarce, was of vital importance throughout the forest tracts: 'when mahua flowers are scarce...the Bhils are in a very bad plight, finding the greatest difficulty in keeping body and soul together.' A couple and three children, by one estimate, could be supported for a month on two maunds. And a mahua tree yielded around 6–8 maunds of flowers, and in exceptional cases as much as 30 maunds. The flowers were used not only as food but for distilling liquor, and mahua seeds provided an oil for cooking, known as *doliu*.

While Bhils kept most flowers for consumption, Koknis sold the bulk of the dried flowers to merchants, or bartered it for other goods. This may have been because Koknis were marginally better off than the Bhils, and did not have to use the flowers as extensively for consumption. But it may also have been because mahua flowers could be used for producing liquor, and this gave a particular inflection to flower collection. Of course, most families required so much of the mahua for food that there was only a little left over for distillation into alcohol. But let us not equate meaning with quantity: that little was what constituted the aesthetics of mahua collection. The mahua season was (and to some extent still is) treated as a period for an exceptionally pleasant state of drunkenness. Dangi fondness for mahua liquor in particular, and drinking in general, was part of colonial lore: 'as long as [they]...have

any property or money—they live in a state of perpetual intoxication—
and when these are exhausted they are reduced to starvation.'

The consumption of liquor, and especially the celebration of excessive
consumption evoked in the whole spirit of the mahua season, was
also at odds with dominant strands in upper-caste thought. To participate enthusiastically in mahua collection and consumption was to
affirm a particular conjuncture of wildness and pleasure; to distance
themselves from it, as at least some Koknis did, was to articulate an
ambivalence towards the predominantly Bhil conjuncture of pleasure
and wildness.

HUNTING AND MASCULINE WILDNESS

Hunting, another major source of livelihood, constituted a very distinctive aesthetics of pleasure where both affinity and distance from
plains values was clear. When there was no other work, or when enough
people had been collected, individuals or large groups ventured out for
a hunt. There was nothing fixed about the period which might be spent
in hunting. A hunter might occasionally not go hunting for weeks, and
might at other times go hunting on several consecutive days. It was this
very ascription of impetuosity to the hunt that constituted its aesthetics
of pleasure.

The hunt was also bound up with the enactment of a masculine
wildness. This was not because hunting was an activity carried out by
men. Women were involved in beating the forests and flushing animals
out; occasionally they were also part of the group that killed the animals.
One well-known Mughal miniature depicts a night-hunt by a Bhil
woman and man, with the woman using a bell to attract animals, and
holding a torch so that they could be shot by the man. We should not,
then, take the masculine wildness of hunting to be some simple reflection of or correspondence with a sexual division of labour. Rather, it was
a particular way of imagining or figuring the activity, one that excised
the involvement of women and foregrounded men instead.

Ebba Koch has argued that for the Mughal nobility, hunting was
associated with daring, strenuousness, and adventure; the mastery of
wildness demonstrated the fitness of the hunter for kingship. The
association of hunting with kingship was articulated in the understanding amongst the Mughal and Rajput nobility that the killing of
tigers and lions was a largely royal prerogative. Other South Asian plains
traditions of kingship, it is likely, made a similar association between
kingship and the wildness of hunting. There are evident affinities

between Dangi understandings and this plains celebration of the association between hunting, kingship, and wildness. Certainly, they emphasized the daring, strenuousness, and adventure involved in it, and excellence in it secured the admiration of other men. There is an endless fund of goth centred around ancestors who are remembered as particularly good hunters; and great kings are almost always cast as good hunters too. It may have been because of these affinities that both the Mughals and the Rajputs, and the former especially, were fascinated with Bhil hunting—the Bhil hunter was to be a staple of miniatures.

But in contrast to the Mughal practice of reserving tigers and panthers as royal game, there was virtually a prohibition amongst Dangis on killing tigers and panthers. The spirits of dead ancestors were believed to take the form of these animals and roam the forests; also, tigers and panthers were treated as forms of Vagdev, a tiger-god. In refusing to kill tigers and panthers, maybe Dangi men underscored their distance from plains communities. While for the latter, the affirmation of masculine kingly wildness involved mastery over tigers, panthers, and lions, for the former the affirmation of masculine kingly wildness occurred through alignment with the power of these animals. After all, even the martial prowess of groups like Bhils was thought to derive from their knowledge of esoteric spells that allowed them to invoke the forest spirits, deities, and animals. Again, then, the affirmation of the wildness and pleasure of hunting was, as transgression, in an agonistic relationship to upper-caste plains values rather than simply convergent or antagonistic.

THE PROBLEMS OF FEMALE WILDNESS

Nowhere possibly are the affinities with upper-caste values more clearly evinced than in the ambivalence towards women's enactments of wildness. Women's participation in wildness was unproblematic only in activities where affinities with dominant plains values were most marked, such as shifting cultivation, grazing, and fishing. Elsewhere, there was much more ambivalence. While women were involved in collecting mahua flowers, and even in distilling liquor, their consumption of it was regarded with hostility, though in the nineteenth century they did still occasionally drink mahua with the immediate nuclear family or even publicly (there are some colonial reports of drunken women at darbars and bazaars). Similarly with hunting—women were not only excluded in the imagining of *shikar* and goth about it, but they were also less likely to eat meat than men, for this could on occasion lead to charges of witchcraft.

This ambivalence towards female wildness was most marked in gathering, the principal source of livelihood in the two to four months after the monsoons started—a period when grain and mahua stocks would have run out and hunting and fishing were no longer easy, and agricultural operations for the next season had just started. While men often accompanied women on gathering expeditions, and several men knew as much as women about where to find particular kinds of leaves, tubers, fruits, or herbs, the activity was constructed as female, and associated with female wildness.

The ambivalence towards gathering may have been because it was construed as potentially re-figuring the forests with a female wildness, and potentially also re-figuring women with the female wildness of some of the forest spirits. For example, *dakans* [witches] were often thought to be especially good at gathering. Maybe because of this ambivalence, it was not associated with pleasure. Like cultivation, rather, it tended to be subsumed under metaphors of drudgery. But in the case of cultivation, the ascription of drudgery had been part of an agonistic relationship with upper-caste values. With gathering, it was an acknowledgement of the affinities with upper-caste values. That is to say, in their opposition to these values, most Dangis affirmed either a masculine wildness or a wildness that was not sharply gendered: the claim to wildness itself was intended to be enacted primarily by men, and women were intended to be the site for the acknowledgement of affinity with upper-caste norms.

Still, this was not a consistent rejection of female wildness. After all, there is the fact that gathering persisted as a form of livelihood and men participated in it, and this when greater effort in other modes of subsistence such as hunting, agriculture, or mahua-collection could have substantially reduced dependence on it, maybe even eliminated it altogether, at least in good seasons. Besides, [...] many women affirmed a female wildness that was profoundly disruptive and destabilizing of both upper-caste and dominant Dangi norms.

KINGSHIP AND CASTE

At the very beginning of moglai, according to many goth, there was one raja and one *naik* (lieutenant). In other accounts, there was only one raja. He is sometimes identified as Paharsinh Dongarsinh (both words that, without the suffix '*sinh*' (lion), mean hills), sometimes as Chitangan, and sometimes as Janak raja. Each of these figures is associated with different stories. But quite as often, narrators do not know who the first raja was, and this is not regarded as especially worrying. What is clear is that whoever the first raja was, he gave *raj* to the Bhils. Moglai was a time of Bhil raj, literally, the reign of Bhils. Though Bhil raj continues even after the *mandini* in many goth, it is certainly most strongly associated with moglai. Bhil raj was a time when Bhil chiefs ruled in the region, and when values espoused by dominant Bhil groups were very influential.

One parallel to Bhil raj could be the point that in eighteenth- and nineteenth-century Dangs, as well as in large tracts of Rajputana, Bharuch, Surat, and central India, power was wielded principally by chiefs from forest communities such as Bhils, Kolis, Girasias, Vasavas, Naikdas, and Bhilalas, and that furthermore such chiefs were very powerful in plains areas. But it is not enough to stop with this, for forest chiefs not only wielded power but often did so through a distinctive discourse of wildness.

This discourse poses some knotty problems for the way we usually understand kingship, and to some extent even caste. It is now recognized that caste had to do not so much with purity and pollution 'but rather with royal authority and honour, and associated notions of dominance and order'. Indeed, the king was 'a central ordering feature in the social organization of caste'. This point is well taken, but we should be careful not to presume that the centrality of the king rests on classical textual constructions which associate kingship with Kshatriya values. True, such associations were widespread in western India, with the claim to be Kshatriya often being conflated with that of being a Rajput. Thus, to recall a famous example, after the Maratha chief Shivaji had established his political authority, he hired priests in order to construct for himself a genealogy that denied his more humble origins and traced his descent from one of the most illustrious Rajput clans. Many of the smaller kingdoms in Gujarat and central India had similar genealogies. Because such claims were often made even by Bhil chiefs and other similar forest groups, it may seem that kingship in these communities too conformed broadly to this model. In Dangs too, there were often claims to Rajput descent, and the *bhauband* of dang Amala now often claim the suffix Suryavanshi—that is to say, descent from the legendary solar dynasty of Kshatriya rulers.

Nevertheless, the departures from Kshatriya kingship, both in Dangs and elsewhere, may be more important than the convergences. Rao, Shulman, and Subrahmanyam have shown how in Nayaka-period Tamilnadu, 'the Sudra now proudly claims the summit.' Similarly, it seems likely that the ideology of Maratha *svarajya* represented a significant departure from either Kshatriya or Mughal models of kingship. In Dangs, while we do not know whether the word Bhil raj was used in the late eighteenth or early nineteenth century, there was a distinctive Bhil style of kingship that diverged profoundly from dominant understandings.

Bhil relations with ritually powerful groups like Brahmins—whose ritual authority Kshatriya and classical kingship was supposed to complement and even sustain—were often tense and even hostile. And Bhil kingship involved rule by a community lower down ritual hierarchies than even Sudras. Such kingship, with its privileging of wildness and very distinctive forms of political power, often constituted a powerful alternative to Brahmin- or Kshatriya-centred claims to social power. Furthermore, this style of kingship was not confined to forested areas such as Dangs: it often spilled over into the 'mainstream' plains areas, and may actually have inhibited the influence in these regions of Brahmin- and Kshatriya-centred ways of claiming power. In surrounding plains too, the power of kings may have been derived to a substantial extent from their association with the wildness of forests and forest chiefs.[...]

KINGSHIP, PARTICIPATION, AND LACK

In telling goth of Bhil raj, one motif now is that of shared kingship—every Dangi man, and certainly every Bhil man, was a raja. In the nineteenth century, kingship was widely shared. Several terms carried connotations of a widespread Dangi participation. Amongst these were *girasia* and *mewasi*. The Girasias or Girasia Bhils were a community living in the hills around Mewar, depending on both cultivation and raids in the early nineteenth century. More broadly, girasias referred to those groups or communities which, like Dangi chiefs, claimed political allowances called *giras* from plains villages, and attacked these villages if the allowances were not paid. In this sense of the word, [...] many Bhils, Rajputs, and Kolis in western India were girasias. Mewasi, it is speculated, was an appellation introduced around the twelfth century, deriving from an Arabic root which meant 'to oppose' or 'to rebel'. By the late eighteenth and early nineteenth centuries, it was quite routinely used to describe even submissive hill or forest chiefs. Both terms were often used to describe the Dangis, the Bhils of Rajpipla, or other Kolis and Rajputs who held giras rights.

The very names of the *jatis* (castes) with which the most powerful forest polities were associated carried connotations of political power. This was most strikingly the case with two names: 'Koli' and 'Bhil'. The Kolis were a large and amorphous community quite like the Bhils, for the most part concentrated in central and north Gujarat, practising a little agriculture, but depending crucially in the late eighteenth and early nineteenth century on raids and attacks on plains villages.

This association of entire jatis with political power was because power was very widely shared. As nineteenth-century colonial officials came into intensive contact with Dangs, a refrain developed, one which even finally elbowed its way into the *Khandesh District Gazetteer*: all Dangi Bhils regarded themselves as rajas. Part of the emphasis was surely because of the quixotic and distinctly ludicrous texture of the fact to officials ensconced in social–evolutionist categories—the primitive Bhil laying claim to the insignia of royalty! Yet they had inadvertently made a very important observation about the eighteenth- and nineteenth-century forest polity. Kingship was deeply shared in Dangs, and 'every Bhil from the humblest to the most haughty expects the term [raja] applied to him when spoken of, and every one of them is proud of the fact that he is a Bhil or raja. Let it be remembered that the two terms Bhil and raja are synonymous among all the people of the Dangs.'

Hardiman has shown how ties of kinship could have been extensive enough for the bulk of Bhils to consider themselves rajas. In 1954, there were 668 persons officially listed amongst the bhauband—a word which can for the present be glossed as the principal adult male Bhils associated with the ruling chiefs. Working with the very reasonable assumption of five members to each family, he points out that around 3140 Bhils, around a quarter of all Bhils in Dangs, were of 'direct royal lineage'—and this was only the most immediate family circle! Since the bhauband intermarried a lot with ordinary Bhils, quite evidently the majority of Bhils would have been at least related to bhauband.

And there certainly was explicit recognition of ordinary Bhils as rajas in the nineteenth century. No Bhil had to pay agricultural tax for the cultivation they undertook—an exemption that affirmed their status as a community which owned the land. Of the giras dues that the Ghadvi chief received from the neighbouring state of Baroda, Rs 30 was distributed amongst all the naiks of Ghadvi Dangs 'including all Bheels of Dhang Ghadi'! While it was surely not distributed to all Bhils, a payment so designated may be regarded as a symbolic recognition of the extent to which all Dangi Bhils were rajas.

What do we make of this extensive participation in Bhil raj? In some other Asian contexts where widespread sharing or participation in kingship has been noticed, explanations have put the principal king at the centre of their explanations. Here, the king is the ultimate source of authority, and shared kingship basically amounts to participation in the substance of this authority. Thus, in Dirks' argument about

Puddukottai, participation in authority or sovereignty was basically through receiving royal gifts of lands or other markers of power, and it was proximity to the king which was the principal source of power. Simultaneously, by making gifts, virtually to the limits of his abilities, the king created his own power. In a different vein, Geertz emphasizes how the king's rituals created his authority in the Balinese state, and how that ritual was extended to include lower levels of the chiefly hierarchy. Though deeply insightful, such a centripetal view may sometimes be 'overly formal, top-down' and 'largely unresponsive to "ground up" centrifugal tendencies which threatened to undermine it.'

Nor however can this view simply be replaced with a perspective that emphasizes ground-up, centrifugal tendencies involved in kingship. In the context of societies like Dangs—after all conventionally described as 'tribal'—this may be a move especially fraught with danger. By emphasizing centrifugal tendencies, we run the risk of drawing implicitly on that liberal model of society before (or, more precisely, just after) the social contract: a society of fully formed, independent men, with each man his own master, conceding only some of his power to the chief. In this model, well-developed hierarchies are a sign of civilization and development. This commonsensical image has been very influential in thinking about a wide range of societies, from 'feudal' ones to those like Dangs, which are often described as 'stateless' or 'primitive' societies, or, in Clastres's memorable phrase, 'society against the state'.

Maybe goth can suggest an alternative way of thinking about the sharing of kingship. In accounts told by vadils, there is fierce dispute on the question of which group of bhauband (brotherhood of chiefs) is seniormost. The ruling bhauband of Ghadvi, Amala, and Pimpri tell a goth which begins similarly, almost identically. According to it, the god Vishnu visited each of the five principal chiefs—those of Ghadvi, Amala, Vasurna, Pimpri, and Deher—disguised as a mendicant. He asked that they give what was most precious to them. But the various goth diverge on the question of how each chief responded to the request. Narrators from each group of bhauband claim it was their ancestor who offered his life, while those of other groups baulked at this ultimate sacrifice. Each group goes on to claim that in recognition of this ultimate gift, Vishnu recognized their ancestor as the principal chief of Dangs. The giving of one's own life—the ultimate gift possible after all—is here a means of establishing hierarchies. There are innumerable goth in this vein which tell of how relatively minor bhauband rose to prominence, and how their dangs grew alongwith; or how major bhauband were marginalized. That is to say, there is a profound, almost constitutive, under-determination of political hierarchies in goth—hence the intense uncertainty and debate about which bhauband were seniormost.

Taking my cues from the emphasis in goth on both shared authority and contestation, I suggest that widespread participation in Bhil kingship was associated with a politics of lack—a lack, that is to say, of self-sufficient loci for kingship. Because of this lack of self-sufficient loci, kingship resided in no one place, and there were multiple hierarchies of kingly authority. In order to situate what I mean, consider the enactment of kingship in Dangs.

OF BHAUBAND AND MULTIPLE HIERARCHIES

The *gadi*, or seat of power, was held by the head of the group of bhauband who controlled a dang—he was the raja in the most restricted sense of the word. [...] while dang symbolized the forest communities and forest polities in general in relation to the *desh* or Gujarat, within the dang there were several entities called dangs.

In the early nineteenth century, the most powerful dangs were those of Ghadvi, Amala, Vasurna, Beher, Kadmal, and Pimpri. Between them, the bhauband of these six dangs possessed nominal suzerainty over most of the Dangs. The Ghadvi bhauband was the most powerful of these six. This may well have been a recent development, partially because the Ghadvi chief who held the gadi had used his resources to employ Makranis and Sidis. The Makranis and Sidis had formerly been part of Maratha forces, but the disintegration of Maratha armies in the late eighteenth century resulted in many of them migrating into Bhil areas. Here, with the assistance of their more powerful horses and weapons, the chiefs who employed them quickly gained dominance over other Bhil chiefs.

But the holders of the gadis of these dangs were in no sense unambiguously on top of a clear hierarchy. Almost comparable in power to them were their close bhauband. While many bhauband were related to each other, the bhauband should not be thought of as a local instantiation of that anthropological construct, the lineage of patrilineal descent. Blood relationships or genealogical ties were not necessary to being part of the bhauband. Being a member of the bhauband was rather about a metaphorical kinship and kingship, about ties created through participation in political authority—this, after all, was the sense in which all Bhils were rajas.

Most narrowly understood, the bhauband were those closely associated with ruling chiefs in the various dangs. These principal bhauband were not much better off than ordinary Bhils. In the early nineteenth century, none of them possessed a permanent house; they moved with other Bhils for fishing, hunting, or mahua collection; and they were almost as vulnerable as ordinary Bhils during seasons of want. But they possessed considerable authority over ordinary Bhils. When Daulat raja, one of the principal members of the Ghadvi bhauband, confronted a large group of Bhils and beat up two persons, nobody retaliated because, they said, he was a raja and they were poor people.

The major bhauband's participation in kingship was very extensive. The various dues and revenues received by Dangi chiefs were distributed principally amongst them, with every powerful member of the bhauband getting a share. The participation of the bhauband in the power of the principal chiefs was evident when merchants tried to secure leases of timber in the Dangs forests in the 1830s and 1840s. In almost every case, the agreements were signed by several members of the bhauband together, and the principal chiefs even claimed that they did not possess the authority to sign agreements without first securing the consent of their bhauband.

The bhauband were quite independent of the local chiefs. Each group of bhauband stayed in a village or group of villages separate from the chiefs, and they often collected revenue directly from these villages. They paid only a token share of the revenue to the principal raja as a mark of their submission. So marked was this independence that many bhauband held smaller dangs within the larger dang. Thus, part of dang Ghadvi were the chiefs of dang Kirli, dang Sivbara, and dang Malangdeo; part of dang Dherbhavti was dang Palasvihir, and so on. More than half the Dangs villages were part of such dangs within dangs, some consisting of just one or two villages.

As powerful actors, the bhauband could demand to share in the authority and resources of the principal chief; if he did not oblige, they could seriously undermine, or refuse to constitute, his authority. Contestation was marked both during succession disputes and in more everyday interactions. Sometimes the heads of subordinate bhauband regarded the authority of the dominant raja as illegitimately obtained, and laid claim to the gadi themselves. Similarly, challenges could also come from within the principal chief's own bhauband: from brothers, uncles, nephews, or other followers who disputed his right to the gadi.

Because of this kind of power of their bhauband, the holders of the gadi had to share authority with at least some bhauband. If the principal chief did not do so by distributing resources, his authority would be quite quickly undermined. To extend or maintain his dominance, he had to enter into alliances with other bhauband, and this involved sharing his resources and authority—it was the very process of sharing authority that constituted his kingship. This sharing of resources and kingship was always represented and perceived in different ways: by the principal chief as grants from above, and by the bhauband as their rightful share which the chief could not keep away.

The power of the bhauband should not however lead to the mistake of thinking of them as self-sufficient loci of kingship; their authority too was characterized by a pervasive lack. Not only was it unclear who was a member of the bhauband (since all Bhils were rajas), but the bhauband too needed to participate in the power of the principal chiefs and other bhauband. Certainly, support from senior rajas could create bhauband. Amongst the bhauband were jagirdars and *amir umraos* (military retainers), figures who had attained their status through grants from powerful chiefs. Thus, for instance, when Nawji naik, one of the amir umraos of Vasurna, was killed in the early nineteenth century during an attack by his chief Aundya Raja on Rajhans Raja of Ghadvi, Nawji's wife, who was at the time pregnant, was promised the jagir if she gave birth to a male child. She did, and the jagir was granted. These territories secured as jagirs were sometimes referred to as dangs. The principal chiefs could also unmake members of the bhauband, as could unfortunate circumstances. Senior bhauband or holders of gadis regularly took back villages and other grants from those they considered rivals and from former grantees who had offended them, backed the wrong side in a dispute, or had simply lost the power to sustain their grant. Daulat Raja took back Vahutia village from a naik; his father Rajhans took back Jhari Gharkhedi from another bhauband.

As all this suggests, the rajas and the bhauband were not part of a single neat hierarchy. There were often attempts made by powerful groups to assert such a hierarchy, but they did not make much headway. Most rajas or bhauband owed allegiance and had close ties simultaneously with several chiefs. Because of this, even the boundaries of a dang were not always clear. While at one level the naik of Kakadvihir owed allegiance to Ghadvi and his village was part of Ghadvi, at other times there are references to dang Kakadvihir. Many smaller dangs like Kakadvihir both were and were not dangs. Sometimes, a smaller dang owed allegiance simultaneously to two larger dangs. Even the six principal dangs were, because of this, distinct but overlapping entities. Amala and Vasurna had originally been held by the same group of bhauband, as had been those of Ghadvi and Deher. In the mid-nineteenth century, similarly, Ankus Raja of Deher divided villages with the Kadmal chiefs in order to avoid quarrels. Such fission occasionally resulted in some villages being co-shared, with each group of bhauband possessing rights in them but collecting their revenue independently.

There was thus a profound lack in loci of authority: at every level, ties and alliances with other chiefs and bhauband were essential to construct or sustain claims to kingship and authority. With pressure from above and below to share kingship, the ties and alliances of shared kingship were in constant flux; they were constantly being made and negotiated. The profusion of intermeshed hierarchies is evident in the malleability of titles of the principal chiefs. For example, it was broadly accepted that only the most important chiefs and their close bhauband had the term 'raja' regularly attached to their names; the other chiefs were to be called naiks. Another suffix was *kuver* or prince, and it was meant to be used by those bhauband who had claims of succession to the gadi. But even important figures like the chiefs of Pimpri or Vasurna were sometimes referred to as naiks; conversely, several minor naiks were often referred to as rajas. Who was a raja, who a naik, and who a kuver?—these were difficult questions in a situation where all Bhils were rajas.

OF BRIDEWEALTH AND *DAKANS*

There was also an even more pervasive lack involved in nineteenth-century Bhil kingship—a lack in the authority of Bhil men because of what was perceived as the power of Bhil women. In comparison to surrounding plains societies at least, both Kokni and Bhil women were quite powerful. Consider the complexities of bridewealth. When one of the Ghadvi bhauband, Chipat, wanted to marry a woman from the village Masli, he came to visit her father with around twenty friends, and Rs 5 worth of mahua liquor. Chipat's proposal was accepted, and the men drank the liquor—often a way of marking a friendship or alliance. In Dangi marriages, it was customary for the prospective groom to visit the father of a girl and offer him mahua liquor and an amount in cash. This gift formalized the engagement or *pen*, which was followed later by marriage.

Certainly, some meanings of bridewealth enacted the subordination of women. Thus, bridewealth transformed marriage into a relationship between men—here, the prospective groom and the father of the woman—through the exchange of the woman. In Chipat's marriage, an alliance was established between him and the bride's father. That is to say, the bride was 'the object that both consolidates and differentiates kinship relations'. 'Given as gift...from one patrilineal clan to another', the woman is the 'conduit of a relationship rather than a partner to it'; 'the bride functions as a relational term between groups of men; she does not have an identity, and neither does she exchange one identity for another. She reflects masculine identity precisely through being the site of absence.' In addition to establishing in this way a relationship between men, bridewealth also enacted the control of women's labour by men. Thus, in goth, the payment to the father is often described as a recognition of his loss of a valuable pair of hands for labour, and of the gain of that pair of hands by the groom. In these ways, it may seem that bridewealth staged the subordination of women to men in Dangi society.

However, in many ways these meanings of bridewealth were also subverted. It was quite common for Bhil women especially to elope with men, or to marry men of their choice, rather than participating in a regulated exchange. Such actions undercut the postulated absence of women in these exchanges, and made that absence into something that had to be established post facto, usually by the man paying bridewealth to the woman's parents after the elopement. Similarly, there was the relative ease with which a woman could separate from her husband, either to go back to her affinal village or stay with another man. In the former case, her parents paid back the bridewealth to the husband in settlement of his claims, and in the latter case the new husband or man did so. Here, then, the relationships that bridewealth sought to establish—between men exclusively—were disrupted by the foregrounding of relationships between women and men, or in other words by women refusing to assent to their absence.

Nor did the control of women's labour by men, whether as fathers or husbands, actually prevail. In comparison to most women from surrounding plains societies, Dangi women had a striking degree of control over their own labour and its products. True, they had little independent access to land or control over the disposal of crops produced through a significant contribution of their labour. Still, women had considerable control over resources obtained through gathering, fishing, and mahua collection. In the Rewa Kantha area, inhabited by forest communities similar to Dangis, women referred to the mahua tree as their parent, because they used the money generated by their sale of mahua flowers to buy goods they required. Other forms of livelihood over which they had some independent control included forest produce and, for Kokni women, milk products from cattle. Through the sale or barter of these, women could secure goods quite independently of men. This ability, however limited, to disrupt the meanings of bridewealth as a relationship between men, to displace these with other meanings, was precisely what constituted the greater power of Dangi women in relation to women in surrounding plains societies.

But while Dangi women were relatively more powerful, that power was a deeply contested one, and was often considered illegitimate.

Contact with them was in many ritual contexts believed to be polluting. The perceived autonomy of women in choosing partners remained on the margins of appropriateness, which may be why it was associated most of all with clandestine liaisons. Most strikingly, there was the celebration of abducting women as a way of securing a wife. When such abduction took place, the woman's parents and affinal family would give chase. If they did locate the couple, a serious clash could ensue. Usually, however, only a perfunctory search was made before the man's relatives or friends approached the woman's parents and offered a bridewealth payment—more than normal—as settlement. With this, the marriage would be regarded as formalized. Such abductions were considered quite honourable acts, and several folk songs celebrated the daring involved in these; further north in the Central Provinces, there was even an annual fair, Bhagoria, where such abductions were supposed to occur. Indeed, abductions were so accepted a means of marriage that the abduction itself was often gestural: the girl would go or be taken to the boy's house with the knowledge of people in her village, and stay with him publicly. Later, her parents would visit him and fix a bridewealth; if this failed, she would return to her parents. What makes the language of abduction all the more striking in these situations is the fact that it took place most of all in those cases where women had previously indicated interest in or developed liaisons with the men who 'kidnapped' them—where women had exercised a significant degree of autonomy in the choice of their partners. In other words, the rhetoric of abduction erased women's agency and transmuted it into its opposite at the very moment they exercised it most visibly.

The tension between the power of women and its illegitimacy is most visible in the image of the *dakan* or witch. In principle, any woman could become a dakan. Usually, it was the older and more articulate women who were suspected of being dakans. There were two or three such suspect women in some small villages. Dakans were regarded as extremely malevolent and dangerous, capable of killing people through their spells. This malevolence and power was thought to derive from their proximity to malevolent female forest spirits like *joganis*—in this sense, dakans were the epitome of female wildness.

Sanctions against dakans could be brutal. Quite often, when Dangis suspected witchcraft, they consulted a *bhagat* to identify the dakan. The violence of the dakan was conceived of as gratuitous, or not socially determined. This was why consultations with the bhagat were necessary; his enhanced sight enabled him to see the violence that was independent of social causation. He would identify the dakan. After this, the male members of a village would try to mobilize social opinion for action against a suspected dakan.

If they did succeed, she was seized and her eyes usually tied shut with a cloth containing ground chillies. This was amongst the several 'tests' to determine whether she was actually a witch—if she was innocent, her eyes would water. After this test, she was suspended by her feet from a tree or a pole between uprights, and a fire lit under her, her body just beyond the reach of its flames. This treatment continued for three days, though most women died long before that. If they did survive, they were freed, and permitted to stay on, since they were thought to have been deprived of their powers of witchcraft.

Such swingings were not very common. Many relatives of a suspected dakan, especially her agnates, were likely to stand by her, and protect her against swingings. Attempt to override them could lead to disputes and clashes. As a result of these fissures, dakans often stayed on unharmed in villages for long after they had been identified as such. But even if they were not very common, swingings had an air of rightness to them as far as most Dangis were concerned. It was the most appropriate way to take action against a dakan and to deprive her of her power.

Yet dakans were respected in some ways, or at least regarded with ambivalence. Many Bhils 'to protect themselves from the consequences of being bewitched will not marry into a family in which there is not a reputed witch to defend them from others of her species....' Even a whole village could benefit from witchcraft: in the 1940s, the health of the cattle of one village was attributed to the protective presence of a witch. Besides, it could benefit entire communities: 'Konkanas (Koknis) and Warlis are afraid of Bheels. They think that Bheels are expert in magic and witchcraft.' And the witches of forest communities like the Chodhras, Naikdas, or Dublas in other areas of western India were so feared that many 'moneylenders will have no dealings with these early tribes.' A dakan's reputation sometimes 'secured her a free supper of milk and chickens', by itself quite a considerable benefit in a poor society. Often,

through fear of offending her the village people supply the witch with all articles of everyday use. As even things praised by a witch do not thrive, presents are made to her to secure her absence from marriage and other festive occasions. She is also free from a share of the articles collected for the use of travellers and moneylenders.

Whatever their reasons—maybe because of the resources and respect they secured, or because this was one of the few means by which they could claim authority in Dangs—many women in fact claimed to be witches.

The power of women threatened always to draw attention to Dangi masculinity as a prosthetic reality—'a "prefixing" of the rules of gender and sexuality; an appendix or addition, that willy-nilly, supplements and suspends a lack in being'. It is striking that the belief in dakans, as well as the practice of swinging them, was so much more marked amongst the forest communities of western India than it was amongst neighbouring plains communities. As I have argued at greater length elsewhere, it was the paradox of the great power of women, and the simultaneous illegitimacy of that power, that was articulated in Dangi images of the dakan. The dakan was the figure above all who threatened to reveal the prosthetic dimension of Dangi enactments of masculinity.

BHIL RAJ AND MASCULINITY

It is in the context of this considerable but illegitimate power of women that the enactment of the bhauband's authority in the nineteenth century has to be understood. In many ways, Dangi chiefs enacted Bhil raj as a denial of this prosthetic reality, as a claim instead to an accentuated masculinity. That is to say, the masculinity of Bhil raj was meant to challenge and control the presumed power of women.

For example, bhauband constructed a distinctive masculinity in their marital relationships. There was a concerted effort amongst them to control the meanings of the bridewealth they paid, and to cast women as conduit or absence. There was much more concerted effort than amongst ordinary Dangis to confine it to one exclusive meaning—that around the relationship between men which it created. Senior members of the bhauband often had as many as 'a dozen wives'. This was usually depicted as a matter of status, an indicator that the bhauband was powerful enough to support that many wives, but it may also have had to do with the multiple alliances senior bhauband were likely to be involved in—each marriage allowed, after all, alliances with additional groups of bhauband. The honour and authority of the bhauband was intimately linked with transforming affinal or agnatic women into conduits for relations amongst the bhauband. Such women had a less active role in the choice of partners: their marriages were intended to construct alliances with other prominent bhauband. One of the wives of Daulat Raja, a major mid-nineteenth century Ghadvi chief, was the daughter of a prominent member of the Vasurna bhauband, Purtea Raja. Daulat's elder brother, Devisinh, was married to the daughter of Trimbak Naik, the chief of Pimpri dang.

Of course, as daughters, women within a family were persons to be given away, and an abduction, though a serious provocation, could be transformed into an alliance between the male bhauband involved. When in the early nineteenth century, the Ghadvi raja Rajhans—elder brother to Devisinh and Daulat—carried away the daughter of the Vasurna Raja, Aundya, the latter initially retaliated by attacking Rajhans, but the two later converted the abduction into a marriage alliance. But the abduction of wives was a more serious matter—they had been taken into the patrilineal family, and honour was directly involved in retaining them within it. In cases where such women fled to rival bhauband, the kind of settlement with the new husband that was ordinarily possible became difficult. When Somee, the 'kept woman' of a senior Vasurna bhauband, Shendia Raja, abandoned him to live with his arch-rival Bapu Raja, the son of Aundya, he was so enraged that he sought her out and killed her.

Nor was it only in the context of their individual relationships with women that a distinctive masculinity was claimed. The bhauband would, when any marriage took place within their dang, claim a marriage tax. It may not be too far-fetched to interpret the tax as an acknowledgement of the role they were supposed to play in sustaining appropriate relations between men and women. Certainly, we know that controlling dakans was one of the major responsibilities of the bhauband and the rajas. Once a dakan had been located by a bhagat or priest, they played a major role in mobilizing crowds and swinging dakans. Villages in which dakans had been located were also expected to pay a tax to the bhauband.

The bhauband were also more involved in those activities which Dangis associated with a masculine wildness. In goth by vadils, the Bhil chiefs or bhauband who are most celebrated are cast as figures who excelled in hunting, a masculine activity. It was they above all who invoked male ancestors to traverse and transform the forests. Their warfare involved secret spells that they learnt as male warriors from forest gods and spirits. And it was they, with their claims to a distinctive masculine wildness, who were most deeply involved in controlling dakans—after all the epitome of a dangerous female wildness.

SOME RESERVATIONS

Two lacks, then, involved two strategies. The lack of self-sufficient loci for kingship was associated with the participation and inclusion of all Bhil men in kingship. In sharp contrast, the lack of Bhil masculinity was associated most of all with its denial, with the exclusion and subordination of women, with the enactment of Bhil kingship as distinctively masculine.

But is this neat formulation too easy a dichotomy? Did these re-
figurings and extinctions of the wildness of women succeed? Going by
the prevalence of dakans, the ways in which women continued to
exercise power and subvert dominant meanings of bridewealth, maybe
not. Though Bhil raj should have been, in dominant Dangi understandings, only the enactment of masculine kingship, that masculinity
continued to be haunted by apprehensions of its prosthetic nature. The
power of figures like dakans was not simply part of some illegitimate
margin: recall the role they played in protecting village cattle, in re-
straining the power of moneylenders, or in marking out the distinctive
power of the dang.

We do not know much about Kokni women, but Bhil *ranis* or queens
figure in goth of moglai in more than the relatively trivial sense that
many Bhil ranis effectively ruled their dangs after their husbands died.
Consider for a moment goth of a dispute between the Ghadvi and Kadmal bhauband which, we know from records, occurred around 1799.

Fatehsinh raja was the brother of Bada Udesinh [a Ghadvi chief]. He had two wives.
Of them, the younger one, Chauti, she was from Vasurna, she left him and went
away. She went to Virsinh raja of Kadmal, and said, 'will you keep me?' He told her,
'I will not keep you. But I will give you a bullock, and you can sell that and wear
bangles.' She said, 'I do not want the bullock.' But then she took the bullock and
went away. On her way, she met some Bhils. She told the Bhils, 'take this bullock.'
The Bhils took it and ate it. Then they said, Virsinh raja will not keep you, but go to
Gondu raja [another Kadmal chief] and he will keep you.' So she went, and Gondu
raja kept her.

[After several months] Gondu raja asked the rani, 'there is no shortage of food in
my house, but you keep getting thinner. Tell me why.' She said, 'your face and
Fatehsinh raja's face are the same. Maybe he will kill you, or you will kill him. I do
not know, and this is why I grow thin.' Then Gondu raja told her, 'do not worry, I
shall kill him'.

Fatehsinh raja had gone to cast nagli. The others who were with him went out
into the jungle to hunt. Only one old man remained with him. He heated water for
the raja to wash his face. Just then, the people from Kathikaldar came and killed the
raja. When everybody came back from hunting, the old man said, 'you go away for
hunting, and look what happens. The raja has been killed.' Dasari rani [Fatehsinh's
senior wife] was called. They told her, 'the raja is calling you.' The rani came. She
pulled off the sheet, and saw that he was dead. Then the body was burnt.

Then Dasari rani went to the Baduda [Baroda] *sarkar*. She said 'My raja has been
killed. Now you put the *nishan* [flag] of the Gaekwad in my raj and help me catch
them. Do not put the nishan elsewhere, but put it up in my raj. You may put it
elsewhere later.' So the nishan was put up. This showed that Ghadvi was the first of
the rajas. Then the Gaekwad came and helped the Ghadvi raja kill Gondu raja and
others.

Quite evidently, ranis are important here not simply as interchangeable substitutes for rajas. They enact rather a very distinctive politics. The actions of Chauti rani negate any notion of women simply being the means of constructing ties between groups of bhauband; rather, Chauti not only leaves Fatehsinh but actively seeks out other bhauband who will keep her, thus constructing relationships both between herself and potential partners, and between bhauband. As for Dasari rani, it is she who is associated most of all with what is regarded in many accounts as an event of especially great importance: the establishment of close relations between Gaekwadi officials and Ghadvi. It is this relation which in many goth is identified as the cause of the dominance of Ghadvi bhauband over other bhauband.

The power of Bhil ranis may also have had to do with their distinctive wildness as women. Let me briefly summarize a goth [...]. During moglai, a Kokni village headman, Ghobria patil, challenged the authority of one of the most feared bhauband of Amala, Rajhans Raja. The latter was initially confused as to how to retaliate. He came back with his wife, Jegi Rani, who tied a rope to Ghobria's neck, got him down on his knees, and rode him around the village as she would have ridden a horse. This *dosh* of being ridden by a woman (with all its obvious sexual innuendoes) led to Ghobria patil's death, from mortification and shame, the next day. In this way, one of the most powerful Kokni patils, who had till then without reprisals defied the most powerful Bhil bhauband, was finally subordinated by a Bhil rani. Maybe then, Bhil raj was not only about the masculine power of the bhauband, maybe it was also about the wildness of Bhil women.

Time, Self, and Community*

Veena Das

In this chapter I examine the construction of the Sikh militant discourse in Punjab, with special emphasis on the place assigned to violence within it. This discourse was part of the political language being evolved by the militant movement, of which the purpose was to create a politically active group and forge effective unity among the Sikhs. Thus a 'we' group was being created out of a heterogeneous community to function as an effective political agency within the context of the modern state structures in India.

This discourse functions through a series of rigorous dualisms in which masculine and feminine, Hindu and Sikh, and state and community function as counter-concepts. Not all these concepts have the same status. Some oppositions, such as masculine and feminine, are seen as belonging to nature; others are seen as products of history. These rigorous dualisms, as part of an unstable, evolving, political language, are new; they bear the stamp of contemporaneity, and some may well become neutralized in course of time. So it is important to note that while the militant discourse sees the sacred and the eternal as an essential element, it emphasizes those aspects of the eternal which break their way into modern political events. This is characteristic of

* Originally published in Veena Das, *Critical Events: An Anthropological Perspective on Contemporary India*, New Delhi: Oxford University Press, 1995, pp. 118–36, as 'Time, Self, and Community: Features of the Sikh Militant Discourse'. In the present version, all notes and references have been deleted. For the complete text, see the original version.

the language through which linguistic and political self-recognition is sought to be created among the Sikhs; but this language is, equally, a part of contemporary political culture in India rather than a trace element or remnant of the past.

The emergence of a militant movement among the Sikhs, both in India and among emigré Sikhs, is an important phenomenon [...] what concerns me here is the period between 1981 and the end of 1984, when Sikh leaders led a series of mass civil disobedience campaigns against the Indian government for the fulfilment of several demands, while simultaneously propagating the use of violent means to achieve these ends.

Their demands had been most clearly articulated in the document known as the Anandpur Sahib Resolution. This had been adopted by the Working Committee of a major regional party of the Sikhs, the Akali Dal, in 1973. Depending upon the context in which this document is being articulated, it can be read as either asking for greater autonomy for Punjab within the federal structure of the state in India; or, alternatively, for an independent state of Khalistan. For example, in defending the resolution within the forums of all the opposition parties, Sikh leaders have argued that this resolution asks for greater autonomy to all the different states in India. But in meetings addressed by militant leaders in many *gurudwaras* the same resolution has been explicitly articulated as providing the charter for a Sikh struggle to forge a separate homeland. It is the political context of contemporary India that invests the words 'Sikh' and 'Hindu' with socio-political plenitude. This context stamps the discussion with contemporaneity by the use of such terms as 'minorities' and 'cultural rights'; and yet it also creates the illusion of history as a series of resemblances in which modern conflicts are seen as nothing but a repetition of earlier conflicts.

I shall analyse a selection of the written and oral discourse which was produced in the period 1981–4 by Sikh militants. My analysis of the written discourse is taken first from the monthly magazine *Shamsher Dast*, which was the organ of the All India Sikh Student Federation till it was banned in 1982; second from some of the published reports of the Shiromani Gurudwara Prabandhak Committee; and third from two prominent publications entitled *Khalsa Times* and *Akal Times*. For the analysis of the oral discourse I have depended upon lectures given by Bhindranwale and various other militant leaders in the gurudwaras, especially at Mehta Chowk and Amritsar. The recordings of these meetings in which the lectures were delivered are not easily available at present, but they enjoyed a wide circulation as recorded lectures during the period under discussion.

It is characteristic of written discourse that it strives towards a rational organization of ideas. Further, the tone of written discourse often varies according to the assumed addressee. At one level, the 'you' of oral discourse is directly present to the speaker, which gives his speech the character of a performance and allows the use of many kinds of rhetorical strategies using voice and body. At another level, oral discourse also addresses certain absent others, wherein the people present become audience to an imaginary conversation between the speaker and a presumed addressee. This is especially true when the state is sought to be addressed. Both the cases I discuss belong to such a political rhetoric; there are certain imperatives embedded in both these kinds of discourse, making them closer to performative forms of speech acts. The emotional role of several tropes, such as synecdoche, irony, and metonymy in the organization of such discourse, has been noted by several authors and is amply demonstrated in the militant literature.

TIME, SELF, AND THE OTHER

In the most direct forms of speech, the aim of the militant movement is expressed in terms of an anxiety over the preservation of a separate Sikh identity. The greatest threat to this identity is seen to be the Hindu character and the state in India. Through a series of interesting slippages these come to stand for each other.

The movement for the preservation of Sikh identity is framed in a language which immediately places it in the context of modern nation states, for it is replete with references to the rights of minorities, international covenants, and the centrality of territory as a means of preserving identity. Yet, this struggle is also represented as a continuation of a series of struggles that Sikhs have historically had to wage in order to preserve their identity. By imputing an identity of events and the return of certain key constellations in Sikh history, contemporaneity is established between non-contemporaneous events. The function of language here is to create an optical illusion between contemporaneity and its other. Language functions more to *produce* a particular reality than to *represent* it. In this sense neither Sikh nor Hindu identity can be treated as possessing an unchanging essence. Rather, these are identities being produced anew in every period, and narratives of the past are a part of the process of producing these identities.

In such narratives the contemporary Sikh community is defined with reference to certain key events of the past which emphasize the building up of the community on the basis of its heroic deeds. The construction of memory is here strongly tied up with the construction of a concrete identity. As Assmann has noted, this has a positive aspect (*that is how we are*) and a negative aspect (*that is our opposite*). In other words, the Self is given shape and form by opposing it to Other/s.

Two communities are posited as counterpoints of the Sikh community, as the relevant Others, in the episodes of this narrative. The first are Muslims who, as holders of power in the medieval period, symbolize the unjust practices which the Sikh gurus consistently defied. However, the position of Muslims in the modern period as a minority resembles the position of Sikhs. This is an interesting example of the manner in which political exigencies have led to a redistribution of attributes in the triad of Hindu/Sikh/Muslim. For a long part of their history, the Sikhs represented historical events in terms of the antinomies between Sikhs and Muslims, in which scenario Hindus were the weak partners of the Sikhs. These antinomies played an important role in the construction of popular imagination, right until Partition. It is therefore significant that the historically strong opposition between Sikh and Muslim is now neutralized in contemporary militant discourse.

The second opposed community are the Hindus, who are represented as weak, effeminate, and cunning. These are people towards whom Sikhs are shown to have had contempt, but whom they have consistently protected. The emergence of this particular dualism reflects a process quite the reverse of that which neutralizes the Sikh/Muslim dualism. The Self of the Sikh, as it emerges from this particular organization of images, is that of the martyr whose sacrifices have fed the community with its energy in the past, while the Hindu is weak and effeminate or cunning and sly. In both cases the Hindu character is envisaged in terms of the danger it poses to the masculinity of the Sikh.

Even when there are differences of emphasis, an important image in all these texts is that of *charkhi chadhna* and *khopdi utarvana*—that is, being slowly ground to death over a churning wheel, or offering one's head at the stake—punishments that defiant Sikhs are said to have suffered under the Mughal emperors.

Consider the following example in which the construction of the past and the construction of the Self appear as conjoint themes.

History has always been repeating itself. Sikh people passed through such a critical phase after the death of Banda Bahadur Baba Gurbakash Singh in 1716, that some historians called it the darkest period of Sikh history... Time again took a new turn with the martyrdom of Bhai Mani Singh in 1734...In this way began once again the era of struggle for the Sikhs which subsequently was converted into the golden age of the Sikhs. Which sacrifice is there in the history of the world that Sikhs had not to pay for this conversion? A terribly dark route from the teeth of '*charhi*' to the edge of the sword was traversed. Every inch of the land where we today have assembled was covered with the precious blood of the Khalsa, then and then only could we harness the days when Kashmir, Jamraud and Ladakh bowed before the Kesri Nisan Sahib and Nanak-Shahi coins could replace the Muslim one's [*sic*].

Just as the heroic character of the Sikh is sought to be established through a particular reading of Sikh history in which defiance of powerful Muslim rulers is privileged, so the character of the Hindu, the negative Other of the Sikh, is established through a historical narrative of the modern period pertaining to the nationalist movement. It is a consistent complaint of the writers of these journals that the contribution of Sikhs to the creation of modern India have been undermined by Hindu chroniclers of the nationalist movement. By a careful choice of episodes, which occurred primarily in Punjab, they are able to argue that the sacrifices of Sikhs were far weightier than the sacrifices of other communities; and yet Sikh symbols, such as the *nishan sahib* (the flag) which used to fly over Lahore in the time of Maharaja Ranjit Singh, were given no recognition in modern India. The people responsible for this denial to the Sikhs of their rightful place in history are in these accounts the Hindus. They have bestowed modern India with their own 'effeminate' and 'cunning' character via their dominance of the state apparatus as well as the ideology of the nation.

Let me take, as example, a, poster circulated by the All India Sikh Student Federation entitled *Lala Lajpat Rai di maut kiven hoi?* (How did Lala Lajpat Rai die?) Addressed to the Sikhs, the first paragraph reads as follows:

The politicians of India have always tried to keep the minorities suppressed. We have a well-known saying that a Hindu does not kill a snake. He asks the Muslim to kill the snake. The meaning of this is that if the snake dies, an enemy dies. But if the snake bites the Muslim then its meaning will also be that an enemy will die. This saying makes the character of the Hindu crystal clear—of what temperament are they the masters.

The poster then goes on to exemplify the character of the Hindus through discussion of a historical event. It mentions the visit of the Simon Commission in 1928 and the decision taken by several prominent politicians in Punjab to boycott it. According to this poster, a procession was organized by the Akali Dal, with the help of several Muslims and Congressmen, to greet members of the Commission with black flags. Thirty thousand people came to protest against the visit of the Simon Commission, of which nineteen to twenty thousand were Sikh. One of the leaders in this gathering was Lala Lajpat Rai. According to the poster, the story of Lala Lajpat Rai's so-called heroism is roughly as follows.

The procession was being led by Master Tara Singh, Lala Lajpat Rai, Satpal Dang, and Abdul Kadar, when a lathi-charge against it was ordered. According to the poster, Gopi Chand, Satpal Dang, and Abdul Kadar were wounded. Lala Lajpat Rai received one lathi blow on the head but was protected by his umbrella. This is why he could continue to lead the procession till its final destination. The procession was organized on 30 October 1928. Lala Lajpat Rai died of heart failure on 17 November. Yet his death was linked with the lathi-charge, and it was circulated that, as he lay wounded, he had uttered the famous words that every lathi falling on his body would become a nail in the coffin of the British Raj.

Even though the misrepresentation of events in this and several other such posters would be easy to show, the truth that history books linked this episode with Lala Lajpat Rai's death and the protest organized by the Congress, understating or ignoring the contribution of others in the movement, can hardly be denied. Indeed, as many historians, especially those writing under the genre of Subaltern Studies, have pointed out, there has been a tendency in nationalist history-writing to assimilate local histories into the master narrative of nationalist history, with agency being vested in the nationalist leadership alone. What is interesting from my point of view, however, is that the author of this poster is not content to challenge the national narrative and expand the consciousness of the reader by giving voice to the silences in this narrative. There is a further move to establish that the history of Sikhs, which is inscribed on the body of the martyr, is a reflection of Sikh character; while the history of the Indian nation, in that it takes the character of the Hindu as paradigmatic, becomes nothing other than a writing of Hindu history. This point becomes clearer if we turn our attention to the construction of masculinity as the defining feature of the Sikh community.

COMMUNITY, KIN, AND MASCULINITY

Anderson has drawn attention to the fact that the style of thought in which large collectivities, such as the nation, are invested with the status of a 'natural' entity often involves the use of kinship terms as metaphors for defining the relationship between individual and collectivity. Such metaphors are used extensively in the oral discourse of militants to create a sense of community. What is specific to the Sikh militant discourse, however, is the emphasis on ties between *men* as the defining ties of community. In one of his speeches Bhindranwale argued:

Khalsa *ji* (you, who are the pure ones), the Sikhs are the son of the true king Guru

Gobind Singh *ji*. Now you know that a son must resemble his father. If the son does not resemble his father, then you know the term used for him. If he does not behave like his father, then people begin to view him with suspicion. They say the Sikhs are the descendants of Hindus. Are they pointing a finger at our pure ancestry—how can a Sikh bear to be called anyone else's son?

In the written discourse the position of Mahatma Gandhi as the Father of the Nation is contested on the grounds that the sacrifices of Sikhs brought independence to the country. In the oral discourse there is a palpable anxiety about non-violence and passivity within a movement based upon those principles, largely because of their feminine character. In one of his speeches Bhindranwale propounded the idea that it was an insult for Sikhs to be included in a nation that considered Mahatma Gandhi its Father, for his fighting techniques were quintessentially feminine. His *charkha*, the spinning wheel, was a symbol of women:

Can those who are the sons of the valiant guru, whose symbol is the sword, ever accept a woman like Mahatma as their *father*? Those are the techniques of the weak, not of a race that has never bowed its head before any injustice—a race whose history is written in the blood of martyrs.

The construction of the past in terms of a genealogy of father–son relations is also a construction of the Self and the Other. Through this particular narrative web of Sikh history as a history of martyrs, a Sikh character is sought to be simultaneously created within which the negative counterpart is the Hindu. The dangers of a 'Hindu' history are not just that Sikhs are denied their rightful place in history, but also, as many of the authors state, it looks like a conspiracy to make of martial Sikhs a weak race:

the Sikhs have been softened and conditioned during the last fifty years to bear and put up with insults to their religion and all forms of other oppression, patiently and without demur, under the sinister preaching and spell of the narcotic cult of non-violence, much against the clear directive of their Gurus, their Prophets, not to turn the other cheek before a tyrant, not to take lying down any insult to their religion, their self-respect, and their human dignity.

The danger is not of a heroic confrontation with a masculine Other, but that the feminine Other will completely dissolve the masculine Self of the Sikh. 'With such an enemy,' says one warning, 'even your story will be wiped out from the face of the earth.'

In view of this particular articulation of community as the community of *men*, it is not surprising that there are direct exhortations in the oral discourse to the Sikhs to shed all femininity. The most visible sign of masculinity in this discourse is the sword. In many speeches, there is the simple exhortation: '*Shastradhari howo*' (Become the bearer of weapons). In one of his speeches Bhindranwale gives an example from the mythology surrounding the saint–poet Tulsidas. Pleased with the poet, Lord Rama appeared in person before him to give him *darshan* (a privileged viewing). Tulsidas, however, saw that Rama did not have his bow and arrow with him, so he refused to bow before him, saying, 'Tulsi's head will only bow before you when you have the bow and arrow in your hand.' How this militant Sikh leader took an example from what is considered a sacred Hindu text is presently not at issue; for the moment I want to juxtapose it with stories of a different genre, which derive from the experiences of modernity.

In another of his speeches, Bhindranwale referred to the fact that Indian Airlines and Air India do not allow Sikhs to carry their swords into airplanes. 'If a Hindu can wear his sacred thread (*janeu*) which is his sign, why can't a Sikh carry his sword?' he asked. Note one of the main characteristics of this discourse, namely, the juxtaposition of non-contemporaneous events as if they formed a contemporaneous reality: Rama's carrying of a bow and arrow exists on the same plane as airline regulations on the carrying of weapons in aircraft.

The other visible sign of Sikh masculinity is a beard. Bhindranwale exhorts Sikhs to grow these:

If you do not want beards then you should ask the women to become men and you become women. Or else ask nature that it should stop this growth on your faces. Then there will be no need to exhort you to wear long beards. Then there will be no need for me to preach [*prachar karna*], no need to break my head on this [literally, *matha khapai karna*] matter.

Another leader, a functionary of the Akali Dal, stated that the flowing beard of the Sikh man is a direct challenge to the authority of the state. When the threat to the Sikh community is articulated, it is often said that 'they' have their eyes on 'your' sword, on 'your' beard (*ona di nazar twadi kirpan te hai—ona di nazar twadi dart te hai*). So, once again we are back with a familiar theme: the feminine Other destroys the community by robbing it of its masculinity and bestowing upon it a feminine character.

TIME, REPETITION, AND WILFUL FORGETTING

The construction of past and present deploying the mode of 'repetition' is a major cognitive tool by which a single and rigid character is sought to be bestowed upon the Sikh community on the one hand, and the Hindu community on the other. There is no willingness to subject the character of the community to the chances of transformation or change. This is directly tied up with an obsession in such discourses to provide mechanical analogies which relate new events to a limited stock of past events. Such a view of the past does not allow freedom from arrested preconceptions about a monolithic Sikh character. From this emerges the *idée fixé* that every event repeats the past and can only be understood within the framework of repetition. For example, the assassins of Indira Gandhi are seen as reincarnations of two assassins, Sukha Singh and Mehtab Singh, who had similarly avenged the desecration in 1752 of the Harmandar Sahib (the Golden Temple in Amritsar) by a small Muslim chieftain, Massarangara. In the same vein, even the sacrificial death of young Sikh children is eulogized as evidence of the heroic character of the Sikhs, a repetition of past sacrifices made by the two young sons of Guru Gobind Singh. This is not to say that outrage at such events does not exist, but that it becomes a muted link within the master narratives of Sikh history and Sikh character.

As may be expected, such a unified master narrative, which absorbs in itself all the voices within a community, cannot be built without a systematic 'forgetting'. In the master narrative of Sikh history, this amnesia pertains essentially to the close links between Hindus and Sikhs. Bonds of language, a common mythology, shared worship, and a community created through exchanges in everyday life are selectively forgotten. This is no different, really, from the way in which Sikh bonds with Persian, Urdu poetry, important elements of Islamic ideology, and everyday relations with Muslims were forgotten in the traumatic period of communal violence during the late 1940s in Punjab. In fact, the participation of Sikhs in the communal riots against Muslims, testimony of which is not only present in history textbooks but also in the personal lives of people still living, is not acknowledged at all. All the darker aspects of the past are purged by being projected on to Hindus.

As one example of this kind of forgetting, incidents of communal tension from the 1920s are discussed primarily in terms of Hindu–Muslim conflict, as though the Sikhs did not figure in these at all. Under the sub-heading 'It Happened Before', the White Paper prepared by the SGPC, entitled *They Massacre Sikhs*, says:

This phenomenon in which Sikh religious sensibility is calculatedly outraged and their human dignity cruelly injured has its historical antecedents in this part of the world. It was in the late twenties of this century that a cultural ancestor of the present anti-Sikh Hindu urban crust wrote and published a small book, purporting to be a research-paper in history under the title of *Rangila Rasul*: 'Mohammad, the pleasure loving Prophet'.... The entire Muslim world of India writhed in anguish at this gross insult to and attack on the Muslim community but they were laughed at and chided by the citified Hindu press of Lahore...But the process of events that led to bloody communal riots in various parts of India till the creation of India and Pakistan and the partition of the country itself, with tragic losses in men, money and property, is directly and rightly traceable to a section of the majority community exemplified in the matter of *Rangila Rasul*....

The first act of wilful forgetting, then, is related to the purging of the community of evil, which is now projected on to 'the citified Hindu majority'. The second act of forgetting is the construing of all acts of violence—whether directed within the Sikh community in institutional practices such as feuds, or directed outwards in communal violence—as the violence of martyrdom. Finally, there is the assumption that the state is an *external institution*, in fact a Hindu institution which has been imposed upon the Sikh community rather than created through practices within the region itself.

There are finally two other processes which allow the Sikh community to absolve itself from all blame by projecting corrupt state practices on to the Hindu character, and I now come to these.

INDIVIDUAL BIOGRAPHY, SOCIAL TEXT, AND VIOLENCE

By what processes does a community suppress from its collective memory the individual memories of certain apocalyptic events? By what means can a section of the Sikh community erase the participation of Sikhs in riots, abduction, and rape at the time of Partition, even as it sanctifies other memories, such as police oppression and contemporary illegalities against the Sikhs? To my mind this question is intimately related to the issue of how individual biography becomes social text.

One of the most important characteristics of Sikh oral discourse is its use of detailed local knowledge through which people are recognized, named, and their individual misery transformed into the misfortunes of the community. In every meeting addressed by Bhindranwale there was detailed use of local examples. For instance, he would say, 'Ajaib Singh from village Todda, who is present here—the police came one night and dragged his son away and the whole night they tortured him with hot iron rods. Is this not a sign of the *gulami* (slavery) of the Sikhs in India.'

Sometimes expression is given to the most tabooed subjects if these relate to police excesses. For example, in one meeting Bhindranwale

pointed to an old man who was present in the congregation and said
the man had been dragged to the police station in Ferozepur along
with his daughter and been forced to have sex with her (*onane pyo dhi
vich sambandh karaya*: literally, they made the father and daughter have
a relation). It would seem from these examples that local knowledge of
police atrocities and their reiteration in narratives of the community
are very important. They show how the state comes to be experienced
in everyday life, and how this experience is transformed in the making
of a violent community.

Once the community becomes the conduit through which the
individual experience of having been violated can be seen as the experience of the *whole* community, then the next step is to explain all violence
committed by the community as a response to injustice. References to
such violence abound in the speeches of Bhindranwale and other
militant leaders. These are usually framed by the creation of active and
passive solidarities around victims of violence who belong to the Sikh
community. For example, in one of his speeches Bhindranwale refers
to some villagers who came to Guru Tegh Bahadur, exhorting him as
their true king to protect them from marauding Muslims. After repeatedly representing their case for three days, they were given an answer
by the guru: he did not wish to hear that they had been raided, he
wished to hear what reply they had given the raiders. This is followed
by Bhindranwale's exhortation to his audience: those who insult the
Sikh faith, burn the sacred book, and make Sikh women naked can
only be made to 'board the train' (his favourite colloquial expression
for killing/assassination).

The juxtaposition of these stories of how Sikhs were insulted and
oppressed, the allusions in them to mythology and folklore eulogizing
Sikh heroism, and then the exhortations to violence, are skilfully done
for the purpose at hand. Where active agency is vested in the Sikh as
killer, it is framed within the community's fight for justice. Corresponding to this is the imperative that an armed Sikh should not kill the
unarmed.

It is well known that many killings by militants have entailed not
heroic confrontation with an armed adversary but an ambush against
unarmed people who have been shot unawares. There is considerable
ambiguity in the references made to these sorts of killings: they are
represented as the acts of people who went out of control. For instance,
the murder of Lala Jagat Narain by armed militants is justified by the
argument that he was publishing insults against the President of the
SGPC (Shiromani Gurdwara Prabandhak Committee); that he had

written an article saying the SGPC President's passport should be impounded; and that even after being warned he continued to write ignobly about Sikhs in his newspaper. As Bhindranwale said in his speech, 'Finally some lover [of the Sikhs] could not restrain himself and made him mount the train.' In the written discourse the more formal language—'finally his murder happened'—replaces colloquial usage. The common point, however, is that in both cases agency is deleted.

These efforts to justify violence are further supported by reflections on the nature of the present. It is repeatedly stated that this particular moment in history is pregnant with new possibilities. It only requires conviction and a capacity for sacrifice to ensure that the brief period of Sikh glory during Sikh rule can be brought back. Precisely because the nature of time is seen as extraordinary, it is also assumed that ordinary morality does not apply. In various warnings, both written and oral, issued to people perceived as enemies of the Sikhs, the threats were framed by references to the particularity of the historical moment. 'We would regret it if something were to happen to you—but the time is such that every action has to be geared towards the recovery of lost Sikh glory.'

By what process does the state, which is seen as the major aggressor, come to stand for the city-corrupted Hindu? First, by creating a genealogy and ancestry for holders of office. Indira Gandhi, who was Prime Minister at the time, is always referred to as '*Pandatan de ghar jammi*'— she who was born in the house of the Pandits. Others are either referred to as born of Brahmins if they belong to the high castes, or as belonging to groups which suffered all kinds of ritual humiliation—those who did not have permission to wear the sacred thread; those who were not permitted to ride a horse; those who had to perform weddings at night because they were not allowed to take bridal parties through the streets in the morning, etc. In either case, such people's right to rule is declared illegitimate because of their ancestry. The Brahmin's task was not to rule but to provide ritual service, while the lower castes were subservient in both ritual and power hierarchies. But typical of this discourse is also the juxtaposition of this reasoning with logic derived from contemporary democratic societies. Thus, Indira Gandhi's rule was illegitimate not only because she was born in a family of Pandits, because she was a woman, and because she was a widow; but also because she had said in a speech that if Sikhs demanded a homeland, then Sikhs outside Punjab would be subjected to civil violence. She had thereby admitted that the state of which she was in charge was unable to protect its citizens.

There is a huge mistrust of alternative definitions of the Sikh community. This comes to the fore in the relationship between Sikh militants and communities on the peripheries of Sikhism. One such community is the Nirankaris, who may be considered a sectarian development within Sikhism. Since the followers of this sect worship a living guru, this being contrary to orthodox Sikh teaching, they were declared enemies of the *panth* in 1973 by the priests of the Golden Temple. In April 1978 some of Bhindranwale's followers clashed violently with the Nirankaris on the holy day of Vaisakhi in Amritsar. There were deaths and injuries on both sides. Some Nirankaris were arrested but were later found to have acted in self-defence. In April 1980 the Nirankari guru was assassinated and the murder of several Nirankaris followed. In the reports of these episodes in militant literature, the very use of Sikh symbols by Nirankaris is seen as an insult. Though it is acknowledged that they *were* a historical sect with close connections with the Sikhs, their present forms of worship are considered unacceptable; they are declared 'counterfeit Nirankaris'. By an exchange of images, the Nirankaris are not seen as the victims of violence by the militants; rather, the Sikh community is shown to be the victim. Further, the Nirankaris are declared to be agents of the Hindu government, whose only mission is to destroy Sikhs.

Yet a certain ambivalence towards the violence directed against the Nirankaris is discernible in the phrase with which the killing of the Nirankari Baba is described: '*Akhir ona da katal ho gaya*' [literally, finally his murder happened]. The use of an impersonal voice signals a distancing from the act of violence, as though couching some dim recognition of the violence this does to the notion of the community itself.

CONCLUDING COMMENTS

We can now pull together the main strands of argument on the features of Sikh militant discourse. These features are: (a) the use of rigorous dualisms to define Self and Other; (b) the creation of contemporaneity between non-contemporaneous events; (c) the weaving of individual biography into social text through the use of local knowledge; and (d) the justification of violence with reference to both mythological motifs and contemporary political practices. These features are best brought together by focusing on the notion of time in militant discourse. The present, in this discourse, is the site of the militant movement. It is the pregnant moment which may give birth to a resplendent future. However, this very characteristic of the present makes it subject to manipulation, since the rules of normal morality do not apply. The ambivalence of such a position is reflected in the deletion of agency when abhorrent events, such as murders, are described and justified.

In its construction of the past, the Hindu and the Muslim may be described as the feminine Other and the masculine Other respectively in relation to the Sikh Self. As the feminine Other, the Hindu is seen as part of the Self. Weak and effeminate, the Hindu needs the protection of the Sikh, the protective masculine half of the Hindu. Stories of the past are replete with incidents in which insults to the Hindu faith and Mughal injustices to Brahmins are avenged via the martyrdom of Sikh gurus. In contrast to the Hindu, the presence of the Muslim in the past is as the masculine Other. Heroic confrontation with the powerful Muslim kings or chiefs, even when it leads to defeat, confirms the heroic Self of the Sikh.

The danger to Sikh identity in the contemporary period is the danger that the masculine Self faces from a feminine Other. In confrontation with a masculine Other, militant discourse seems to postulate that the travails a Sikh faces may lead to physical extinction, but yet to an affirmation of the Sikh Self. The danger of the feminine Other, on the other hand, is the seductive possibility of becoming totally merged in the Other and being gifted with a false Self: hence palpable anxieties about the 'narcotic' cult of non-violence, and fears of merger in a nation which takes the feminine Mahatma Gandhi as its Father.

In relation to this past, the present is spectral. It has memories of the Muslim as the oppressor, but these are now transformed by the notion of minority communities endangered by a 'Hindu state'. Sikhs and Muslims are both said to face this danger, in which a modern discourse of state, minorities, and cultural rights is permeated with a second discourse of Sikh history. In the latter discourse, Sikh gurus inter-penetrate present political events, and the reincarnation of Sikh historical personalities guides and alters the course of history. The emergence of novelty is thereby subsumed within repetition, and the coevalness of events chronologically distant is established through the magical realism of language.

Does this construction of Hindu identity in militant Sikh discourse reflect back on the Hindu's own conception of his Self? This question is of great importance, for the emergence of a militant discourse among Sikhs has to be understood within a political context where a new militant Hinduism is emerging which claims complete ownership of the Indian state. I propose to tackle this in some detail in time, but meanwhile several important contributions regarding this emergence of Hindu militancy have been made [...] which permit an opinion.

This is that in relation to (a) the 'feminine' identity of the Hindu, and (b) the relation between Hinduism and the culture of the state, the militant discourse of Sikhs is refracted, if not reflected, in the modern political movement for a re-crafted Hindu identity. [...] epistemological proximity of myth and history as modes of claiming the past is likely to be found in the construction of all collective pasts. And though the literature on a Hindu past which has been constructed by militant Hindu movements differs in its constitution of the 'herioc' Self from that in militant Sikhism, both kinds of militancy create an image of the community which depends upon a violent expulsion of the Other. Hence, both inscribe their truth upon the bodies of innocent victims. We have evidence from such discourses, therefore, that communities which experience a tremendous loss of their organic connectedness, of a past which is slipping away from them, can become sources not of rejuvenation or the replenishment of their denuded life, but sadly of violence against each other. Yet they are not the only sources of violence in contemporary India. The various modern institutions within which bureaucratic, judicial, and scientific discourses appear embedded are also sources for new kinds of suffering. [...]

PART four

Culture and Power

The pairing of culture and power in this section—and, indeed, throughout this volume—should not be surprising. If the rethinking of culture has been at the core of historical anthropology, an important role here has been played by the ways in which such reconsiderations have emerged bound to the increasing appearance of issues of power in significant strands of the humanities and social sciences. Of course, this has also meant that across the disciplines the two terms continue to be discussed and elaborated in distinct ways.

Here I do not wish to lay down overarching definitions of culture and power. Amidst much else, such an exercise would run counter to the productive possibilities that have been opened up by the plural renderings of these categories. Rather, I refer the reader to my exploration in the Introduction to this volume regarding the importance and implications of the probing and articulation of culture and power in anthropology, history, and historical anthropology. There, I also provide my own understandings of these notions. Without claiming that the authors of the chapters in this section would agree on every detail with my delineation of the concepts, I am nonetheless confident that they would all sympathize with the spirit of my efforts. Equally, my own arguments regarding culture and power are in tune with the varied emphases of the chapters ahead concerning, on the one hand, the acute interplay in social practice between the conventions and actions of approaching and ordering the world, and, on the other, the relation-ships and matrices of authority and domination within which such processes occur.

Our deliberations open with the formidable ethnographer team of Ann Gold and Bhoju Ram Gujar focusing on that metaphorically and materially charged object and indicator of rank and repugnance, the shoe. Everywhere, the shoe encapsulates and unravels the labour and production of culture and power, whatever the manner in which these terms might be defined in historical anthropology today. This could not be truer of South Asian societies, which imbue shoes and feet with palpable resonance. Here, Gold and Gujar bring to life the myriad implications of the shoe in the past and present, the last half century, of the Sawar kingdom of Rajasthan in western India. In their hands, compelling fieldwork is conjoined with playful writing, narrative is interwoven with method, and ethnography becomes theory.[1]

In the chapter, the presentation of elegiac accounts as well as acerbic vignettes registers and reveals the simultaneously symbolic and sub-stantive salience of the shoe in schemes of status and shame, sovereign and subaltern, purity and pollution, work and worship, and approbation and argument, which are all constitutive of culture, power, and their enmeshments. Here are to be found shoe stories that follow comple-mentary pathways and traverse crisscrossing routes. From those encapsulating the violent work of local hegemony in the form of a special oversized shoe, 'one and one-quarter hands long', that hung on the wall of forts of kings, and beatings with which were administered by a *bhangi* ('untouchable sweeper') through to others evoking the scandalous shoes of well-shod king's men insolently stomping through a potter's kitchen and a farmer's garden; and from telling tales of simple shoes on the poor feet of common folk turning into an immense outrage for well-heeled superiors through to a painful parable of bare feet that resolutely bore, on a scorching earth under a burning sun, the heavy (emotional and physical) burden of the rulers' (incorrigible and whimsical) wishes.

Staying with the significance of such stories, rather than readily tearing them up for their historical veracity, allows Gold and Gujar to grasp the pervasive rules of the shoe game as based on 'complex emotions' of honour and dishonour and the linkages of these con-figurations with those of purity and impurity. Moreover, it permits them to track incessant insinuations of the shoe in wide-ranging worlds of labour and leisure and in dense designs of dominance and defiance. Finally and above all, the affective empathy of the authors with story and subject brings to us the tangible textures of passion and pain, insult and

injury, honour and humour, drudgery and drama, the embodied attributes and intense sensuousness of culture and power, encoded in and
expressed through sensitive stories of the singular shoe and several
shoes.

In the following chapter, Nandini Sundar puts the spotlight on the
fifteen-day long annual festival of Dussehra held in September–October
in Jagdalpur town in the Bastar region of central India. Her principal
concern is with the place of Dussehra in the elaboration of hegemony,
that category of categories in discussions of the mutual entailments of
culture and power. Sundar makes an elegant case for the development
of Dussehra in Bastar as not only illuminating the standard political
chronology of the region but as encapsulating in a single ritual 'the
dialectically produced and historically sedimented relations between
subaltern and sovereign' there. Thus, the ritual festival and its accretions
through time serve to reveal 'the establishment of royal hegemony, its
transformations under indirect colonial rule, and the manner in which
both have been accepted and contested.'

Sundar provides us with a textured description of the festival. The
account moves across the existence of Dussehra as a royal ritual,
including the key place here of the relationship between the sovereign
and the goddess Danteshwari; its integration of different social groups
through labour, which suggests a homology between revenue service
and ritual contribution to the state; and the events and rituals of the
festival that have remained more or less constant over the last hundred
years. At the end, Sundar succinctly narrates the accretions to Dussehra
in Bastar under colonial and postcolonial regimes. These include the
introduction of British modes of legitimating indirect rule, the translation of imperial rituals into local idioms, and the initiation in 1906 of
the 'Muria Darbar' to establish communication between the administration and the public, all of which could yet retain 'indigenous rituals'
and provide a window to the concerns of the people. They extend to the
inauguration and institutionalization of a government exhibition and
the sports day during the festival, introduced under late colonialism in
1938–9 but carried over into the independent era, so that today state
departments continue to display their success in promoting progress
and the Anthropological Survey of India participates in staging the
authenticity of tribal culture.

Next, K. Sivaramakrishnan takes us back to inaugural moments of
the construal of the colonial state, the shaping of forests, and the making
of tribal places in nineteenth-century woodland Bengal, eastern India.
Imaginatively intervening in debates in recent environmental studies
and colonial discourse theory, he brings to bear on historical anthropology

the perspectives a critical historical geography, itself shoring up an innovative environmental history. Understandings of space and spatiality —and of territory and territoriality—have a key role here. Rather than treating space as a prior presence, always given, already there, a mere backdrop to human action, Sivaramakrishnan attends instead to the construction of space as part of historical practice, transcending, too, facile distinctions between metaphorical and material space.[2]

Specifically, the chapter shows that colonial labours—for example, of state surveys, tree plantations, and timber conservancy—entailing forests and their inhabitants were simultaneously the representations of space and the practice of spatiality, ever inflected by the diverse and dependent settings through which they worked. It is in this way that we witness not only the production of landscapes as historical spaces and places but the concomitant production of societies and cultures. Put another way, the partitioning and transformation of landscapes by colonial discourse and practice was accompanied by the compartmentalization and alteration of the peoples inhabiting these mutating environments. Significantly, these simultaneous processes indexed their enactment within weighty operations of power.

The main focus of the chapter is on the making of tribal places among the Paharia and Santhal groups of southwestern woodland Bengal, turning on the conjunction of projects of people and landscape classification. Here key convergences were established between the space of primeval landscapes and their human inhabitants in the imagination of important imperial agents. These found acute expression in the precepts, policies, and practices of colonial administration. If the making of tribal places was predicated on distinguishing their inhabitants from Hindus, it was crucially based on restricting the practice of shifting cultivation, a situation where distinct patterns of deforestation made for divergent histories of the Santhals and the Paharias through the nineteenth century.

Together, by the 1870s there was a confluence between two important elements of imperial policy in the shaping of woodland landscapes and their inhabitants, a convergence further reinforced by the spread of forest conservancy. One involved the speeding up of 'the gradual transformation of wildlands and wastelands into an ordered terrain of fields and groves', redefining tribal relations with forests, reducing the diversity of forest use, and thus establishing effective governmental control over forest produce and management. The other entailed 'a concerted effort by sections of the Bengal administration to prevent tribal people from losing their lands and homes', to paternalistically mitigate the exploitative influence of non-tribals on tribal society.

Working in tandem, the two stratagems participated in the making of tribal places within geographies of empire, located on the cusp of culture and power.

The section closes with John Kelly's incisive exploration of questions of colonial power, entailing issues of race and sexuality, gender and violence, class and order, and the body and the law. Set in the indenture period in Fiji during the first decades of the twentieth century, the chapter's protagonists are Indian indentured women and men, colonial officials, and colonizing subjects. Kelly complements Sivarama-krishnan's emphases in the preceding chapter to go beyond invocations of the omniscient authority of the colonial gaze in discussions of dominance. In a manner all his own, he lays down the requirements of supplementing the presence of the gaze with the equally visceral but more tactile place of the grasp in understanding projects of power. In the chapter, thickly textured narratives are not only intermeshed but critically interspersed with presciently probing theory. It is through such layering that Kelly presents new insights for the study of culture and power, the practice of historical anthropology.

Beginning with the figure and the records of Adolph Brewster Joske, a stipendiary magistrate in a remote courthouse in a hinterland province of the largest island of the Fiji group, the chapter leads the reader 'to the world of law, order, and violence in indenture Fiji'. Here we witness Indian indentured women subject to sexual, physical, gendered, and epistemic violence of fellow indentured men and superiors of Indian and colonial provenance. Here we meet Indian indentured men caught in crushing hierarchies and exploitative webs of race and class, men ever seen as expressing their 'animalistic' essence and 'sexual jealousy', just like their compatriot women subalterns. Here we encounter white men and their sexual, voyeuristic, predatory, and colonizing gaze and grasp. The colonizer figures were neither all knowing nor all powerful. The indentured subjects not only resisted but also laughed.

At the same time, the magistrate's records and writings also confront the reader with the rather particular judicial gaze of Joske, helping to 'clarify, and complicate, general questions about the constitutive powers of colonial gazes', especially as supplemented by formative considerations of colonial grasps. Now we find the acute limitations of aggrandizing claims repeatedly made in authoritative scholarship regarding the all-(en)framing Christian or colonial or masculine gaze. Now we follow the formidable tracks of positivism, scientific and legal, the differences between the two, and the implications of these dif-ferences for the study of colonial social fields and the legal codifications there. Now we face the scientific discovery and speech of a doctor as pinning down something palpable yet unable to lead to clear conviction in courts of law. Now we muse over agents of law as not only gazing but ever grasping, as steering clear of all ambiguity, as imposing their categories in specification of crime and motive, and yet as incapable always of resolving the facts.

Thus, we are left to think through how 'Gazes don't scar. It is grasps, from the furtive to the righteous, to the dispassionate and scientific, to the wilful, official and legal, that cut and leave the deepest marks on real bodies, as in the typical indenture horror story...' Kelly's deep, provocative tracings of the enmeshments of culture and power critically grasp colonial projects and historically gaze on Indian nationalism, also providing a linkage to the next section on empire and nation.

NOTES

1. This is true not only of the chapter, but the wider work from which it is derived. Ann G. Gold and Bhoju Ram Gujar, *In the Time of Trees and Sorrows: Nature, Power, and Memory in Rajasthan* (Durham, Duke University Press, 2002).

2. Even wider considerations of these questions are contained in K. Sivarama-krishnan, *Modern Forests: Statemaking and Environmental Change in Colonial Eastern India* (New Delhi, Oxford University Press, 1999), from which the present chapter is derived.

Shoes*

ANN G. GOLD AND BHOJU RAM GUJAR

[...] The shoe was ready for everyone, whether they did something wrong or not.... Whatever the village crier [*ganv balai*] or the king's man says, it is always the Truth. 'Why did you piss in front of the sun? Let's beat him!'.... Whoever was happy was happy, and whoever got the shoe, got the shoe, and kept on getting it.

—*Mumtaz Ali, interview, 1997*

In the last days of the kingdom of Sawar, shoes were what American cultural and symbolic anthropologists in the 1970s might have named a key or regnant symbol ordering coherent galaxies of meanings as well as shaping praxis. In the 1980s, we might have traced shoes, playfully or dolefully, as a narrative trope—noting the intertextualities loosely knitting individual testimonies into a discourse of power where shoes are fluid signs of hegemonic rule, abjection, and, at times, muted resistance. As we think about shoes from the vantage or despair of the thoroughly post-all present, they may serve as evocative if elusive media of contested power in its multiple refractions. Shoes—depending on which hands wield them, or which feet they grace—generate fear or pride, surrender or defiance, and, on occasion, black

* Originally published in Ann G. Gold and Bhoju Ram Gujar, *In the Time of Trees and Sorrows: Nature, Power, and Memory in Rajasthan*, Durham: Duke University Press, 2002, pp. 105–25, as 'Shoes'. In the present version, all notes and references have been deleted. For the complete text, see the original version.

comedy. There are quite a few Rajasthani jokes about shoes, but much that they represent is not really funny.

RULE OF THE SHOE AND RULES OF THE SHOE GAMES

In this chapter we consider several distinctive modalities of shoe power. First, we conjure the violent essence of local hegemony lodged in an oversized shoe, a crushing sanction against resistance to despotism. This shoe may have hung in the royal forts of Sawar and in neighbouring kingdoms. Second, we show how ordinary shoes—taken for granted on nonchalant privileged feet—become outrageous. We hear of occasions when well-shod kings' men stomped insolently into farmers' kitchens or gardens without slipping off their shoes. The latter act is a given of common courtesy and mutual respect automatically performed even today. The *darbar* [ruler], we heard tell from one probably unreliable source, even wore his shoes into the temple; but he was the darbar and hence, by virtue of birth and nature, incorrigible. The troubling obverse of this second dimension of shoe power is the way that low-born persons (including all females) were subject to punishment if caught wearing shoes in the presence of superiors. To our imaginations, stirred by these histories from below, the most poignant aspect of shoes is lack: their absence from the naked and suffering feet of the poor and of women. In closing this chapter we apprehend the hated abjection of forced labour, or *begar*, with a painful story of bare feet.

Speaking the language of shoes, our aim is to pace off gross and subtle parameters of hierarchy and its underpinnings in the last half-century of Sawar's history. Shoes are partially about display. They are leather, and may be embroidered; they have attributes of colour, shape, and smell, as well as function. But the discourse of shoes/power is interlocked with several other discourses that are less tangible: shapeless and odourless, if not purposeless. Prominent and heavy among those discourses meshed with the language of shoes is that of honour—*ijjat*. To simplify: a shoe-beating, if administered, would destroy honour. But to resist a shoe-beating is to sustain honour, and hence to rise in others' estimation. Wearing shoes in front of superiors affronts their honour, and is accordingly insufferable. If persons offended do not act against the challenge, they themselves lose face.

The rules of the shoe game were based on complex emotions having more to do with honour and shame than with violence and pain. No one ever spoke of pain in connection with shoe-beatings, only dishonour. Bare feet, at times, were an acknowledged source of physical suffering. Of course, the personal pain experienced on violated honour may be as or more acute than the pain experienced from a beating. Haidar Ali, a Muslim shopkeeper in Ghatiyali, bluntly states that shoe-beatings dishonoured their victims. He was not one to mince words in his critique of the time of kings. Bhoju asked him about justice in the old days, which many persons praised in contrast to the prolonged, costly, corrupt legal system of modernity. Haidar Ali had this to say about 'justice' under the kings:

It was nothing, it was just that whatever the boss (*hakim*) said people did, and nobody wondered, 'Is it true or just?' Whatever he said, that's correct...Today we can go court, but it used to be that the great kings had a shoe for beating, and they would dishonour people with it [make people *beijjat*].

Beyond honour, more implicit than explicit in our Sawar narratives, another domain of shoe talk would have to be located within the anthropologically famous Hindu concern for purity [*pavitrata; suddhata*]. Shoes are, of course, doubly impure: first because they go on feet, which are lowly in myth and function; and second because they come in contact with the literal filth on the ground: faeces, saliva, and other bodily effluvia, all prime sources of pollution. Note, however, that not one of our interviewees ever spoke directly of impurity in connection with shoe-beatings. The result of a shoe-beating was always interpreted not as pollution but as dishonour. I think pollution is salient in helping us to understand why it would be such an outrage for the king's men to wear shoes into a potter's kitchen (where he is likely to have his family deities enshrined) or into a gardener's plot (which he himself thinks of as a Shiva temple, and where economic damage is likely to compound the purity violation). Purity is evidently linked with honour: to have one's purity defiled, without resisting, is to lose face.

The language of shoes expresses some blunt, obvious assumptions of rank: ruler over subjects, master over servant, male over female. Shoe-beatings were threatened sanctions, stylized violence. In terms of its efficacy in upholding a king's regime, the shoe in Sawar may be reminiscent of the concept of *danda*: the stick, defined by Kautilya in his *Arthashastra* (the classical Hindu guidebook for rulers, which was composed during the first centuries of the common era). Danda, as 'the coercive power of the state' consists in fines and punishments. Fines were part of the ruling apparatus in Sawar too. In fact, sentences of beating were often commuted to fines through rulers' acts of clemency. But I think it would be an error simplistically to equate Sawar's shoe with Kautilya's stick. The shoe in Sawar seems to be more subtle and more polyvocal, its calculated violence psychological rather than corporal.

DISHONOUR DOUBLED

In 1993 persons we interviewed often alluded to the sanction of shoe beating in the context of our questions, which we frequently focused on the protection of forests and wildlife under the *raja-maharajas*. Assembling the basic details from numerous accounts, I can offer a composite, speculative description of the situation. I stress that neither Bhoju nor I were ever able to corroborate all the details to our perfect satisfaction.

An untouchable 'sweeper' employed in the fort was 'ready' to administer a 'shoe-beating' to anyone who defied the Court's orders. These infractions included game poaching and wood cutting. But they might be any violations of a requirement stipulated by power, however petty or arbitrary, as Mumtaz Ali so eloquently expresses it in the epigraph to this chapter. While some of our recorded accounts specify 'two shoe-blows', others refer to 'five hundred'. Significantly, far more persons tell of threatened than of administered shoe-beatings.

The sweeper, whose blows personified dishonour, was almost universally referred to in our interviews by the degrading caste name Bhangi. I was struck by this because, at least in my company in the 1980s and 90s, it was far more common for people to use the polite 'Harijan' in ordinary conversations. I believe that, in the context of explaining the genuine potent efficacy of the shoe-beating sanction, the degrading caste name Bhangi was required as a linguistic marker. To speak of a beating by the hand of a Harijan would simply not evoke the powerful repugnance immediately conveyed by Bhangi. Evidently, what inspired public fear of the shoe was not physical pain but intense humiliation.

The shoe itself was often described as special, oversized ('one and one-quarter hands long', *sava hath lamba*), and dedicated to the purpose of punishment. It was not an everyday shoe, and was kept ready—hanging on the wall in the fort (in each fort, that is, for Sawar was not the only place where the shoe ruled). Some persons located it specifically in the stables. As a symbolic, unworn shoe it is more dignified, courtly, and less polluting in the common 'dirty' sense. Yet a beating with it, held in the hands of the untouchable sweeper, would be no less dishonouring. A few embellished accounts included the notion that the especially long shoe had little bells on it. Perhaps the little bells would jingle insolently when beatings were administered. Perhaps the entire village could hear them ring and thereby know that something degrading was happening to whomever had been so rash as to disobey the authorities. This fanciful detail does not appear in any recorded interview, and I am not sure who planted it in our minds. I am, however, pretty sure that the jingling of little bells from inside the fort would not easily reach the ears of villagers below. Nonetheless, the aural image is compelling.

The effective power of the combination of polluted Bhangi and polluted shoe seemed limitless, if not mythic. As we conversed about it while these histories unfolded, Bhoju coined the term *jute ka raj* ('rule of the shoe') to describe the time of kings. For royal authority to be vested in shoe and sweeper was emblematic of ugliness and abjection, as if all that upheld the court's grandeur in that time were degraded. But there were, of course, other sides to the story of rule.

The other recurrent, narrative motif involving shoes—who may and who may not wear them in front of whom—also has to do, less dramatically but more immanently, with dominion and abasement, with symbolic enactments of rank that are equally an everyday violence. Real shoes either adorning and protecting or absent from real feet are indicators, both abstract and material, of caste and gender hierarchies in that time. Very simply, the rules are that persons of rank wear shoes anywhere, but persons of no account must go barefoot—at least when near superiors. Who wears shoes in whose presence indexes rank. No human being should wear shoes in the presence of God. In every household the kitchen is a pure place where no person wears shoes. Gardeners hold their garden plots to be like Shiva's temples, and therefore their caste customs forbid shoes to be worn into gardens.

The ban on wearing shoes in the company of rulers, or any social superiors, was one among many bans (*pratibandh*)[....] These pratibandh included bans on wearing gold and silver adornment, on wearing finely woven cloth, on eating or serving guests foods cooked with white sugar or white flour, and on bridegrooms riding a horse through the village streets on their wedding day. For the sake of argument, we might bracket the emotional investment such display items definitely hold, and their consequent weight as sources of prestige, clout, and honour. Given this, all these restrictions might well strike outsiders as deprivations of what were, in any case, rare luxuries. For the poor, as many of our interviewees bluntly stated, these prohibitions truly were symbolic. Most persons forbidden them could not in any case afford them. The extreme example of this was a ban on building *pakka* (brick or stone) houses, which many frankly laughed off when we asked about it. In those days people could barely fill their stomachs, we were told, so where would they find the resources to build houses?

The ban on shoes differs from the other bans. Shoes are not as costly as gold, horses, or fine cloth. Although they do represent an investment of scarce resources, their practical value, enhancing physical capacity for productive work, makes them 'worth' it in a way different from adornment. Bare feet cause obvious discomfort and represent health hazards in mud, hot sand, or winter chill, all of which are met in the Rajasthani seasonal cycle. Unshod persons are vulnerable to thorns, snakes, worms, cuts, and blisters.

In the sections that follow we speak first of shoe-beatings avoided and received; and second of shoe bans where the subservient behaviour demanded of subjects before rulers is immediately parallel to the behaviour required of women before men.

SHOE-BEATINGS MANQUE

Many of the shoe-beating tales we were able to elicit with any amount of realistic detail were of shoe-beatings avoided—threatened but never ultimately inflicted.

In a 1993 interview, Ugma Loda told a comical story about an abortive shoe-beating. Ugma was a farmer, almost sixty-six years old. He told us he had first grazed cows; then studied for two years; then left school to join his father in farming, which has been his metier ever since. He related his story in the context of describing sanctions for wildlife protection. In this particular case, however, the infraction was sheer disobedience.

Ugma: And the wild animals destroyed our fields and we could do nothing.
Bhoju: If you killed an animal, then what?
Ugma: Well, if they found out then they would call us and punish us, but if no one knows, then, no matter! And they had a Bhangi who would beat people with a shoe: this was the worst punishment, to be beaten by a Bhangi!

Once they called Gopal Chamar to the fort, and he couldn't come.

[Chamars, like Regars, are leatherworkers and also stigmatized as untouchable, but they would hold themselves superior to sweepers. Presumably the Chamar was called to perform begar or unpaid work by the king's men.]

So they called him the next day, and they asked him why he had not come before, and he said, 'Because my children were hungry and their mother wasn't there.'

They said, 'You must be punished; we will have you beaten with the shoe.'

So they sat him down, and several hours went by and they didn't beat him or let him go; so he begged them, 'Please beat me with the shoe if you're going to beat me, I'm late!' So they started to laugh, and they let him go. At that time he was the only earning person in the family.

What might this anecdote reveal about the 'rule of the shoe'? That good humour and a patronizing compassion mitigates its severity, or that the arrogant bosses have amassed sufficient symbolic capital to enable them to be generous, arbitrarily, on whim? Which of these morals, we might wonder, did Ugma Loda want to convey to us with this tale? We were too new at the game then to probe further, but I suspect it would be both. There is also a whiff of trickster resistance here, which emerges more sharply when we contrast this episode with another.

Amba Lal Loda, also in 1993, narrated another episode of an averted shoe-beating, this one involving a direct appeal to the darbar, and perhaps a veiled heroic challenge to the darbar's sense of honour. This is evidently a risky game, but in this case the proud peasant succeeds in winning. Whereas in the preceding episode a Loda tells with mingled humorous compassion and slight scorn a story about a Chamar, in this case we hear a Loda speak with pride of another Loda who stands up fiercely for his honour. His triumph is shared by his community, and there is clear relish in narrating it. The subject of the story, Dhula (now deceased), belonged to a highly respected and prosperous family in the Loda community, and he was the father of Ladu Loda, who appears elsewhere in these pages.

Although in the first anecdote the king's men are the deflected punishers, seen as vulnerable to self-deprecating trickster tactics, here the darbar himself is an actor. He is portrayed as responsive—displaying appropriate compassion and magnanimity. He dramatizes his own humanity and compassion; he recognizes and appreciates his subject's gutsiness. He maintains authority through a charmed combination of all these gambits.

Amba Lal is describing the 'sorrows' of those times and the particular duties of Lodas vis-à-vis the Court.

Amba Lal: If he [the Court] had a guest, then he would say, 'Hey, I have a guest, so bring me mattresses and cots!' And suppose we [Lodas, farmers] didn't do this work, what would happen? He would have the Bhangi apply the shoe to us!

Bhoju: When he had the shoe applied to us [Bhoju uses an inclusive 'us' speaking as a fellow-sufferer from the broader peasant community], could we take our opposition (*khilaph*) to a court of law or some such thing?

Amba Lal: No no no! Nobody went to the courts. Once something happened: Dhula Loda, he refused to do something, to give a cot or something, and the darbar called him to the fort, and gave an order to the Bhangi: 'He didn't do my work, so give him two blows with the shoe.'

So at this time Dhula Loda said [to Vansh Pradip Singh directly], 'Only you can beat me. If the Bhangi beats me, I'll kill the Bhangi, or I'll kill myself, but I won't let him beat me.'

So the darbar let him go, and he didn't beat him. The darbar said, 'You have made mistakes one hundred times, and I forgive you, but never come here again as an offender!'

This is a no-fault conclusion; everyone maintains their honour. Of course, the darbar has an imperial edge, but at the same time he is portrayed as appreciative of Dhula's stance. There is a hint that Dhula's self-respect has gotten him in trouble more than once, but also a hint that the darbar respects this strength of character.

Note the striking difference between these two narratives. Dhula the clean-caste farmer escapes the shoe-beating by standing on his honour, even though his threats of suicide and murder are likely to have been understood as bluffs by all the players, including himself. By contrast, Gopal the untouchable leather-worker evades the shoe through apparent simple-mindedness. Moreover, his single-minded concern for his children, his absent wife, and hence his consequently emasculated house-husband role, all contrive to make him a figure of amusement for the nobility. He does not avoid this identity, but rather exploits it to his advantage.

WAS THERE A SHOE?

In 1997 we sought to flesh out our understanding of the foundations of authority in pre-Independence Sawar. If it truly rested on a shoe one and one-quarter hands long, we wanted to document this. But we found that it was extremely difficult to obtain specifics. Almost everyone was vague. Some, especially Rajputs, denied with fair regularity the very existence of a shoe, asserting its chimerical nature. Many others said that there was indeed a shoe but it was never used, or at least they had never witnessed its use. One man claimed that beatings had taken place in Ghatiyali's fort by a man belonging to a known Harijan family, and he named names. But we were unable to confirm his account because the named persons were deceased.

Early in 1997 we spoke with Bankat Singh Kamdar Shaktavat, a member of the Court's own lineage who lived near the Dark Garden ('Andhera Bagh', a lovely tree-filled park belonging to the Sawar royal family) in the Sawar Ravalo just below the fort. He gave his age as about sixty-nine years old. In his youth, as a Kamdar, he had been an active participant in the administrative apparatus of the darbar.

Bhoju: I heard about a shoe, one and one-quarter hands long, with little bells on it.
Bankat: No one has seen it and no one was ever beaten! [His swift denial strikes me as rather abrupt.] It's just that the darbar would say, 'Have the Bhangi give him one hundred blows!' But he never carried it out. I never saw it.

Bhoju's interpretation of this denial, proffered as we transcribed the tape, epitomized to me one important aspect of the 'rule of the shoe.'

He suggested that 'people understand that there was no such shoe, and no Bhangi would apply it, but still they were afraid.' In a way, whether there was or was not a shoe is of no import. In collective memory the regime's credibility was fuelled by the idea of a shoe. Nonetheless, we have enough accounts of actual events to convince both of us that shoe-beatings probably did occasionally, if rarely, take place in Sawar in the twentieth century.

The following short tale, told by Kishan Lal Gujar of Sawar in 1997, reveals that pride and bravery and bluffing did not always succeed in fending off the shoe.

Bhoju: Did the Bhangi really beat people? Was that real or just a fear?
Kishan: No, it's true, the Court did have people beaten by the Bhangi. Once...the manager was Saman Singh, and our Kalyan Gujar said to him, 'Please distribute the grain quickly, because we are troubled at the threshing ground.'

And they had a fight—Kalyan Gujar and Saman Singh. So, Saman Singh had him called in, before the Court, and the Court had him beaten by the Bhangi. And Kalyan Gujar said, 'The Court is here with us now, but if I ever meet you alone I will kill you.' [It is not clear whether he is speaking to Saman Singh or to the Bhangi; and we were unable to trace more details or learn the aftermath of this tale.]

From a Sawar Brahmin that same month we heard another tale of a shoe-beating averted for the sake of honour. Sampat Lal, the narrator here, came from a Brahmin family affiliated with the fort as royal priest. He told us he had reached an age of understanding (eleven or twelve) when Vansh Pradip Singh was ruling. His father, Ganpat Lal, had been *Tehsildar* (sub-collector of revenue). At this point in the interview we were discussing a judgement the darbar passed on a sexual offender. This was one of the few crimes the darbar himself abhorred sufficiently to punish with more than threats. Sampat Lal states:

There was also a Jain Mahajan [member of the merchant community] who was misbehaving [doing *badmas:* may mean any kind of naughtiness in children, when applied to adults it implies sexual misconduct]. The Court did not send him to jail, but he fined him. This was Bhavar Lal's father. The darbar condemned him to five hundred shoe blows.

The other Mahajans requested, 'Don't let the Bhangi do it, it will hurt our honour [ijjat].' So he gave a five-hundred-rupee fine instead. The Court threatened, and because of this people were afraid.

In this case the offender was a member of the merchant class, for whom the dishonour of shoe-beating, particularly as administered by a Bhangi, would have been an unthinkable fate worse than death. Moreover, the shame was not confined to the individual; his entire community would have been implicated, as the darbar well knew. Thus, in spite of his rage at sexual misconduct, the Court responded with clemency, commuting the sentence to a steep fine.

Chalak Dan, a Charan in Rajpura, just outside Sawar, told us he was still a child when the darbar died. He testified to actual shoe-beatings, but without providing details of case or name.

Chalak Dan: During the time of Vansh Pradip Singh the peasants were very sorrowful (*dukhi*). Chotu Bhil used to come to our village, and people used to bring him cups full of milk, *ghi*, yogurt because he was the king's man, the Court's Bhil! [enunciated with scorn]. That's how afraid people were!

[Bhoju comments: 'They paid him as much attention as today they pay the chief of police!']

At that time there were many wild pigs, and the darbar still didn't kill them, and if someone else did then he called them into the fort and had them beaten terribly.... If the farmers slept then the pigs would destroy their crops.

Bhoju: Didn't they complain?

Chalak Dan: If they did, he beat them with his shoe: 'The pigs are eating your crops, you eat this!'

As noted above, the verb 'to eat', coupled with blows, combines incorporation with humiliation and degradation. The parallel structure here confirms the salience of eating in this locution: to eat shoe blows is to internalize the degradation of a shoe-beating.

Chalak Dan, whose entire interview revealed hostility to the Court, does not bother to pose a Bhangi as intermediary, or even to employ the causative 'to have beaten with a shoe' rather than the transitive 'beat.' He makes it sound as if the shoe would be in the Court's own hand, which is quite unimaginable.

Ganga Ram Mina was very close to Bhoju's family, and since 1980 we had interviewed him many times on a variety of subjects. He possessed an enormous store of knowledge about festivals and myths, agriculture, and local history. In 1997, having farmed for fifty years, he had 'retired' from physical labour and was regularly to be found sitting on the raised platform surrounding the Mataji temple, just a few yards from Bhoju's house. Often he was knitting (not a common occupation for men, but after a lifetime of labour it troubled him to sit idle).

We probed him about the source of the raja-maharaja's authority: why would people agree to work without pay?

Bhoju: Suppose someone said, 'I won't do begar.' What then?

Ganga Ram: No, he had to do it, and if he refused, the shoe fell.

Bhoju: Yes, I've heard there was a shoe and he had people beaten by the Bhangi—is it true?

Ganga Ram: Yes, it is true. The Bhangi used to beat. He always stayed in the fort, and whenever any boss wanted to have somebody beaten, the Bhangi would do it in the place where horses were tied. They would tie him [the offender] up and have him beaten.

From this we gather that a lowly location, the stable, was used as the setting for the degrading punishment. It is also realistic, as members of the sweeper community performed their conscripted labour in the royal stables.

Speaking with another long-time friend, Gokul Mali, in his field in 1997, we covered the by now familiar nexus of the darbar's conservation policies, his protection of trees and wildlife, and the threat of shoe-beatings. Gokul told us he was in his teens at the time of Vansh Pradip Singh's death in 2005 (*Samvat* Era); he is still a vigorous and active farmer in his sixties.

Bhoju: Were there a lot of animals?
Gokul: Yes a lot. And no one else [besides the darbar himself] could kill them. If someone did, they [the king's men] would have that person beaten. If someone killed some animal, then he was beaten.
Bhoju: Did the Court know about this?
Gokul [sidestepping the question]: They called us into the fort and had the Bhangi beat us.
Bhoju: I have heard there was a shoe that was one and one-quarter hands long (*sava hath lamba juta tha*).
Gokul: Bhajjalal Bhangi [his son Gopi Lal still lives in the fort and takes care of the darbar's horses]—this was the Bhangi who did the shoe-beating.
Once, a boy, Bhura Mali, Bhagirath Mali's son, he killed a boar. He was the leader, and the knowledge came to the fort. Everyone ran away, but they caught Bhura. Someone from the fort caught him. And they took Bhura along with the pot of meat he was cooking [boar meat]. They took him to the fort and beat him badly (*khub pita*). And they also fined him.
Because the darbar scattered grain for them [the pigs], and set up water tanks for them, by the fort and on the hill.

Gokul's account includes a youth of his own community who was punished with a terrible beating for pig poaching. There is no rescue, no sentence commuted, no honour upheld in this story. Perhaps because it is a 'boy', the blemish is less acute to recall. Note the deliberate contrast set up here between the Court's kindness to pigs and his cruelty to the Mali boy.

From a respected Muslim shopkeeper, Mumtaz Ali (with whose words I prefaced this chapter), we gleaned some powerful critiques of the kings' rule. Bhoju asked him about the bans (pratibandh):

Bhoju: I heard that...they didn't let you wear nice clothes, was it like that?
Mumtaz: Yes, even if we did not greet the guards and chiefs and bosses [*syana sardar hakam*], then they beat us with shoes.
Bhoju: Did they beat people in Ghatiyali fort?
Mumtaz Ali: People say that they beat.
Bhoju: I know that the Malis had to do forced labour.
Mumtaz Ali: It wasn't about Malis or whatever...the shoe was ready for everyone, whether they did something wrong or not.... Whatever the village crier [ganv balai] or the king's man says, it is always the Truth. 'Why did you piss in front of the sun? Let's beat him!'.... Whoever was happy was happy, and whoever got the shoe got the shoe, and kept on getting it. In those times, the poor were dying, and today too, they are dying; and those rich people who were blissful then, today too they are blissful.

Although Mumtaz is one of the most acerbic in his critiques of the former rulers, he waffles slightly nonetheless on the actuality of beatings in Ghatiyali: 'People say they beat.' He has no personal testimony, no witnessed moments, to offer. He is also more cynical about the genuine 'trickle down' impact of democratic reforms than many other speakers are.

The oversize shoe—myth or reality—was not unique to the kingdom of Sawar. In Mehru we spoke with Ram Dev Regar from Choti Mehru, who was then about fifty-one years old. His *thakur* [darbar], a Charan (or royal bard), was Pratap Dan (Singh) Charan. We asked Ram Dev about forced labour (begari) in Mehru:

Bhoju: Did you have to go there [for begar]?
Ram Dev: I had to go, and if I didn't go, then he sent a worker to call: 'This person, why didn't he come?' And, he had a one-and-one-quarter-hand-long shoe and he would bring us there and give five *jute* [five shoe-blows]. The shoe was kept hanging in a special place.

POWER'S INSOLENCE AS SHOD FEET

Our conversation with Polu Ram Kumhar in 1993 serves as an introduction to the second form of shoe violence. A potter by birth, Polu had, through a riverbed gardening venture, attained an economic status beyond most of his caste fellows. A reflective, articulate, and successful man, Polu spoke thoughtfully. His train of thought makes a rapid transition from offensive shoes in the kitchen to the shoe for beating—revealing how close the two shoe complexes are in thought; they are very nearly the same shoes.

Bhoju: What kind of work did you do in begar?
Polu: My son! We gave water to forty horses in this fort! We took water from the

reservoir, we took water for forty horses up to the fort. And for their baths and water we also brought, on top of that.

Twenty-four hours a day, two of us sat here with our ears turned toward the fort; at anytime they can call us, 'O Potters, come for begar!' And we would go, and if we didn't go they would *beat us with the shoe*, and that's why we kept our ears turned toward there.

Sometimes we are boiling milk on the cooking hearth, and if someone in the fort needs the milk they will *come with their shoes on*, and walk in the kitchen, and take the milk and go, and we can't stop them.

If we stop them, they have a shoe one and one-quarter hands long, and they beat with that shoe.

And suppose our child is sleeping on a cot and some guest comes, they won't even wake up the child, they will just take it off the cot and take the cot. That's the kind of work they did. In this way all castes were sad, believe me.

Kalyan Mali, in 1993, also told a story of offending shoes on the feet of the powerful—or at least of a person imbued with power by association with the Court. The story also highlights his own resistance, as did all of his well-spun tales. Instead of using the standard interview format here, I have reworded his story and told it in the third person. This is because my notes were made after the fact, rather than directly transcribed from a recorded interview, and I do not want to attribute words to Kalyanji, [...] who has a unique storytelling style.

One day Kalyan Mali was busy running the *charas*: the laborious and tedious irrigation system in which the farmer drives his oxen backward and forward, yoked to a pulley system that lowers leather buckets into a step well, hauls them out full, and spills the water into irrigation channels. The king's servant, whose title was village crier, came past the well and walked into Kalyanji's garden with his shoes on. In the process he broke plants and picked vegetables without asking permission. Kalyan said to him, 'Take off your shoes when you enter the garden-temple.'

The village crier answered, 'I'm measuring and I need my shoes.' Kalyan repeated, 'Take off your shoes.'

'Who are you to tell me?'

Kalyan Mali became angry and responded, 'Your mother this-and-that' (*teri man aisi ki taisi*) and, 'You are like a Regar!' [both offensive insults]. And he picked up a stone to throw, and the crier ran away. He ran and told another of the king's men, 'Kalyan Mali beat me!'

So two men came and dragged him to the fort. Akka Singhji [a well-known *kamdar* in Ghatiyali] asked him, 'Why are you beating my Balai?' and added that he was going to beat him in return.

Kalyan Mali replied, 'If you want to beat me, fine, but first listen!'

'Okay, speak.'

So Kalyan Mali said to Akka, 'Do you let us go in your royal neighbourhood (*ravalo*) wearing shoes or not?'

'No we think it's very bad.'

'Well,' Kalyan Mali said, 'My garden is like your ravalo.'
Then Akka Singh told the Balai, 'It was your mistake.'

Once again a bold farmer is justified, vindicated, and goes unpunished. His boldness, moreover, extends to comparing himself with the Rajputs, making an analogy between his garden and their neighbourhood. It works. But note that Balais are very low in the social hierarchy. Had Kalyanji's dispute been with a Rajput manager and not the lower crier, things might have developed quite differently in this encounter and given it a different outcome.

ABJECTION AS BARE FEET

In all of our interviews, only one account directly links the shoe-beating theme with the shoe-wearing ban, and it is a second-hand narrative that was probably pure fabrication. However, it is worth examining for its several idiosyncrasies, and as an interface of the two shoe-power matrices. It was among the few testimonies we heard that declared that a specific shoe-beating to a named individual was actually administered.

This episode emerged during a conversation with a group of Regars in Devli Gaon, one of Sawar's *tehsil* headquarters. We had been speaking with Ram Lal Regar, who was quite elderly and extremely articulate. There were several others present, including another senior Regar and a youth of the same community, probably in his late twenties. He was therefore too young to have witnessed those times or even to have appreciated the conditions that prevailed during the rule of kings. Although the older men present had already narrated acutely painful personal histories of abasement and suffering, they hotly denied this youth's second-hand story of a beating.

Bhoju: Did they ever call you into the fort to have you beaten with a shoe?
Ram Lal: No, I never heard of that, and I never saw it either.
Regar youth: There was a man in Devli named Hanuman, who does sewing. One time, Hanuman was telling me, 'I walked in front of the fort wearing my shoes and the big shots (*thakur saheb*) were sitting there, and I said '*Jai Sri Ji ki*' to them, and I went along my way. [This is a polite greeting, 'Victory to Shri Kalyan ji,' referring to the deity Shri Kalyan ji, of whom the royal family were devotees. It would be the polite and proper thing to say.] Then they called me back, and a Bhangi was working there, and they called him over, and he took off his shoe and struck me twice.'
Ram Lal [and another older listener, speaking almost simultaneously]: This is a lie! It didn't happen; such things did not happen.

This story is so unlike the usual references to shoe-beatings, in several ways, that I am inclined to share the elder men's scepticism. First, the shoe is not a special shoe kept in the fort as a reminder of potential sanctions, but a real shoe on a real Bhangi's foot. No symbolic filth this —it is beyond the pale. Second, the episode does not take place in the seclusion of fort or stables but on the street. Finally— although punishment is meted out for the offence of a low-caste person disrespectfully 'wearing shoes' in the presence of nobility, the anonymous Bhangi, who happens to be on the scene, himself happens to be wearing shoes— handy to take off and beat with but contradicting the narrated event's total logic. This contradiction seems to discredit the entire story: 'Such things did not happen.' Yet I found this anomaly provocative. Bhoju and I searched for a Hanuman among the Regar tailors in Devli City, but we never found one. During the same session in Devli Gaon, from the elderly Ram Lal Regar we heard what struck me as the crudest account of the abusive nature of the forced labour system involving bare feet. It is not at all likely that in this case bare feet signify anything more than poverty. Ram Lal makes his painful trek all alone, and he might have worn shoes if he had owned them. Yet the pain of Ram Lal's memories suggests not only physical suffering but an abjection of the spirit that is difficult to bear recalling, even fifty years later:

I was my father's only son, and once they sent me from Devli to Napa ka Khera with a case of Coca-Cola (*koka koyala ki peti*). The manager wrote a note with the name of someone from Napa ka Khera [to whom it should be delivered]. So, it was my duty to take it to Napa ka Khera, and it was the hot season, June. It was my turn, and I didn't have shoes; they put the case on my head and gave me the note, and I had to take it to Napa ka Khera.

I had a very miserable time (*bahut paresan hua*). My feet hurt, but I couldn't put it down because if I put it down who would put it back up? And I was very thirsty, but I couldn't drink.

I was the son of a poor man, I didn't have shoes, and when I walked into the river [that is, the dry river bed], I got blisters on my feet [from the hot sand], and I was crying. But what could I do? I had to bring it there. There was a Mina in Napa ka Khera. There I wrapped cloth bandages around my feet, and returned home with great difficulty.

Such was our condition in the time of the *raj*!

Ram Lal's pointed concluding words indicate that he has deliberately given us this story for our history. As if he were saying to us, 'You asked me what things were like, I'll tell you.' This episode also may not recall an event exactly. Coca-Cola, I am told, could not have been available before 1947. But it does not really matter what was in the case; what is salient is that the disempowered, barefoot Regar goes thirsty and anguished while carrying as a head burden a bottled luxury drink destined for kings. He is unable to lower this burden.

Women, when asked to describe the strictures on their behaviour in the old days, often spoke of not wearing shoes in front of men. Although the term pratibandh is not used here, this struck me as a direct domestication of the courtly ban on anyone of low rank wearing shoes in front of nobility or those associated with nobility. Gender hierarchy evidently mirrors other power configurations. For women, too, this ban was inconvenient and health-threatening. Shoes protect feet, and women were always walking—often, like Regars, carrying heavy head-loads.

In the barber's spacious courtyard we talked with a group of neighbour women in 1997. Ratni Nain told us, with some humour but little nostalgia, about the ways women had to behave in the old days in front of elders and males. To signify respect was necessary even if the men were not actually present. Women had to show respect for the men's meeting place by passing it barefoot and veiled when no men were there. Ratni Nain states: 'We kept our faces veiled. At the men's meeting place (*hathai*), whether men are there or whether no men are present, even so we cannot pass it with our shoes on; even if no one was there, we veiled our faces. And if there *were* men there, we would pass it with our backs turned [a sign of respect as well as modesty, and a way of keeping *purdah* even in the street].'

When Bhoju asked Dhapu, a very old Mina woman in Napa ka Khera about the kind of modesty she used to practice in her in-laws' home in the old days, it was shoes that she first thought of in responding:

In those days it was different, not like today. In that time, if my father-in-law saw me wearing shoes, and if I was just this far from him, he would let out insults. He would say, '*Yu yu yu*...she seems like she is climbing on my head' [that is, quite literally, getting uppity].... And when we went to the field, and if there were four or five men, we had to take off our shoes before those men; that's how much etiquette [*kayda*] there was in those days.

The old woman's memory of her father-in-law's taunt, '*Yu yu yu*...she seems like she is climbing on my head', is expressive of this chapter's main themes. Shoes have to do with one person putting himself or herself above another, and with the Court and his men holding themselves above all, but never without a modicum of give and take, and never without a toll of rebellious resentment.

The Dialectics of Dussehra*

NANDINI SUNDAR

[...] ENCAPSULATING HEGEMONY HISTORICALLY: DUSSEHRA OVER TIME

The fifteen-day long annual Dussehra festival, which takes place in Jagdalpur in September–October, is critical to the understanding of the Bastar polity. It illustrates the establishment of royal hegemony, its transformation under indirect colonial rule, and the manner in which both have been accepted and contested. At the same time as Dussehra illuminates the standard political chronology of Bastar, it also provides an alternative history—one that is not laid out in linear time, but as several co-existing and contestatory stories; one that subsumes in a single event the dialectically produced and historically sedimented relations between subalterns and sovereigns in Bastar.

First, Dussehra encapsulates the process of state formation under the Kakatiyas—both spatially and historically. Spatially, Dussehra incorporated all the areas within the kingdom—conversely, as different *garh*s and *zamindari*s were alienated from Bastar, their people continued to attend the Bastar Dussehra for a while and then gradually drifted

* Originally published in Nandini Sundar, *Subalterns and Sovereigns: An Anthropological History of Bastar 1854–1996*, New Delhi: Oxford University Press, 1997, pp. 47–76, as 'The Dialectics of Dussehra: *Raja* and *Praja* in the Bastar Polity'. In the present version, all notes and references have been deleted. For the complete text, see the original version.

away. Each ritual of the festival provides a glimpse of the textured construction of hegemony through time, for example, the manner in which the organized and orderly routines and imagery of imperial darbars was based on and refashioned 'old regime' assemblies; how 'sports days' and agricultural exhibitions co-existed with the wild dance of the *devi*s in possession; and, finally, how the Collector and the Commissioner, the MLA and the MP have succeeded to the mantle of the king in this disenchanted but not de-hegemonized world.

Second, Dussehra has always been and remains a performative act of legitimation, a process whereby, to paraphrase Corrigan and Sayer, the state states—it defines individual and collective identity. Within the agricultural mode of production, Dussehra was an extension of the village *jatra*—local festivals necessary to preserve fertility and avoid sickness. The king was seen as necessary to the performance of this function for the kingdom as a whole. In turn, by the incorporation of different groups as participants and contributors to the ceremonies, the Kakatiyas simultaneously ensured their contribution in terms of corvée and revenue to the more mundane and regulated aspects of state construction and sustenance. The latter was the real service the people performed for the state, but its ritual overlay—Dussehra—came to be seen as equally central to the continued existence of the polity.

While Dussehra was a moment for the expression of public loyalty, it was simultaneously contingent on the king's proper behaviour and acknowledgement of the role of his subjects. Moreover, their loyalty could fracture, as happened in 1876 and even earlier in 1774, when the Halbas of Dongar rebelled against the king, Daryaodev, led by his half-brother, Ajmer Singh. The establishment of hegemony is not a one-time accomplishment, but something which is ceaselessly contested, and constantly re-established.

DUSSEHRA AS ROYAL RITUAL

Elsewhere in India, Dussehra is also celebrated as Durga Puja, or Navratri (nine nights), held as it is on the first nine days/nights of the lunar month Asvina (September–October). The tenth day was known as Vijay Dasami or victory day, of which the common mythological referents are a commemoration of the victory of Ram over Ravan, the protagonists of the epic, Ramayana, or the Goddess Durga over Mahishasura, the buffalo-demon. However, in Bastar, as elsewhere, the central place of Durga was taken by Danteswari, the tutelary Goddess of the royal family, and Dussehra was celebrated as the state festival par excellence. Following the worship of professional tools, especially arms, throughout the festival, and their processional honouring on the ninth day, the tenth day traditionally marked the beginning of military campaigns (which aiso made sense in the context of the ending of the monsoons). The other ubiquitous features of Dussehra are the sacrifice of animals, especially buffaloes; the entrusting of the well-being and safety of the kingdom, usually in the shape of a sceptre or sword, to the Goddess (or an ascetic) for the period of the festival; and the ceremonial of processions and assemblies (darbars) which required the attendance of all notables and invited the spectatorship of all commoners. The central theme of the Dussehra festival, taken generically, is said to be the worship of the Goddess by the king on behalf of the kingdom, in order to ensure its well-being. However, the various rituals of Dussehra in Bastar are multi-layered accretions of different meanings going back to different historical periods and events, and drawing upon different ensembles of tradition—some pan-Indian and high-Hindu, and some specific to Bastar.

VILLAGE RITUALS AND STATE PERFORMANCES

Jatras are village festivals held to appease the local Mother Goddess through sacrifice, so that she feeds off the animals and not human lives (by causing death through sickness and drought); and to invoke her aid in the well-being of the village. The *majhis* and *pujaris* whom I interviewed in 1992 had similar explanations for Dussehra—with the benefits being intended for the area as a whole rather than a single village. This suggests that in the popular imagination, the direction of cosmological understanding goes from the rootedness of village life and everyday experiences upward to the state, rather than the other way around, as Fuller claims. In his view, village rituals were minor replicas of royal rituals, with a village headman assuming the king's function.

Dussehra is also similar to a *mandai* (the *pargana*-level equivalent of a village jatra) in that it is a meeting place for gods and humans, albeit on a much larger scale. In 1992, 88 village mother goddesses were invited to attend Dussehra in Jagdalpur. The ritual division of labour between different groups for Dussehra parallels that of different lineages in the propitiation of village gods. However, it is essential to remember that groups living closer to the capital are naturally far more involved through the assignment of specific tasks than those further away. Although people came to attend Dussehra from all over the state, often walking several days and several hundred miles, it is not the central festival in people's lives, as is often claimed, but a royal or political ritual—one that binds people to the state. For instance, from 1930–6, due to the Queen's illness or absence from Jagdalpur, Dussehra was not held. It would have been inconceivable for any important village ritual to go uncelebrated that long. The leading headmen who were consulted by the Administrator on due procedure replied that although they were anxious to celebrate the event, its main significance for them was the opportunity to see the Queen, and they would rather not celebrate the festival in her absence. The Queen, too, seemed piqued to think it could be held without her. After Pravir's death and the internecine quarrelling among the remnants of the ex-royal family, the royal place on the chariot was taken by the umbrella of Danteswari held by her senior priest. This turned what was centrally a royal ritual into a religious festival, and elevated Danteswari to cardinal importance.

DANTESWARI

The history of Danteswari embodies the history of the region, and, in understanding how she came to power, it is possible to understand how the Kakatiya dynasty came to power. In the received wisdom, Danteswari was seen as the chief goddess of the land, and the king merely owed his power to his role as her chief priest. According to popular legend, Danteswari came with the Kakatiyas from Warangal. She asked Annam Deo to proceed in front. As long as he could hear the sound of her anklets, she is said to have told him, he was not to look back. All the land that he could cover in this fashion was to be his. At Dantewara, however, the sands of the Sankini and Dankini rivers muffled the sound of the anklets. When the tinkle ceased, the king turned around, whereupon the goddess stopped still in her tracks and refused to go further. Hence a temple was built on the spot (Dantewara) and another shrine established in the palace at Jagdalpur, for the king's convenience.

However, a closer look at both the rituals of Dussehra and the actual distribution of Danteswari shrines across the state suggests that her position as Chief Goddess is tenuous, and had to be constantly reinforced during Dussehra, as a part of the process whereby the king reinforced his own power over subordinate forces. Danteswari's position has to be seen through a hall of mirrors. Like mother goddesses elsewhere who were appropriated from indigenous cults and adopted as tutelary goddesses by royal families, she represented what Kulke calls the integration rather than displacement of tribal elements in the development of 'nuclear areas of sub-regiona' power'. Ultimately, it was this fusion which helped legitimize rule in these areas. The site of the Danteswari temple, according to the inscription in front of it, represents the spot where one of Parvati or Sakti's teeth *(dant)* fell, as her dead body was being carried by her husband Siva across the land, and is thus one of the *sakta-pithas* (Sakti cult centres) of India. But the sakta-pithas themselves result from a process whereby the original object of worship —an animal or tree spirit and then a local mother goddess— is first worshipped through different, more pan-Indian rituals (flowers and incense as against animal sacrifice and medium possession) and then associated with one of the goddesses of the Hindu pantheon, generally Durga/Kali/Sakti in order to form regional cults. The phenomenon has been well described by Nandi for the Deccan and by Eschmann for similar deities in Orissa.

However, local manifestations of Danteswan all over Bastar are refractions of the royal deity and not the other way around. Simeran Gell notes of Muria cults in the north that while both Tallur Muttay (Earth Goddess) and Yayal Muttay (Danteswari's local name) are part of a unified cosmology, 'the Muria cults of *pen* and Tallur Muttay are transactional cults between men and other worldly beings in which the effort is to achieve a sort of balance between demands on both sides; hierarchy is however intrinsic to the cult of Yayal Muttay.' In south and southeast Bastar, Danteswari is just one of the many devis, but she is superior to the other goddesses in the area, and at mandais where all the Devis and their mediums are assembled, they go to greet her rather than vice versa. In other words, Danteswari is worshipped locally only because the king was able to establish and maintain his political power, and gradually assimilate Dussehra and the worship of Danteswari to local festivals like mandais.

Thus, when I say that Danteswari's position has to be seen through a hall of mirrors I mean that the rulers adopt 'tribal' gods and change them, and the tribals in turn adopt these changed gods and change them...and so it goes on in endless mimesis. What is 'tribal' here, and what is 'Hindu'? Contra Ghurye, who used the phrase 'backward Hindus' for aboriginals, we might equally see the Hindus as over-determined aboriginals. For the same reason, the concepts of 'Sanskritization', 'Kshatriyzation' and the newer variant, 'Hinduization', popularized within the South Asian literature to refer to scheduled caste or tribal imitation of Brahminical, dominant caste or Hindu customs, are not adequate to capture the nature of mutual appropriation and the resultant contradictions that co-exist in popular religion. Paraphrasing Sontheimer, one might instead use the term 'religious (re)configuration'.

Yet another complication in Bastar is the long history of state formation. By the time of the Kakatiyas, the search for the *adi vasi* or original inhabitant becomes highly problematic with the influences of Sanskritic Gods and multi-caste territorial assemblies preceding animistic worship and tribal clan divisions on occasion. Even if the Nagvanshi kingdom was just an enclave of agriculturists surrounded by hunting–gathering groups, there must have been a mutual exchange. In understanding the relation between the Kakatiyas and the defeated Nagvanshi kingdom, the relation between Danteswari and Manikeswari (locally known as Mawli), whose temple is across the road from the palace in Jagdalpur, is of particular interest. Manikeswari appears to have been a Nagvanshi goddess, though the existing literature on this as well as local knowledge is most confusing. It appears to me that Mawli, who is deemed older than Danteswari by local tradition and whose unanthropomorphized shrines are found all over the state, became the Nagvanshi Manikeswari through the process of appropriation described above. However she also stayed in her form as Mawli, meaning simply 'Mother'. With the conquest of the Nagvanshis, their Goddess Manikeswari became subordinate to the Goddess of the Kakatiyas, Danteswari. Yet, as part of the process of achieving hegemony, the defeated had to be accommodated, albeit in a subordinate position: thus while the festival is seen as dedicated to Danteswari, Manikeswari or Mawli is acknowledged in every ritual of Dussehra.

In all the events of Dussehra, the procession must follow a route from Danteswari to Mawli, which suggests that the latter is somehow senior. According to the Mawli pujari, when there was a ruler all the major rituals that now take place in the Danteswari temple used to take place in the Mawli temple. The chariot's path is further determined by the position of the Mawli and Jagannath temples—which it must circumambulate. The Mawli Parghav event in which Danteswari is welcomed from Dantewada, and which is one of the bigger events of the festival, is also suggestive of the importance of Mawli's role—except that once again there is no consensus on the precise meaning of it.

As part of the same process of hegemonic reconfiguration, the priests of all the temples in Jagdalpur (for example, Malkarnath, Kalkanath, Karnakotin, Sitala, Kankalin, Telangin, and Mawli) who used to be ab-original or low caste, have been replaced by Brahmins within the living memory of people. The Mawli priest (a Dhakad, aged approximately 60) remembers that a Dhurwa priest used to look after the Danteswari temple, but died with the raja in 1966. Lallu Pujari's Oriya Brahmin family then took over. In short, the history of the rise of any group to power can be read through the history and relative position of their gods, and vice versa. Similarly, the recent adoption of Ram and Hanuman in Bastar is an index of the power of their devotees—the migrant traders and officials—over the lower classes.

DUSSEHRA: INTEGRATION THROUGH LABOUR

Every single group in the kingdom, however small in number, has some role in the festival—ranging from the small groups of Mundas in and around Potenar, the Saonras in Bade Umargaon and its environs, to the more populous Murias and Marias. Certain functions are carried out on a caste basis and certain others on a regional basis—for instance, there may be several castes in a particular village which is assigned to bring wood. Upto the mid-twentieth century, the villages in a pargana would pool resources and send rice, goats, and other presents to the king through the majhi. Certain parganas contributed supplies, while others contributed labour. For instance, in Kachorapati pargana, two kg rice and eight annas per household were collected, of which approximately forty to sixty kg and one goat were marked for Dussehra contributions. The rest was kept for pargana events. A Dussehra tax was levied at the rate of three paise per rupee of rent in Jagdalpur *tahsil*, and anywhere from eight annas to three rupees per village elsewhere. This cess was similarly collected through the majhis. The supplies thus collected would be used to feed people who had specific functions to perform at Dussehra. Today, ironically, when there are no cesses or special taxes levied, the mass feeding is not seen as an act of largesse (as it was during the days of the king) but the fulfilment of a duty on the government's part. In 1938 the state contributed Rs 5600 annually for the festival, which was managed by the Palace Superintendent. By 1992, the budget had risen more than forty-fold, albeit in nominal terms, to Rs 2,13,500. Except for a brief period in the 1960s when the festivities were managed by the king and his supporters on their own, all arrangements have been co-ordinated by the tahsildar's office in Jagdalpur. Currently there is also a Dussehra committee comprising of majhis and former supporters of the king—men and women known as members and membrins respectively—to formally oversee the arrangements. While expenditure has increased, people complain of skimpy portions, nostalgically looking back to the liberality of the king, at which time, they claimed, an extra sack of rice would be thrown in now and then. There are also accusations of corrupt government officers and MLAs; whether true or not, in view of inflation and the fiscal oversight exercised by the Dussehra committee, these accusations are symptomatic of the present-day status of the state. In short, although people still come voluntarily and suffer the income loss of fifteen days or more away from home and work, and say they would 'jump on the *sarkar*' if the festival were not celebrated, the most striking feature about Dussehra as it is celebrated today is the extent to which it is regarded as a government responsibility (*Sarkari Dussehra*) rather than a people's event.

In 1992, the Dussehra festivities started on 26 September and continued till 10 October. Preparations, however, began at least two months earlier—in August, with the construction of the chariot. According to popular legend, the chariots date back to the period of Purushottam Deo (AD 1407–39) who made a pilgrimage to the temple of Jagannath at Puri. He prostrated himself along the entire route, and so pleased the Lord Jagannath that the Lord gave him a twelve-wheeled chariot for the return journey. However, since the original chariot was too big to be easily pulled, it was divided up into two smaller chariots, a four-wheeled one and a bigger eight-wheeled one. Purushottam Deo started Dussehra in his then capital at Dongar, where even today a minor version of the event is held.

Every year, one of the chariots is made afresh. The entire process of construction is carried out through the cooperation of different villages. In 1957, an effort was apparently made to give out a contract for chariot-making but the lessee had to withdraw in the face of popular resentment. Each stage in the construction of the chariot is marked by certain offerings and sacrifices: for example, the *pata* jatra which inaugurates the work, when people from village Billori bring logs of sal to Jagdalpur for the construction of the pata (wheels). Different parts of the chariots are given different names and made of different woods—for instance, the base is known as *magar muhi* and is made of sal wood brought by the villages of Pandripani, Bade Marenga, Bade Morathpal, Lendra, and Rajur; and the roof is made of dhaman wood brought by Tondapal, Badebadam, Chilkuhuti, and Dongriguda. These villages are given special forest passes for the purpose. The coal for smelting the iron to be used for the joints of the chariot is brought by another set of villages, as are the siadi creepers to make the ropes to pull the chariot. In all, some 72 villages appear to be involved in bringing construction materials for the chariots alone.

The entire carpentry and construction, which takes about 15 days, is supervised by the Saonra Naiks of Jhar Umargaon and Beda Umargaon, who have been traditionally designated for the task. In 1992, there were 65 men of different castes from Beda Umargaon, and 43 from Jhar Umargaon at work. Muria ironsmiths make the nails and the dragging ropes are plaited by Dhurwas. In the days when the king took part, Gadbas carried the king's palanquin to the *kalas-sthapan* ceremony (installation of sacred water) at various temples. Halbas, as the militia of old, carried swords alongside the chariot, while Bhatras bore bows and arrows. The four-wheeled chariot is pulled by 50 or 60 men from each of the 40 assigned villages near Jagdalpur. These men belong to different groups: Bhatra, Dhurwa, Muria, Halba, Dhakad, Mahara, and Sundi. The eight-wheeled chariot is pulled solely by Marias from the villages of Killepal pargana. The division of labour is so specific as to detail every possible function—even the people who put up the ladders to ascend and descend the chariot are from a specific village.

DUSSEHRA RITUALS

Despite variations and accretions over time, as modes of representing authority changed and darbars and sports shows were added on, the Dussehra programme has remained more or less the same over the past century. In the following account, I try and bring out some of the distinctive features of the traditional Bastar Dussehra like the *Kachan Gadi* ritual, *Jogi Bithai*, *Mawli Parghav*, and the *Kumdakote* kidnapping. The other features are more standard, though also part of an ensemble of beliefs developed from Mother Goddess cults.

Dussehra Programme (1992)

Days	Time	Events
1.	Evening	Kachan Gadi ritual
2.	Morning	Kalas-Sthapan
	Evening	Jogi Bithai
3–9.	Morning	Navratri Puja
	Evening	Small chariot procession
10.	Morning	Durga Ashtami/Mahaashtami
	Evening	Nisha Jatra
11.	Morning	Kunvari Puja
	Evening	Jogi Utthayi
	Night	Mawli Parghav
12.	Morning	Bheeter Raini Puja
	Evening	Big chariot procession
13.	Morning	Bahar Raini Puja (Kumdakote)
	Evening	Chariot returns to palace
14.	Morning	Kachan Jatra/(Ran Jatra)
	Evening	'Muria' Darbar
15.	Morning	Gangamunda (Kutumb) Jatra
	Afternoon	Ohadi: Farewell to village deities
16.	Morning	Farewell to Danteswari

Source: Official Dussehra Programme, 1992, Tahsildar's Office, Jagdalpur.
N.B.: Exhibition runs throughout the festival

The Kachan Gadi takes place in the evening, on the last day of the waning moon in the month of *Kunwar* (September–October), which elsewhere is observed as *Pitramoksha Amavasya*, when people make offerings to their departed ancestors. In Bastar, it marks the start of the Dussehra, with permission to hold it being taken from Kachan Devi. In the ritual, a pre-pubertal Mrigan girl becomes possessed by Kachan Devi in the course of circumambulating a swing made of thorns seven times, accompanied by a group of singing women. Once possessed, she engages in a mock fight with a man from the Khati caste. After defeating him, the girl (in her role as Devi) is laid down to swing on the thorns, apparently without ill effects. The king (or, since the death of the last king, Lallu Pujari holding the umbrella representing Danteswari) puts his request through the priests of the temple, which is granted when the Devi takes off her garland and gives it to them. According to the Mawli priest, the significance of this is the symbolic exchange of the king's weapons and the safe-keeping of the kingdom in return for the garland during the period of the festival. In royal times, apparently, a darbar was held at night, whereby the king 'abdicated'—exchanging his clothes and ornaments for the simple clothes of an ascetic. In this guise, he could perform ceremonies in the temples of Danteswari, Mawli, and Kankalin.

[...] Scattered speculations aside, the Kachan Gadi ritual represents one moment of inversion in the entire year, when the Maharas/Mrigans are given some recognition in the polity. This suggests, in turn, a situation of power that while normally subordinated or held in check, still needs to be acknowledged.

In the ritual known as Jogi Bithai (seating of the ascetic), a 'jogi' is incarcerated sitting cross-legged in a pit dug in the *sirasar* for nine days, during which time he can neither eat nor move. The public comes and sees him and makes money offerings. The logic behind the ritual is that the jogi is a substitute ascetic for the king, who would otherwise have had to perform similar penances during Dussehra. This is strongly suggested by the fact that the king and the jogi never see each other. However there are other less serious philosophies behind the mutual abstinence, which indicate that there is often a wide gap between the high philosophy behind ritual and its popular reception. One such allegation is that a jogi once soiled his seat, and the raja who went to pick him up got soiled in the process, and thereafter refused to have anything to do with him.

The four-wheeled chariot begins to circulate from the evening of the third day and this is kept up for six days. It now creaks its way around the central market winding up again in front of the palace, preceded by the Munda and Panka musicians, a group of women waving incense before it and shouting *jai*, and, as is inevitable in this modern day and age, a brass band! For night processions they have fire torches and tubelights held by rows of men and trailed by a generator on a push cart. Getting the chariots, especially the eight-wheeled one, around street corners is an unwieldy task and the rope pullers have to invest much energy. There is great shouting and excitement. As the chariots turn, people also run around trying to escape being run over. If the chariot breaks down, the circuit is completed by jeep, replacing the elephant of former times. The streets as well as the rooftops of shops and houses are lined with crowds, especially on the last two days that the big chariot emerges.

People say that formerly (presumably in the late nineteenth, early twentieth century), there used to be a massive sacrifice of one hundred and eight goats on the eighth and ninth day. Nowadays, only about 40 goats in total are sacrificed at Dussehra. The buffalo sacrifices stopped about 25 years ago. The Mawli Parghav, referring to the welcome of Danteswari, which takes place on the eleventh day, is the first major crowd puller of Dussehra. The events preceding this are mostly attended only by townspeople or neighbouring villagers. In royal times, the king (now replaced by the Raj Guru), went some distance barefoot to receive the palanquin of Danteswari which had been carried on foot all the way from Dantewara, 57 miles south. He would then carry it back to the palace. Following internal family quarrels after Pravir Chandra's death, the palanquin was kept in the Danteswari temple. In 1992, this event was followed by fireworks and performances. There was a dance by a group of Marias—the male drummers with their distinctive horned headgear, and the women all in red sarees, as well as other non-local popular entertainment like acrobatics. The big daytime events are invariably accompanied by hawkers selling ribbons and rope, tobacco and knives, combs and earrings to local youth. At the beginning of the twentieth century, when local traders were fewer, merchants would come from as far as Calcutta and camp in Jagdalpur for the festival.

The big chariot emerges on what is elsewhere celebrated as Vijay Dasami. As long as there was a king, the Mawli (Manikeswari) image— a golden, eight-armed Durga, said to be a very old statue—was brought to the darbar hall and placed on the throne. The king ascended the chariot from this hall and came back to it, where he was re-enthroned after his nine days of asceticism, followed by a darbar. On the twelfth day of Dussehra, as it was celebrated in royal times, the king (and chariot) was 'kidnapped' to a place called Kumdakote, to the east of Jagdalpur, where his subjects presented him with gifts such as cash, game, fruit, brooms, mats, and hawks. The practice was known as *joharni* (*johar* being a term of greeting in Halbi). It is also a time when the king partook of new grains (*nayakhani*). In the context of the quick-ripening millet and coarse paddy grains of the shifting cultivation cycle that was prevalent all over Bastar, Dussehra made sense as a harvest festival. The Mawli Pujari claimed that the offering of forest produce represented an assurance to the king that the people, and hence he too, would not starve even during drought; but Menon writes that the ceremony resulted from the tribals feeling aggrieved that they, the majority of the king's subjects, could not take part in the essentially Hindu celebrations. They wanted their own Dussehra, 'which, they said, could only be held in their own home, the jungle.' So they kidnapped the king when asleep and took him and his chariot to Kumdakote, which was a dense jungle then. The king came to some understanding with them, and rode the chariot back in triumph. As various observers have noted, there was often a mutual feeling of possessiveness and loyalty between monarch and subjects bred by the paternalist relation. In yet another interpretation, I read the offering of grains and first fruits as a symbolic assertion of the people's rights to the forest in the first place.

The Kumdakote, nayakhani makes it possible to read Dussehra as an act of negotiation between people and king. The king legitimized his own position as essential to the well-being of the land through the ritual eating of the first grains and fruit, sacrifices, and other rituals. The subjects, in turn, subordinated the kingship to their own ends of preserving fertility and avoiding sickness—treating Dussehra as a state extension of village mandais and jatras. They also asserted, through this, their rights to the land and its produce, and the king's dependence on them for his own livelihood.

THE 'MURIA DARBAR': 'REPRESENTING AUTHORITY' IN COLONIAL AND POSTCOLONIAL BASTAR

Under colonial rule, there were accretions to the festival which reflected British modes of legitimation. This reworked Dussehra proved the ideal form for the ritual display of indirect rule. Cohn describes how British attempts to work through Mughal and other indigenous idioms of rule, such as the giving of gifts by nobles, led to continuing tensions over titles, forms of address, questions of precedence, and even dress. While grappling with these forms, colonialism inevitably changed their meanings to more contractual relations. Eventually, the British substituted their own forms of legitimation: the laying of foundation stones, coronations, jubilees, the ranking of princely states by gun salutes, not to forget cricket matches and agricultural exhibitions.

Yet the language of custom remained. Describing the celebrations for the silver jubilee of King George V and Queen Mary in Bastar, which included 'processions, illuminations, fireworks displays, and aboriginal dances with distribution of goods to the poor and sweets to the school children', Hyde claimed that there was considerable enthusiasm: 'Indians know all about Rajas and Emperors and greatly enjoy "*tamashas*" associated with them.' Thus empire was translated into local rituals, and indigenous rituals now added to the greater glory and diversity of empire.

The 'Muria Darbar' was first begun in 1906 as part of the Dussehra programme as a means of communication between the administration and the public. Since then, it has served as the real microcosm of the polity. The scale was evidently never large, and a specification in the 1947 programme gives us a glimpse: 'Uniform, darbar dress or clean clothes will be worn so far as those attending the darbar may be in possession of such.' All officials, zamindars, and majhis were required to attend, and the majhis were given red turbans to signify their authority. In later years, this symbol too became a site of contestation as Pravir Chandra appointed his own majhis and gave them blue turbans as against the red-turbaned majhis who were supports of the state. Since approximately 1923 onwards, the Darbar speech was given by the administrator rather than the sovereign. Although the state still formally functioned in the royal name, this was as close to a ceremonial public acknowledgement of a de facto transfer of power as one might get.

The various issues raised by the administrators, though couched in a language of administrative largesse, provide a glimpse of the concerns of the people. From 1906 to 1947, complaints and queries regarding the reservation of the forests, grazing and commutation dues, *begar*, and purchases of supplies by officials at less than the market rates (*bisaha*) were routine. At the same time, the colonial state presented its own version of the truth to its subjects. Just after the rebellion of 1910, the raja castigated his subjects for not cooperating with the administration and maintaining a 'universal conspiracy of silence' with respect to the rebellion. In a situation where several villages had been burnt, hundreds of villagers flogged, large fines extracted, and people were still fleeing to neighbouring provinces, it would seem odd to us if they had done anything else. In these Dussehra speeches, colonialism emerges as an essentially patriarchal phenomenon—the wise and stern, all-knowing priest or father giving advice to wayward folk on the need to extend cultivation, look after the forest, accept inoculation, attend schools, stop drinking, and desist from running off with marriage partners. Year after year, exhorted to virtue or castigated for their vices, the assembled adivasis either kept silent, or concurred heartily, sometimes perhaps a shade too heartily.

EXHIBITING THE STATE

The Government exhibition, started in 1938/39, along with a sports day that concluded the events, represented the colonial administration's 'improvement' drive to supplement the indigenous rituals of Dussehra. The exhibition was designed to encourage local manufactures such as carpentry by aboriginal youth. The games included archery, elephant rides, and lotteries. A livestock exhibition was also held. As Burton Benedict argues, exhibition displays were not about the actual products on exhibit at all: 'Systems of classification revealed differences in national views of the ideally constructed world.' Thus 'British exhibits tended to show colonial products and the use of native labor to obtain these products', that is, natives in the service of empire and commerce. The French, on the other hand, concentrated on showing natives as natives, while the American exhibits showed natives as having been transformed into good, civilized Americans.

Like everything else, the exhibition was continued over into the postcolonial state. The main government exhibition runs parallel to the evening events almost throughout the festival and is perhaps the best barometer of the state of the state in its most reformist mode. Each department (Health, Tribal Welfare, Education, Fisheries, Forest, Seri-culture, Irrigation, Electricity, Municipality, and Archaeology) has its own stall, paid for out of its own budget. These provide information and advertise their achievements. There are also dances and other items performed by different schools. Similar exhibitions are held in the larger mandais—such as in Narainpur. The Anthropological Survey of India, which has its offices next to the exhibition grounds in Jagdalpur, has its own exhibition of 'tribal' artifacts, which are really made by non- tribal artisanal 'castes'. As Alfred Gell points out, these items are increasingly being seen by outsiders as symptomatic of the authentic tribal, while the tribals themselves have been taking to consumer items produced elsewhere, in a process that has gone on much longer than is commonly thought. To paraphrase Clifford, the pure products have been going crazy for a while, and therein lies the predicament of culture. [...]

Geographies of Empire*

K. SIVARAMAKRISHNAN

[...]

Representations—the confluence of ideology and knowledge—achieve consistency only by intervening in social space and its production. Thus botanical surveys, tree plantation, and timber conservancy were measures that entered the colonial repertoire for knowing and ordering the landscape at the same time, by the beginning of the nineteenth century. Where they occurred, persisted, failed, shrank, and enlarged are all aspects that set colonialism off against its 'historical and geographical particularities'. We have to describe, therefore, the production of landscapes as historical spaces and recognize the concomitant production of societies and cultures that takes place. Tribal people were associated with tribal places, and the production of these places had as much to do with the history of these people as it had to do with the geography of their lands. When landscapes were partitioned through colonial survey and policy, their inhabitants were also compartmentalized.

[...] This brings me to the making of tribal places in woodland Bengal. Tribal places were made, not only by curbing practices like

* Originally published in K. Sivaramakrishnan, *Modern Forests: Statemaking and Environmental Change in Colonial Eastern India*, New Delhi: Oxford University Press, 1999; and Stanford: Stanford University Press, 1999, pp. 80–90, as 'Geographies of Empire: The Transition from "Wild" to Managed Landscapes'. In the present version, all notes and references have been deleted. For the complete text, see the original version.

shifting cultivation but by assigning them a specific terrain which was designated the place of tribes unredeemable from 'backward agri-culture'. Key administrators, scientists, and other influential imperial agents joined to imagine a significant congruence between the space of primeval landscapes and their human inhabitants. Their scientific criticism of *kumri* and *podu* (forms of shifting cultivation in south India) aimed at regulating patterns of settlement and production such that British control over forests was facilitated and agendas of pacifica-tion by rule of law were accomplished. 'Tribe' and 'caste' ultimately became the main categories of colonial sociology in India. By the end of the nineteenth century they were still being parsed by prominent colonial ethnologists exasperated by the blurring of lines between them. Thus Herbert Risley, the authority on Bengal tribes and castes, wrote in 1901:

all over India at present there is going on a process of the gradual and insensible transformation of tribes into castes...the main agency at work is fiction...I hope the ethnographic surveys will throw a great deal of light on these singular forms of evolution by which large masses of people surrender a condition of comparative freedom and take in exchange a condition that becomes more burdensome.

[...] But the numerous studies of social categorization inadequately deal with the integral spatial components of such colonial discourse. Both literary critics and historians have studied the objectifying gaze of colonialism, but confined their analysis mostly to its impact on the body, occasionally to consequences for the appropriation of space, but rarely focused on *the body in space*. Even recent studies of tribal sedentar-ization in India, both in the pre-colonial and British period, do not note the making of tribal places.

I would, therefore, like to emphasize the confluence of projects of people and landscape classification. This is important because

it is now widely acknowledged that what were until recently regarded as hunting and gathering tribes were in many cases reduced within the last hundred years or so to an economic condition in which they are forced to survive by foraging, begging, thieving, and such activities.

Such alteration and degradation of subsistence production for certain tribes was accompanied in the colonial period by their confinement to certain spaces through force or voluntary movement and settlement. When it came to forest management, therefore, people were not so much unyoked from ecology, as Arjun Appadurai has it, as they were classified by relation to ecology. We may see this clearly in the following discussion about the creation of the Santhal Parganas district.

Santhals and Paharias certainly came to belong in the tribal world of Bengal designated by colonial ethnologists and administrators. But they were differentiated by their place in a regional agrarian economy. Paharias invited greater official opprobrium and suffered gradual impoverishment as the landscape of the new Santhal Parganas district was partitioned into areas fanned and forested. They were the group on the hilltops most obdurately resistant to sedentary cultivation. Santhals, in contrast, emerged as the apparently successful pioneers who first extended and then stabilized the cultivated arable land. But this was made possible by creating an enclave—far from complete—for Santhals, viewed as tribes sufficiently imbued with a developmental spirit. Other Santhals left for a variety of reasons to work in tea gardens and other plantation economies in north Bengal and Assam. They more often became deracinated labour in far-off places. In those situations it was not their potential to become developed (read incipient caste-like qualities) that came to be valorized but rather their tribal 'hardiness and simplicity'.

DISCERNING AND MAKING TRIBAL PLACES

The work of [August] Cleveland with the Paharias in woodland Bengal marked the first instance where the need for administrative exceptionalism was recognized. Like the Paharias, their neighbours the Santhals are reported to have lived by hunting and raiding lowland farmers. Grain, salt, tobacco, cattle, and goats were generally taken in these raids. William Hodges describes Paharia raiding at its height. 'Like those of all savages, their incursions were merely predatory...entering villages by night, murdering husbandmen, drove off their cattle and then secured themselves in the hills.' Curbed by British rule in such practices, they were established in their own areas to till in peace. Soon there emerged a clear distribution of Santhals in valleys and Paharias on barren hills, in what became after 1855 the Santhal Parganas district, an area of 5500 square miles taken from Bhagalpur and Birbhum.

After Cleveland's pacification of the Paharias in 1782, disputes over grazing, forest products, and boundaries of the hill people's terrain continued between Paharias and lowland *zamindars*, leading to John Ward's demarcation of the Damin-i-Koh in 1832. Rapid Santhal migration and settlement in the skirt of the hills followed, as official encouragement thickened an earlier flow. Between 1838 and 1851, Santhal villages increased from 40 to 1473, their population from 3000 to 82,795, and their revenue payments from 2000 rupees to 43,918 rupees. The Santhal Parganas, marked by masonry pillars, became a particularly well-delineated case of the exceptionally administered district, where government was to rely on indigenous forms of village organization. These forms, characterized by the hierarchy of village *manjhi, des manjhi,* and *parganait* (*pargana* head), were considered sufficient justification to persevere with the policy of a segregated Santhal province as the question of revenue settlements and letting *dikus* (outsiders) into the provincial land markets repeatedly came up in later decades. As one Santhal officer, an ardent advocate of protecting their place, wrote in 1881, 'to let in the dikus for the purpose of breaking up Santhal tribal unity would be like drugging a spirited horse...instead of taming him by good riding.'

If the Santhal system re-created the Paharia stipendiary chiefs and self-governing councils, in some respects it also divided the integral landscape of Rajmahal into hill and plain. Paharias confined to the hilltops soon became impoverished, and in the 1880s the inquiries of the Dufferin Committee revealed as much. Carstairs, the Deputy Commissioner of Santhal Parganas, wrote, 'Mr. Grant, SDO Godda,...searched fifty Paharia houses and did not find so much as food for the evening meal of the day. They were waiting for the return of women who had carried firewood for sale to the market and would bring back food.' In contrast the Santhals seemed prosperous with their terraced rice fields, pigs, poultry, goats, cattle, and liberal access to small game and the fruit and seeds of *mahua* (*bassia latifoia*), *sal,* and *kendu* (*diospyros melanoxylon*) from the forests.

The divergent futures of Paharias and Santhals through the nineteenth century were built on distinct patterns of deforestation. In the hills, Paharia territory, shifting cultivation persisted but in the foothills and plains of the Damin, forest clearing established Santhal agriculture. Even by the early decades of the nineteenth century, when Buchanan–Hamilton toured the Bengal districts, the view of the Rajmahal hills was one of mostly stunted trees. It was a landscape created by shifting cultivation, firewood removal, *sal dhuna* extraction, and annual fires for both pasture regeneration and amelioration of the air. The Paharias clearly managed forests for what came to be known in the jargon of forest conservancy as minor forest products. They grew sesamum and *kurthi* (a pulse), in clearings around preserved kendu, palas (*butea frondos*), asan (*terminalia tomentosa*), and mahua trees. The flower of the mahua was a valuable food, while the asan was used to breed the tasar silkworm. Even though *ghatwals* and other elite had sought monopolies of tasar silkworm breeding by surrounding the activity with rituals of purity (like vegetarian observances), the poor Paharia was still the source of cocoons that were skilfully gathered while foraging in the forest. In addition to cocoons and charcoal, which they made abundantly, Paharias traded millets, sorghum, and pulses grown in their *jhums* for salt, iron, and clothes. The northern Paharias also grew some cotton.

The making of tribal places, in which restricting shifting cultivation was a key strategy, was a pacificatory tactic that compelled close observation of landscape use. Even the critics grudgingly noted that cutting down trees was only one among many ways forests were utilized in these places. An account otherwise largely sceptical of tribal villagers' management of forests, especially shifting cultivation, records, with refreshing candour, that villages tended to be embowered in groves of fruit trees containing mango, tamarind, peepul (*ficus religiosa*), and surrounded by extensive forests, providing shade, food, small timber, and fodder. To ensure a liberal supply of fodder these forests were interspersed with grasslands. In the long run, pioneering settled agriculture differentiated the relatively 'successful aboriginals' from the unsuccessful ones.

One commentator noted, 'Though the Kolarians, particularly the Santhals, cherish religious groves, they seem unable to stand the sight of fine old trees and invariably cut them down.' Clearly at this point in the history of land settlement, and its conversion to what were colonially sanctioned 'productive uses', Santhals were a class of aborigines appreciated not for their love of trees but their willingness to cut them down in the service of agriculture. It was this aspect of their reputation that earned them their place in British India, carved out in the skirts of the Rajmahal hills. Sutherland, the Joint Magistrate of Monghyr wrote in 1817, after investigating tenures in the Rajmahal area, that 'very extensive forests...have been brought under gradual cultivation by industrious Santhals.' But the Santhal migration and clearing of the hills was itself impelled by the spread of settled cultivation. E.G. Man, a contemporary chronicler of this process, portrays the Santhal as a primitive backwoodsman who cleared and prepared the land for the advancing Bengali. A cycle of reclamation and dispossession seemed to be at work. The creation of the Santhal Parganas was an attempt to break the cycle and reward Santhal enterprise.

The making of tribal places was also predicated on distinguishing their inhabitants from Hindus. Manbhum, a district carved out of the former Jungle Mahals district, was largely populated by Bhumij cultivators even in 1865. Dalton had classified them as Kolarian and Munda, after observing their ceremonies, language, and marriage practices. Manbhum was thus part of the larger tract running from the hilly areas west and south of Bengal, Bihar, and Benaras to the frontiers of Hyderabad, and many of the aboriginal zamindars of the jungle mahals were described as becoming Hinduized because they aspired to Rajput status.

To the first colonial chroniclers of their fortunes, the rajas, mankis, ghatwals, and other privileged status holders in Chotanagpur and its adjoining areas had attained an exalted standing and prosperity that had followed their Hinduization. Dalton expresses this viewpoint clearly when he says:

left to themselves the Kols increased and multiplied, and lived a happy Arcadian sort of life under their republican form of government for many centuries; but it is said a wily Brahmin at last obtained a footing among them and an important change in the form of government was the result.

What was this change? The chief alteration of aboriginal society was its division into the Hinduized and the others, with the former coming to dominate the latter through service tenures and office. Further, rural hierarchy was introduced by the rajas who appointed revenue farmers and favoured Brahmins and Rajputs with land grants, the cumulative effect being the erosion of Munda and Manki authority as the collective proprietary land system they presided over was dismantled. A related problem was the migration of Santhals and other tribes out of regions where outsider (non-tribal) jagirdars and *thikadars* (rent collecting intermediaries) obtained rent contracts over them and raised rents. These trends both ousted Santhal parganaits (chiefs of parganas) and increased rental demands.

As one exasperated Santhal officer put it, no sooner is a village rescued from its primitive jungle by the labours of the Santhals and brought into a tolerable state of cultivation than it is given in farm to some jobber or other, and the Santhal sent to the wall....' Through this narrative of aboriginal dispossession the 'tribal' officers of Bengal carved out tribal places as zones of paternalist, local knowledge-based direct administration in a region increasingly subject to bureaucratic and rationalized governance through standard laws, codes, and procedures. Disturbed in some respects by the permeability of the boundary between tribe and caste, these administrators sought to create and preserve the defining characteristic of tribes, which may be summed up as 'a matter of remaining outside of state and civilization.'

By the 1870s, the southwestern parts of woodland Bengal—the emerging tribal heartland—were taking shape as a landscape where two important elements of policy converged. The spread of forest conservancy reinforced this convergence. One element worked to hasten the gradual transformation of wildlands and wastelands into an ordered terrain of fields and groves. The patchwork of forests and fields, supporting the varied demands made on them, demonstrated the processes whereby villages were formed in the jungle areas. The chequered landscape of embanked fields, uplands, and jungle indicated a transition zone. Forest dependence for the mostly tribal cultivators of these areas had an ecological basis. They tilled poor soil, which meant that a high proportion of largely rainfed agriculture was on uplands that had to be fallowed (for three to five years) after every season of cultivation. These lands could yield only coarse rice or millets.

The tenants of these lands often did *begari* (forced free labour) for zamindars since they paid no rent on occasionally cultivated lands. The aboriginal agricultural classes played a key role in this managed transition, and they were least amenable to standard forest rules. They participated in what Dalton saw as a double civilization process of the land and of themselves. In his words, 'to throw into their country a staff of forest conservancy officers' was guaranteed to arrest this civilizational momentum. The other element was a concerted effort by sections of the Bengal government to prevent tribal people from losing their lands and homes. Dalton and other officers were joined in this campaign by missionaries. They were all votaries of administrative exceptionalism in these tribal places and argued that loss of land and traditional polity were destroying aboriginal society and thus undermining British rule itself.

The combination of these themes focused attention on the locus of governance and its relation to complex patterns of transformation in the landscape. Efforts to preserve 'tribal republics' and the patchwork of forest and field considered their 'natural habitat' came to distinguish the administration of the southwestern region in woodland Bengal. An anonymous tract, dedicated to creating the tribal history consonant with these efforts, thus records that

according to traditions the Kols, in their two tribes of Munda and Oraon, were the first inhabitants of Chotanagpur…from ancient times they live in patriarchal style under heads of villages and heads of districts (munda and manki) each ruling over one or more villages.

This document goes on to note the types of tenures—*rajhas* (paying rent to the king), *bhuinhari* (rent-free), and *majhas* (land granted to *majhi* or villager in charge of rent collection). When Chotanagpur came under British rule in 1818, the area was opened to 'Mahomeddans, Hindus and vagabonds', who as thikadars and jagirdars began oppression of the Kols.

In the next fifty years British curiosity expanded into neighbouring tributary states. Kols who had migrated away from oppression into the

isolated hills and dense sal forests of Bonai and Gangpur were living by
girdling sal for the resin *dhuna* and raising tasar silkworms on its
associate, the asan tree. Such images of tribal idylls in the forests only
spurred certain Bengal officers to secure the continuation of traditional
forms of local governance. They argued that mankis and mundas should
be restored to their original authority and possessions, and since this
was not possible under existing Bengal regulations, special provisions
like the Chotanagpur Tenures Act were introduced. In these measures
we may find a modified reiteration of the discourse of frontiers discussed
elsewhere.

Arguably, the principle animating these mid-nineteenth century
discussions of what were coming to be distinguished as tribal places
was one of first naming them. Naming schemes for the landscape
expressed a state of expectation. Paul Carter evocatively portrays the
explorers of rural Australia who assiduously located objects of cultural
significance: rivers, mountains, meadows, plains of promise. Like them
the pioneers of colonial administration in woodland Bengal searched
for hints of the habitable, the glimmer of exchange value. Their lexicon
for the landscapes they discovered was constructed from agricultural
and tenurial usage. An aborigine, in this context, was the first clearer of
the land for cultivation. Such a claim was strengthened by further
claims, in most cases, that these first clearers were previous occupants
of the land who had subsisted on forest products. These original settlers,
defined by the transformation of landscape that gave them their name,
were also mobile. Their sedentarization was both a loss of territory and
a territorialization prescribing how they would cultivate and where.

In a fine-grained study of agrarian relations in Chotanagpur, Prabhu
Mohapatra has shown that a widely subscribed official view was consolidated during the cadastral survey and settlement operations of the
early twentieth century. According to this position, there were customary
and community rights over land in Chotanagpur that preceded property
and tenure rights granted under the Permanent Settlement of 1793.
Missionary anthropologists like Father Hoffman, the author of *En-
cyclopaedia Mundarica*, were important to the spread of this idea. The
khuntkatti (agnatic kin-based village settlement) system epitomized
this collective land control by tribes and village communities and its
variants were found among the pioneer tribes who had cleared the
jungle. In these villages, even wood for domestic purposes from forested
wastes adjoining fields could be taken only with the consent of the
extended family of first clearers. Sacred groves were created to appease
bongas (spirits) believed to be disturbed by forest clearing, and the *Pahan*
(priest) carried out all ritual and religious functions on behalf of the

village. Thus there was a separation between secular and sacred leadership between Munda or Pradhan and the Pahan.

The headman (pradhan/munda/majhi) was the representative of the corporate village group and through him the villagers expressed themselves in economic matters such as reclaiming waste for cultivation or rights in jungle lands. Landlord villages marked the breakdown of the khuntkatti system, but there too ordinary rent-paying cultivators enjoyed usufruct rights in jungles and the right to reclaim jungles at privileged rates. As recently as the 1930s, a Bihar officer, who came to be renowned as an ethnographer of Santhals and other tribes of the region, recalled his encounter with such first clearers like the Kharias en route to a bear hunt through thick sal jungle. The identification of land clearance with tribal groups entered the expressive forms of tribal unrest, as exemplified in the Tana Bhagat movement of 1918, with its cry that title deeds were embodied in 'my spade, my axe, and my plough'.

It is worth noting that becoming native to a place was always preceded by a movement into that place, voluntary or forced, that is often described as migration, sometimes being characterized the original migration. Both recent migration, as in the Santhal case, and long processes of sedentarization followed by stratification, as in the Munda case, established tribal places in southwest Bengal. But in all cases tribal relations with outsiders were similarly treated by the British. Colonial rulers sought to mitigate the exploitative influence of non-tribals on tribal society. Concurrently they redefined tribal relations with forests, to reduce the diversity of forest use, and thus establish effective control over forest products and management. Both strategies characterized the British making of tribal places. [...]

Gaze and Grasp[*]

JOHN D. KELLY

Adolph Brewster Joske was the stipendiary magistrate in a remote courthouse at Nadarivatu in Colo North, a hinterland province of the largest island of the Fiji group. His station had originally been set up to monitor and, if necessary, intervene in what the British called 'the Tuka cult', a hinterland religious complex that the British regarded as intrinsically disorderly. By the time that Joske took up his station, Tuka had been officially suppressed. The prophet-priest Navosavakadua and hundreds of his followers were in exile on distant islands, officially designated as 'dangerous and disaffected natives' in need of rehabilitation. In fact Joske's court had little Tuka business over the years. Relations between the colonial government and the hinterland Fijians at last grew more routine. But like most magistrate's courts in the indenture period in Fiji, his was overwhelmed with criminal cases emerging out of the plantation 'lines' housing South Asians brought to Fiji, people committed by contract to five years of labour.

In 1915, the Fiji government proscribed official use of the word *coolie*, part of a reform effort designed to impress India. Until then (and indeed,

* Originally published in L. Manderson and M. Jolly (eds), *Sites of Desire/Economies of Pleasure: Sexualities in Asia and the Pacific*, Chicago: University of Chicago Press, 1997, pp. 72–98, as 'Gaze and Grasp: Plantations, Desires, Indentured Indians, and Colonial Law in Fiji'. In the present version, all notes and references have been deleted. For the complete text, see the original version.

for quite a while after) the Indians were generally called and imagined to be 'coolies', and the rural magistrate's courts in cane-growing areas came to be known as the 'coolie courts'. These courts were a focus of indenture-contract discipline, the site where fines were levied and indenture times extended for violations of the labour contract such as failing to complete tasks, insolence, refusing to work, absence from the 'estates' without permission, and other violations of labour law carrying penal sanctions. These courts were also the sites of charges laid for extraordinary numbers of violent crimes, crimes also emerging from the plantations and 'free' Indian settlements nearby.

Among all the magistrates of these courts, Joske kept by far the clearest and most detailed records. He was unique among his peers for the meticulously typed documentation of all testimony that he presented to the Supreme Court. His records will lead us into the world of law, order, and violence in indenture Fiji, and his very specific juridical gaze will help us to clarify, and complicate, general questions about the constitutive powers of colonial gazes.

IN JOSKE'S COURT

Supreme Court case #12 of 1907 began in Joske's court. An indentured man named Surajvali was charged with a brutal assault on a woman who had been living with him. According to police testimony, the police found the weapon, the scene of the crime, and, in a distant hut, the victim, because the accused brought the constables to them. An Indian constable testified, 'The accused came to the police station. He said I have cut my woman...I have offended against the Government. Arrest me.' The investigation then commenced.

I have often wondered, when examining the records of this typical sort of case, whether these police narratives of confession were sheer fiction. The eerie story, repeatedly represented in Fiji's court records, is of indentured immigrant men launching brutal public attacks and then immediately seeking out the police to confess. Was this story merely the constabulary's efficient means of shaping the necessary evidence, or was it a report of surrenders and confessions that actually occurred? Joske's records, here, are very helpful. We can track, through the clear detailing of Surajvali's interventions in court, something of what he did and did not care to make clear about his own actions. Surajvali, present for all the testimony against him, cross-examined no one but the victim, Jaine. Jaine testified from her hospital bed, describing her jewellery and its origins, and describing the attack on her. He asked her, 'Did I ever neglect to feed you or take care of you, or do anything to pain you?' She replied, 'I am too weak to answer and my mouth is sore and I cannot talk.' After this, the court asked her a question, not recorded in the documents, to which she replied, 'I do not know if I shall recover or not, that God will decide.' (I also do not know if she survived.) Surajvali made only one other intervention in his own defence during the evidentiary proceedings. When her jewellery was introduced as evidence, before her testimony, he insisted that the thick silver necklace (Exhibit C) had been given to the woman by Sundar. 'Sundar showed her the necklace and she ran away from me.' None of her jewellery was given by Surajvali; her other necklace, the small one, she said was a gift from a man 'now in Suva gaol'.

The overseers, the inspectors of immigrants, the magistrates, and other government officials were well acquainted with this type of crime. The Fiji government had decided, after investigations in the 1880s and 1890s, that the cause of crimes such as this was 'sexual jealousy', and they explained it as an Indian racial trait. Surajvali confessed in court: 'It is the fault of the woman. It is true that I beat her. Had she not gone to the house of Sundar I should not have struck her. That is all.' Sundar did not testify, and not surprisingly, Surajvali was found guilty by the Supreme Court and was sentenced to seven years and 24 lashes. This is what makes this case typical: a hopeless, self-justifying confession publicizing a never-concealed, extraordinary act of violence by a man against a woman with whom he once had a sexual relationship, leading to severe punishment by the court, generally death if the victim had died. As in this case, there was often at least one male rival involved; sometimes the rival was the victim of the violence. As in roughly half the cases, in this case no 'European' man was alleged to have been involved, either as a sex partner or as an assigner of rights to women.

THE SEXUAL VIOLENCE OF INDENTURE IN FIJI

From 1879 through 1920, over 60,000 people were recruited in South Asia and brought to Fiji to work as plantation labourers, under five-year indenture contracts with penal sanctions. Violence was fundamental to the indentured labour system and plantation life in Fiji [...] [Those] who frame the struggles of the Indians in Fiji within the boundaries of political economy, explain violence as a response to labour exploitation, focusing on rare labour gang riots and attacks on overseers, and they have often repeated the colonial explanation of men's frequent attacks on women and on other indentured men, and the frequent suicides, as products of 'sexual jealousy'. To the colonials, the whole explanation for the violence lay in this terrible 'jealousy', a package of racial traits thought to include violent temper and a cool willingness to die, un-leashed by the lack of 'traditional' restraints of caste and village in Fiji, and exacerbated by the fact that indenture brought over only 40 women per 100 men.

Here I will reject the racist story of an instinctual unreason, this jealousy narrative, but I will accept the colonial designation of the violence as sexual, although this latter choice is problematic. This violence obviously has other dimensions as well, even if our conceptions of sex and sexuality are broad. As I have argued earlier, indentured men found it harder to establish marriages and households—in effect, to constitute patriarchal domestic places privileging themselves—than they did to find sex partners. We could seek a non-sexual centre to the facts here, and emphasize the degree to which the real story was one of gender domination and a broader struggle over domestic rules. But accounts of pure reason, clean reconstructions of measured utilities and interested calculations, are not really more plausible than stories of constituting instincts. Despite the danger of colonial stereotypes of animalistic lust creeping back into our accounts, I think we should seek more than an antidote depiction that makes the agency of these indentured men seem reasonable—especially agency that is so delib-erately destructive of others and self.

In any case we cannot follow colonial accounts. The ruling colonials were astonishingly unable or unwilling to generalize about their own role in the violence, no matter how often white overseers were implicated in the stories told of men fighting over rights to have women. Fiji 'European' accounts varied by genre and distance from the lines. Europeans with personal experience of the plantations seem generally to have been aware not only of the alleged Indian instinct for 'sexual jealousy', but also of frequent sexual liaisons, paid for and otherwise, between European men and Indian women. Walter Gill, in his memoir of his years as an overseer in Fiji, provides ample evidence of this awareness. But the formalities of the courts became mechanisms for bureaucratic repression and denial. When European overseers were snarled in the circumstances of a violent crime, the courts generally ignored those aspects of defence evidence. In egregious cases, especially when the European was losing control over the Indians, court cases were avoided altogether, and the European was transferred or asked to resign, and not infrequently was sent back to Australia. But when general accounting for the violence was called for, the European authorities (including Gill) reproduced the narrative of 'sexual jealousy'. When Europeans were involved, blame was laid almost always at the feet of the Asian siren, to whose wiles the European had succumbed. Gill provides a window into the fantasies of European men on plantations, mixing imagery of nature, primitivism, and the Oriental exotic in his extensive descriptions of Indian women in indenture Fiji. Life in the lines, to them, was dangerous but exciting for those who could maintain control. The fantasies of the plantation Europeans about the Indian women gained far greater social extension than did news of their own actions. How, exactly, did this happen?

To understand these facts, we need more than a science of political economy or any other method for reconstructing 'practical rationality'. Can we capture the contours of this reality, instead, as the history of some sort of gaze? We can identify various kinds of colonial gaze operating in the stories, from these fantasies of the plantation whites to the formalities of the judges examining witnesses. But which gazes had what effects? What was made real, if we 'deploy' a bit more contemporary vocabulary, when which gazes 'inscribed' what, where?

GAZE POWERS

Attention to the colonial gaze has done much to open studies of colonial power to relations and effects that do not follow mechanically from production or other pragmatic exigencies. However, exclusive inquiry into gaze has had the unintended consequence of presuming too much about the powers of the gazer. This essay will join inquiry about the colonial gaze with inquiry about the colonial grasp, especially regarding the constitutive powers and limits of both in relation to the sexual bodies of indentured Indian women in Fiji. Court records, especially those of A.B. Joske, provide a window into the ambiguities of official attempts to investigate and regulate. Questions will also be raised about Indian resistance and also Indian initiatives in the constitution of their own and colonizers' bodies, but my main focus here will be the powers, modes, and limits of colonial agency.

Critical scholarly inquiry into powerful gazes can be found in many disciplines. Much could be said about the complex trajectories of critical psychoanalytic reformations of the scientific self and its positively empirical gaze—from Freud to Lacan, Kristeva, and others. More influential in current scholarship on colonial culture and history are Foucault's magisterial syntheses, especially his crystallization of a distinction between a modern, panoptic mode of discipline, in which a dominated body is incited to interiorize the disciplinary gaze in a self-disciplining subjectivity, and (allegedly) all earlier forms of discipline, wherein spectacles of punishment were arranged instead to produce fear and submission to specific external authorities. I will return

both to Foucauldian scholarship on colonial culture and history, and
to nineteenth-century positivism. But let me start with an art-historical
touchstone of gaze theory from John Berger's *Ways of Seeing*, where he
suggests problematic conventions that entail the following:

Men act and *women appear*. Men look at women. Women watch themselves being
looked at. This determines not only most relations between men and women but
also the relation of women to themselves. The surveyor of woman in herself is male:
the surveyed female. Thus she turns herself into an object—and most particularly an
object of vision: a sight.

As he criticizes artistic representations of nude women, Berger distinguishes a European tradition with roots in Christian conceptions of
shame from the tradition of nakedness in Indian, Persian, African, and
pre-Colombian art, where 'nakedness is never supine,' and which is
more likely to show 'active sexual love as between two people, the
woman as active as the man'. Thus, Berger finds a sexual gaze at the core
of a Christian tradition of gender difference, men surveying and objectifying women, and women interiorizing their own surveillance, and
he gives us a brief glimpse of a vast, lost Garden of Eden beyond the
West, in which genders were equal and sex was free and active.

Foucault and Berger deliver us two different versions of the social
history of the powerful, other-transforming gaze. To simplify, let us call
them *modernization* versus *original sin*—a story of an axial modernity of
overwhelmingly different and new powers versus a story of a Christian–
European long run of moral inscription. When we take up problems of
sex and gender in colonial culture and history, however, the larger
patterning of agency stays the same whether we bring with us a story of
European culture as original sin, a story of modernization, or a synthesis
of the two: we script the colonized from the outset in the position of
patient and victim, and tend to grant the colonizer all active powers.

Consider Timothy Mitchell's *Colonising Eygpt* (1988). Mitchell tells
us that Egypt's modern colonizers had novel powers to 'enframe', a
uniquely envisioning and vision-insistent way of ordering space, time,
and people which enabled the colonial agents to remake the place in
their own image of it, a kind of power that only a postmodern and
postcolonial consciousness like Mitchell's own could actively understand and confront. In contrast, Michael Taussig, in inquiring into the
space of death on the colonial frontier, argues that the 'good speech' of
the colonizer was deformed, the efforts of even the most critical of
colonial observers to depict the real scene generally failed, and
visualizing faculties were taken over by cascading fantasies of evil and
violence that overcame other ordering schemata. But again one might

synthesize and fit Mitchell's and Taussig's accounts into a story of
colonial ordering: at the beginning, and on the edge, there are failures
and deformation, but eventually and centrally the colonial gaze will
reshape its world and inscribe even the subjectivity of the colonized. A
counterpoint to this resolution, then, is Ranajit Guha's argument against
the idea that colonial regimes, and that of the Raj in India in particular,
were ever actually hegemonic. Guha argues forcefully that the British
in India never succeeded in constituting a civil order that made their
domination seem unquestionably natural, inevitable, necessary, or even
simply good for India. The colonial projects failed to establish a rule of
law that actually constituted citizens, law with consent and collaboration of the governed. By Guha's argument, European 'bourgeois culture
hit its historical limits in colonialism,' as its willed self-alienation from
the colonized contradicted its promise to lead, rather than simply
dominate, people it regarded as Others. Precisely as they reorganized
towns and gridded out new, antiseptic cantonments or quarters exclusively for the ruling whites, and made their 'modern' vision real, in
Guha's view the European colonial states ensured that they would not
achieve the hegemonic ordering powers found, for example, in the
nation-states of Europe.

We are already far from Berger, and from gazes that are frankly
sexual. Let us return to Gill, the *randi-wallah*, or overseer, and his gang
of indentured women workers:

As a gang they gave a minimum of trouble. It was as if they wanted me as part of their
strange coolie lives. When we squatted together on a headland at midday, one or
another of them would shyly offer me a 'roti' or 'chupatti' from her meagre ration of
thin unleavened bread. And they would discuss themselves and me, bawdily, yet
naturally, shrilling like starlings at their own crude humour. Though still 'The Sahib',
I was their particular sahib; part of them and of their lives.

The routine seldom altered. To them the act was fresh each time they went into
it.

'How old is he?' Chini would ask in the vernacular, peering at me from the fringe
of her sari.

'Old enough.' The girl who said it would giggle and wriggle her hips.

Muniamma's snicker was contagious. Invariably we heard it before she asked,
'Do you think he's a virgin?' And because opinion was divided, and none of them
could prove I was not, they would argue among themselves. Then a long, skinny
Tamil, with an unprintable nickname, would wonder what I would be like in bed.
This was their chance to cackle over individual fantasies. It was erotica uninhibited,
and because it was also part of them, something to be revelled in. And because
nobody knew what I was like physically, there would be a shaking of cloth-covered
heads and a cracking of knuckles in long, brown fingers, until one of them would
tell a fantastically intimate story of an experience all of us knew never happened.

And then at last old Latchmi would wrap it up, saying, 'Arre! He'd be just like the rest of the sahibs,' and she would look over her shoulder and down her back with a surprised expression. 'Two shoves like a rooster, and the hen left without a tail-feather ruffled.'

I have been told I should have got up and walked away—there was something about my dignity and the prestige of the white man—yet I could never understand why.

In his fantasy that he was experiencing 'erotica uninhibited... something to be revelled in', women speaking 'bawdily, yet naturally', Gill, like Berger, imagined an Eden of active eroticism beyond the strictures of European morality. Later, Gill did arrange a regular sexual liaison for himself with an indentured woman, as discussed below. Here, I suggest we attend to the gazes, not only to Gill's image of these women, their natural, Oriental eroticism in his gaze, but to their active gaze on him.

Even if this active, speculative female testing and imagining of his sexuality occurred partly in Gill's imagination, I doubt that he wholly invents it. I suspect that the women did playfully test which sexual rules, plans, and taboos would emanate from their young sahib. They could not address it or approach him directly. They certainly could not grasp him or even touch him on their own initiative. Later in his text, Gill described being grabbed by an indentured woman shocked by nearby lightening in a storm: 'Her action confirmed her fear. To have touched me, unless stimulated by something uncontrollable, would have been impossible for her as an Indian.' It was difficult even for them to address him directly. Note the shyness when he was addressed directly, or when food was proffered, food being highly significant in South Asian cultural marking of rank and social boundary. Trapping his attention with their 'act' and watching his reactions, trapping him in their gaze by putting on a theatre for him, may well have been both their tactic and their pleasure.

But I want to keep hold of something else here too: Gill's internalized sense of being observed. Women watch themselves being looked at, but what of white men? George Orwell, in his essay 'Shooting an Elephant', tells of his duty to act, as a police officer in Burma, once trapped in the gaze of a crowd of 'natives' who had called him forth to see an elephant on rampage:

A sahib has got to act like a sahib; he has got to appear resolute, to know his own mind and do definite things. To come all that way, rifle in hand, with two thousand people marching at my heels, and then to trail feebly away, having done nothing— no, that was impossible. The crowd would laugh at me. And my whole life, every white man's life in the East, was one long struggle not to be laughed at.

Gill's account of his raucous luncheons, in contrast to Orwell's report of his grim march, suggests what might have made Gill an interesting puzzle to the women in his gang: his resistance to a 'duty' not to see or hear such things as he did, the duty that made being *randi-wallah* the job for the most junior man, 'something about my dignity and the prestige of the white man'. Gill claims not to have understood this, but in fact he knew that he 'should have got up and walked away' if he wanted to appear respectable. Who and what was at risk in the sexual joking of the women's gang?

According to Berger, a woman's every action 'is also read as an indication of how she would like to be treated.... Only a man can make a good joke for its own sake.' British colonial men, so possessive of their own 'prestige' and 'dignity', could not tell a good joke for its own sake except in the confines of their own race, class, and gender, at their clubs or military camps, and some could not even do so there. We need not doubt that self-surveying was a crucial matter for Indian women who wished to appear respectable and good in character to Fiji Europeans. But let us also notice more than the transforming power of Gill's colonizing gaze, as he monitored his prestige, dignity, and authority (risking all to pursue his own pleasure, but aware of the precariousness of his position), while his gang made up, and frequently re-enacted, good jokes about his body and sex life in a vernacular he could not always follow, and laughed about him in his presence.

SEXUAL VIOLENCE AND THE END OF INDENTURE IN FIJI

The sexual exploitation and violence endemic in the lines played a role in the demise of the system. As the best historians make clear, not all plantations in Fiji were the same. They varied in the frequency, stability, and degree of permitted coerciveness in the sexual liaisons between European men and indentured women, and the prevalence and top-down tolerance, support, and investment in open prostitution in the lines. Gill's gang did have consequential things to learn about him, as well as a chance for pleasure at his risk. The greater risks were those faced by the women, especially when the Europeans' interests extended beyond gazing and joking. The scenarios alleged in court testimony strongly suggest that the violence—brutal assaults, murders, rapes, and suicides—can be connected to the plantations where the European planters and overseers were living out the vision of exotic sensuality and predatory promiscuity intrinsic to the nature of the 'indentured' women.

Gandhian nationalists in India told a story about Fiji quite different
from any told by Fiji Europeans. The Gandhians told stories of virtuous
women struggling to protect their chastity in an atmosphere of coercive
evil. With evidence from supporters in Fiji and research expeditions,
they were able by the 1910s to marshal overwhelming anecdotal and
medical evidence of real evil there. Faced with outraged public opinion
in India, Gandhi called India's first national *satyagraha*—insistence on
the truth campaign—and the colonial government of India put an end
to indenture and to all labour migration to Fiji.

A crucial part of this story, the collapse of a very profitable labour
regime, was the official reluctance to look. For decades, protests about
abuse of Indian women were directed at the colonial government of
Fiji both from within Fiji and from India, even from official India. By
the 1910s, the inquiries from official India were frequent and increasingly insistent. But official Fiji never took new initiative to look into
what it generally saw as the sordid business of Indian 'sexual jealousy'.
When forced to, it conducted cursory investigations only, mainly to
prove that complainants were of low moral character, untrustworthy
as witnesses, and unworthy of sympathy.

This reluctance to look is all the more odd when we juxtapose it
with the willingness to inquire minutely into the details of employment—something more like the 'panoptic' or 'enframing' colonial
state now familiar to us in the literature on colonial power. By the late
1900s and the 1910s, Fiji's Immigration Department was issuing very
detailed annual reports on Indian labour immigration and work
practices on each plantation (held in the National Archives). Wading
into the vast table that is Appendix D to the report for 1909, for example,
we learn that 1.75 (mean number) female immigrants worked on the
tiny Lau 'plantation' in Rewa, working 86.98 per cent of the days, missing
0.68 per cent for Unlawful Absence, 0.26 per cent Absent with a Pass,
0 per cent in Court or Gaol, 11.41 per cent for Sickness, 0.45 per cent
for Bad Weather, and 0.22 per cent for Holidays. They (the 1.75 of
them) earned 7.42 pence per working day, or 8.53 pence per days
actually worked. Summarizing for all plantations, the report concluded
happily,

The various returns comprised in this Report support the view that the general
condition of indentured immigrants in the Colony is in the main satisfactory and
one of gradual improvement. Comparing 1899 with 1909 the following figures
show that the average number of days worked upon and the daily wages earned are
higher than in 1899, and that the improvement during the past few years has been
constant and progressive.

In the course of delineating both immigrant mortality and immigrant crime, the reports do include data about violence. By 1914 this included a ten-year murder rate summary: the general murder rate (actually, murdered rate) from 1905 to 1914 varied from 0.006 percent in 1911 to a high of 0.066 percent in 1908. Yet they saw no need to figure the percentages specifically of adult women killed (between 1905 and 1914, 29 women as against 12 men, despite the reverse sex ratio of 2.7 men to 1 woman in this period). They do not calculate, as I have from their data for 1905 to 1918, when the lines were emptying, that (in their terms) 0.11 percent of adult indentured women were murdered each year (this leaves out those 'grievously wounded,' and 'free' women wounded or killed)—in effect that one out of 185 women was killed during a five-year indenture in this period. But the reports do show that an extraordinary number of indentured labourers, especially men, committed suicide (at least 62 indentured men and 5 indentured women between 1909 and 1914, for example—and I am missing the report of 1911—while over these six years 20 women were murdered). Using the report statistics for the period between 1909 and 1914 (not including 1911), 79 indentured men were either murdered, executed for homicide, or committed suicide, a rate of roughly 1 per 115 over a five-year period of indenture.

These rates are extraordinarily high, and the Fiji government knew it. Its reluctance to generate more illuminating summary statistics was no doubt partly strategic. Indenture was under a cloud, and officials sought to write reports with conclusions like the one above: news about rising incomes was definitely putting their best foot forward. But there was more to this. They knew that indentured Indian men were killing Indian women, other Indian men, and especially themselves, at extraordinary rates. And they didn't need to investigate because they already knew why: 'sexual jealousy'. The 1909 annual report of the Immigration Department gave two-sentence summaries of its ten suicides. It found one case of 'home-sickness'—Sambhar, register number 39803, committed suicide two days after arriving at his plantation—one case of derangement, three cases cause unknown, and five which were, one way or another, matters of 'sexual jealousy'. 'Shankar...had previously threatened to kill his woman or to take his own life'; 'Murari...Evidence pointed to jealousy of his woman'; 'Ganganna...Depression of mind owing to desertion of her husband was proved'; 'Goviden...had quarrelled with and been deserted by his woman'; 'Ramadhin...clearly due to the conduct of his woman who had been enticed away by another man'. The report summarized as follows:

The number of cases in which the cause of suicide appears to be attributable to sexual jealousy and disappointment is as usual large. It is connected with the disproportion of the sexes at present existing on most plantations, and the consequent facility with which women abandon the partners to whom they are bound by no legal ties for others who offer a better inducement. Among the 'free' Indian population, where the disproportion of sex is becoming obliterated, cases of suicide from this cause are comparatively few.

The theory of sexual jealousy was a routinized, bureaucratic alibi. It filled the space of explanation. Opprobrious about women making choices ('abandoning partners'), and generally silent about top-down involvement in the cases, the reports depicted—when they offered an account at all—a sad reality governed by Indian racial natures, about which little could be done. The report for 1910 made no general comment on suicides. The last to explicitly mention 'sexual jealousy', the report for 1912—'it is probable that in the majority of cases sexual jealousy was the principal factor'—also introduced a new generalization into suicide reporting: 'In the remaining cases owing to lapse of time or other reason, the cause for the act could not be clearly ascertained, but no evidence as to ill-treatment of any individual immigrant as the cause for suicide was either proved or alleged at the inquiry.' As criticism mounted in India and official Fiji was pressured for explanations of this violence in its system, the reports stopped commenting about 'sexual jealousy' or other causes; after 1912, the reports either made no general comments about suicide, or repeated a version of the 'no evidence of ill-treatment' sentence. Evidence was getting to be a dangerous thing for official Fiji in these cases, but the government had begun long before to resist the responsibility for gathering it.

RESPECTABILITY, DIGNITY, AND RESPONSIBILITY

A dynamic of distinction between an ordinary Indian of suspect motives and the extraordinary Indian of demonstrated 'good character' was in place very early in indenture Fiji. Only the latter was thought by most Europeans to be worthy of their recognition or compassion—thus the curious official tendency to pursue evidence first of all about the character of a complainant, not an accused, in most official allegations of sexual abuse. But distinguishing among the Indians was a real problem.

Europeans like Gill, as we already know, were much more willing to involve themselves with all manner of Indians than were their more squeamish seniors. Gill did not restrict himself to respectable people and situations. At one point, he claims, vague guilt almost led him to

cut off a chance conversation with a shy young *ayah* (nanny), who
appeared to be interested in him. But 'then it seemed to me that if I did,
I would be allowing the white women to make an unwarranted intru-
sion; interfering in a situation beyond their understanding.' Here and
elsewhere Gill blamed white women for an impinging moral code
that would lay down a sexual colour bar. Gill provides us with a detailed
account of his relations with this ayah, Appelema, who was not married
but lived with a man in the lines.

It was a strange set-up. I was grateful to her, and because, for her, life was a nightmare
of poverty, she eagerly accepted the few shillings I was able to let her have. She never
spoke of the man except once, to assure me that he would do as she told him. From
then on she came on two nights a week, arriving about eight and leaving when it
suited her—invariably before ten. When she came she would go to a mat in a corner,
and sink down on it crossed-legged, with her skirt spread around her and her hands
in her lap. Then we would talk of the little things in her life, and of the people
amongst whom she lived. Soon I was made to realize that the mat was hers; by the
little pat of invitation if I lingered, and by the strange intimacy of the three folded
garments on its lip when she undressed.

The image Gill constitutes is of a delicately, mutually negotiated space
and time of sexual exchange, outside of any morality but squarely
founded in the economics of indenture. Europeans gossiped about it, 'But
the small islands of resentment, invariably married women, in the end
meant nothing.' What meant more was Appelema's resentment, when
she believed false gossip in the lines about Gill and another indentured
woman and stopped coming. 'In four weeks I only saw her once, but
because of a gaggle of white women on their way to tennis, I shied from
speaking.' And then Gill proved how asymmetric, in many ways, were
his and her powers to control social space and time. Gill's recounting
is apologetic, but in an extraordinarily vague and limited way.

For a few more days I held out, and then of all people I must choose Abdullah Saib
to bring her to me....I would have chosen my words more carefully if I had
remembered certain things....It was possibly the most stupid combination of words
I ever uttered.

His *sardar* (Indian work boss) Abdullah Saib, sent to 'fetch her here;
that's all,' dragged Appelema screaming past the company office and
other overseers' bungalows. Gill claims that he was able to restore his
relations with her, especially because of his sexual fidelity, but that he
was unable to discipline the sardar.

Next morning Abdulla Saib salaamed and then said, 'You want to speak to me?'

I did, but I knew the answer. 'Remember what you said about carrying out orders? Was it my fault she wouldn't come? Anyway, that's what a woman's hair is for. And it's just as well she's a Muslim, or I would have been rough.'

He told the head sirdar that working for me and holding a mongoose by the tail were the same thing. I got no sympathy from Baili Khan either. He said there were few Europeans who had a man as faithful as Abdulla Saib. And I had to agree.

In short, Gill was more constrained and responsible in his relationships with the men of the plantation hierarchy, including the Indian work bosses who were truly 'faithful' to him, than he was in his relations with either the white women or his paid lover. He presents himself as if coerced, as if he 'had to agree,' but it is Gill who plants the misogynistic joke about hair in the sardar's imaginary speech.

Throughout his depictions Gill insisted on the notion that the good overseer was simultaneously careful to learn to know and to distinguish between the different kinds of Indians, and careful to avoid 'bringing himself to coolie level'. One new overseer spoke Hindi with actual fluency, but talked 'too much.... The Indians were getting on top and knew it,' and the India-born white man was soon sent off to Australia. Gill moralized, 'Perhaps the kindest way of putting it would be that an Australian does not necessarily have a flair for working with Australians.' It was no accident that Appelema had not come from Gill's gang, nor that his relations with the sardars were less malleable. Gill loved, hated, and paid women, but gave and took responsibility with men.

If this was how Gill and perhaps many other Europeans made their way in the world of the lines, the situation was different when Indians, especially women, needed to deal with Europeans who were not plantation people. These Europeans needed a simpler, safer code of distinctions, and often dealt with Indian women or men in terms of a simple binary of respectability. Indians, both indentured and 'free', frequently sought to use their good reputation with one European as an avenue of mediation in their dealings with another, leading to curious interventions, especially by churchmen, in affairs of business and government.

A particularly elaborate example of this process is provided in Bhagwan Singh's family history and life story, My Father's Land. Singh's grandparents, Ram Chander and Padam Kaur, were indentured labourers in Fiji. Twists of fate and the mediation of a Christian education led to a clerical career for their son in Fiji and then in India. Their grandson, Bhagwan Singh, rose bureaucratically in India, and finally became, from 1971 to 1976, India's High Commissioner in Fiji. It is not an average family history, and Singh narrates it with a strong sense of the propriety of distinguishing those worthy of special treatment, especially as he narrates the events that first put his grandmother into contact with the Catholic mission—her struggle for justice for her husband.

The way Bhagwan Singh tells it a century later, Ram Chander became embroiled in a feud between two work gangs on his estate, a feud that could in part be traced back to shipboard rivalries, and probably included insults to Padam Kaur. When the sardar of the rival gang pressured Ram Chander to help suborn perjury to keep members of his gang out of jail, Ram Chander refused, and the men were convicted. A few months later, in June 1890, a fire destroyed this sardar's house, and members of his work gang identified Ram Chander and others of his group as arsonists. Ram Chander was convicted and sentenced to 15 years in prison.

This sardar, Dost Mohammed, and the members of his gang who testified against Ram Chander, were assaulted on their return to Ra province, the site of their plantation. Four men were arrested and brought to A.B. Joske's court, charged with the assault. 'For lack of evidence, Joske dismissed the case though he noted on the file that he had no doubt to the moral guilt of Bernard and Budhia in the attack on the complainants.' The next month Padam Kaur's indenture contract expired, and she was sent to Suva (Fiji's capital) with a letter, drafted by a literate line-mate, to a Roman Catholic missionary.

The missionary took her in. She converted to Catholicism, changed her name to Parbotti, and began a succession of efforts to secure her husband's release. Her husband's letters, written in 'Urdu and a particular dialect of Hindi spoken around Agra', each page topped with 'Lord Ram is Ever Helpful,' provoked no new inquiries, but her appeals gathered more attention. After living at the mission she was able to arrange to stay at the Immigration Depot, whose superintendent, H.J. Milne, wrote to the Governor that '[s]he appears to be a superior sort of woman, very respectable.' She had a European barrister write a formal petition, and the governor ordered an inquiry. 'Unfortunately the Magistrate who conducted the enquiry utilized the services of Dost Mohammed as an interpreter. For obvious reasons, nothing new came out.'

Parbotti then found a new witness who would testify that Dost Mohammed told him that Ram Chander was innocent, and managed to recruit a new barrister, the influential G.J. Garrick. Garrick wrote in a memo to the Governor,

I have prepared this petition and am forwarding it not in a professional capacity but from a conviction of the innocence of the prisoner of the crime he was convicted of.

I have had considerable experience of the principal witness for the Crown and believe him unworthy of credit.

Not in twenty years at the bar, he added, was he more convinced of a false conviction. The governor then instructed, 'Let the Superintendent of Police make the most careful enquiries and give a report with as little delay as can be.'

BACK TO JOSKE'S COURT

Singh then provides us with a fascinating glimpse of the fastidious Joske reversing his previous decision:

The Superintendent passed on the file to A.D. Joske [sic], the Stipendiary Magistrate at Ba, who carried out an extensive enquiry. He visited Penang [the plantation] and interviewed Coster, the Assistant Manager, Birja, the new Head Sardar, and numerous labourers. In his report, he reversed his own previous defence of Dost Mohammed's character and pointed out that the 'public Indian opinion at the Estate was that it had been a trumped up charge.' He concluded by saying that although in such cases it was nearly impossible to pin down anything positive, particularly at such a late stage, he strongly recommended clemency.

In May 1893, close to three years after Ram Chander's conviction, the governor pardoned him. He and his wife began new careers as workers at the depot, then as warders in the Suva gaol, and their son received a good Christian education. The Christianity did not stick, but they had become well known as people of good character.

The case gives a strong feeling for the difference made by moral sponsorship, a phenomenon hardly unique to indenture-period Fiji, but perhaps particularly important across the colonial colour line. But what interests me most is the powerful, aphoristic line attributed by Singh to Joske, simultaneously an apology for his earlier opinion of Dost Mohammed's evidences, and justification for vast revisions upon learning the governor's leanings: '[I]n such cases it was nearly impossible to pin down anything positive.'

A very interesting aphorism, not only for its invocation of the 'positive', a sign of extraordinary power in European epistemology of the nineteenth and early twentieth centuries, but also for its verb. The positive facts here are not known by sight, but have to be pinned down, not a visual but a tactile metaphor. Not a matter of gaze, but of grasp. How could court officers constitute the facts in these matters of arson, grievous wounding, and murder? How, indeed, was one to constitute positive information out of the testimony of the people denigrated as 'coolies', who surely hated the courts more than they were hated? Testimony sometimes conflicted wildly, other times seemed arranged in lock-step, because it was. Was it more suspicious when all witnesses agreed or when they disagreed? How could one monitor even the translation process? Who or what was worthy of trust?

We proceed now to the case that motivated this essay, another charge of violent crime passed on to Fiji's Supreme Court by Joske in 1907. It is the case from Fiji that I find most unforgettable, although I still am uncertain what to say. Unlike most of the cases I have addressed here and elsewhere, no one died or was hanged, but the form of injustice involved has bothered me more than that in any of the other cases. It is a story of the power of European sexual fantasies, but also of the limits and powers of gazes quite different from those of the lascivious European overseers—the magistrate's gaze of meticulous A.B. Joske and the medical gaze of Hospital Superintendent G.F. Dunckley. It is a case about the power, the limits, and the will of scientific and legal authorities to resolve the facts.

Almost everything I know about the case, and all the testimony I quote below, comes from the record assembled by Joske for the Supreme Court (Supreme Court #24 of 1907). The case was also mentioned in the *Fiji Times*, Fiji's main newspaper, on 7 December 1907. In the local news column, much space was taken by the story of a drunk indigenous Fijian 'roosting' on a Suva rooftop. This story was followed by the news that Hon. D. and Mrs. Robbie had returned from their trip to Europe. 'Both are looking well.' Then came the paragraph about the Supreme Court sitting, then news that Messrs. A.M. Brodziak and Co. were the successful tenders of the native tax on kava (*yaqona*) for 1908, and the news that at the first meeting of the newly constituted Suva Town Board, 'His Worship the Warden suitably welcomed Mr R. Crompton as the newly elected Councillor.' In the midst of these more detailed items was the court summary:

The criminal sessions of the Supreme Court continued on Wednesday, Thursday and Friday during which time five cases were heard, viz., a charge of rape (discharged), horsestealing for which an Indian was found guilty and sentenced to two years hard labour, arson, by two Indians, (5 years), wounding (18 months and 24 lashes) and wounding (2 years and 24 lashes).

We turn to the charge of rape, prepared by A.B. Joske against Ramdial and Kurkut, and a trial that passed through colonial Fiji's public culture leaving barely a ripple.

AN INDETERMINATE AND UGLY STORY

Let us begin, as Joske's proceeding did, with the testimony of the complainant, Janka:

I am an Indentured Indian woman under agreement with the Colonial Sugar Refining Coy., at Tavua. I know the defendants here present before the Court. Their names are Ramdial & Kurkut. They raped me Wednesday of last week 19 June. It happened on the Company's Estate at Tavua. I went about 2 or 3 chains from where we women were working to the river's edge to stool. I did that, washed myself & returned to work. As I returned I saw Ramdial & Kurkut. Ramdial lifted me up & carried me into the acacia scrub I cried out & Kurkut shut my mouth with a cloth. Ramdial had connection with me first & penetrated me. Then Kurkut had me. He penetrated me also. Patun & Sertaji saw Ramdial seize me by the hand. They ran away. I went home at five o'clock & I then told my husband. He went to the Sirdar who told us to go to the Manager, Mr Thomas. It was 10 A.M. when these men raped me. I went to the Hospital Superintendent & was examined by him. The only part that I was bruised on externally was one of my toes.

Defendants did not cross-examine, but the court did. The woman's testimony went on as follows:

Defendants did not pay me anything. I made no assignation with the men. Ori is the woman's sirdar. I did not go & tell him as on a previous occasion he had beaten me for going to stool without telling him. I was afraid of the Sirdar. Cheddi heard Sertaji & Patun tell the Manager that they had seen Ramdial take me by the hand. That is why I have mentioned him as a witness lest those two should go back on me.

In her answers we can hear something of Joske's questions, and in the questions the stipendiary magistrate's lines of doubt. Indian witnesses were widely accused of lying, frequently disparaged, and harshly cross-examined in Fiji's courts. As Janka demonstrates here, she too seeks to foreclose the options of those whose testimony can help her, fearing that they would 'go back on her' in the hostile courts of colonial Fiji. There were other lines of doubt: Was she a prostitute? Was her story coherent? Why didn't she tell the authorities sooner? Her answer, that she was afraid of her sardar, suggests how little space and time she could control, if her story is true: she was unable to report a rape because she would have to admit to leaving work 'to go to stool'. 'The Sirdar beats us if we go away to stool,' noted another witness, one of the few uncontested claims in the evidence of the case.

Patun and Sertaji, the other women, testified and backed up Janka's story. Sertaji testified unambiguously that '[h]e seized her forcibly.' Patun was more ambiguous: 'I heard Janka say that she would tell about it.'

'Whether he was going to force her or whether she was willing I know not.' Ramdial cross-examined; the question was not reported. Answer: 'I did not hear you arrange with Janka to meet her on the river bank at 10 A.M. as we went to work at 5 A.M.' The only other Indian, apart from the defendants, to testify was Mullu, Janka's husband, who told the story of hearing about the rape from his wife and then going to the authorities—testimony entirely supportive of Janka's own.

Both Ramdial and Kurkut testified in their own defence. Ramdial told a story of simple prostitution, with a pre-payment of four shillings, that was complicated when Patun and Sertaji saw Janka at work and announced their intention to gossip about it. Kurkut told an incoherent story, perhaps because he sought to agree both with Ramdial's testimony and with the testimony of the manager, Harold James Thomas. Thomas had already reported that on the night of the event, once confronted with news of medical evidence, Kurkut confessed to having forced sex with Janka 'because Ramdial told him to.' Kurkut claimed in court that Ramdial had told him beforehand of a sex-for-money arrangement, then admitted confessing to Thomas, and then claimed that Ramdial had forced Janka but that she had invited him to sex.

This case, Supreme Court Case #24 of 1907, is unusual in the Fiji archives, not least for the fact that the Supreme Court found the Indian defendants not guilty. I have little doubt—though I must admit, no positive proof—that the most important testimony was that of George Frederick Dunckley. What, indeed, did he see?

POSITIVISM

Before delivering Dunckley's version of the truth, I want to delve more deeply into the background to the questions I have raised here about gazes, grasps, and quotidian colonial knowledge and power. In particular, remembering Joske's reported aphorism—'in such cases it was nearly impossible to pin down anything positive'—I seek a better feel for the very idea of 'positive knowledge', an idea credited with vast and general influence in nineteenth-century Europe.

Let me explore further the differences between Joske and Dunckley, the magistrate and the doctor, in their forms of surveillance and truth-telling. What happened to the positive knowledge of the doctor, the knowledge that enabled the plantation manager Thomas to obtain a confession, when it was examined in the court? This requires some retelling of the stormy history of relations between positive procedures in science and positive procedures in law.

Law involves different challenges than does science, many authorities tell us. Whereas a positive science can aspire to eventual clarity, unity, and completion, positive law must be capable of adequate adjudication, which is to say consistent and predictable application with respect to both the facts of real cases and the code of the law. The law courts cannot, especially in the lower rungs, choose which matters to attend to in what order, and must render judgements on all matters. The legal positivists led by John Austin had to add a clear and unambiguous definition of what law was to the positively seen and known universe. Law was not only a product of reason but evidence of will. Austin argued that for law to exist, it had to be, in the first instance, the command of a sovereign power.

Both scientific and legal positivism sought to banish all theology and metaphysics, to scrub away all the murk at their foundations. They could recognize in each other a kindred spirit; each descended from August Comte's quest to cease all argumentation and conflict caused by metaphysical vagaries in depiction and explanation. But there was lots of room for misunderstanding and arguments at cross-purposes between these two vast developments of 'the positive philosophy'. Legal positivism found doctrines of natural law (as well as unwritten constitutions and doctrines of equity, fairness, and customary rights) themselves to be metaphysical. To be positive, the law required dogmatic categories, provided by sovereign will; thus, for example, so-called customary law could be properly, positively adjudicated only after it had been codified. In short, while scientific positivism sought to erase mistaken doctrines imposed upon nature by human will and to reveal pure order in nature, legal positivism sought to erase mistaken doctrines of nature imposed on to human will, to enable pure ordering by will.

From this complex history, the point can now be made to seem very simple. Recent scholarship from the social sciences has tended to treat the modalities of colonial power as if they were a *scientific* monolith. But an enormous amount of crucial work in the ordering and reordering of colonies was done by professional lawyers. In the social sciences, we think about law and order far too reflexively to gain a really clear understanding of what went on in the European colonial empires.

I think it is time that scholars of colonial societies stopped being satisfied with their discovery of such a will to order in colonial legal codifications, as if it were a secret (or the bedrock of a Nietzschean, Foucauldian human nature). We need to pay more attention to the political wills in plain view, to official, especially legal, decisions about where and how to apply sovereign will so positively; and, contrarily, to various kinds of denial, to where and when colonial sovereigns refused to act or even to look. As Kaplan has argued, invention of disorder was as crucial as invention of tradition in colonial 'constituting moments', as in refusals to see law, order, or pre-existing sovereign power in the institutions of the colonized. Here, we track the exercise of judicial will in the microcosm of individual cases, as courts in quotidian operation ponder what they do and do not, can and cannot, know about the morals and motives of witnesses across a colonial colour line. What do judges and other government officials do when 'it [is] nearly impossible to pin down anything positive'?

I find more than one 'gaze' operating—we have clearly tracked four: the Gill-style overseers' moral-sexual fantasies, the gaze pressure felt by the dignity-preserving colonials, the codifying but also sometimes refusing-to-look gaze of legal and other official reporting, and Dunckley's allegedly expert eyes of science. But I also want to test whether we might be better served by supplementing theorized 'gaze' powers with other metaphors of power. The gaze might be the phallic, leering, vital vehicle for the ramification of desire, or the vehicle of a claim to transcendence and virtual omniscience, but in all modes it flies through space, too ambiguous in its attachments to handle all the transactions and transcursions of real power.

I suggest then that grasps are at least as well worth thinking about as gazes, as we try to write about power. Equally and more viscerally embodied than gazing, grasp is nevertheless neither more nor less intrinsically material. It is, like gaze, yet in a different way, another vehicle for inscription, embodiment, and objectification, for realization of representations in self and world. As the Indian intellectual tradition has been more keenly aware, it is equally capable of empowering abstract application.

Thinking about gaze as a modality of grasp, or about legal positivism as a gaze-theory solution to a grasp problem—the maintenance and extension of effective sovereignty—might lead us to reconsider a great deal. As Hackshaw points out, Austin's definition of law was 'inherently circular, in that "law" could only exist by the will of a supreme and unaccountable sovereign, who governed an independent political society,' while such a body politic could exist only if it recognized a sovereign and laws. Dogmatic insistence on that circularity was what cleansed positive law from muddier grounding, made it nothing other than what it said it was, and enabled it to define or inscribe every entity into its terms—whatever things and people found their way into legal proceedings. In democratic nation-states, such legal inscription might to varying degrees inform the subjectivity of citizens, make more and more modes of action into matters of rights, law, and order, with increasing participation of a wider field of agents in the mechanisms of law.

But what of a colonial social field, with its Others? There, as Guha already alerts us, a contradiction was sharply revealed. The promise of positive, productive, extending circularity could only be realized at the cost of inviting into legal agency the colonial subjects, even the colonized subjects. The oxymoron of the democratic state, constituted in the metropolis as the powers of grasp were made to seem a mere consequence of the powers of gaze, was not felt to be possible in the European colonial world, where the grasp increasingly held others down and out, where cleanliness, of law as much as of household, seemed to depend upon limiting 'their' access.

Finally, we also might want to take very seriously the unevenness of talent, training, and intention that was part of the actual gazing and grasping of the colonial state. On the one hand, the colonized world included modes of knowledge and order beyond the ken of the Europeans—leading among other things to the various legal efforts to codify 'customary' or 'personal' law . On the other hand, the colonizers were nowhere all masters of the arts and sciences of their own civilizations. I would not suggest that in the Fiji courtroom, Janka or Kurkut were particularly empowered by the philosophical discourses of South Asia, any more than Dunckley can be expected to have benefited from Renaissance artwork. Consider the problem that arose with one peripheral witness in the first case discussed above: 'Sanicheri the next witness cannot be sworn as she does not know whether she is a Musulamani or a Hindu & does not know the meaning of religion having been born in Fiji.' (She was cautioned to tell the truth and warned of the consequences of giving false evidence.) Dunckley will show more mastery of both medical and courtroom techniques, more control of his own role. But from this we shouldn't generalize too hastily. If we are to believe Fijian Indian accounts, and I do, it wasn't only the lack of typewriters, but also because some of the European magistrates could barely read and write, that several of Fiji's district courts left behind little or no written trace. Remembering this, let us return to colonialism as it actually existed, to the long arm of the law and the manners of its grasp, in the Magistrate's Court of A.B. Joske, in Colo North in 1907.

DUNCKLEY'S GRASP OF THE FACTS

What did Dunckley do on the night of the incident? What did he see, and how did he understand it? How was it that his inquiry was powerful enough, via the Estate Manager Thomas, to impel Kurkut to confess at least partially, and then, in court, powerful enough to negate the confession? Here is his evidence in its entirety, as recorded by A. B. Joske:

Am Hospital Superintendent on the Colonial Sugar Refining Company's Estate at Tavua. At the request of the Manager Mr Thomas I medically examined the woman Janka on Wednesday last the 19 June. It was in the evening. I discovered an internal wound in the lower part of the vagina. It looked very much like a tear as if a portion had been torn away. I then called Mr Thomas to see it also. The tear was certainly due to violence. There was a distinct tear & clot of blood on it. I do not think the tear was due to excessive copulation. By all appearances it was due to violence. I could not say whether the wound was self-inflicted, but it was fresh made within twenty hours.

The unstoppable, privileged gaze of power: the hospital superintendent, investigating the vagina of the possible rape victim, decides to call in the Estate Manager to see the evidence too. Horrible enough. But they were investigating violent crime, and no doubt felt justified, especially when they found what they were looking for. One story was consensual sex. The other was rape. Call in science: was there evidence of violence? Science triumphed: reasonable men concurred on the evidence, a wound that was fresh. There was violence, 'by all appearances'. Something positive was pinned down. But it was not enough evidence to finally vindicate the complainant. Why not? The law was not only long-armed and beyond common decency; it was also, sometimes, incapable of resolving the facts, even when it was in complete control of both the means of measure and the terms of reference.

On the Wednesday night the evidence of violence seemed compelling enough to pressure a confession out of the weaker of the accused. But in the court, alternative narratives each strove for momentum. Lawyers and judges have no option but to play speculatively with stories of motive, as they 'engage in the activity of placing the already described act into legally relevant categories,' especially 'categories of culpability'.

Even in the face of uncertainty about motivation, the lawyer nevertheless must provide reasons for deciding cases one way or another, and must do so within the framework of these categories. In doing so, the lawyer may need to construct a 'theory' or narrative of the case which accords with the evidence and provides an explanation of the intentions of the persons involved which can then be used as the basis of a classification in terms of the 'dogmatic' legal categories of culpable action.

Joske brought the charges and sent the case up the line to the cool, comfortable chambers of the Supreme Court in Suva. Without records of events or deliberations there, we cannot speculate too much, but it seems very likely that the court had to decide whether there was sufficient plausibility to the accused's narrative—the story of prostitution—to create doubt that rape actually occurred. Science had spoken. Clearly, there had been violence. Yet Dunckley had added, 'I could not say whether the wound was self-inflicted, but it was fresh made.'

What could make reasonable the bizarre speculation that lay behind this line of inquiry? By Janka's story, she was raped, feared to complain all day, was forced to complain and then to endure colonial examination in order to save her marriage, and then saw the assailants go unpunished. The other story is that she sold sex for money, was discovered, and then did violence to herself to dazzle the gaze of science, to save her marriage, and to protect herself. Here, precisely, is where the legal gaze must look beyond science. Here is the kind of problem of order that science does not solve: the immediate duty of a judge to render a consequential judgement. A judge cannot view ambiguity benignly and look forward to further research, but has to decide what to reach and grasp with the law's long arm.

The agents of law have no choice but to impose their own categories; they must not only gaze but also grasp. But which categories, in the specification of motive? Aggressive courts that force a lattice of economic reason, 'rational choice' and its interests and responsibilities on to all parties, courts that look for contracts and ignore ignorance, can make people live and act by their terms, can call their categories into being. But a very different social synergy required the Fiji courts for its maintenance and extension. In operations from the enforcement of penal labour laws to hostile encounters with witnesses to cases in which violence is measured, the Fiji courts found, made judgements about, and sought, in effect, to will into being a lattice of premises about what was conceivable as motive and action in otherwise unknown in- dentured Indians. The world of Gill's 'animalistic' Indians, the world of 'sexual jealousy', violent passions, and female promiscuity, needed the support of the courts to go from fantasy to legal presumption, the basis for law and order.

On the plantations themselves, the indentured Indian women in Fiji were the object of pernicious, denigrating, lascivious gazing. But these gazes did not simply create their truths across clean, open, unbridged spaces, virtual or real. There were also real struggles between strong and weak, in public and private, grasps taking possession, taking pleasure, seeking embodied facts, and leaving their figurative and all too literal marks and scars. Gazes can inscribe, say scholars insisting on the constitutive powers of representation. But I am not so sure that gazes, by their nature, can generate the finality that the metaphor of inscription suggests. Gazes don't scar. It is grasps, from the furtive to the righteous, to the dispassionate and scientific, to the wilful, official, and legal, that cut and leave the deepest marks on real bodies, as in the typical indenture horror story, in its movement from jewellery to a knife attack to a noose.

GAZES AND LAUGHTER

We cannot win with our words battles that are mainly lost by exploited people in the real world. But the indentured labourers had other weapons with which to fight rape than reliance on the constabulary and courts. [...] the archives provide several accounts of very visceral public humiliation of targeted, abusive European overseers—attacks that, perhaps deliberately, reduced the prestige and dignity of a European overseer and certainly demonstrated his loss of control. As far as I can tell, from admittedly scanty and anecdotal materials, overseers bombarded with shit, or held down and pissed on, were invariably transferred or sent back to Sydney. And I have never seen a record of anyone charged in court for such an attack.

There were also friendlier transactions between Indians and Europeans. After retiring as magistrate and later district commissioner, A.B. Joske became A.B. Brewster, amateur ethnographer and memoirist, often invoking Kipling. The Indians basically fell out of the stories he told of the Fiji of his memory, but some do appear once in a while in his most famous book, *The Hill Tribes of Fiji*. One was Joske's cook for thirteen years, 'the faithful Ferdinand' with his 'great culinary skill'. Otherwise, Joske's first mention of the Indians is as the source of Fiji's only real crime. But he also remembers how frequently he assisted the Indians in obtaining land leases, 'many of which I pegged out myself...on account of the scarcity of duly qualified surveyors.' Indian hands prepared his food; his hands pegged out their land. 'I left Fiji in May 1910, and it seemed to me then that our settlers from Hindustan were the happiest of people...the proof of their contentment was that ninety-nine percent of them elected to remain.' Actually 40 per cent went back to India, even though they had to stay in Fiji ten years to be eligible for free return passage, but the point here is Joske's moment of nostalgia. When Joske himself prepared to depart from Colo North, a delegation from the local Indian community presented him with a silver tea set, a token, they said, of appreciation for his service as their magistrate, 'a very great tribute of their affection as I was leaving them for good, and they could have no hope of any favour from me in the future.' Lots of sinister political things can be said about tea in the maintenance of British bodies and about this sort of gift within the body politic, but not in comparison to the things we have been considering.

Remembering, then, that there was terrible violence, some limited but successful resistance, and a social field with more benign relations as well, I finish with another look at an official gaze and some laughter.

In Fiji the highest-ranking government officer with specific responsibility for the welfare of the immigrants was called the agent-general of immigration. In late 1910 or early 1911, the colonial secretary received a letter in Tamil (dated 23 September) from 'the Madrasi Coolies of Wainunu Tea Estate'. The letter was successfully translated in late January 1911, and sent to the agent-general of immigration for investigation. The writers alleged that a 'Jiroj', as it came through in the translation, was abusing workers and raping indentured women: 'Our females are compelled to be victims to his debaucherous character.' This complaint itself, about 'our females', concerned both rape and medical exams, and was a patriarchal objection to science as well as crime: 'We haven't married our wives to be so disgracefully treated in allowing a male, to examine females right through.'

P.R. Backhouse, Labasa inspector of immigrants, was sent to the remote plantation to investigate, and found that George High, the overseer accused, had been dismissed in December for drunkenness. Noting that 'his past record is far from clean,' Backhouse recommended that High be watched if employed elsewhere. But it was not necessary to proceed further with these charges, because 'everything seems to be running smoothly' on the estate. Backhouse also reported, with evident satisfaction, that the letter was 'very exaggerated'. He had mustered the women and then all the labourers, and asked which of them had a complaint to make. Only one woman made a public complaint, 'and she had not any witnesses to support her statement.' Two men complained about conditions on the estate, but they had just served prison time, 'and their manner and bearing did not at all influence me in their favour.' Otherwise 'the appearance of the labour at the muster was quite satisfactory.'

On his way back to Labasa from this estate, Backhouse was laid up for a week at Levuka, where, on his own initiative, he held a muster of 'all the time expired immigrants on Ovalau' Island. He found that many of them could not produce their C.C.D. or C.I.R. documents, the documents that would certify that they had completed terms of indenture. He 'left all particulars' with the local constables, to inquire further and arrest all suspected deserters. His own unfounded suspicions but not repeated allegations by indentured Indians, merited and received further action.

The uncorroborated complaint of the woman never became a charge of rape in court. In his report, Backhouse rendered his own judgement: 'That High had illicit relations with the woman, I think there is little doubt, but I am inclined to believe that the woman was a willing party.' We know that Backhouse was not out of step with the rules, written and unwritten, of the Immigration Office. By 1919 he had been promoted to agent-general. And we may never know any of the judgements or other comments rendered about Backhouse by the workers of the Wainunu Tea Estate, and especially by the indentured women. Backhouse, very much the colonial official, observed the scene at the estate, but maintained a far greater distance than did Walter Gill:

The appearance of the muster was quite satisfactory & they seemed very happy and contented. When I was leaving the estate I noticed them laughing amongst themselves. The people were well and cleanly dressed.

He was too much the inspector ever to know what, or whom, they were laughing about.

PART five

Empire and Nation

If empire and nation have been familiar to—and formative of—
anthropology and history as disciplines over the past two centuries,
it is also the case that these concepts, entities, and processes have
been critically reworked in historical anthropology in recent times.
The chapters that follow undertake at least three critical sets of tasks.
First, the metropolis and the margins, imperial Britain and colonial
India, appear here as part of shared analytical fields, where each of
these elements is seen as constitutive of the other. Second, militating
against modular apperceptions of scholarly schemes, empire and nation,
and politics and religion, emerge as intimately entwined, shoring up
and assiduously shaping each other. Third and finally, empire and
nation—and politics and religion—are rendered in this section in terms
of their everyday expressions and quotidian configurations. Together,
there are many gains toward newer understanding and several losses of
received wisdom.

In the opening chapter, Peter van der Veer crucially conjoins developments in the metropolis with those in the colony, turning on the
mutual fashioning of empire and nation and the formidable dynamic
between religion and politics. Unsurprisingly, his considerations begin
with the debate and doubt concerning secularization and secularism
in modern India, which are sieved through key relationships between
state, nation, religion, and empire. Here, van der Veer makes the critical

claim that as part of the wider nationalization of Protestantism and
Catholicism (in Britain, for instance) and of Hinduism and Islam (in
India, for example), not only the modern subject and its discrete
conscience(s) but the modern public and its distinct sphere(s) were
profoundly shaped by religion and its transformation(s). There were
shared features but also salient differences in the interplay between
religion, state, and nation in Britain and India, two sites of one empire.

Peter van der Veer traces two major religious developments that
connect nationalism and religion in nineteenth-century Britain: 'the
enormous growth and impact of evangelicalism on the entire religious
culture of Britain'; and the 'inclusion and enfranchisement of Catholics
in the nation'. Covering a wide range of ideas and imaginings, precepts
and practices, evangelicalism not only played an important role in
producing modern individuals but it had a significant political impact.
Indeed, evangelicalism emerges in the chapter as a 'typical nationalist
movement that tries to combine enlightenment with romanticism',
rationalist thought with religious sensibilities. These thoroughly modern fusions informed the conjunctions of church and nation-state in
nineteenth-century Britain, together exercising significant influence
in the spread of middle-class values—through public activity—over the
larger population in the metropolis and in expressions of the civilizing
mission of empire in its outposts, binding together 'home' and colony.

At work was a 'shift from an Anglican exclusivist vision to an
inclusivist nationalism', acutely reflected in emancipation of Catholics,
the second major religious development of the period. On the one
hand, in the first half of the nineteenth century contending expanding
movements among the Protestants and the Catholics nonetheless
served to make possible and shore up nationalism. This nationalism
had distinct imperial and missionary attributes. On the other hand, in
the second half of the century the 'internal rivalries, animosities, and
political conflicts within British Christianity faded into the background
of what came to be seen as the difference between British Christian
civilization and the barbarity of the colonized peoples.' Now race became
the dominant element in an imperial and civilizing nationalism.

Building on this discussion, the chapter turns to the Indian colony,
where, across the nineteenth century, religion and race found complex
and critical manifestations. Starting off with the debate between
Orientalists and the Anglicists in the early decades of the period, van
der Veer shows that whatever the differences between the missionaries
and the state, their interests, articulating a shared colonizing project,
colluded in the crucial fields of education and reform, much as they
had done at home in Britain. Despite the official proclamation of

religious neutrality, the British interfered 'with every aspect of Indian religion and society', revealing the Christian roots of colonial policies.

All this set off various changes in Indian religions, and van der Veer's chapter focuses on Hinduism, especially finding parallels between the creation of a public sphere by 'reformist organizations' in India and the activities of the evangelicals in Britain. Telling familiar stories to unravel their unusual implications, van der Veer writes of the endeavours undertaken by Raja Rammohan Roy, the Brahmo Samaj, Swami Vivekananda, Dayananda Saraswati, and the Arya Samaj. It is in these ways that the chapter reveals the mutual constitution of the metropolis and the colony, politics and religion, and empire and nation. Along the way, van der Veer thinks through binaries of a secular West and a religious East, further highlighting the differences of the modern state in metropolitan Britain and imperial India as being predicated on the figure of the national citizen in the former and that of the colonial subject in the latter.

The issue of imperial intervention in Indian society is approached through complementary yet distinct filters in the next chapter, Nicholas Dirks' excursus into the policing of tradition under colonial rule. The chapter begins with the two reasons on account of which the imperial proclamation by Queen Victoria of non-interference in 'religion' and 'custom' on the subcontinent fell apart: 'the first was that the British did not know how to define either religion or custom, and the second was that the phase of high imperial rule required the state to appropriate the civilizing mission from the church, to justify itself both at home and in the colonies.' It followed that the doctrine of non-interference led to a heightened concern of imperial knowledge with its Indian subjects, so that by the late nineteenth century colonial rule increasingly took on an anthropological cast of mind. The imperial state now emerged as an ethnographic state, where anthropological knowledge replaced historical learning as the principal modality of rule.[1] All this had profound consequences for the delineation and transformation of Hinduism and caste under empire, especially in the wake of the subjecting of Indian tradition to colonial discipline.

Here, Dirks focuses on aspects of the hookswinging controversies in southern India in the second half of the nineteenth century. Following the opinion of British officials and Indian notables—and against the desires of missionaries—the government refused to abolish hookswinging. But individual magistrates, possibly responding to missionary pressure, at times used their discretionary power to prevent the practice from taking place. L.C. Miller, the acting district magistrate of Madurai, was one such administrator. In June 1894, he decided on his own authority to prohibit the annual hookswinging in Sholavandan. This resulted in much protest from local residents, including a petition with more than a thousand signatures of members of different castes that was presented to the government. With ethnographic acumen, historical sensibility, and literary sensitivity Dirks untangles the braiding of distinct idioms in this petition, also laying the basis for a critical reading of colonial sources. In this way, he makes an incisive case for the transformations of the meanings of hookswinging as part of wide-ranging changes in definitions and deployments by colonizer and colonized of custom and tradition, non-Brahminical and Brahminical Hinduism in the nineteenth century. These processes occurred within fields delineated by the British, who 'displaced their own politics into such domains as custom and tradition...endowing them with new meanings and applications.'

The mutations of religion under empire acutely informed the formations of nation on the subcontinent. Scholarly conventions of history writing have for long construed two opposed narratives concerning the Indian nation and its partition, the former signalling the story of the ascendancy of secular nationalism and the latter telling the tale of the descent into communal conflict. But in actual enactments of historical practice, the two narratives and the practices they entailed were endlessly entwined, the one turning on the other. This is brought home by the next chapter, Shail Mayaram's imaginative exploration of the violence and its subjects that shaped partition and nation in the princely states of Alwar and Bharatpur in the Rajasthan region.[2]

Mayaram's focus is on the Meos, a marginal–critical community, and the official–state violence directed against these people. In an innovative and important move in conduct of historical anthropology, her account is based not only on oral testimonies of the Meos but on those collected during fieldwork among erstwhile state officials. Appropriately, the chapter begins with the recounting of 'operations' against the 'Muslims' (Meos) by a Captain in the Alwar army, before moving on to other accounts offered by military officers and everyday actors, a state poet and the home minister, nationalist leaders and Congress sympathizers. Here are to be found chilling narratives that foreground the collective ritual dimensions of violence as embodied in logics of kinship and gender and masculinity and femininity, the ideology and practice of *shudhi* (purification) writ large on the bodies of Meo women and men, and the genocide against them. At the same time, if the formative violence of the nation is ever gendered, so also can its victims construe new idioms of gender and kinship as they re-negotiate community and identity in the aftermath of trauma. Such are the stories with which Mayaram ends the chapter, telling tales of Meo women and men that enact selective speech and strategic silence, witness to fractures of language in the wake of violence, betokening rigours of nation and survivals of community.

In the closing chapter of the section and the book, we return to the thread of cloth and clothes, first picked up by Bernard Cohn to initiate *Historical Anthropology*, but this time as stitched into textures of Indian nationalism. Emma Tarlo's point of departure is Gandhi's pulling out of *khadi* from the 'political closet' in ways that made clothing choices a moot moral issue, 'the subject of more rigorous criticism and public scrutiny than ever before'.[3] Tarlo weaves poignant stories about the distinctions of khadi—as manifested in its textures and its fibres—as well as problems of its plainness. The latter posed gendered conundrums, which extended from women's aesthetic sensibilities and their very identity as offended by a dull uniformity through to the association of white khadi with widowhood. The solution came in the form of 'a wide variety of coloured, printed and decorated khadi *saris*, sometimes embroidered, sometimes bordered with silk': yet if this rescued the fabric from monotony, it also increased its potential for revealing social and economic differences.

There were other distinctions that were woven into the warp of khadi: dyeing the fabric became a means of distinguishing between various groups within anti-colonial nationalism; and different religious communities used khadi unto discrete styles of dress. Conversely, in the precise bid to untangle Indian society from British influence, khadi could cover up regional distinctions and local traditions. Together, lending itself to different interests and varied practices, the use of khadi fashioned paradoxical motifs and sartorial spin-offs in the unravelling of fabrics of nationalism. The clothing question only continued into India after independence, a pattern that Tarlo deftly traces from the clothes (and accessories) of the Nehru family through to textures (and caps) of the present.

NOTES

1. These arguments and emphases are worked out in detail in Nicholas B. Dirks, *Castes of Mind: Colonialism and the Making of Modern India* (Princeton, Princeton University Press, 2001), from which the present chapter is derived.

2. The chapter is excerpted from Shail Mayaram, *Resisting Regimes: Myth, Memory and the Shaping of a Muslim Identity* (New Delhi, Oxford University Press, 1997).

3. The chapter is derived from Emma Tarlo, *Clothing Matters: Dress and Identity in India* (Chicago, University of Chicago Press, 1996).

The Moral State*

PETER VAN DER VEER

[...]

In recent years much doubt has been thrown on the secularization of India and the ultimate triumph of secularism. The anthropologist T.N. Madan has, for instance, argued that 'secularism as a widely shared worldview has failed to make headway in India. Since Indians are Hindus, Muslims, Buddhists, or Sikhs, they are not Protestant Christians. They cannot and will not privatize their religion.' Madan points out that in sociological theory, especially that of Max Weber, there is an essential linkage between Protestantism, individualism, and secularization. He argues, accordingly, that secularism is a 'gift of Christianity to mankind' and that it is part of Europe's unique history. Madan expresses what appears to be a general consensus among both social scientists and the general public that the modern West is uniquely secular and the East uniquely religious. The problem is that this reduces complex and diverse histories to the binary opposition of secularity and religiosity. [...] the history of secularity in Western societies is

* Originally published in P. van der Veer and H. Lehmann (eds), *Nation and Religion: Perspectives on Europe and Asia*, Princeton: Princeton University Press, 1999, pp. 17–40, as 'The Moral State: Religion, Nation, and Empire in Victorian Britain and British India'. In the present version, all notes and references have been deleted. For the complete text, see the original version.

varied and complex; the same can be said about the development of
religious institutions in India. Nevertheless, the appeal of these essential-
izations cannot be dismissed by providing ever more complicated
narratives of social change. It is in fact hard to go beyond theories of
modernization and secularization, however much one tries to get away
from them. One is forced to address the conceptual complexities and
contradictions involved in them.

In my view the crucial relationship to be analysed is that of state,
nation, and religion. The modern state is a nation-state; the hyphen
indicates that the modern state requires a nation and vice versa.
Although Britain and India are now both nation-states, in the colonial
period only Britain was a nation-state, whereas India was a colony.
This, at least, seems to indicate a time lag, in which colonizing Britain
was an established nation-state and colonized India became one—
perhaps as a result of colonization. However, one has to remember that
the nation is a nineteenth-century historical formation, so that the
time lag is relatively minor. [...] a notion of time lag, in which blueprints
of a finished nation-state are exported to less evolved societies via
colonialism, may lead us to miss the gradual and differential nature of
nation-state formation—and to miss that this process involved Britian
and India simultaneously, within the same historical period.

[...] That religion is important in producing the modern subject
should not sound too strange for those familiar with Weber's discussion
of the Protestant ethic. That it is also important in producing the modern
public is perhaps more startling, especially if one stresses that in the
nineteenth century not only was Protestantism nationalized but also
Catholicism and many other religions, such as Islam and Hinduism in
India. [...] In other words, in the eighteenth and nineteenth centuries
there were major changes in religion underway that affected its organization, its impact, and its reach. These changes had to do with the rise
of that hyphenated phenomenon, the nation-state.

Implicit in my argument thus far is that the modern subject is
produced together with the modern public. Consequently, religion is
important not only in the shaping of individual conscience and civilized
conduct, but also in the creation of the public sphere.

[...] In this essay I look at the nationalization of religion in Britain
and India. I hope to show that developments in the metropolis and in
the colony had important features in common, but that there were also
substantial differences that had to do with the way state, nation, and
religion are related in these two sites of the empire.

THE MORAL STATE IN BRITAIN

In nineteenth-century Britain two major religious developments connect religion to nationalism. The first is the enormous growth and impact of evangelicalism on the entire religious culture of Britain. The second is the inclusion and enfranchisement of Catholics in the nation. Let me start with evangelicalism. Evangelical Revival starts conventionally with John Wesley in the first half of the eighteenth century, but there was an important second wave in the 1790s, which lasted into the nineteenth century. The growth of evangelical movements in the first half of the nineteenth century is spectacular, but more significant than these numbers is the considerable impact evangelicalism had on religious groups and individuals of every kind. [...] evangelicalism aimed at inward conversion, but also at an outward activity in converting others. Itinerant preachers and later Bible and missionary societies reached far and deep. What one has here is a strong civilizing and educational effort aimed at transforming people's personal lives. There can be little doubt about evangelicalism's importance in producing modern, civil, and hard-working individuals.

At the same time evangelicalism had a very significant political impact. Obviously the term 'evangelicalism' covers a broad range of ideas and attitudes, but its campaign for the abolition of slavery in the first decades of the nineteenth century shows how evangelicalism, despite its diversity, could have a strong political message. Here we see also how evangelicalism at home was connected to the empire, as exemplified in the words of William Wilberforce, one of the leaders of the evangelical Clapham sect:

I consider it my duty to endeavour to deliver these poor creatures from their present darkness and degradation, not merely out of a direct regard for their well being...but also from a direct persuasion that both the colonists and we ourselves shall be otherwise the sufferers. The judicial and penal visitations of Providence occur commonly in the way of natural consequence and it is in that way I should expect the evils to occur.

David Brion Davis suggests that the abolition of the slave trade in 1807 and of slavery in 1833 were 'genuine rituals,' evoking fantasies of death and rebirth, and 'designed to revitalize Christianity and atone for national guilt.'

These attitudes toward the rest of the world were new and thoroughly modern. Until the 1790s there was hardly any interest in missionization abroad. The 1790s proved a turning point, however, perhaps best captured in the title of William Carey's book *An Enquiry into the Obligations of Christians to Use Means for the Conversion of the Heathens*. A great number of missionary societies were founded, including the well-known London Missionary Society (LMS) and Church Missionary Society (CMS). All saw themselves engaged in a battle against idolatry and an endeavour to save heathen souls. Not only were these souls thought to go to hell, if not saved, but it came to be seen as a Christian duty to save them. One can only wonder about the extent to which Christian imagination in Britain was fuelled by the imagery of the poor Hindus, Muslims, and others being lost for eternity. We do know that one of every two missionary speakers at provincial anniversary meetings of missionary societies between 1838 to 1873 came from India. There can be little doubt that the simultaneous evangelical activities of Bible societies, missionary societies, and Sunday schools created a public awareness of a particular kind of world and of an imperial duty of British Christians in the empire.

I see evangelicalism as a very broad, religious force, active both within and outside the established church. By 1850 about one-third of Anglican clergymen, including many of the best and brightest, could be designated evangelical, and so could the vast majority of Nonconformists. I take this to imply that the earlier strong divide between the established church and Nonconformism was, to some extent, bridged by evangelicalism. This divide obviously continued to exist in political debates about church-state relations, but Dissent appears to have lost its radical anti-establishment politics within evangelicalism, which basically promoted a middle-class piety with strong elements of civil and frugal behaviour and national honour. Certainly, one can point at the extremist elements within the movement with their millenarian, adventist antinomianism that seem to perpetuate the earlier characteristics of eighteenth-century Dissent. These elements remained significant throughout the nineteenth century and into the twentieth century. In a number of cases their outbursts of religious fervour pushed influential men, like the Liberal leader Gladstone (1809–1898), from evangelicalism toward High Church. Nevertheless, one can see in Gladstone a strong evangelical streak that informed his political views and actions. Similarly, several generations later, C.F. Andrews (1871–1940), missionary and later friend of Tagore and Gandhi, left the Irvingite congregation, in which his father was a minister, for High Church, only to become a missionary and later a moralist supporter of Indian nationalism. Andrews did not feel close to the religious atmosphere in which his father, who had the powers of prophecy and healing, conducted his services. Nevertheless, he became a missionary who soon felt the constraints of High Church Anglicanism as too limiting. One can easily see the influence of evangelical moralism in C.F. Andrews's positions.

In mainstream evangelicalism, religious enthusiasm was channelled into public activity, spreading middle-class values over the larger population. By and large it does not seem correct to see the evangelical movement as anti-rational. Rather it tried to combine rational thought and religious feeling, sense and sensibility. In that and other aspects I interpret it as a typical nationalist movement that tries to combine enlightenment with romanticism. While there is constant debate between utilitarian liberals and evangelicals, there is considerable evidence of the common ground between them in the way John Stuart Mill tried to distance himself from his father's hyper-rationalism. The evangelical project was to convert the people to a morally inspired existence, in which individual conscience of sins and atonement are catchwords, within a nation with a mission.

Gladstone is an interesting example of the combination of liberalism and evangelical moralism. Brought up in a devoutly evangelical family, he began his career under the influence of the poet-philosopher Coleridge's book *On the Constitution of the Church and State*. To defend the established church in the aftermath of Catholic Emancipation, he wrote a book titled *The State in Its Relations with the Church*, in which he endowed the state with a conscience that transcends that of individuals. In this treatise he not only argued for a strong tie between church and state, but endowed the state with high moral qualities:

[T]he State is properly and according to its nature, moral....It means that the general action of the State is under a moral law....In the government and laws of a country we find not a mere aggregation of individual acts but a composite agency....This composite agency represents the personality of the nation; and, as a great distinct moral reality, demands a worship of its own, namely, the worship of the State, represented in its living and governing members, and therefore a public and joint worship. To sum up then in a few words the result of these considerations, religion is applicable to the State, because it is the office of the State in its personality to evolve the social life of man, which social life is essentially moral in the ends it contemplates, in the subject-matter on which it feeds, and in the restraints and motives it requires; and which can only be effectually moral when it is religious. Or, religion is directly necessary to the right employment of the energies of the State.

Since Gladstone later in his career became a defendant of the rights of Dissenters and Catholics, it has been argued that he completely repudiated his earlier views. I would, however, suggest that we see in Gladstone a shift from the early-modern view of the public church to the moral nation-state, in which not the state bureaucracy but individual and national conscience were paramount. What remains constant is the moral/religious nature of political activity. Instead of excluding others from this moral life of the nation, he wanted to include them all. This meant a repudiation of a strictly Calvinist notion of the 'few elect' to be replaced by a moral universalism that extended grace to all the inhabitants of the world. This vision of a national church or the nation as a church goes beyond the visible, institutional Church of England.

Such a fusion of church and nation-state was also crucial to the civilizing mission, as envisioned by Thomas Arnold in his *Principles of Church Reform*. While Arnold was still doubtful of the desirability of including Roman Catholics (Irish barbarians) and the chance that dissenting groups would join this Christianizing and civilizing mission, these concerns were soon overtaken by new realities. The liberal doctrine of the improvement of society fits extraordinarily well with Arnold's Christian moralism. He derived his ideas from Coleridge, who also influenced Gladstone and, interestingly, John Stuart Mill, principal spokesman of liberal ideas in the nineteenth century. In Gladstone, there is a liberal view of progress instead of the usual evangelical views of damnation and the end of times, but added to this is the notion that progress is the Christian improvement of society and that in such progress we see the hand of God. This mixture of liberal and evangelical ideas leads to a quite general emphasis on the moral character of the English people and their duty to lead the world. These views of progress and grace for all were not confined to the British isles, but included the 'white man's burden' to bring the gospel to the colonies.

The shift from an Anglican exclusivist vision of the nation to an inclusivist nationalism is reflected in the other major religious development of the period, the emancipation of the Catholics. Eighteenth-century England had been very much a Protestant state, but the creation of the British nation-state required the inclusion of the Catholic minority. There was a considerable history of anti-Catholic hostility in England, which resulted in excluding Catholics from most areas of public life. From 1800 Roman Catholicism, like evangelicalism, experienced tremendous growth. In England this was the result of both an increase of English Catholics and a great influx of Irish immigrants. In Ireland there was an expansion of Roman Catholic activity, marked by the foundation of an Irish priest-training college at Maynooth in 1795. Roman Catholicism, like evangelicalism, also had an influence outside its fold. This is most clear in the Oxford movement (also called the Tractarians), from 1833 onward a movement toward emphasizing the Catholicity of the Church of England, called Anglo-Catholicism.

John Henry Newman (1801-1890), one of the movement's luminaries, replaced 'Anglo' with 'Roman' in 1845 and rose to become a Roman Catholic cardinal in 1879.

Evangelicals saw the growth in numbers of Roman Catholics as a threat that was compounded by their understandable fear of 'the enemy within' constituted by the Oxford movement. In the 1820s the political struggle was about Roman Catholics' right to sit in the united Parliament of Great Britain and Ireland, which was decided in 1829 by the emancipation. Not only were Roman Catholics now allowed to become part of the nation, but also Dissenters whose civil disabilities had been revoked by the Test and Corporation Acts in 1828. One has to interpret Coleridge, Arnold, and Gladstone in the light of these events, which definitely served to transform the religious and political character of British society in significant ways.

The enfranchisement of the Catholic minority in the British isles did little, however, to prevent the strong connection that grew between Roman Catholicism and Irish nationalism. This connection emerged very clearly in the repeal agitation of 1843, in which the Roman Catholic clergy and Irish nationalists worked hand in hand to attack the legislative union between Britain and Ireland. This movement, supported by Roman Catholic organizational structures, drew huge popular support. It is not exaggerated to see Irish nationalism as the strongest example of religious nationalism in Greater Britain. The emancipation of Catholics had thus not succeeded in drawing in the Irish Catholics into the British nation, which continued to have a too strong English character. Likewise, the Scottish Presbyterians were not immediately inclined to be part of an English/British nation, which was marked by the disruption in 1843, when half the established church's clergy left to form the Free Church of Scotland. As in England, evangelicalism worked here to promote the cause of nationalism, but this time it was Scottish nationalism. The main inspiration to form the Free Church was an evangelical urge to be close to 'the people', but, as a corollary, the disruption was marked by anti-English sentiments (which remain strong until the present day) as expressed in opposition to Westminster as well as to Anglicized landlords. Not nearly as strong as in Ireland, nationalism in Scotland was nevertheless also marked by religious overtones. The same may be true for the connection between Welsh linguistic nationalism and Nonconformist religion.

The Catholic Emancipation undid any illusion people like Thomas Arnold may have had about Britain as a Protestant nation. Anti-Catholic feelings among the Protestant majority did not prevent Roman Catholics from becoming the largest single church in England in the twentieth century. At the same time, building 'Greater Britain', including Ireland, into a nation proved impossible in the face of the successful combination of Roman Catholicism and Irish nationalism. Anti-Catholicism was very strong in the evangelical movement, but I want to emphasize that both Catholicism and evangelicalism—in a dynamic fed by mutual rivalry—expanded substantially in the first half of the nineteenth century. Both movements were simultaneously expanding and trying to dominate an emerging public sphere, which made nationalism possible. Evangelical Awakening and Roman Catholic Revival are most profitably seen as two connected movements that derived much of their expansionist energy from their mutual rivalry. In this connection it is interesting to note that evangelicalism, despite its anti-Catholicism, even influenced the nineteenth century's most famous convert to Catholicism, John Henry Newman, as he candidly admitted in his *Apologia Pro Vita Sua*.

From the 1830s to the 1860s anti-Catholicism and anti-ritualism within the Anglican Church were major themes of what John Wolffe has called 'the Protestant Crusade'. This implied widespread agitation and popular mobilization of both Protestants and Catholics. Again, I would suggest that we see them in their interaction. Both evangelicals and Catholics were eager to underline their nationalism. Protestants in particular liked to emphasize their link to the paramount symbol of imperial nationalism, Queen Victoria. While Irish Catholics obviously emphasized their Irishness, English Catholics were trying even harder to distance themselves from allegations of anti-national allegiance to the pope. My contention is that both movements helped significantly in creating an imperial and missionary nationalism, characterized by superior national qualities of a ruling race: a nation with a mission. As Mandell Creighton, Anglican bishop of London, asserted at the turn of the century, 'the question of the future of the world is the existence of Anglo-Saxon civilisation on a religious basis.' Creighton explicitly had the Church of England in mind when speaking about the conquest of the world, but I would suggest that religious diversity was encompassed by a notion of the duties of a superior race.

The notion of racial superiority in the second half of the nineteenth century depended to an important extent on comparison. Civilization was defined by its antithesis, barbarism or savagery. The internal rivalries, animosities, and political conflicts within British Christianity faded into the background of what came to be seen as the difference between British Christian civilization and the barbarity of the colonized peoples. The biblical affirmation that humankind was one, derived from a single pair in the Garden of Eden, as well as the Enlightenment notion of universal sameness and equality, were rapidly giving way to ideas of radical racial difference in the second half of the nineteenth century. Philologists like Renan and Max Müller equated race and language, and Renan asserted the right of superior races to colonize inferior ones. Where Thomas Arnold had been very concerned about the relation between religion and nation, his son Matthew Arnold, the author of *Culture and Anarchy*, relocated that concern by emphasizing a racialized view of culture.

[...] It is important to note that Arnold was the inspector of schools and in that capacity responsible for the education of the British in the nation's new racialized mission. Modern science supported this ideological formation of national culture, in which language and race took central stage and the culture of the colonized was turned into an object of academic study, with its own university chair. Gradually race came to take precedence over religion as the dominant element in British nationalism in the second part of the nineteenth century.

THE COLONIAL MISSION IN INDIA

One of the great policy debates in the East India Company in the early nineteenth century was between Orientalists who argued that the Company should continue its policy of supporting native religious and educational institutions, and Anglicists who argued that there was little of value in these native institutions, which should be replaced by the more civilized and advanced institutions of England. This was clearly a complex debate, more or less decisively won by the Anglicists, when Thomas Babington Macaulay's *Minute on Indian Education* of 1835 was accepted as the basis of official policy. In this battle evangelicals sided with Anglicists. Evangelicals, such as those of the Clapham sect (William Wilberforce, Zachary Macaulay, John Venn, Samuel Thornton, Charles Grant) prominent in the anti-slavery campaign, were indignant at the support the Company had given to Hinduism and Islam in India. They concurred with the utilitarian Anglicists in their disdain for the native institutions and literatures of India. William Wilberforce told the English Parliament that the Orientalists were as sceptical about Christianity as the French revolutionaries whose actions it regarded with horror. Not only should the Company allow missionaries to work in India (which it did after 1813), but it should stop the support of native institutions.

In the early decades of the nineteenth century the Company was still giving patronage to Hindu temples and festivals, especially in the south. Under strong pressure from the evangelicals the Company had to withdraw from that policy. It did so very hesitantly. Even as late as 1838 a committee had to be formed in England for the purpose of 'diffusing information relative to the connection of the East India Company's Government with the superstitious idolatrous systems of the natives, and for promoting the dissolution of that connection'. We have to see this as a withdrawal of sorts, however, since the British became active in setting up systems and committees to manage religious endowments. These committees became important arenas for organizing the public sphere, for both Hindus and Muslims. As such, it was another instance of a new colonial politics of representation that replaced the older patronage networks, in which the Company had participated to further its prime purpose: trade.

Utilitarians and evangelicals agreed that the religious institutions of India needed to be dismantled and replaced by Christian civilization. They disagreed, however, on how to bring civilization to the natives. Religious neutrality was seen as essential, first for trading purposes and later to British rule in India. The Company continued to resist direct support for missionary projects. The Anglican Society for the Propagation of the Gospel in Foreign Parts (established 1701) had always been a colonial church providing clergy for the British in the colonies until it was transformed in the 1830s under evangelical influence. Serious missionary activity among the natives originated only in the nineteenth century outside the Company in evangelical circles, which raised money from the British public. The Company's neutrality, however, did nothing to prevent attempts to reform Indian society through education, an endeavour fully supported by the utilitarian Anglicists. This, however, turned out to be a field in which missionaries were extremely active.

Whatever the debates between evangelicals and utilitarians—and they were considerable—none of them would have denied that civil society and the forms of knowledge on which it was based were ultimately part and parcel of Christian civilization. Gauri Viswanathan has argued forcefully that the teaching of secular English literature, as recommended in Macaulay's *Minute*, amounts to a relocation of cultural value from belief and dogma to language, experience, and history. This relocation can be detected in the intellectual differences that simultaneously divide and connect Matthew Arnold and his father Thomas, as well as Thomas Babington Macaulay and his father Zachary. Despite their differences, these people occupied the same moral universe. Their differences were not about the moral mission of the state, but about matters of policy. The developments in that universe were similar in Britain and among the British in India. For evangelicals and utilitarians the world was no longer limited to England or Greater Britain. The anti-slavery campaigns had made the British public aware of Britain's role in a larger world. This role had to be one of reform and uplift, friend and foe agreed.

However much the British tried to hide the Christian roots of their colonial policies behind the mask of religious neutrality, the colonized 'natives' were not to be fooled. It is often observed that there were great differences between the operations of the missionary societies in India and those of the state, but these were within a shared colonizing project. It is certainly true that the officers of the Company and later the colonial state looked down upon the missionaries and that, in general, there was a substantial social gap between them. Nevertheless, their concerns colluded in the crucial fields of education and reform, as they did back home in Britain. The real difference was, obviously, not between the colonial state and the missionaries but between the colonizing British and the colonized Indians. Where in Britain the state would gradually occupy the social spaces opened up by the religious organizations, in India these spaces were occupied by rival religious organizations of native 'subjects'. Their ideas and actions could not be incorporated in a British nation characterized by its Christian civilization. In due course they became oppositional toward the colonial state and, by the same token, bearers of Indian nationalism.

Despite the official policy of religious neutrality, the British interfered with every aspect of Indian religion and society. Considering the nature of the colonial project there was actually no choice and the tropes of withdrawal, secularity, and neutrality only tried to hide that discursively. I have to limit myself here to a discussion of the British involvement with Hinduism and its consequences, but I want to suggest that the developments that took place in Indian Islam and Sikhism were not altogether different. British policies set off a whole chain of reformist reaction in Hinduism. As in the case of the evangelical Awakening in Britain, the causalities involved are extremely complex and reform should not be viewed merely as a reaction to the colonial project. I would like to draw attention to the creation of a public sphere by re-formist organizations in a way that reminds one of the evangelical activities in Britain. I want to look briefly at the construction of Hindu spirituality in the Brahmo Samaj and the Ramakrishna Mission as well as at the construction of the Aryan race in the Arya Samaj.

One of the early instances of a Hindu public responding to colonial rule is the abolition of *sati* (widow immolation) by the British in 1829. Sati was perhaps the most definite sign of Hindu depravity and Christian moral superiority that evangelicals could get. Consequently they focused their campaign against native institutions on the abolition of this particular practice. They succeeded in convincing Governor-General William Bentinck, who later also enacted Macaulay's Anglicist proposals for Indian education. A statue for Bentinck, erected soon after his departure from India in 1835, showed a sati scene under Bentinck's stern figure, and in an inscription on the rear of its base it was recorded that Britain was now committed to 'elevat[ing] the moral and intellectual character' of the Indian subjects. Beneath the evangelical moralism, however, one may well detect a sexual fantasy of 'white men saving brown women from brown men'.

More important than the evangelical actions and the government's responses is the position taken by 'enlightened' citizens of Calcutta. Rammohan Roy (1772–1833), sometimes called 'the father of the Bengal Renaissance', wrote a great deal on this subject between 1818 and 1832. In January 1830 Rammohan, together with three hundred residents of Calcutta, presented a petition to Bentinck in support of the regulation prohibiting sati. Rammohan rejected the practice on the basis of his reading of Hindu scripture. He distinguished authoritative sources (such as the Vedas) from other sources. It is interesting to note that he did not refer to any authoritative interpretation of these sources by learned gurus but relied entirely on his private, rational judgement. This is certainly an important step in the laicization of Hinduism. What we also see here is that scriptural authority can be referred to by a layperson without mediation of a sacred interpreter. One of Rammohan's most important objectives was to abolish the rules of the caste-based, hereditary qualification to study the Veda. Following Lata Mani, I would suggest that the colonialist insistence on the unmediated authority of written evidence for Indian traditions, enabled by the Orientalist study of these texts, made possible a gradual shift in emphasis from the spoken to the written in Hinduism. I would add, however, that the centrality of the text was also insisted upon by the evangelicals who railed against the *sati* practice. Rammohan's position participated in both the Orientalist and the Protestant ways of thinking. His privileging of his own rational judgement, based on reading and discussion, enabled the rise of a public and a certain kind of public debate in Habermas's sense.

Rammohan was strongly influenced by English and American unitarianism, a Christian creed characterized by a rational and universalist theology as well as a social reformist conscience. He contributed to its theology an interesting tract, called *The Precepts of Jesus*, published in 1820. He was very interested in Christian theology and, to a certain degree, he was a Unitarian, but, as his involvement in the sati debate

shows, he also remained a Hindu. In 1828 Rammohan founded the
Brahmo Samaj. This was a small movement, propagating a deist and
universalist kind of religion, based, however, on Hindu sources and
especially the Upanishads and the philosophical commentaries on
the Upanishads (together known as the Vedanta). It was particularly
opposed to 'superstitious customs' of 'ignorant people', deceived by
their Brahmin leaders. The deception by Brahmins is a crucial point.
It is, of course, tempting to see it as a straightforward adoption of
British attacks on Brahmins, as, for example, in James Mill's *History of
British India*, but I would suggest that it is a bit more complex. Roy
himself came from a Brahmin family and his attack is based on his
reading of Brahminical sources. The British attack on Brahmin priests
gave support to a particular argument against priesthood in a Brahminical
debate about religious authority. Christian rational religion and certain
Brahminical arguments of long standing fitted together quite well as
the basis of a Hindu rational religion. Reason and 'the dignity of human
beings' became as important as for its Christian counterparts in Europe.
Also interesting was its attempt to come to a universal religion, reminiscent of the deist view that the great truths of religion were all universal
and that true religion was ultimately natural religion, not bound to
particular historical events of revelation that divided one religious
community from another.

I would like to stress the strong parallelism of the development of
Indian and European 'rational religion'. There is, however, a crucial
difference: whereas the European Christians tried to universalize their
Christian tradition, Indian Hindus did the same with their Hindu
tradition. This reproduced the Hindu–Christian opposition, which was
also the colonized–colonizer opposition. Colonialism provides the
discursive frame in which Hindu rational religion emerges. As Ranajit
Guha demonstrates, this is also clear in the work of someone outside
the circle of the Brahmo Samaj, the humanist thinker Bankimchandra
Chattopadhyay (1838–1894), who was very much influenced by August
Comte. Bankimchandra (again a Brahmin), like many European
thinkers, centres his view of 'humanness' (*manusyatva*) on the notion
of the perfectibility of man. In contrast to European thinkers, however,
he thought it possible to give examples of *Adarsa Purush* ('ideal man'),
whose perfection had to be emulated. These examples were taken from
Hindu religious history with, at the highest rank, the god Krishna. The
most perfect man was thus a Hindu god. The Enlightenment question
about the nature of man had found in the colonial setting a particular
answer in terms of religious nationalism.

The intellectual Vedantic and unitarian views of the Brahmos left them to an important extent isolated from the larger Bengali Hindu society. In this larger environment a particular Bengali brand of Vaishnava devotionalism had become important since the sixteenth century. This devotionalism focused on the god Krishna and on gurus who descended from the disciples of the great sixteenth-century guru Chaitanya. It is interesting to see that in the second half of the nineteenth century this devotional tradition had begun to exercise considerable influence on the rational religion of the Brahmos. In the 1860s Keshab-chandra Sen (1838–1884), one of the most influential Brahmo leaders, introduced devotional singing in the Brahmo congregational meetings. He also no longer spoke English but Bengali. He moved to the rural outskirts of Calcutta and introduced an ascetic lifestyle among his followers. The next step seems to have been his encounter with the contemporary guru Ramakrishna (1836–1886), a priest in a temple for the mother goddess Kali in Calcutta. In his two newspapers (one in English, one in Bengali) he introduced Ramakrishna to the wider, reading public as a true saint in the authentic Hindu tradition. In that way he authorized this illiterate Hindu ascetic as an acceptable guru for the Hindu middle classes. In a recent book on Indian nationalism Partha Chatterjee portrays the meeting of these two personalities as constituting the 'middle ground' occupied by the emergent middle classes, between European rational philosophy and Hindu religious discourse. In his view, this 'middle ground' enables the anti-colonial nationalists to divide the world into two domains: the material, outer world, which is dominated by Western science, and the spiritual, inner world of the home, which is dominated by Hindu values.

The spirituality of Hindu civilization, however, is not only signified by the home, but also by reformist and political action, such as much later in Gandhi's non-violent action (*satyagraha*). The theme of Hindu spirituality in opposition to Western materialism definitely becomes the principal theme in Hindu nationalist discourse from this period onward. A major step in the popularization of Hindu reformist ideas was made by linking it to emergent nationalism. Hindu spirituality had to be defended against the onslaught of colonial modernity. Perhaps the most important expounder of the doctrine of Hindu spirituality has been the founder of the Ramakrishna Mission, Vivekananda (1863–1902).

[...] The typical strategy of Vivekananda was to systematize a disparate set of traditions, make it intellectually available for a Westernized audience and defensible against Western critique, and incorporate it in the notion of Hindu spirituality carried by the Hindu nation, which was superior to Western materialism, brought to India by an aggressive and arrogant British nation. His major achievement was to transform the project to ground Hindu spirituality in a systematic interpretation of the Vedanta (the Upanishads and the tradition of their interpretation). This project, started with Rammohan Roy and which had produced rational Hinduism, was now combined with disciplines to attain perfection from the ascetic traditions in what Vivekananda called 'practical Vedanta'. The practical side also included participation in social reform.

[…] A major element of Vivekananda's message was nationalist. He saw his project very much in terms of a revitalization of the Hindu nation. In 1897 he founded an ascetic order, the Ramakrishna Mission, to make ascetics available for the nationalist task. National self-determination, social reform, and spiritual awakening were all linked in his perception. The Ramakrishna Mission established itself throughout India and also outside India. It did not become a mass movement, but Vivekananda's rhetoric of spiritualism exerted an immense influence on the way Hindu gurus in the twentieth century came to communicate their message. Vivekananda transformed Hindu discourse on asceticism, devotion, and worship into the nationalist idiom of 'service to the nation' for both men and women.

Vivekananda's construction of Hindu spirituality gave the notion of self-sacrifice a new meaning that drew simultaneously from Hindu traditions of devotion (*bhakti*) and evangelical notions of female morality. In this complex mixture, femininity is the signifier of Hindu spirituality, while actual women should be self-sacrificing in accordance with both Victorian notions of domesticity and Hindu notions of total devotion to their husbands. The abolition of sati by the colonial government thus set a far-reaching series of Hindu responses in motion, which ultimately led to the formation of a modern conception of spirituality through which the Hindu nation got defined.

While gender was the dominant issue in the prohibition of sati and crucial to the definition of Hindu spirituality with its emphasis on feminine devotion and self-sacrifice, race and caste formed the dominant issue in the formation of Hindu Aryanism. The mutiny of sepoys of the Bengal army and the ensuing revolt in northern India in 1857 as well as its suppression in 1858 contributed immensely to the notion of racial and religious difference between the colonizers and the colonized. In this period of great anxiety about the loss of control over India, stories about inhuman atrocities inflicted on British women and children were rapidly circulated throughout Britain and confirmed the general view of the barbarity of the Indians already established in the depiction of sati. The suppression of the revolt demonstrated once and for all to the British that they were a superior race.

[...] Evangelicals, however, argued that the British had not taken their civilizing mission as a superior race seriously enough. They took the events as divine judgement upon Britain for her sins as a nation. These sins consisted largely of a neglect by the Company to promote the gospel. On Sunday, 7 October 1857, a great number of churches in Britain, both Anglican and Nonconformist, participated in 'a day of national humiliation', proclaimed by Queen Victoria. In the sermons of that day almost every preacher agreed to the necessity of wiping out that humiliation, repressing the revolt by military means, and inflicting retribution on the Indian population. The Christian qualities of some of the British officers during the revolt were extolled at great length, just as Henry Havelock attributed his victory at Fatehpur 'to the blessing of Almighty God on a most righteous cause, the cause of justice, humanity, truth, and good government in India'. In the longer run, however, the revolt convinced most colonial officers that conversion to Christianity was an uphill struggle and reinforced the idea that religious neutrality was essential to colonial rule. For them it became difficult to see how the Indian barbarians would ever become equal to British Christians. Lord Canning dismissed the evangelical Herbert Edwardes, commissioner of Peshawar, as 'exactly what Mahomet would have been if born at Clapham instead of Mecca'. Racial difference between the British and the colonized, and among the colonized themselves, became the explanation and legitimation of colonial rule.

While this re-invigorated racism in India colluded with the rise of racial nationalism in the metropolis, at the level of scientific thought the notion that the higher castes of India belonged to the same Aryan race as the British was widely accepted. In India the idea of race had to be combined with that of culture or civilization to explain why the British as 'younger brothers' of the Aryan family had to guide the 'older brothers' to civilization. This intervening cultural element continued to be religious difference. The story of the Aryan race in India was a story of decline, caused by a variety of things, such as racial mixing or climate, but especially by the inherent barbarity of Hindu polytheism.

[...] The Aryan race theory was taken up in northern India by Hinduism's most important reformist movement, the Arya Samaj. Its founder, Swami Dayananda Sarasvati (1824–1883), was one of India's many gurus in the nineteenth century. He was initiated in the order of the Shivaite Dashanamis, a prestigious Hindu ascetic order that allowed only Brahmins to take the ascetic vows. Like other ascetics of his order, Dayananda travelled through India, visiting sacred places. He became rather successful and seemed on his way to form his own, limited community of ascetic and lay followers. In 1872 Dayananda visited the Brahmo leader Debendranath Tagore in Calcutta for four months. This visit seems to have transformed his style. He abandoned his ascetic robe and exchanged his use of Sanskrit oratory for Hindi.

[...] It is not possible to follow here in any detail the development of Dayananda's thinking and of the movement, Arya Samaj (the Society of Aryans), which he founded in Bombay in 1875. Let me just summarize the points that made Dayananda's Aryan religion (*Arya Dharm*) a radically new religious programme. First of all, he proposed to get back to the basic Vedic texts, to supersede the traditional commentators of these texts. He provided his own Sanskrit commentaries to these texts, in which he sought to show that all the scientific knowledge of the West in fact was already present in the Vedic revelation. He spoke of the Vedic teachings of telecommunications, about the construction of ships and aircraft, and about gravity and gravitational attraction. The importance given to science and its appropriation is, of course, extremely significant. Vedic religion was a universal, rational religion of an Aryan people. It was the cradle of all human civilization. In this we can see the influence of the rational religion arguments in Calcutta.

Like the Brahmos, Dayananda argued that the Vedic revelation was monotheistic. A monistic argument could very well be developed from an early medieval interpretation of the Upanishads by Shankara, the founder of the Dashanamis, the order to which Dayananda belonged. Moreover, there is also a monotheistic tendency in the ascetic orders that focus their meditation on one god. Dayananda, however, wanted to obscure the reference to many gods in the Vedic hymns. He did not use the traditional Hindu argument that one particular god is higher than all the other gods (or that he encompasses all the others). He wanted to get rid of the Hindu pantheon and the practice of image worship.

In the nineteenth-century European evolutionary worldview, monotheism was seen as the highest form of religion. A religion had to be monotheistic to be rational and to allow a scientific understanding of the world. In that sense Dayananda's discourse on Hindu monotheism looks derivative, but I would like to draw attention to the very specific Hindu discursive underpinnings. The reference to the Vedas, the monism of the Vedanta, and the monotheism of the Shivaite and their depreciation of image worship are all present in Dayananda's thinking. The lay response to Dayananda's message was also very much predetermined by existing Hindu discursive frames. Dayananda's rejection of image worship limited the appeal of his message considerably. Image worship is dominant in popular Hinduism and it is inconceivable that a radical iconoclastic movement would succeed in India. The Arya Samaj did, however, have a considerable following in the Punjab, where one finds a long history of imageless worship.

Second, an important point in Dayananda's programme was an attack on the caste system, which he saw as a degeneration of the original, natural ordering of Vedic society in four functional groups: priests, warriors, traders, and servants. This natural order was entirely rational and functional, if only because it was based on achievement rather than ascription. Dayananda's privileging of this ancient social hierarchy may have been related to the fact that the census operations, starting in the 1870s, tried to use it to rank actual castes (whose social relations were only salient on a regional basis) hierarchically on an all-India basis. As Bernard Cohn has powerfully argued, the census operations enhanced the importance of caste distinctions in the new arenas for competition created by the British. Dayananda's solution to take over the all-India grid of the census, explain it in functional terms, and do away with actual hereditary caste relations was original and radical. It was used much later in Gandhi's social philosophy to include the untouchables in the Hindu nation.

More than anything else this meant in the Arya Samaj that everyone —regardless of caste—could become priest and officiate in the principal rite of the Arya Samaj, the Vedic sacrifice, which is commonly the strict prerogative of Brahmins. Despite his emphasis on Brahminical scripture and Brahminical ritual, Dayananda launched a direct attack on the ritual hegemony of Brahmin priests. Dayananda continued a discourse on priesthood that, as we have seen with Rammohan Roy, has its roots both in Brahminical debates and in colonial attacks on Brahmins. Dayananda took his attack one crucial step further by allowing non-Brahmins to perform the Vedic sacrifice. While this had a *Wahlverwantschaft* with the aspirations of a new class of English-educated Indian officials, Dayananda's programme was too radical for many. Again, it had most of its appeal in the Punjab, where religions like Sikhism had done away not only with the worship of images but also with Brahmin priesthood. We have to see the radical novelty of Dayananda's programme: the Arya Samaj became a religious community in which all religious power gravitated toward the laity. After his death, Dayananda was not succeeded by another guru but by a committee of lay members.

A third important point of innovation was the great emphasis the Arya Samaj put on education. A large number of schools were founded in the Punjab and elsewhere that continue to attract many non-Arya

Hindu students. This kind of social activity made the Arya Samaj into a strong competitor of the Christian missions. Following the Arya Samaj a great number of religious movements, with or without a core of ascetic gurus, entered the quickly expanding fields of education, social welfare, and medical care. The Arya Samaj had discovered the larger Indian public as the target of internal missionization. Special rituals were devised to purify those who had been converted to other religions and to bring them back to the Hindu fold. The larger Indian public also came to include those who had left India as indentured labourers to work in British plantations overseas. Arya Samaji missionaries were sent to these areas and had considerable success in them.

What we see here is that the Arya Samaj became an important factor in creating a Hindu public. It brought the debate about the nature of Hinduism in a much more direct manner to the popular masses than Rammohan or Bankim had been able to do. Dayananda's message developed in the colonial context from important Hindu discursive traditions and remained close to them. Dayananda was a prolific writer and talker, constantly in debate with other Hindu leaders, following again an old tradition of the public contestation of religious opinion (*shastrartha*). At the end of his life he found the revolutionary issue— the protection of Mother Cow against British and Muslim butchers— which introduced mass participation in the public sphere.

CONCLUSION

I hope to have conveyed that (1) religion has been crucial in the making of the modern nation-state in both Britain and India; (2) the processes of nation building in these two countries have been connected through empire; and (3) the imperial relation has affected the location of religion in Britain and India. The modern state depends in liberal theory on the formation of a civil society, consisting of free but civilized subjects, as well as on the formation of a public sphere for the conduct of rational debate. In that theory the notions of freedom and rationality are defined in terms of secularity. I have tried to show that, contrary to theory, religion is a major source of rational, moral subjects and a major organizational aspect of the public spheres they create. Anti-slavery societies, Bible societies, anti-Catholic agitation, anti-sati petitions, Ramakrishna Missions, cow-protection movements—what they all have in common is the creation of public spheres of political interaction central to the formation of national identities. The moral tenor of these movements is essential to understanding the mission of empire as well as the mission of anti-colonial nationalism.

I hope also to have demonstrated that the supposition that the British polity is secular and the Indian religious is false. I have suggested that a sharp, structural distinction between nation and state cannot be made. In the modern period the nation-state is produced as a hyphenated entity, that is to say that they go together. There is, of course, a liberal notion that the state is outside civil society and can be criticized by civil society, which limits the power of the state, but it seems to me that the modern state is not an entity but a nexus of projects and arrangements through which society is organized. The externality of the state is an effect of these projects. It is especially through the project of education and through legal arrangements that the modern subject is formed. As Mauss suggested, language, race, and religion are also constructed in the process of nation-state formation. This is true for both the metropolis and the colony.

[…] Obviously, the crucial difference between the modern state in the metropolis and in the colony is that in the former, political legitimacy is in terms of the nation, citizenship, and national identity, whereas in the latter, the subjects are excluded from citizenship, while their national identity is either denied or denigrated. Religious and racial difference are both legitimations of differences of power. That is why anti-colonial nationalisms are not only struggles for power in the political arena, but also attempts to counter the cultural hegemony of the colonial theory of difference. They often do so, as in the cases discussed here, by posing an alternative interpretation of the grounds of hegemony, whether religion or race. Vivekananda posed the superiority of Hinduism's spirituality over and against Western materialism. In doing so he denied that Britain's Christianity possessed a superior morality that allowed the British to rule India. Britain's ascendancy was, in his view, only a material one, which had in fact jeopardized the spiritual value British Christianity might have had. Dayananda took the Aryan race theory over from Orientalism, but instead of accepting the theory that Christianity was to redeem the 'fallen state' of Hindu civilization, he proposed a return to Vedic religion, which had preceded Christianity and was the very origin of all morality.

The Policing of Tradition*

NICHOLAS DIRKS

THE DOCTRINE OF NON-INTERFERENCE

Victoria's proclamation had announced, unambiguously, that the British would no longer seek to impose their 'convictions on any of our subjects', and that she would 'strictly charge and enjoin all those who may be in authority under us that they abstain from all interference with the religious belief or worship of any of our subjects on pain of our highest displeasure.' She had further declared that in the 'framing and administration of law, due regard would henceforth be paid to the ancient rights, usages and customs of India.' But although it was clear that the British intended by this never to repeat the provocations that were seen to have led to the revolt—explicit government support for missionization, regular usurpation and annexation of ancestral and princely lands, and the introduction of military requirements that entailed choices between discipline and pollution—it was equally clear that the British had little idea what non-interference would really mean. Although colonial rule retreated from its active phase of colonizing properties and souls, it could hardly stop interfering with India during

* Originally published in Nicholas B. Dirks, *Castes of Mind: Colonialism and the Making of Modern India*, Princeton: Princeton University Press, 2001, pp. 149–72, as 'The Policing of Tradition: Colonial Anthropology and the Invention of Custom'. In the present version, all notes and references have been deleted. For the complete text, see the original version.

the years after the rebellion, when Britain sought to consolidate its control and make permanent the assumptions and institutions of imperialism. The notion that 'religion' and 'custom' could be genuinely exempted from any interference fell apart in the face of two fundamental flaws in colonial reason: the first was that the British did not know how to define either religion or custom, and the second was that the phase of high imperial rule required the state to appropriate the civilizing mission from the church, to justify itself both at home and in the colonies.

The policy of non-interference thus necessitated a new commitment to colonial knowledge about the subjects of its rule. The rebellion put an end to debates over a history that had been seen earlier to justify the state's claim over revenue and land control, but it made the anthropologization of colonial knowledge necessary for several reasons. Such knowledge could help explain why the rebellion took place; it could suggest how to avoid such disaffection in the future; it could delineate ways to claim the loyalty of subjects on the basis of custom and culture; and it could serve to differentiate the autonomous and proper domains of religion and custom. Armed with such knowledge, the British could not only avoid interference but, in time, become the primary protectors of India's tradition. Even as the history of colonial conquest could now be conveniently erased and rewritten, the primacy of history in the rhetorical debates of imperial policy could yield increasingly to other logics and imperatives. It is in this sense I have argued that colonial rule took on an anthropological cast of mind in the late nineteenth century.

The anthropologization of colonial knowledge proceeded slowly, and in the context of myriad other interests and processes in this period. It can hardly be accidental, however, that the decade of the 1860s saw a veritable explosion in the production and circulation of gazetteers and manuals that now included as a matter of course extensive reports on the manners and customs of the castes, tribes, and religions of the specific regions being studied. Colonial authors continued to write history, even as they sought with increased concern to adumbrate the moral and material progress of the imperial domains through these and other writings. For the first time, however, they began to compile ethnographic facts systematically, as if they were administrative necessities rather than antiquarian curiosities. Indeed, as this chapter will demonstrate, much of the new ethnography emerged as part of the requirements of administration rather than as independent research, at least in the early phases. Much official ethnography, later reported in manuals and then in ethnological catalogues, when it did not come from early missionary accounts emerged out of administrative and policing concerns in the late nineteenth century as the British struggled time after time with the problem of non-interference. In the story that follows, missionaries played an important role off-stage, generating sufficient publicity for a crisis to develop around the question of what the colonial state could countenance: was colonialism on the side of barbarism or civilization, and were there occasions when the colonial power had to take a stand? Or, from our perspective more than a century later, did the policy of non-interference hold up under the demands of late-nineteenth century high imperialism, when colonial greed and grandeur had to be clothed in the vestments of a civilizing mission, when the moral charter of Christian prosyletization had to be secularized and nationalized as the ground of and justification for imperium? Could an autonomous and sacrosanct sphere of religious belief be separated from a wide range of customs and practices that periodically leaked into public view and made imperial disinterest appear shocking, even barbaric? And what happened when Indian tradition itself became the subject of colonial discipline?

The debate that followed involved the delineation and redefinition of 'Hinduism' as a religion rather than as the simple denomination of the myriad practices and customs that could be catalogued across the subcontinent. Despite the demise of Orientalism, high Sanskritic texts and Brahminical testimonies were taken, with the help of a new generation of Orientalist administrators, as the basis on which to decide what would count as Hindu religion and what could be consigned to a world of custom. In southern India and elsewhere, Brahmins came to have particular authority as the arbiters of confessional belief. As a result, Brahminic prejudices about local customs increasingly came to inform the administrative decisions that were made on a regular basis about questions of interference, even when it was clear that rural Brahmins occasionally practised these very customs. And it no longer appeared either practical or morally feasible to protect custom in the same way as was appropriate for 'proper' religion. As it turned out, Victoria's proclamation was sharpened to exclude from its provisions any form of custom that seemed either dangerous to the colonial state or offensive to the various agencies—from missionaries to social-reformist groups—that took on a relationship to the colonial state based on the use of petitions during the last decades of the century. In the process, Hinduism became increasingly Brahminic, even as Brahminic definitions of religion used Christian categories and logics to characterize the domain of belief and practice that counted as the core of Hinduism as a world religion. Such redefinitions and redeployments of religious and customary meaning would have dramatic effects, both in relation to India's modern history more generally and in the specific regional theatres where, as in southern India, an anti-Brahmin movement would soon emerge.

COLONIAL SUBJECTS AND INDIAN TRADITIONS

In late October 1891, the *Madras Mail* brought dramatic attention to the fact that 'the barbarous and cruel custom of hookswinging to propitiate the Goddess of Rain, which has been obsolete for some time, has been revived at Sholavandan near Madura.' The newspaper provided an account of this event in tones of scandalized disapproval:

The manner in which this horrible custom is carried out consists in passing iron hooks through the deep muscles of the back, attaching a rope to the hooks, and (after the method of a well sweep) swinging the victim to a height several feet above the heads of the people. The car on which the pole is placed is then drawn along by large ropes in willing hands.... Full details of this hookswinging affair are too revolting for publication.

The person swung from the hooks was selected by lot from a larger group that represented a number of the villages sponsoring the festival. [...] It is impossible to date the beginnings of anthropology in India: the need to understand custom and tradition began with the first early state, and developed with renewed intensity under the British from the early days of their rule. Notions of custom were fundamental to the establishment of revenue systems and legal codes, and thus much early anthropology can be read in early settlement reports and other colonial records. Given colonial reliance on forms of knowledge, it should come as no surprise that the anthropological knowledge of India finds some of its first bearings in the files of administrators, soldiers, policemen, and magistrates who sought simply to control and order Indian life according to the demands of imperial rule and what these agents of empire considered to be basic and universal standards of civilization. But in the late nineteenth century, the efforts to understand custom and to better rule Indian society became linked to the development of official anthropology in new and important ways.

[...] I came across the newspaper account quoted above because it was enclosed in a file that initiated a series of governmental investigations and reports on the festival. The government was clearly embarrassed by the newspaper's charge, motivated at least in part by missionary pressure, that even though it had been apprised of the event it took no steps to prevent it. The subject had come up several limes before, most recently in the 1850s, but those officials who looked into it had assumed that the festival was dying out on its own, and that delicate issues such as government's declared intention not to interfere in any aspect of native religious practice would be raised. As investigations in both the 1850s and the 1890s soon revealed, however, there was no clear legal mechanism to suppress the ritual on the neutral ground of physical (as opposed to moral or religious) danger. Not only did the victims voluntarily submit to the ordeal (indeed, they often seemly extremely anxious to do so), they seemed to escape the hookswinging with no grievous bodily harm.

[...] For the most part, British officials and Indian notables agreed that however desirable the suppression of hookswinging might be, it would be unwise to legislate its abolition; it would be better to rely instead on moral persuasion and official disapproval. Nevertheless, the Madras Missionary Conference strongly advocated outright abolition. In a memorial dated 13 November 1893, it recorded that 'this practice is barbarous and revolting; and that its public exhibition must inevitably tend to degrade and brutalize the community among which it takes place.' The missionaries particularly cited the festivals that had been conducted in Sholavandan and written up in great detail in newspapers in Madurai and Madras. Although the government refused to abolish hookswinging, and essentially concluded that Section 144 of the Indian Penal Code could not be applied to do so, individual magistrates did occasionally use their power to prevent hookswinging from taking place, perhaps responding to pressure such as that mounted by the missionary conference. In June 1894, L.C. Miller, the acting district magistrate of Madurai, decided on his own authority to prohibit the annual hookswinging in Sholavandan.

THE MEANINGS OF HOOKSWINGING

Miller's intervention in Sholavandan occasioned a great deal of protest from local residents. A petition with close to a thousand signatures was presented to the government, arguing that the villagers should have been allowed to conduct their normal ritual festivities. The signatories included representatives of a great many castes including Brahmins (Aiyars), upper-caste non-Brahmins (Mudaliars and Pillais), as well as Kallars, Maravars, Valaiyars, Paraiyars, and Pallors. The petition was well written and argued, and appealed clearly and cogently to the concerns and assumptions of governmental officials. For example, the hookswinging festival was glossed as a proper ritual, or *ootchavam*, and thus made to look as if it had a Sanskritic genealogy and high religious justification. The petitioners went on to argue that no physical harm had come to any of the men who had been swung, 'even though in the natural course of events it is impossible that the man should not be grievously hurt'. Instead of arguing that the concerns about the physical welfare of the swinger were misplaced, the petitioners used the lack of injury to sustain the religious merits of the 'penance'. 'Your humble Memorialists attribute this most remarkable state of things in the selected man coming down from the pole in full consciousness and without any serious injury whatever, to the act of the Almighty, in whom full belief is placed not only by the selected man, but by the whole mass of worshippers who attend the festival.' The petitioners further reversed the arguments of the missionaries that the exhibition served only to 'degrade and brutalize' the community, by suggesting that 'this act is calculated to inculcate in the minds of the ignorant masses in a practical manner that firm faith in God and God alone, and full belief in his Divine Revelations, cannot but bring home to the believer the greatest amount of happiness and prosperity.' The petitioners were clearly writing with full knowledge of the dominant missionary and colonial discourse, though they also invoked the more standard argument—with all its internal contradictions—that the swinging was performed to promote the prosperity of the community at large, noting that since they had begun to celebrate the said festival in 1890 'the seasons were more favourable, the crops more abundant, the mortality less appalling, and the dire diseases less virulent.'

The petition then objected to the brutal suppression of the hook-swinging festival. In telling this story, the petition made a number of interesting claims. Some claims directly echoed fragments of official British opinion. For example, the petitioners noted that far more dangerous events were regularly countenanced by government, such as 'balloon ascents, parachute descents, circus feats, horse racing, etc.' Other claims seemed to subvert this very point, by including fire walking as well as 'the compulsory shaving of a young Hindu widow's head under which other circumstances would amount to grievous hurt, being a permanent disfiguration of the face according to the IG code.'

Perhaps the most interesting claims relate to our earlier discussion of the agency of the swinger. The petition stated:

the said Malayandi who had been worshipping in the temple having been inspired by the Goddess Mariyamman to have the hookswinging festival, and being in a state of 'Aveesam' (in a state of unconsciousness of his real self got therefrom), besmearing himself with ashes and carrying a copper plate in his hands containing bits of lighted camphor, and went round the temple to make the holy *Pradakshanam*, saying that Goddess has come to him and inspired him to have the hookswinging festival performed.

The petition then specified that he was in an 'unconscious and un-controllable state of mind, for which he was not responsible.' When he was in this vulnerable state the police arrived and carted him off to jail. What the petition had thus established was the religious character of the hookswinging; the swinger was said to be in a state resembling possession (*caamiyaattam*), which both absolves him from responsibility and sacralizes his person. Indeed, the petition implied that when a worshipper is possessed his agency becomes that of the deity itself, which clearly invokes a different discourse of victimization, agency, and responsibility than would normally be considered relevant in colonial debates. The discourse of the petition appeals both to the trans-valued nature of religious action during hookswinging, and the potential liability of the swinger to police action. In more general terms, the petition intended to invoke a sense of legitimate religious practice, and in the colonial context correctly represented hookswinging as a legiti-mate extension of Sanskritic religion through the use of terms such as ootchavam, pradakshanam, and aveesam. The logic of the petition was thus multiple, employing arguments that both appealed to and no doubt mystified the British, making legitimating claims that involved a large range of religious understandings and forms, and demonstrating the strategic character of subaltern agency in the colonial situation. These subaltern petitioners, far from being paralysed by their lack of choice under the weight of custom, could not only speak but also write. In the face of colonial efforts to anthropologize the meanings of custom, the petitioners deployed tactical appeals to colonial reason, while making strong, polyvocal claims for their own.

The government did not intervene on behalf of the petitioners, and in the end—for reasons that had nothing to do with the arguments in this particular petition—they did decide that Section 144 provided a rather flimsy basis for outright prohibition of hookswinging. So although in an indirect sense the petitioners might be seen to have won their argument, if only for the very short term, they began to lose control over the meaning of the event in their very engagement with the official apparatus of governmental regulation. What might be called the petition wars of the nineteenth century ranged widely in subject matter: they concerned such matters as land and irrigation rights, customary law, local taxes, and management rights in temples, to mention only a few. But all these controversies worked to secure colonial discursive hegemony over the taxonomies, legitimacies, and meanings of local social action. Although the petitioners did not actually use all the right forms and idioms, and clearly resisted others, for the most part they attempted to appeal to the legitimating conceits of official colonial discourse.

It is difficult to recognize some of the shifts that took place because we assume that colonial categories had always been in place. For example, the categories of, and more particularly the rigid separation between, low popular and high classical religion were in fact produced in colonial contexts such as the one described above. Indeed, the petition does not represent a more accurate or authentic understanding of popular religious practice than the colonial version, because the petition was necessarily imbricated in colonial discourse—but it can still be read as a measure of subaltern agency. After all, the petition was written specifically to persuade colonial officials to allow the hookswinging to continue. But the uncritical assumption that colonial sources can illuminate pre-colonial meanings when read through conventional interpretive lenses is as problematic as the faith in anthropological intuitions that confer the ring of truth to standard interpretations. Colonial sources constituted a truth regime both for official knowledge and [...] the conventional wisdom of early professional anthropology.

Nevertheless, the petition reveals certain elements of the ethnographic location of hookswinging in south Indian society, thus raising questions about colonial views and providing the basis for critical and oppositional readings of colonial sources. First, the issue of agency that was so fundamental to colonial discourse turned out to be conceptualized in terms that related to the ritual logic of divine possession and the instrumental effects of ritual action, in part because of the specific salience of possession and trance to any event such as hookswinging, and in part because of the need to argue against the criminal culpability of either the swingers or their impresarios, the priests and temple managers. The colonial obsession with agency was no doubt seen as peculiar, but the petition clearly reveals that it was also significantly connected to official attempts to find fault, round up the culprits, and assess both criminality (the significance of which we will come to later) and barbarism. Second, the clear separation between Brahminic and non-Brahminic domains of religious life is challenged by the fact that the petition was signed by many upper-caste members of the village, as well as by the petition's demonstration that it was clearly possible (whether or not fully plausible) to construct a Brahminic gloss on and justification for hookswinging. Nevertheless, the clear assumption in the governmental files was that Brahmins and other members of the upper castes would have had nothing to do with such barbaric rites. The upper-caste consultants and informants for the British were, at least officially, complicit in the reading of hookswinging as non-Hindu and barbaric, even though many of these same consultants probably had multiple ritual connections to 'popular' ritual practices. Indeed, as I have elsewhere demonstrated. Brahmins who still lived in rural areas in the Tamil country in the late nineteenth and early twentieth centuries often had 'low' village deities such as Aiyanar and Mariyamman for their tutelary worship. Although many Brahmins would have kept some distance between their own ritual practices and popular events such as hookswinging, it was also the case that most Brahmins worshipped in temples where hookswinging was performed, and in which animal sacrifices and other 'low' ritual forms were regularly practised.

The heavy recruitment of Brahmins into colonial administration, and the not unrelated alienation of many Brahmins from their local rural roots—which had facilitated a level of tolerance for and participation in 'non-Brahminic' religious activities—created the basis for increasing collaboration between certain Brahminic precepts and Victorian morals during the nineteenth century. Upper-caste notions of respectability and religious scruple became increasingly Anglicized, as Brahmins and other high castes were clearly incited by circumstance and conventions of colonial acceptability to define more strictly, and exclusively, the provenance of 'Sanskritic' and 'Brahminic' domains. Less ironically than in the instance where Brahmins helped fuel the critique of priests, it was this very privilege that helped to create the basis for the generalized antipathy against Brahmins that fed into the anti-Brahmin movements of the twentieth century.

The meanings of hookswinging were thus transformed in rather complex ways during the nineteenth century. The debates over hookswinging played an important role in constituting certain notions of agency and free will as fundamental to the evaluation of local ritual practices, and in redefining the relations between Brahmins and peasants and between Sanskritic and popular religion. And it was precisely because of the incitement to participate in these debates that upper- and lower-caste Hindus both were drafted into a colonial discourse that touched far more than the attitudes of a number of British administrators. In the past, these acts of public devotion had on occasion been supported by kings through tax-free *inam* land grants; increasingly in the nineteenth century the swingers were either paid by the festival organizers or were encouraged to believe that private vows would most efficaciously be fulfilled by participation in these public events. Whereas kings had once sanctioned and supported these occasions, colonial rulers now disapproved of them. Whereas agency had once been multiply constructed around notions of kingly sovereignty, collective interdependence, social forms of (often oppressive) power, and complex technologies—and social relations—of trance and possession, agency was now the index of individual criminal culpability. And whereas religious customs had been shaped by historical forces in which local power had been closely associated with institutions of local ritual, custom became now the object of new forms of knowledge, control, and classification. Even if the meanings of such intimate experiences such as fear, pain, and belief may never be fully understood, we can be sure that they, and certainly the contexts in which they took place, could not have been totally exempt from the transformations we have surveyed here.

In the end, the governmental reversal of L.C. Miller's action suppressing hookswinging was temporary. Finally, in August 1894, a hookswinging performance in the village of Bheemanaickenpolien on the outskirts of Trichinopoly led, it seemed, to a fatality; it was alleged that a fever that killed one of the swingers was the result of the suppuration of his back wounds. A report circulated in late September of the same year proclaimed that sufficient evidence had been garnered to prove that hookswinging could in fact be abolished on the basis of Section 144, given the lethal consequences demonstrated in this episode. Once a death took place, tradition could he policed effectively, in the name of the public good rather than religious interference. The hookswinging debate was over.

CUSTOM AND COERCION

When it became clear that the hookswinging victims were victimized less by corrupt managers and greedy priests than by their own belief, British officials believed in turn that tyranny resided as much in the dictates of custom as in the actions of those who manipulated it for their own ends. This is not to say that the British ever conceded very much to the world of custom—they continued to seek evidence of manipulation and oppression and sought to defend the gullibility of all who had been designated victims—but custom was the unsettling ground on which the alterity of the colonized resided. Custom also worked to resolve the issue of agency oppositionally, by creating a world in which agency, and individuals, did not exist, thus simultaneously disparaging the traditional world as uncivilized and heralding European modernity as the only haven within which agency was possible and individuals could achieve proper autonomy. Agency can thus be seen as a profoundly problematic category precisely because it disavows the possibility of consent—or anything resembling purposive individual action—outside of particular cultural worlds, at the same time that it uses this condemnation as the pretext for dismissal, surveillance, and control. Even when consent was monitored and debated, it was never really thought that sufficient evidence could exist to document it in the contexts in question: sati, hookswinging, firewalking, and so on. But the focus on consent and agency worked to mask the coercion of colonial power itself, its capacity to define what is acceptable and what is not, what is civilized and what is not, and why it is that the extraordinary burden of knowledge and responsibility is arrogated by the colonizer. Those who pursued colonial forms of knowledge continuously disavowed their own interests, while feeling compelled to enlarge the knowledge of custom as if it was a neutral mechanism for the protection of the colonized. Within a world dictated by custom, agency was held out as a tantalizing promise of freedom, but it was held out by a colonial state that used the term to adjudicate the difference between criminality and barbarism—certainly not to open up any genuine opportunities for freedom of choice.

Even as custom became the site on which the British displaced their own regulative power, custom also became something that was utterly changed and transformed when it was held to be both totalizing and invariant. In the case of the ritual forms and socio-religious categories that surrounded the hookswinging controversies, we can detect significant change that was a direct result of colonial intervention. What M.N. Srinivas has characterized as 'sanskritization', a natural social process in India that involved the emulation of Brahmins and Brahminic social customs by upwardly mobile groups, was in fact officially legislated over and over again in the nineteenth and twentieth centuries. This legislation was the result of British officials using Brahmins as informants and seeing Brahmins as the carriers of high culture. Not only were practices such as hookswinging not voluntarily dropped, they were actually constituted as examples of low ritual practice that should be prohibited if possible and at the very least officially discouraged. In certain temples in south India, the customary practice of widow remarriage within certain castes was discontinued after the government took over the management of temples and outlawed the use of these temples for rituals not deemed to have support from the sastras. In myriad other examples, governmental officials—British and Indian alike—used agencies of government that were meant simply to manage and protect instead to legislate newly defined codes of conduct that were part of the colonial construction of appropriate Hindu practice.

The great debates over the agency of victims in such arenas as
hookswinging served not only to miss but also to obscure a far more
fundamental result of colonial intervention in India: the continual re-
invention of the subjectivity of the colonized by and through the
technologies of colonial rule.

[...] Governmental debates about activities such as hookswinging
thus sought to identify the proper place of tradition in popular social
and religious life at the same time that they reconstituted the terms by
which tradition was identified and evaluated. It was not so much that
tradition was invented as that a new operational category for it was
constructed. This new sense of tradition created a hierarchical relation
between folk and classical tradition, and accorded primacy to the
classical tradition in certain contexts of discomfort or dispute.

[...] The British displaced their own politics into such domains as
custom and tradition, simultaneously endowing them with new
meanings and applications, and absolving themselves from the recognition that power was being deployed by them rather than by the fixity of
the hold of the past, seen as custom or tradition rather than history. But
increasingly the norms of custom were established by official
anthropologists who claimed the scientific status and neutrality of their
discipline while working directly for the colonial state. By the late
nineteenth century, anthropology became the official discourse in
which the policing of tradition was transformed into the knowledge of
tradition. [...]

Partition and Violence*

SHAIL MAYARAM

[…]

The 'communal riot' narrative fails as a description of violence in Alwar and Bharatpur, [of] the intervention of the state's overwhelming power to facilitate re-territorialization and annihilation. The following account of a Captain in the Alwar army, who was deputed for 'operations' to the Tijara 'sector', provides more clues:

I was the ADC to HH Tej Singh. We were with the RSS. It had been decided to clear the state of Muslims. The orders came from Sardar Patel. He spoke to HH on the hot line. The killings of Hindus at Noakhali and Punjab had to be avenged. All the Meos from Firozpur Jhirka down were to be cleared and sent to Pakistan, their lands taken over.

Horror stories were coming in with the refugees from Pakistan, he said. 'We did whatever was happening there, like parading women naked on the streets in Tijara and Naugaonwa after their families had been killed.' The performative display suggests the mimetic nature of violence, a common language shared by right-wing organizations, both Hindu and Islamic.

* Originally published in Shail Mayaram, *Resisting Regimes: Myth, Memory and the Shaping of Muslim Identity*, New Delhi: Oxford University Press, 1997, pp. 179–98, as 'Partition and Violence in Mewat: Rites of Territorial and Political Passage'. In the present version, all notes and references have been deleted. For the complete text, see the original version.

The ground had already been prepared by the training of thousands of RSS volunteers in camps by the army of the Rajput state: 'Like Godse who killed Gandhi,' added the captain. But when 'the CBI Inquiry was held we did not tell anything.' The trouble with the Meos went back to 1942, when Maulvi Abdul Qaddus organized the Kishangarh Meos against payment of land revenue. A *patwari* sent to collect it was tied with ropes to a tree; the guns of the police party were taken. When Tijara, Govindgarh, and other areas also revolted, the maharaja sent the army. The violence was not the outcome of an idiosyncratic ruler and a right-wing organization: it had to do with demographic rationality for the postcolonial Indian state. Governmentality required an ethnically conducive, subject population. Revenue and demographic rationality for the princely regimes were entwined. 'Disorderly' groups were problematic: they eroded the fiscal and productive base of the state.

The captain detailed the account of the Clearing Up (*safaya*) and Cleaning Up Operations. Alwar had been divided into four sectors under different army officers to clear the state of Muslims:

I was sent on Special Duty to Tijara. The Hindu–Muslim riots had started. The Alwar state had run out of ammunition. We did not have such sophisticated arms. Sardar Patel supplied us with reinforcements from the Second Lancers who were returning to England [names an elaborate stockpile of weaponry]. In Tijara the Hindus—Jats, Ahirs, Gujars joined us.

Ten thousand Meos led by Ayyub Khan and Maulvi Qaddus fought the battle at Tijara. The army won after reinforcements arrived on the second day.

I went ahead and posted the force on a hill—below was the valley through which they were to pass. We killed every man, all of them. The next four days we had to do the 'Clearing Up' operation. My men and the villagers dug men's graves, threw their bodies in—there was such a stench and then a danger of disease from the dead cattle and men.

The calculated planning occasionally took cognizance of exceptions: Muslims who were part of the state apparatus or who were suitable candidates for 'subjecthood', already having proved their loyalty, such as the captain's Muslim gunner: 'The skin of his hands had peeled off because of the heat of the gun, but still he kept firing. Wherever he is, Abdul Hamid, *khuda usko jannat bakshe'* (may God grant him heaven). He could have killed me while I was driving the jeep.'

Intelligence reports and the drums beating in the hillside brought the captain to villages, where they announced, 'Either be killed or show a white flag and convert, become Hindus.' Then they would enter the village and collect the men. The accompanying *shuddhi* squad would right away shave the men and make them eat a piece of pork.

The women—if they were of marriageable age, were all taken. They were *shuddh* after drinking *ganga jal* [sacred water of the Ganga river] and could be taken. No, the Meos were not Muslims, they were half-Hindu. In their marriages they had both *pheras* and the *nikah* (Hindu and Muslim rites). They were not with the Muslim League. They did not want to go to Pakistan. But we had orders to clear them. Not a single Muslim was left in Alwar. Alwar was the first state to clear all the Muslims. Bharatpur followed. The rulers used to consult each other. Yes, Bharatpur also supported the RSS—Bacchu Singh organized it.

The act of domination was signified by a range of activities: by military control over women's bodies, who were raped or absorbed into families after a perfunctory purification with sacred Ganga water; by the re-inscription of the Meo body by the Arya Samaj shuddhi squads; and by giving the 'half Hindu' Meo males the choice of becoming fully 'Hindu' or being killed. The 'Hindu' was constituted not by criteria of inclusion —that is, absorbed into the Hindu fold—but by exclusion from Islam, signified by the eating of pork. Later, when the task of recovering abducted women was initiated, officials were only taken to villages where there were few women, and villages with large numbers of such women (many had by then given birth to children) were avoided.

The army had been sent to the 'Tijara sector' for the coercive reclamation of territory. The culmination of the operation was the massacre at the Kala Pahar:

Naugaonwa was a large Meo stronghold. We butchered them. That was the last battle of Mewat. Their resistance was over. After Naugaonwa they went to Sohna, Taoru. Upto Dharuhera is the Kala Pahar. That was their objective—all the Muslims fled there....We thought that till they remained there they would keep coming (back). We made a three pronged attack from both sides and the air, using the police and army. It took us more than two months, July, August, during the rains to clear the whole bloody area. Then they flooded Delhi and it was a problem to evacuate them to Pakistan. A book was written for me in which I was described as Alha Udal [the heroes of Bundelkhand whose fight with the Muslim invader is celebrated in *Alha khand*].

The enactment of annihilation by the state enabled the reproduction, through performance, of a nationalist, masculinizing display.

The account of the Clearing and Cleaning Up Operations transcribed above is replicated in several military officers' accounts. In Tijara and other areas, prior to the army's arrival, state officials had already been preparing the ground against Muslims. *Lambardars* (headmen) were summoned and asked to become Hindu. Between 5–7 August, eight

Meo villages west of Tijara were set on fire by unknown persons, who raised the cry that Muslims were attacking them, and who then took refuge near the police station. In Seelgaon, the state forces came with a white flag, promising the Meo ex-army VCOs (Victoria Cross Officers) 'protection' if they would give them their arms. The village disarmed, the VCOs were shot, and men, women, and children 'cut to pieces'. In Alwar (as also in Bharatpur) ex-army personnel and Muslim state officials were made targets: 'loyal Muslims' eroded the construction of Muslim aggression and needed to be eliminated as evidence. A Collector of the Alwar state promised refugees from Bharatpur protection in ex-change for cash. Within an hour of his being given the money, Bharat-pur troops had crossed the river (it is inconceivable that it was without the knowledge of the Alwar government) and attacked the refugee camp.

In the official discourse, the reworking of social space takes place based on the dislocation of body space and a simultaneous relocation. Self-legitimation is inherent in a narrative in which the Meos are projected as a further source of vivisection:

Later when Pakistan was made they asked for Mevistan and a six mile wide corridor to Pakistan. Dr Narayan Bhaskar Khare and Kanvar Raghubir Singh of Jaoli, who was the (Alwar) Home Minister, supressed them. They did great service. In Tej Singh's rule not a single mosque remained. I wrote:

> 'hinduon re pujo pao
> tej singh dujo raj singh maharana na bhao
> shane shane vilaj mlechh mandal ravana bhao'

> [There has been no ruler
> like Tej Singh.
> Hindus be happy you rule.
> Now that the *mlechha* leaves.]

In the Felicitation volume for Khare I wrote [...]

> 'khaskar alvar mlechh sam traskar
> narayan bhaskar nas kar rahyo hai'

> [Specially the Alwar mlechha
> were turned out.
> Narayan Bhaskar
> destroyed them all.]

In the poet's narrative the Alwar riot (1932) was a 'Muslim attack'. Muslims are both stigmatized and totalized as the ritually impure mlechhas, inherently separatist. Hence the valorization of Maharaja Tej Singh and Khare of the Hindu Mahasabha. The former demolishes mosques, but the victimizer's agency is deleted in the passive voice and semantic selection of the Meos who leave. The exodus is rendered a voluntarist act rather than an outcome of coercive collective action.

State officials from both Alwar and Bharatpur, such as the Home Minister, metonymically replicate the account:

The Meos were creating disorder (*mev upadrav macha rahe the*).... The Meos and Muslims wanted a state—a mini Pakistan. All the Meo leaders, such as Yasin Khan and others wanted a state with a route to Pakistan. They wanted a Pakistan. Yes, the Meos and the Hindus fought. The Meos killed a cow. The Bharatpur state began, it pressed from that side and we from this side. We threw them out. Yes, we thought they should go to Pakistan. The people here exploded when they saw a special train from Hyderabad, Sind, full of bloody corpses. They killed the Muslims then. What can you do if people are agitated? Why should Muslims stay here? Another country, Pakistan was made. So go there. It was in the air to send them there. Why are they sitting on our land? The *dhar* came from the villages, they wanted to loot and kill the Muslims. We finished the Muslim League.

In the Home Minister's account of the Meo movement, the killing of a single cow by the Meos causally explained slaughter. The notion of 'criminality' suggests the penetration of the colonial worldview. 'Criminality' as a cluster concept suggests a doctrine of collective guilt; a conception of 'martial' races vis-à-vis the 'primitive' tribes and castes who are liable to disorder (*uddand, upadrav*); and a coalescence of time: the explanation of present behaviour by means of an assumed past. It involves an essentialist formulation of a community defined by a single attribute of criminality (*jurayam aur chori pesha*). Not only do the Meos stand defined, so are Muslims collectively responsible for the train of corpses—a notion reproduced by their corresponding Muslim aggressors.

V.P. Menon offers an explanation of violence in terms of Meo disorder. The Deputy Prime Minister of the new Indian state, Sardar Patel, refers to the Meos who are *'not penitent'*. Paradoxically, his speech at Alwar exhorts Hindus to produce the Muslim girls they are harbouring. Khare had written of the virtual war going on which flared up over a cow and Brahmin being killed in a Hindu temple. 'Naturally the Hindus got inflamed and followed and exceeded Bihar. It is said that the Shuddhi Sangathanwalas have converted about 10 to 12 thousand Muslims to Hinduism.'

Partition, however, was not the outcome of mere cow killing. The Meo conflict with the Jat state dated to the peasant movement. Prior to that, Meo *chaudhari*s had on occasions sided with the government. As a result Maharaja Kishan Singh had appointed Meo lambardars such as

Dundhal, Usman, Hamid, Ghulam, Ajmat, and Chandaka as *zaildars* authorized to collect revenue. But once again in 1936, the Meos and Hindu castes of the *tehsils* of Pahari and Kaman refused to pay *jama* (*sab log phir gaye*). In a patwari's account, Batra, the minister, had told them:

Demand any amount, and enforce it fully, hit them if they refuse....don't reduce it by a single rupee. We would call Meos and say '*de jut*' [beat him]. Any women who left the village were beaten up. In an hour we could collect the jama of Ladamka. Then we went to Papra. The Meos ran into the hills. There were large earthen pots stored with alcohol there. When the military fired at them they burst into flames. The Meos had *desi* [local] weapons but all their *barud* [gunpowder] was burnt up. The Diwan and Batra climbed the hill and told the Meos to come down or they would be shot...The Meos all came out and fell at their feet. The Diwan said, 'either give the jama or I'll destroy the village and take whatever the patwari demands.' In an hour Papra, Dabra, Jutri, Pahari, Jutrula, all paid the jama. In 3-4 days the entire Pahari tehsil paid....This caused friction in Jat-Meo relations.

In 1947 once again there had been considerable signs of disaffection among the Meo peasantry.

THE ORGANIZATION OF VIOLENCE

As communal tension gained ground, the non-Muslim castes in Bharatpur saw the possibility of land. The patwari's account continues:

The Jats held a meeting and stated that the Meos be evicted and sent to Punjab and all the Meo land be redistributed among the Jats. Leaders such as Thakur Deshraj, Tar Singh Ahir of Barsana, Lachi Jat of Kamar near Hathin collected Jats of Punjab and Delhi, Ahirs from Rewari and Yadavs from Mathura. In this way the Hindu dhar was formed. *Tukri*s [companies] of 500–700 persons went to various villages and local Jat leaders and government officials would join them. (Gujars would only join in the loot, for instance, of mustard)....As Kaman was a Hindu stronghold with mixed castes the maximum force, 10,000 strong, was kept here, it made provisions for the dhar along with the people of Kaman. When the dhar came to Kaman in May we arranged for their food. Gosainji called all Hindus and Muslims into the temple and made arrangements for their stay.

Protection to Muslims was conditional on their shuddhi.

Partition violence was a departure in terms of form from the 'feud', the traditional mode of dispute and settlement. Violence had already been multiplied by forms of bureaucratic rationality and the spread of economically extractive technologies. What obtained now was a modern form of political violence in which the mutuality of exchange of feud was rendered obsolete. Logistics of scale were made possible by modern forms of transport and weapons. Forms of communication such as the press and pamphlet, image reproduction through photographs, and speech as mobilizing spectacle in public meetings enabled the rapid multiplication of sites of tension. It helped override both caste and class conflict and equipped the military and crowd with a shared narrative structure in which Meo resistance was presented as the originary cause of counter-attack. All prior memory and resistance were obliterated. Jats of Sinsini attribute the initiative to the Meos (*mevon ki dhar pahle charhi*). They, however, could not explain away the presence of abducted women in their own village, whereas the Meos, according to their own account, had not been able to take away Jat women. The states constituted a regional configuration in which information was shared, strategies planned. Bharatpur, for instance, was in constant communication with Alwar and Dholpur.

Mainstream nationalism seems to have offered scant resistance to the dominant anti-Muslim ideology in the region. In the Praja Mandal lexicon, both the Jat rulers of Bharatpur and the Dholpur Rana (later the *Rajpramukh* of the Matsya Union), as well as the Rajput rulers of Karauli and Alwar, were 'reactionary'. The liberal terminology of 'repression' is used to describe their action. But from all indications there was considerable anti-Muslim feeling in both Alwar and Bharatpur. The Praja Mandal candidate in the Bharatpur election called the Muslim candidate a 'cow killer' in the presence of the revenue minister. The representation comes from the *savarna* or upper-caste idea that meat-eaters are necessarily violent. A former Congress Minister of Alwar told me of the pervasive Hindu sentiment that the killings in Pakistan must be avenged. If the Muslims are not leaving, the military must turn them out. Institutionalized ideology frequently constitutes social action. Princely sovereignty produced an institutional authorization of violence, and its further actions were sustained by the widespread legitimation of violence, including from sections of the Congress.

Some Congressmen were active participants in the creation of terror; others were sympathetic bystanders. Nehru went on record: 'What I am really afraid of is the enemy who is being born right inside our own ranks.' The role of collective silence has been repeatedly pointed out with respect to Argentina, Ireland, wartime Germany, and contemporary Israel. Feldman refers to it as the 'backgrounding of violence' in the informal ideologies of everyday life. A Jat who was MLA of the Congress from Bharatpur described the conflict and his own participation in the dhars that abducted Muslim women:

In the 1947 riots the leadership of the dhars was in the hands of Thakur Dhruv Singh of Pathena who was the next leader after Deshraj. He was most active. He joined hands with Bacchu Singh and his military and they took the Hindu dhar to Mewat and killed people there. The Jats had gone to assist the castes who were being troubled by the Meos. This is why Nagar, Pahari, Kaman were abandoned. The Brahmin-Baniya residents, who were well off, felt threatened by the Meos. The Jats went at their invitation and they looked after the food and drink of the Jats. The dhars had weapons like the *lathi, vallam* [spear], *talvar* [sword] and *pharsa* [axe]. The Meos had *barchhis* [javelins], *ranchangi banduks* [guns]....The Meos began to leave in *bhadon*. No one stopped them. The refugees, mainly Jat Sikhs, had started coming earlier.

Bharatpur's first conflict began on Janmashtami with the looting of the train to Agra which was on the metre gauge. It was stopped a kilometre and a half ahead of Bharatpur. All trains were stopped and people killed....Had it not been for Bacchu Singh, Hindus would not have remained alive in Bharatpur. When he stood for election he said, 'I don't want Muslim votes, only Hindu ones.'

Congress narratives are sometimes hard to distinguish from those of the 'mob'. The ex-MLA's narrative is typical of Jat accounts in its ambivalence regarding the religious status of the Meos. They are 'half Hindu', having only recently become 'clear-cut' and staunch Muslims when Muslim organizations sent *mullah*s; in 1946 they began supporting the Muslim League but its influence among them was marginal ...

Narratives of participants in the dhars authorize domination and legitimize violence. The imagined community of Pakistan, projected by the Muslim League as the 'homeland' of the Muslims, enters popular discourse and deterritorializes the Meo of their 'homeland' (*hamari bhumi*). The sense of a shared regional culture in terms of origin and other myths, ritual and kinship practices, caste and *jajmani* relations, and collective memory are obliterated in the totalization of 'Muslims'. Ironically the name of Krishna, invoked in the slogan 'Girraj Maharaj *ki jai*', was used to kill those who regarded themselves as his descendants.

A Brahmin narrates his experience of the dhar that effaced the long relationship with Meo jajmans, at whose households he performed death rites or the *ganth jorna* (ritual of tying the nuptial knot) at marriages:

I went [to Bilang] with 300–400 other Jats and Bacchu Singh led the dhar. There were 50 persons from the military and other government officials like me. We had already encircled Kaman. It took us the whole day to reach Bilang. Some were in jeeps, others walked. People from villages joined it on the way. Firozpur Agrawali was burnt down. Bilang was besieged.

The patwari recalled his close working with the Meo zaildar Samay Singh. Now they were on opposite sides as they fought during the day:

Women came to our support, brought water and food to the *morcha*, Brahmanis and Mainis. The fighting would stop while we ate. The bugle would play. We went after worshipping Thakurji or devi shouting, 'Bhagwan Ram, Kishan *ki jai.*' We had devised signals, if a Meo was running we would shout *'uttar ko'* [towards the west]. We beseiged it for 3–4 days. Bacchu Singh had to leave. Then the Gujars and Brahmins of Bolkhera came to our help. We burnt the village. The dead could not be counted [*maron ki koi ginti nahin*].

Both dhar and morcha constituted exhibits of a colonizing power. The role of women suggests that gender was not necessarily a significant category that might have created fissures among the victimizers. I will return to the perspective of the Bilang Meos. But the dhar ruptured a shared political and ritual space: the 'brotherhood' of the *pal*, villagers' participation in fairs, *akharas* (gymnasiums) and healing traditions implicit in the worship of Pir Alakh by Bolkhera Hindus.

Ritual was an important aspect of violence. Jats at Sinsini first offered the ritual sacrifice of a goat to their deity, Sinsini. The mythic memory associated with the deity is of its beheading, following an attack by the Turks. The iconic representation of the deity inscribed an initial act of violence that was now to be avenged. Ritual consecrated the totalized memory of Muslim aggression. In Alwar, the sacred thread (*kalaya*) was tied around the wrists of members of the dhar preceding an attack.

The state was the site to express the masculinization of violence. In the election of 1952 Bacchu Singh used the symbol of the *murga* (cock), indicating political practices for the domestication of Muslims. He won. As performative spectacle the dhar replicated state ideology:

A *panda* from Sancholi was a renowned wrestler who held wrestling shows in Punjab and Delhi. The Jats made him the *dulha* [bridegroom] and leader of the procession, of the dhar. In the first week of June they went around fighting and injuring and killing people. He had a fight with his student, Parwal Meo, in which the latter was killed. The Meos reacted by surrounding and killing him. The Jat–Meo conflict now became a Hindu–Muslim one. Wherever the dhar went people from the village joined it. Eventually the people outnumbered the military. Most of the people were Jats, also some Gujars—they did not do the killing and only came afterwards for the loot like of silver and gold guineas, the mustard crop, cattle and other animals, ornaments. They benefitted the most although the Jats got the land.

Violence acquired a phallic image with the masculine wrestler *qua* bridegroom leading a bridal procession. Genocide was engendered and victimhood defined in terms of claiming the feminine, underlining the subordination of bride-givers.

The confessional ideology of shuddhi was inscribed on to the bodies of Meo men and women in a collective ritualization of violence. At

Alwar the shuddhi conducted by Mauli Chand Sharma combined Arya Samaj and Sanatan Dharma ritual. It involved the *yajnopavit* (sacrifice with fire oblations), the wearing of the *janeu* or the sacred thread by the new convert, and also head shaving, keeping the *choti* or Hindu tuft of hair at the crown of the head. Accounts suggest how both the Arya Samaj and the Sanatana Dharma were active 'in bringing our *bhai* (brothers) back'. There was, thus, an exchange of political rites between Hindu organizations. Only those Meos remained who became shuddh.

A former official at Kaman describes the Bharatpur state's organization of shuddhi by the more popular Arya Samaj:

[It] did *makkari* [cheating] in the name of shuddhi. We did it at the Bimal Kund [temple tank] in Kaman to Garhe Gujars, Malkhana Thakurs, and Meos and reconverted them. Raghuvir Singh Dhau, a Jat, got it done at the instruction of the Maharaja. All of us Brahmins were called and told to join in, to eat the food cooked by the Muslims and to feed them. We told Dhau, 'we'll do this, but first you marry their daughter and give yours to them.' He got his daughter engaged to a Gujar from Weir [Bhusawar].

The Meos who did not run away became Hindus. They were made to recite the Gayatri *mantra* [a Rigvedic chant], swear on the Ganga and drink a mixture called *panch gab* that included *gau mutra, gau gobar, gau dudh, gau ghi,* and *gau dahi,* [the five cow products, comprising cow urine, cowdung, milk, clarified butter, and curd]. The Qu'ran had to be put into the flames....We would sing songs like, '*pat hoja hindu phir pakegi khir*' [A wife tells her husband, 'Become Hindu then we'll cook rice in thickened milk']; '*id, bakr id na subhrat pyari, tinon ki aisi taisi sankrant ne mari*' [Neither Id, Bakr Id nor Subhrat are dear, all three have been overtaken by Sankrant (that is, the Hindu festival)]; '*kahe amiran bat kariman sun bahna, 'koran sharif ki koi rakayat ayegi na ari*' [Amiran says to Kariman, 'listen my sister, no verse of the Qu'ran sharif will help you now']; '*nabba ke abba ki main bhi mundva dungi darhi jumme tak sun lena*' [Listen, by Friday I will get the beard of Nabba's father shaved].

The feminization of fear mirrored the phallicization of the state–crowd.

Although there was evidence of the considerable abbreviation of shuddhi ritual, in contrast to that in the early decades of the century, the folklore of Partition details the continuity of some compositions, ritual, and symbols. Shuddhi served to reverse the ritual status of the stigmatized mlechha. But its impact was hardly durable. The official quoted above described how Nazir, a Muslim *rangrez* or dyer, was renamed Narottam. He bathed everyday at the tank and worshipped at the temple, but ran away as soon as he could to Pakistan. Abducted Meo women, on the other hand, were more enduringly absorbed into the families of their abductors after a perfunctory sprinkling of Ganga water.

The abduction of women was a policy of terror, an exercise in which the state-turned-mob transgressed domestic space and invaded the formerly inviolate—women's bodies. As one participant put it:

The Jats of Bharatpur reacted to the Muslim League and what was happening to Hindus in Punjab...This was a time of communal frenzy and passion when people forgot humanism [*insaniyat*]. We took away women. That was the system. Women do not have any religion [*ye to system tha hi, auraton ka to koi dharam hi nahin hota*]. Subsequently, there was an exchange of women and a large number of Muslim women went to Pakistan. Some did not want to go back.

The perception of women as passive and pliable in terms of religious affiliation enabled mass abduction:

Meonis were made shuddh and kept in Gujar and Jat homes, the Meos also took our women. We took hundreds, they took ten–twenty [*hamne saikron le lin, unne das bis lin*]. Any man who did not have a woman took her and kept her, even if he was fifty years old. Any woman was taken, even while she was walking or cutting grass she was lifted, carried over the shoulder. She would not say anything for fear. After a while she would walk herself, they were so scared. No one wants to die, they would come themselves. The gun was shown and they would walk away. Marriage? There was no question of marriage with a *barat* [bridal procession]. After children are born it is like marriage. After shuddhi she became a Hindu, kept fasts and festivals. Gujars and Jats had no problem with Muslim women, eating food cooked by her.

The enactment of violence targets the whole through the part, a few or more victims become substitutes for the community. Its organization in public places and during the day signified command re-territorialization in compressed time. The image of bloody Hindu corpses in trains, which participants of Hindu mobs frequently gave, represented an inversion of what happened in the area. In Bharatpur a large number of attacks on trains carrying Muslims and the army were organized in which, in most cases, the assailants were from the Bharatpur army led by Bacchu Singh. The trains, thus, became moving signs that would prevent the Other from returning.

Public spaces, such as railway stations, streets, and wells, where visibility is ensured to a larger aggregate, had maximal effect. The use of public arenas enables the dead to become signals to the living of the construction of ethnic boundaries. Arendt's contention that violence and communication are mutually exclusive hardly seems valid, considering the lucidity of signification. The locales were carefully selected. Large Meo villages such as Titpuri, Kaimasa, Bichur, and others were specially targeted in order to have a ripple effect on the consciousness of the Other. These are described as the sites of *bhari katti* (heavy slaughter), after which survivors fled seeking shelter elsewhere.

The file 'Framing of Charges' reported, 'The object is rapidly becoming loot and not only communal revenge.' The Chief Commissioner commented on Bharatpur as a place which 'has apparently run completely amock. They have got rid of all the Muslims and consider all those in traffic as legitimate prey'; 'I saw corpses all around....'; 'Thirty thousand were killed, a thousand converted and the rest driven out. The property of Muslims was taken over by the State and auctioned, the sale time proceeds being credited to the State Treasury. The Maharaja is reported to have expressed delight that no Muslim was left in the State.' The violence, lifting of women and cattle, the raiding and killing, continued till October. Charges were never filed or pursued: no one was ready to stand witness. But a discursive inversion was reproduced in official discourse. *Tej Pratap*, Alwar's official newspaper, reported on 8 August that the Meos were *'offering themselves* for conversion' (emphasis added). In most Jat accounts, likewise, the notion that *'they* attacked first' (emphasis added) is widespread. The comment—'Had the Muslims not been cleaned out they would have captured Alwar'— also inverted the safaya operation, which became re-narrativized as a pre-emptive strike.

VIOLENCE AND THE COMMUNITY: MYTH AND MEMORY OF VICTIMHOOD AND RESISTANCE

To recover the speech of victims is, in a sense, to re-invest the victim community with subjectivity. This analysis suggests how the memory of exodus, slaughter, and violence is constructed, transmitted, and reproduced; that the signification of violence is culturally regulated and mediated; and that it has to do with aspects of speech, silence, and language. Occasions of exceptional trauma and holocaust, it has been pointed out, are witnessed by a rupture of language. In Meo accounts, what is particularly noticeable is not only the fractured quality of individual speech but also the breakdown of traditional forms of mythic history through which the community transmitted collective memory and reproduced itself culturally. Both speech and silence also indicate the strategies of re-negotiation of community identity, the attempt at restoration of signification to inter-community relations, thereby remaking ethnic fissures.

A large number of accounts suggest the overwriting of the time of the nation on to community time. Whereas the peasant movement is

computed in Vikram Samvat, *saintalis* (1947 of the Gregorian calendar) is
the referent for Partition and violence, rather than for freedom from
colonial rule. Most Partition descriptions are short, abbreviated, and
condensed, almost all pronouns being deleted in the process. In most
accounts, time is engraved as the time of eviction, a wrenching from
roots, as it were. The journey to Pakistan and back, or to British India and
life in the camp, is hardly referred to at all, although in actual terms it
took far longer than eviction, which was often sudden. *Batvara*
(vivisection) rather than *azadi* (freedom) constitutes a marker of Meo
consciousness.

The division was not only of countries but of extended families as
well. Mehtabi told me, 'Of my eight homes six fled [to Pakistan], two
remained here. My husband went also and stayed with his sister.' For
Mehti, time is figured by the public event of 1947 and by familial time
marked by the birth of her child after she had to flee her village:

My first child was born in the *chaura* [open] during the *bhaga bhagi* [exodus]. We left
everything. The dhar of Gujars, Chamars, Malis, Kolis, Ahirs, and Jats had come. We
fled to the Pahar, my husband and this child in my womb. I was all alone when my
child was born, just me and my husband. No cloth, only an iron grain strainer in
which lie cooked the *rotis* when the child was born. Then the firing began on the
Pahar. They used the *ganj* machine [Bren gun] and the *chilgari* [aeroplane]. But we
were sheltered by a rock. People were killed like in *lavni* [the operation of cutting
fodder generally done by women]. We stayed for two years in Punhana....Many
people went to Pakistan in *kafilahs* [caravans]. But they told me don't come with us
or your child will die on the way.

Partition signified for her a dual pain, of dislocation and of labour, that
brought with it birth yet meant a wrenching from her kin. It was an
event in which her 'normal' world collapsed with its male–female
division of labour, demolishing also the boundaries of inside–outside.
The private event of childbirth thus took place exposed. The exposure
was not just a personal one, but underlined the vulnerability of her
family, her *biradari*, her *jati*, and rendered them vulnerable to military
violence, metaphored in the human onslaught on nature (lavni).

In a large number of Meo accounts, the chilgari is rendered the flying
panoptic presence, the state plane's surveillance marking out places of
hiding prior to swooping down low and opening fire. A disconsolate
Chand Khan trekked through loot and murder for almost a week, with
a bullock-cart carrying grain, and joined the nearly one hundred
thousand people who had congregated from all over at the Kala Pahar.
In his account the dead are measured by corpses spread over a distance
of *kos* (as the enumerative measurement that dominates the early part

of his narrative fails). Then the chilgari gives way to the *chil* (kites)—
both the mechanical and the natural signifying the act of prey:

In the morning our big leader, Chaudhari Yasin, came and told us 'Tomorrow there
will be firing.' Bacchu Singh's chilgari came low and closely surveyed the camp. At
around 12 the next morning a huge dhar came. People were killed for two kos....My
chacha, Dhan Singh, and I were saved because we hid behind a rock. The ganj
machine left none alive. I saw a child suckling at a dead woman, children were
howling....When the military came they cut women's arms for the jewellery. We kept
hiding, the kites screeching.

Tundal's account evokes the speech and the uncertainty of the route,
the closed hostile terrain. His wife Sarupi's concerns were with the
everyday of survival—water, children, hunger, food, on the hostile (in
terms of both nature and man) landscape of the Kala Pahar. She refers
only in passing to the trauma for herself: the blisters and the now
continuous pain that she has in her head:

These children were small, three boys and two girls were with us, the youngest were
one and two and a half years old. What did we have to eat? I left everything when I
ran away, could not even take grain. We ran to Khanpur Ghasoli. We stopped in the
village. And the rest [the *duniya*] was climbing the hill. Who had the time to eat
when we left? I had a few *rotis* in my *khari* [basket]. I told the children to eat them
but there was such a big, black scorpion. When my son told me about it I told him to
throw away the rotis, 'If you eat them there won't even be any water for you.' Then we
went to the Kala Pahar. We climbed straight up and came down along the Dhond-
lond pass. The children's feet had blisters from walking and so I tied the *akhora* leaf
on them and forced them to walk. We had to walk and walk...the people were
running, running with all the belongings they could carry. We had no food, all were
hungry. Some were falling in the stream, some by the hillside. What could they
carry? A few utensils, some clothes for the children—nothing else. Those who hid in
the crevices of the Kala Pahar survived, others were rained bullets by the machine
[gun]...

Sarupi stayed with her sister until she also left, along with her entire
village. But the passage was closed at the (Pakistan) border, so they
could not get into either side. Later, she returned and worked as a
labourer at a farmer's house for fifteen years, pounding pulses, chopping
fodder, and tending the cattle. She earned a rupee a day and stayed till
the single buffalo made three buffaloes:

When I churned the curds I could bring back a bucket of [buttermilk] for my
children. Then those poor ones had something to drink. Then I came back to
Alwar. I don't know what has happened in my head, I have been so ill, I feel I
am crazy...

Several accounts hint at the reinforcement of kinship and community through refuge and survival (though no descriptions of experience with their kin, which are assumed as 'natural', are provided). There were also undeniable fissures with the old and the infirm who had to be left behind, between those who chose to leave for Pakistan and others who preferred to become shuddh. Jamil Khan said:

Bacchu Singh had come with his *paltan* [platoon] and some Ahirs, Gujars and Jats. From Naivado, Pahatvado and Singalvati about 500–1000 Meos came. They had heard a rumour that Maujpur had been surrounded and came to save us. We stayed in Maujpur for 5–10 days then went to my *phuphi's* [father's sister] house in Ranota, tehsil Punhana....We stayed here for six months....My father ran to Maujpur to our relatives, to Chand Khan's father who is our *mama* [mother's brother].'

Islami's concern derived from sacred notions of a uterine space that was invaded by violence: affecting children and women's bodies, their homes and religious practices:

Bacchu Singh came with a dhar of thousands and surrounded the villages. When the dhar moved shouts could be heard from all sides, *'bajrang bali ki jai'* [victory to Hanuman]. All the Meos had come here. Here [in Alwar] too there was hardly a village that was not burnt. All the *batevras* were set on fire. These Kir, Bhangi, and Chamars [dalit castes] really killed people. I saw a child being flung in the air and then caught at spearpoint. One woman was hit so on her neck I saw her body somersaulting. So many were sent to Titpuri and from there they went to Lachmangarh for shuddhi. There were thousands and thousands of cattle in the Itarana and Dautana Runds. The committee then got them auctioned.

Batevras are beautifully crafted stacks of cowdung cakes. Regarded as women's inviolable space, even Meo men are not permitted to touch them.

Transgressions of normal boundaries comprise much of the memory of violence. Body memory figures strongly in Sarupi's account of blisters and the recurrent pain in her head; in Subban's description of a child feeding at a dead woman's breast; and Islami's account of terror unleashed on women and children. Trauma is apparent in the range of intense sound impressions, of gunfire, shouting mobs, what Tundal calls the *rola* or the noise of violence and loot. The intensity of place names suggests how an experiential geography escalates in narratives of violence. The preoccupation with death imagery is constant.

A series of choices were thrust upon the community: between getting killed and becoming shuddh, and between going to Pakistan (taking the *gail*) or staying on in India. Hurmat Mev refers to the choice of his entire village which went to Gurgaon after they were warned that they would either be killed or have to become shuddh. Fateh Singh of Samola and several members of his *pal* made the latter choice:

I was converted with four other Meos. They took us to Titpuri, Lachmangarh. They told us, 'You belong to the [ruling] Naruka lineage.' My father, Khairati Meo, was named Khadag Singh. Water was filled at the well and Sidhji was called who is the father of the BJP [Bhartiya Janata Party] leader, Dharamvir Sidh. The *pandits* were called. My head was shaved and a choti left; I was given new clothes and made shuddh [pure] with ganga jal. The Pundlot *got* has always been close to the Maharaja. He was misguided by Dr Khare. Other people were also involved: the IG, Richpal Singh, the Collector, the Thakur of Garhi, Bhawani Singh, and an SP called Bakhtavar Lal. Mulchand Badhavar was the Collector of Rajgarh and he gave the order to kill....We were saved because we became shuddh.

Mandawar had about 400 Rangad Rajput homes who professed Islam but followed Rajput customs. After their shuddhi, their daughters were taken in marriage by Hindu Rajputs but daughters were not given to them. Even after their ritual 'purification', they were not considered 'Hindu'. Muslims continued to be regarded within communities as sources of pollution.

Ramjani's father underwent shuddhi after his elder son was killed. Bacchu Singh had arrived with over 500 well-armed men. She saw around a hundred people slain on the Ratnaki–Govindgarh road:

Then shuddhi took place, my father was shaved, he was made to keep a *chutti* and sprinkled with ganga jal...Bhairu was installed with vermilion, a lamp and food offering. He is the protector of water. They [Hindus] call him Bhairuji, we call him Khyajakhedar, an *auliya*. But this is the first thing to be done before a well is dug.

In Ramjani's account there was bewilderment as to why Bhairuji, whom the Meos worship anyway, was thrust on them. It suggests the distance between the totalized binary construction of the world and her everyday lifeworld of ritual objects. But strategies of resistance were part of the underlife of collectivized ritual. Several persons got their chotis cut in three or four months. The ritual of purification had been inverted as defilement. [...]

Is *Khadi* the Solution?*

Emma Tarlo

I have done my packing racked with conflicts as to what to take and what
not to take with me—whether to wear khaddar dress there while
addressing the audience or swadeshi silk, the point of which will not be
so well understood...whether to be smart and fashionable as of old or to
be simple and common only. I have at last chosen to be the latter. But it
is taking time and trouble to assimilate the new method.

—*Sarladevi Chaudhurani, 3 May 1920, letter to Gandhi.*

Sarladevi Chaudhurani[1] was preparing for a conference in May
1920 when she experienced this sartorial anxiety. Her letter to
Gandhi reveals that the problem of what to wear was still a thriving
issue in India despite Gandhi's attempts to resolve it. But the problem
had taken a new form. Rather than worrying about the extent to which
they should Westernize their dress, the Indian elite were now worrying
about the extent to which they should simplify and re-Indianize it. Far
from effacing the problem of what to wear, Gandhi had in fact raised it
to unprecedented heights for he had drawn it out of the political closet.
It was no longer relegated to private journals, but was now a much-
discussed public issue. Furthermore Gandhi's particular emphasis on

* Originally published in Emma Tarlo, *Clothing Matters: Dress and Identity in
India*, London: Hurst, 1996, pp. 94–126, as 'Is *Khadi* the Solution?'. In the present
version, all notes and references have been deleted. For the complete text, see the
original version.

the morality of *khadi* gave the problem a new flavour. Whereas in the past it was considered morally and culturally acceptable to alter one's dress to suit the occasion or to wear a combination of Indian and European dress, it was now, according to him, immoral to wear anything but khadi on a permanent and daily basis. Any hope of finding a neutral solution to the problem of what to wear seemed now to have been completely eradicated since Gandhi actively encouraged people to interpret one another's clothes as signs of personal and political belief. The result was that people became increasingly self-conscious about their public image and found their clothing choices the subject of more rigorous criticism and public scrutiny than ever before.

[...] DIVIDED IN KHADI

At a meeting in Devakkottah in 1927, Gandhi was presented with a piece of exceptionally fine khadi woven by a local weaver from very fine hand-spun yarn. Appreciative though he was, Gandhi found himself unable to accept the gift: 'This khadi I cannot wear for the simple reason that it would be against my profession and that I want to have no more than any of the starving millions.' His objection was that the khadi, being so fine, was a luxury item such as the poor could not afford, and therefore, since his duty was to represent the poor, he had no business to wear it. He hoped, however, that some wealthy and patriotic man from Devakkottah would be able to adorn his body in this delicate piece of khadi by buying it for the extravagant sum of Rs 1,001. The following day he found his buyer.

The incident highlights the fact that khadi, intended to eliminate the distinctions between rich and poor, had become diversified according to the fineness of its weave. Those poor villagers (mainly men) who wore white khadi tended to wear the thick, coarsely woven variety, since it was cheaper and more durable. When wealthy townsmen adopted khadi, they may have appeared to be choosing the clothes of the masses but very often they found a means of stressing their own superior refinement by sporting expensive fine khadi which was as costly and prestigious as the famous muslins of Dacca; [...] fineness of cloth denoted not only wealth but also social and ritual superiority. It was worn almost exclusively by those of high social status who could support themselves in prestigious occupations and did not need the hard-wearing clothes necessary for manual labour. It therefore carried the secondary associations of education as well as general refinement. Some high-caste educated people even claimed that their bodies were too sensitive and delicate to support the terrible weight of thick khadi cloth.

It is worth now taking a closer look at the *dhotis*, *kurtas*, and *pyjamas* of the Nehru family. Even in photographs, it is clear that their clothing lacks the crudity of texture characteristic of peasant khadi. Evidence of this may be found in the letters between father and son concerning dress. Writing from jail in 1922, Jawaharlal complained of the quality of his clothing and requested three new dhotis and kurtas of a superior variety. The concerned and loving Motilal responded by sending his son a large stock of high-quality garments, for which Jawaharlal was grateful:

Thank you for the clothes you sent me. I have an abundance of them now. I was at first inclined to return the Andhra dhotis you sent me as they were too fine. On second thoughts, I kept them. They are not as fine as some Andhra stuff. Kripalani used to wear a much finer dhoti. The dhotis you have sent are just right as regards weight. The length too suits me ...

Clearly Jawarhalal was aware that the fineness of these dhotis consorted uneasily with the ideology of khadi, but even in jail it seems that he was unable to resist the luxury of well-made and finely woven garments which clearly set him aside from the average peasant. Later he further distinguished his own identity by adopting the short tailored khadi waistcoat, now known as the 'Nehru jacket'.

Social and economic distinctions manifested themselves not only in the texture of the weave but also in the nature of the fibres employed. Unlike Sarladevi Chaudhurani, many people were reluctant to take the full plunge into cotton khadi, and chose instead swadeshi silk. This, otherwise known as khadi silk, was silk which had been hand-woven and hand-spun in India, using indigenous yarn. Since silk manufacture was restricted to only a few parts of India, and silk thread was finer than cotton yarn, requiring more time for weaving, swadeshi silk was naturally a luxury product, restricted to elite buyers. This disturbed Shrikrishnadas Jaju, secretary of the All India Spinners Association, who wondered whether it was advisable for khadi organizations to sell swadeshi silk at all in view of the fact that it competed with cotton khadi and encouraged a luxury-loving attitude in the wearer. The question of the morality *of* khadi silk was a dominant factor in this debate. At their most lenient, khaddarites felt that the diversity of choice that swadeshi silk provided should be encouraged since it was all part of the khadi cause. At their most puritan, however, people objected not only to the unnecessary luxury of silk, but also to the process by which it was made, which, because it involved the destruction of silk worms, and could thus be defined as a violent act. This finally lead to a new division of types, even within the comparatively small category of khadi silk. A moral distinction was made between 'violent swadeshi silk' and 'non-violent swadeshi silk', defined according to the degrees of violence involved in the production process.

These fine varieties of khadi cotton and silk were never in widespread use, partly because of their cost and partly also because they often did not reach the open market: it seems that Congressmen and other important notables often found means of reserving such pieces for their own use by making special arrangements with people who worked in the khadi shops. Despite the apparent humility of Congress uniform, the sartorial link between politicians and the Indian poor seems to have been less close than it appeared to be on the surface.

There were other problems with khadi besides its coarseness—in particular, the question of its plainness. Male clothing in India had often bordered on the simple in colour and motif, but most women were accustomed to wearing more elaborate materials, decorated with printing, embroidery, dyeing, and woven patterns. Gandhi, who some-times referred to bright colours as 'ugly spots', was opposed to excessive decoration and accused women of being slaves both to their own whims and fancies and to their husbands'. He told them: 'If you want to play your part in the world's affairs, you must refuse to deck yourselves for pleasing men'. White khadi, he thought, was a suitable means of enabling women to enter the public political sphere without appearing sexually provocative or immodest. But for most women the khadi-clad image had little appeal. Even Gandhi's wife Kasturba was at first so reluctant to wear the cloth that she helped other women protest to Gandhi about the unreasonableness of his expectations.

Women's objections related not only to the weight of khadi but also to the threat it posed both to their aesthetic senses and indeed to their sense of identity as women. Aesthetically, some feared that it would stamp out many of the decorative arts which women enjoyed. Certain types of embroidery, for example, required the use of Chinese silk, which was clearly contradictory to Gandhi's philosophy. More gen-erally, women feared the dull uniformity and sombre unattractive image that khadi represented. Kamala Das has recorded her childhood memories of seeing her khadi-clad family. 'I thought Gandhiji a brigand,' she recalls, 'I thought it his diabolic aim to strip ladies of their finery so that they became plain and dull.' Nehru's sister, Vijayalakshmi, also bemoaned the drabness of khadi and felt deprived when the men of the family persuaded her to wear it for her wedding. One woman even expressed the fear that by wearing khadi she might be guilty of leading her husband to 'lose his character' since he might be attracted to other more glamorous women wearing foreign or mill-cloth. Yet perhaps more poignant than any of these aesthetic considerations were the negative associations that plain white khadi evoked. For white was essentially a colour worn by men and, worse still, by widows. Since widowhood was the most feared and least respected state a woman could attain, most young women seem to have been reluctant to embrace so grim an image, however much they sympathized with Gandhian sentiments. As a result, few but the most devout *ashram*-dwellers and some old women adopted plain white khadi saris in their simplest form. Even the most politically motivated women like Kamala Nehru (Jawaharlal's wife) and Sarojini Naidu retained at least some form of decoration in their saris.

There soon grew up a wide variety of coloured, printed, and decorated khadi saris, sometimes embroidered, sometimes bordered with silk, which saved khadi from monotony but which simultaneously increased the possibilities of betraying social and economic differences. The National Council of Women, founded in Bombay in 1921, began making embroidered ready-made garments and items of household use which they hawked from house to house and displayed in khadi exhibitions. These of course sold for considerably higher prices than plain un-decorated khadi, which was already expensive compared to mill-cloth. Rural women, like urban women, were reluctant to adopt white khadi and generally could not afford the elaborate decorated khadi worn by a small urban elite.

Although Gandhi wanted to build *swaraj* on a 'white background', dyeing khadi became a common means of differentiating not only individuals but also various groups within the freedom movement. A special female volunteer corps adopted black saris with orange, green and red borders. These were later replaced by plain orange ones at the instigation of Kamaladevi Chattopadhyaya, who found the previous colour combination distasteful. These women became known as the 'Orange Brigade'. Meanwhile the male Congress volunteers in some cities distinguished themselves by wearing khaki-coloured khadi uniforms. A volunteer corps of Muslims who joined non-cooperation sported either khaki uniforms with the Turkish fez and crescent armbands or else the long green Arab-style robes popularized by the Ali brothers. The Muslim Pathans, on the other hand, wore a distinctive red uniform, and were even named 'Red Shirts' after their dress.

Even when people adopted plain white khadi, they were still able to differentiate themselves if they wished through the style in which they made up their garments. Gandhi hoped that khadi would help to unite 'Hindu–Muslim–Sikh–Parsi–Christian–Jew', but he did not insist that everyone adopt the same style of dress. As long as it was a simple Indian style, he was content. Yet the acceptance of different styles allowed the expression of different interests. Some felt that this prevented khadi from being a symbol of national unity:

The Musalman by putting on khaddar in Muslim fashion may feel that he is injuring British interests but he will never feel that he has become one with the Hindu. That is, he begins to feel politically but not a bit nationally. Pictures of political leaders bunched together appear in newspapers. They are so dressed that the Muslim eye selects the Muslim leader, the Sikh the Sikh. Under these circumstances it is impossible to educate the mass mind nationally.

On the whole, Hindus who adopted khadi wore dhotis, kurtas, and Gandhi caps; Muslims wore kurta pyjamas with a cap or fez; and Sikhs retained their distinctive turbans. Some Hindus, far from uniting with Muslims in khadi, actually refused to wear the cloth because the khadi available in their region was made by Muslim weavers. Parsis and Christians, on the other hand, rarely adopted khadi because they found it primitive and preferred to stick to Western styles. This led one Parsi man to suggest that khadi should be made up into European as well as Indian styles. Even as early as 1921, when khadi was still a comparatively new cause, there were reports of people making it up into Western-style suits, shirts, and trousers, and even dyeing it black to make it visually indistinguishable from European dress.

Where khadi threatened to cover difference, there were often traditionalists ready to object. An interesting example of this was the dilemma of a Maharashtrian woman who wrote to Gandhi in 1928, explaining her difficulty in adopting khadi:

A year ago I heard you speaking on the extreme necessity of everyone of us wearing khadi and thereupon decided to adopt it. But we are poor people. My husband says that khadi is costly. Belonging as I do to Maharashtra, I wear a sari of nine yards long. Now if I reduced the length of my sari to six yards, there would be a great saving, but the elders will not hear of such a reduction. I reason with them that wearing khadi is the more important thing and that the style and length of the sari is absolutely immaterial, but in vain.

In this case the objection to khadi was that it threatened regional rather than religious identity. The desire of the Maharashtrian elders to preserve local traditions stood directly in the way of national unity. When Gandhi harped back to India's mythical past when all had worn khadi, he failed to consider the extraordinarily diverse clothing traditions that had always co-existed among different social, religious and ethnic groups in India. For khadi was in danger of blanking out local Indian traditions just as much as it sought to stamp out British influences. Gandhi's response to the woman's dilemma was that she should sacrifice her provincialism for the wider benefit of nationalism.

The above examples reveal that despite the notions of voluntary poverty, equality, and national unity which Gandhi attributed to khadi, there was a tendency among many khadi-wearers to retain visible signs of their social, economic, regional and religious identity. This is not altogether surprising since many of the people who adopted it did not actually agree with much of what Gandhi attributed to it. Some, for example, believed only in its political value and its ability to hasten swaraj, while others emphasized its power as the counterpart to the boycott on foreign cloth, and yet others believed chiefly in its ability to stimulate cottage industry or to promote a more humane economy. Furthermore, mingled with these various personal beliefs and motivations was the feeling of an *obligation* to wear it, which loomed large on the political horizon for believers and non-believers alike: as the examples at the beginning of this chapter show, the pressures to adopt khadi were enormous, ranging from subtle encouragements, blatant propaganda, regulations, and family pressures to threats of physical violence. But perhaps the greatest pressure of all lay in the explicitly moral association that Gandhi himself attributed to it: his countless speeches on its virtues and the sinfulness of foreign cloth made many people embarrassed to be seen in anything other than khadi.

This pressure led to a bizarre sartorial paradox: the greater the stress on the idea that clothing was an expression of integrity and moral worth, the greater the increase in the use of clothing as a form of disguise or as a mask for a person's actual beliefs. For there were those who found that the combination of moral pressure to wear khadi and moral condemnation if they did not was more powerful as an inducement to wearing khadi than their actual beliefs in the cloth itself. Furthermore, there were not merely the negative consequences of being seen in foreign cloth to consider, but also the positive benefits of wearing khadi. For as the Rev. C.F. Andrews pointed out to Gandhi, khadi was 'a cheap method of gaining popularity'. That the mere act of wearing khadi could earn a person a reputation for honesty, self-sacrifice, and integrity undoubtedly made it a tempting clothing option for those with little belief in its ideology.

It was the combination of Gandhi's moral emphasis and the apparent hypocrisy it engendered in others that caused men like C.F. Andrews and Motilal Nehru to contemplate giving up the wearing of khadi. In

1924, Motilal even accused Gandhi of being 'systematically duped by unscrupulous liars who have ingratiated themselves into your favour by the simple device of pretending an abiding faith in khaddar to the exclusion of all else.' An equally disillusioned khadi supporter wrote from Purulia informing Gandhi of the shallowness of people's khadi faith:

As you are expected to come to Purulia, all the people are buying khadi just to wear it during your stay. Your visit has reminded some of these men of their promise to use khaddar, and some are buying it just to escape public criticism. Now, if a man uses foreign cloth as a rule, but only wears khaddar on certain occasions, he is a hypocrite. And if your visit increases the number of hypocrites, what is its use?

Even Gandhi was forced to acknowledge that 'many self-seeking "workers" have exploited khadi dress. Wearing khadi and having made people believe that they were men of self sacrifice, such workers deceive society and refuse to make any amends. Such khadi wearers disgrace khadi.'

In particular, it was Congressmen who came under frequent criticism for their 'insincere' use of khadi. But if there were wolves in sheep's clothing in the Congress Party, there were also sheep in wolves' clothing in the Indian Civil Service, for the same fear of recrimination that persuaded Congressmen to wear khadi in public also persuaded some khadi lovers to hide their khadi beneath a public facade of foreign cloth. Indeed most of the sartorial antics popular in the nineteenth century resurfaced in the Gandhian era with a somewhat changed emphasis and an explicit moral overtone. No longer were people preoccupied with the problem of how much foreignness to allow into their clothes. Rather, it was a question of how much swadeshi they ought to integrate into their clothing and lifestyles. Like Westernization, swadeshi was usually a matter of degrees rather [than] absolutes.

KHADI TRANSFORMATIONS OF THE PROBLEM OF WHAT TO WEAR

In the pre-Gandhian era many men and women found a relatively uncontroversial solution to the problem of what to wear by wearing foreign cloth in Indian styles. But with the new Gandhian emphasis on khadi, this solution was now considered unpatriotic and immoral. Whereas in the past the style of a garment had been the most important criterion for judging patriotism, this was now the cloth itself, its production, and origin. The result was that some Congressmen, being officially obliged to wear khadi, concealed their lack of khadi faith by wearing mill-made imitations that were mass-produced in both India and Japan. By choosing simple white cloth they could continue to enjoy the comforts of the cheaper softer mill-cloth, while simultaneously reaping the benefits of a sanctimonious khadi-clad image. Some such imitations were pure fake while others were what Gandhi called 'half khadi', that is, fabrics that were hand-woven but with machine-spun yarn. In Simla Congressmen not only bought and wore khadi imitations, but actually sold them in so-called khadi shops. The All India Spinners Association tried to control these developments by introducing its own stamp consisting of a spinning-wheel motif, which guaranteed that their khadi was 'certified'. But 'uncertified' khadi remained a constant problem and there were even reports of dealers sending specimens of 'certified' khadi to Manchester with the intent of obtaining cheap khadi imitations on which they could print the image of the Mahatma's head to attract custom. The inevitable consequence of these developments was that some people who actually intended to wear khadi were clothed in fake khadi without even knowing it.

Another sartorial option, popular in the nineteenth century, was to wear a combination of Indian and European garments. Photographs of crowds in the 1920s and 1930s reveal that this remained a common choice. Gandhi was irritated by the sight of foreign jackets worn over khadi outfits by children in National Schools. 'They should be saved from this miserable condition,' he argued.

Just as in the nineteenth century Indian headwear was often worn with European dress, so the Gandhi cap was often adopted without the wearer Indianizing the rest of his clothes. The cap was cheap and easily obtainable and, as we have seen, people were often coerced into wearing it. But a mere khadi cap was not enough to satisfy either Gandhi or his Muslim co-worker Mohammad Ali. Confronted by a crowd of white caps and assorted clothes at a meeting in Sholapur, the latter proclaimed: 'Personally I don't find anybody clad in khadi.... You must, you have to, bear the burden that full khadi dress entails.'

For many who were not prepared to bear this 'burden' but who none the less wished to appear patriotic, the solution was to maintain two alternative sartorial images through changing their clothes to suit the situation. Always a popular solution, this enabled people to distinguish their public from their private selves. Gandhi's intention, as we have seen, was to abolish the public/private dichotomy altogether by suggesting a permanent sartorial solution corresponding to a person's inner self. In theory this should have ended the necessity of changing clothes, since khadi was the Indian expression of a constant unchanging truth. But far from discouraging constant changes of dress, Gandhi's preaching had the effect of reinforcing the necessity of changing clothes. For with the new Gandhian emphasis on the morality of dress, public appearances were interpreted as realities. This meant that the clothes of the public self were under more rigorous scrutiny than ever before. Whereas in the past people judged one another's loyalties ultimately by the clothes of the private self, they were now encouraged to interpret the dress of the public self as an explicit expression of belief, national allegiance, and moral worth. This inevitably tempted people to present acceptable external images regardless of whether or not they corresponded to their personal beliefs.

The threshold of the house remained an important border for conversion. Those who did not fully believe in khadi, and who retained the idea that European dress was more civilized, cast off their khadi on entering the house and replaced it with mill-cloth or European dress. Many, like Sarojini Naidu, wore khadi only in periods of intense non-cooperation or when attending political meetings. In particular, Congress politicians developed a reputation for wearing khadi only for ceremonial purposes in public events. According to Gandhi, such men had 'become the laughing stock of all,' creating an 'atmosphere of cant hypocrisy and humbug'. Some Congressmen restricted their khadi wearing exclusively to the election period, buying khadi clothes at the last minute to bolster their political image. But worse still were those politicians who refused to invest their money in khadi, yet, wanting the political benefits, borrowed clothes from the All India Spinners Association solely for election purposes and returned them once the elections were over, at which point they reverted to foreign cloth.

To Gandhi it was vital for khadi to remain at the centre of all political activity. Advising someone on how to select a candidate for the Legislative Council, he wrote:

I shall tell you what I should do. I will first of all scan the candidates from top to bottom and if I find that among all the candidates there is not one man who is dressed from top to bottom in khaddar, I will retain my vote in my pocket absolutely sealed. And if I am satisfied there is at least one man who is dressed from top to toe in khaddar, I will go to him in all humility and ask him if he is dressed in this style for the occasion or if he habitually at home and out of home wears hand-spun and hand-woven khaddar. If he returns an answer in the negative, I should again retain my vote in my pocket. If positive, I would ask, 'It is extremely good that you always wear khaddar, but do you also spin for the sake of the masses at least for half an hour [per day]?

Yet even with such elaborate screening, it was not impossible for some stealthy politicians to satisfy their love of foreign cloth. Locating the boundary between inner and outer selves somewhere between their inner and outer clothing, these men retained the comfort of their silky-textured mill-made underwear, safely submerged beneath a coarse external layer of khadi. Reversing the formula, there were other men working in the British administration who put on, beneath their smooth-textured Western suits, coarse khadi underclothes which remained close to their hearts and their inner beliefs both at home and in the workplace.

The only time when Gandhi considered it admissible for someone to change his sartorial image was when that person was going abroad; then it was acceptable for a patriotic Indian to wear European styles as long as they were made from khadi. Advising Dr Gurudas Roy about what to wear on his trip to England, Gandhi wrote:

I am perfectly confident you can do without any European clothing in England and Scotland provided that you take a sufficient stock of hand-spun woollen clothing.... You may not know that Pandit Motilalji when he was preparing to go to England as a member of the Skeen Committee had an entirely hand-spun outfit including his cardigan jackets....I suggest your consulting Satis Babu of Khadi Pratishthan, and if he cannot furnish you with an outfit, I know that the Khadi Bhandar of Bombay can, because that Bhandar has provided many England-going Indians with proper outfits....All your underclothings may well be cotton khadi.

Making khadi up into European styles was one of the most innovative methods of remaining patriotic and loyal to the ideology of khadi without sacrificing one's personal liking for European dress. But although such a solution was more acceptable to Gandhi than the reverse solution of making foreign cloth into Indian styles, it was not accepted by the Indian public, who retained the old idea that the style of dress was the most important criterion of patriotism. If clothes looked European they were likely to be criticized more than Indian-looking garments, even if the former were made from khadi and the latter were not. For, once all the Indian features of khadi had been masked through cutting, tailoring and dyeing, there seemed little point in wearing khadi at all. Those men who wore black khadi suits of the European cut were suspected of British bias as they appeared embarrassed by their indigenous clothing traditions. This suggested that for at least some members of the Indian public a person's physical appearance was actually more important than his or her belief in khadi as an economic and moral solution to India's poverty.

A final example concerning the ever-controversial question of headwear reveals this distinction between Gandhi's emphasis on the morality of the cloth and the public's emphasis on the morality of the clothing style. In 1929 a lawyer wrote to Gandhi concerning the criticism

he had received for wearing a *sola topi* which had been specially made
out of certified khadi cloth:

I was a practising lawyer but non-co-operated in 1921. Circumstances have driven
me back to law but I am a strict khaddarite. I have given up the use of trousers and
ties and attend the court and local legislature in dhoti. As Chairman of my District
Council I am running Famine Road Works, which require my being out in the sun.
Recently I got a touch of the sun and went in for a hat, which has been specially
made of pure khaddar. This has started a controversy. Will you take part in it?

Gandhi replied in *Young India:*

This is an old controversy. My narrow nationalism rebels against the hat, my secret
internationalism regards the sola topi as one of the few boons from Europe. But for
the tremendous national prejudice against the hat, I would undertake to become
president of a league for popularising sola hats....But I know that national likes and
dislikes are not governed by reason....I do not expect Indians to take kindly to the
sola hat. Nevertheless workers like Pandit Durgashankar need not be ruffled by
criticism and may certainly wear khadi imitations of the sola hat. It is in reality an
easily portable umbrella that covers the head without the necessity of one hand
being occupied by carrying it.

Gandhi's liking for the sola topi, which the Indian public rejected with
such vigour, reveals the distinctiveness of his personal belief in the
meaning of national dress. To him a moral and patriotic outfit consisted
of simple, practical clothes made from khadi, preferably though not
exclusively in Indian styles. But for the Indian public, style remained a
central criterion of Indianness. To many the sola topi was as much a
symbol of Britishness as their own Gandhi cap was a symbol of Indianness. The British themselves were well aware of the symbolism of their
topis. Not long after poor Fred Burrows was forcibly khadi-capped by
zealous Gandhians, the British voluntarily removed their own hats.
The ritual was described by Rupert Mayne, who was sailing with the
last British regiment to leave the newly created Pakistan: 'As we left
Port Said and sailed into the open waters, everyone was paraded with
their topees on deck and at the given signal we all flung our topees into
the sea and that was the last of India.' What better final victory for the
Gandhi cap?

POST-INDEPENDENCE POLITICAL SARTORIAL INHERITANCE

Needless to say, the problem of what to wear did not end with the
dawning of Indian independence. And no one suffered more from this

problem than Indian politicians. The intensification of nationalist feeling and moral righteousness that became attached to khadi could not easily be shaken off. [...] Jawaharlal Nehru never shared Gandhi's vision of a non-industrial village-based society, yet during his years as India's first prime minister he continued to support khadi production while simultaneously promoting industrial progress. Successive governments have all followed this line regardless of whether the khadi and craft emporiums ran at a profit or a loss. As with government policy, so with clothes.

After fighting for freedom under a banner of khadi, politicians could not just turn about and forget it once the British had left India, even though the majority of the populace (excluding perhaps artists and intellectuals) did exactly that. Furthermore the moral stigma which Gandhi had so cleverly woven into imported fabrics could not be unravelled any more than the moral integrity which he had so neatly woven into khadi.

Nehru's solution was to carve himself a highly tailored but noticeably non-Western image, while retaining khadi as the fabric of his dress. He therefore opted for the stitched tight pyjama which he wore with either the long *sherwani* or the short, now famous 'Nehru jacket'. It was more or less a return to the pre-Gandhian version of respectable dress, with the difference that Nehru's version was made from khadi. He sometimes wore foreign dress on foreign visits but in India his clothes remained essentially Indian.

Concerned by the post-independence sartorial confusion around him, Nehru wrote an official note on dress, advising those in high grades of government office to steer clear of European clothes 'which marked them out as a privileged, denationalized, and out-of-date class, and to adopt such clothes as would take them closer to the people.' He passed on his own chic notion of swadeshi to his daughter Indira Gandhi, who usually dressed in handloom cotton saris, at least when she was in India. Similarly, her son Rajiv Gandhi threw aside his European dress and aviator's uniform in favour of khadi when he entered political office in 1984, and his wife Sonia is still seen in public in handloom saris. In the run-up to the 1991 elections, most political candidates were wearing white khadi, and one New Delhi candidate was even dressed as Mahatma Gandhi himself. But despite the efforts made to keep politicians in touch with the humble masses, the modern day politician remains a remote and conspicuous figure for most villagers.

[...] It is the long-term association with morality and patriotism that has enabled and indeed forced plain white khadi to remain in politics. No longer everyday dress, it is an obligatory appendage whenever the public political self is most on show. Modern-day sceptics tend to view this phenomenon as a sign of degeneration, of the shallow integrity of contemporary leaders who lack the sincerity of their freedom-fighting ancestors. But, as we have seen, strategic khadi dressing was born in the Gandhian era itself, even at a time when Gandhi was preaching a virtual religion of khadi. It merely intensified after independence when the moral pressure to believe in khadi dissipated, leaving only the fabric itself to stand as an anachronistic but emotive symbol of the humble, caring politician. Most people know that the khadi-clad politician is no more humble than the rest of them, but then, [...] it is sometimes difficult to do things without khadi!

Post-independence Political Heads

A discussion of post-independence political dress would not be complete without reference to the age-old saga of headwear. Jawaharlal Nehru, India's first prime minister, often wore a Gandhi cap, a relic of the freedom struggle, and the same cap continues to sprout on Indian heads today, primarily at times of political intensity or at nationally important funerals. But Nehru had always disliked Gandhi's peculiar way of over-simplifying things, sartorial or otherwise. While Gandhi tried to condense all Indian diversity into a single item of headwear, Nehru instead put into practice his favourite maxim 'unity in diversity', and wore a variety of different things on his head. In the desire to communicate with other nations and ethnic groups, he developed a habit of dressing up in other people's clothes when on political tours; this was 'dressing up' because it was an attempt not so much to adopt the identity of the other as to greet others on their own terms and thus accept their otherness. To this end he generally retained his sherwani pyjama, adding some foreign appendage to his dress, and it was often the headwear of the other that he chose to wear on his visits. It was a means of expressing acceptance of ethnic diversity, even when the ethnic group he was visiting did not look so ethnically diverse! Nehru initiated his daughter Indira Gandhi in the same sartorial practice, and through her it passed to her son Rajiv. Indeed accepting the headwear of the people has now become a common feature of Indian ministerial tours, thereby reversing the traditional practice whereby the ruler bestowed authority on his subordinates through the distribution of headwear. The reversal of the gesture serves as symbolic acknowledgement of the fact that in democratic India it is the people who have the ultimate power to legitimize the authority of their elected leaders.

Despite their practice of using different forms of headwear, the Nehru men did not abandon the Gandhi cap, which they continued to wear for certain official occasions. And the cap has remained an important feature of election campaigning, although its popularity has waned somewhat in recent years. It is also worn by some Indian men at funerals or for important religious rituals when many who normally go bareheaded cover their heads. As we have seen, the Gandhi cap was never quite the symbol of national unity that Gandhi hoped. This is reflected today in the wearing of different coloured caps to represent different interests: some Hindu fundamentalists have taken to wearing orange Gandhi caps, and certain sections of the protesting peasantry green ones. Meanwhile the old-style Gandhian with his white khadi cap has become an increasingly rare sight. [...]

NOTE

1. Sarladevi Chaudhurani was the wife of Pandit Rambhoj Dhutt Chaudhurani, a nationalist leader in the Punjab, and the niece of Rabindranath Tagore. In 1920, she became the first elite woman to adopt *khadi* and was exceptional for wearing it in coarse plain white underrated form.

Contributors

I<small>SHITA</small> B<small>ANERJEE</small>-D<small>UBE</small> is Associate Professor of History, Center for Asian and African Studies, El Colegio de México, Mexico.

L<small>ATE</small> B<small>ERNARD</small> C<small>OHN</small> was Professor Emeritus, Department of Anthropology, University of Chicago, Chicago.

V<small>EENA</small> D<small>AS</small> is Krieger–Eisenhower Professor of Anthropology, Johns Hopkins University, Baltimore.

N<small>ICHOLAS</small> D<small>IRKS</small> is Franz Boas Professor of Anthropology and History, Vice President for Arts and Sciences, and Dean of the Faculty, Columbia University, New York.

S<small>AURABH</small> D<small>UBE</small> is Professor of History, Center for Asian and African Studies, El Colegio de México, Mexico.

A<small>NN</small> G. G<small>OLD</small> is William P. Tolley Distinguished Teaching Professor in the Humanities, and Professor of Anthropology and Religion, Syracuse University, Syracuse, New York.

P<small>AUL</small> G<small>REENOUGH</small> is Professor, Department of History, University of Iowa, Iowa.

R<small>ANAJIT</small> G<small>UHA</small> has held academic appointments in universities in Britain, Australia, and the United States, and now lives in Austria.

B<small>HOJU</small> R<small>AM</small> G<small>UJAR</small> is Headmaster, Government Middle School, Maganpura village, Rajasthan.

R<small>AVINDRA</small> J<small>AIN</small> is retired Professor, Centre for the Study of Social Systems, School of Social Sciences, Jawaharlal Nehru University, New Delhi.

Malavika Kasturi is Assistant Professor, Department of History, University of Toronto, Toronto.

John D. Kelly is Professor and Department Chair of Anthropology, and Master of the Collegiate Division of the Social Sciences, University of Chicago, Chicago.

Shail Mayaram is Senior Fellow, Centre for the Study of Developing Societies, New Delhi.

Gyanendra Pandey is Asa Griggs Candler Professor of History, Emory University, Atlanta.

Late K.S. Singh was Former Director-General, Anthropological Survey of India, New Delhi.

K. Sivaramakrishnan is Professor of Anthropology, Yale University, New Haven.

Ajay Skaria is Associate Professor, Department of History, University of Minnesota, Minneapolis.

Nandini Sundar is Professor, Department of Sociology, Delhi School of Economics, University of Delhi, Delhi.

Emma Tarlo is Research Fellow, Ferguson Centre for Asian and African Studies, Open University, United Kingdom.

Peter van der Veer is University Professor, Utrecht University, The Netherlands.

Susan Visvanathan is Professor of Sociology, Centre for the Study of Social Systems, School of Social Sciences, Jawaharlal Nehru University, New Delhi.

Index